Race, Resistance, and the Boy Scout Movement
in British Colonial Africa

TIMOTHY H. PARSONS

Race, Resistance, and the Boy Scout Movement in British Colonial Africa

OHIO UNIVERSITY PRESS
ATHENS

Ohio University Press, Athens, Ohio 45701

© 2004 by Ohio University Press

Printed in the United States of America

All rights reserved

Ohio University Press books are printed on acid-free paper ⊗ ™

12 11 10 09 08 07 06 05 04   5 4 3 2 1

Library of Congress Cataloging-in-Publication Data

Parsons, Timothy, 1962–

Race, resistance, and the boy scout movement in British Colonial Africa / Timothy H. Parsons.

p. cm.

Includes bibliographical references and index.

ISBN 0-8214-1595-6 (cloth : alk. paper) — ISBN 0-8214-1596-4 (pbk. : alk. paper)

1. Scouts and scouting—Great Britain—Colonies—Africa. 2. Great Britain—Colonies—Africa—Administration. 3. Great Britain—Colonies—Africa—Race relations—History. I. Title.

HS3270.A35P37 2004

369.43'0967'09171241—dc22

2004015380

To Ann Parsons and Frances Marx
Kate, Julia, and Elizabeth Parsons
and to the memory of my father, George Parsons

Contents

Illustrations

Preface

I FIRST STUMBLED ON this project during my dissertation research in Kenya in the early 1990s. As a Fulbright scholar, I had the option of sending a box of supplies to myself through the U.S. embassy in Nairobi. While filling out the standard customs declaration form, I noticed that the Kenyan government listed Boy Scout uniforms along with firearms, explosives, and illegal narcotics as items that could not be imported into the country.[1] My interest was piqued further upon discovering a speech by Kenya's colonial governor in the Kenyan National Archives referring to African Scout troops "infected by Mau Mau." He was essentially suggesting that Scouting had somehow become caught up in the violent struggle against British colonial rule that came to be known as the Mau Mau Emergency. My thinking along these lines got an additional boost from the old men I interviewed for my social history of African soldiers in the British East African colonial army. During the course of our conversations, my informants invariably asked if I had served in the army. In explaining that I had not, I thought about how I had been a Boy Scout. Similarly, my friendship with my primary research assistant, who was my junior by only a few years, grew when he discovered that we both had been members of the movement.

Yet I undertook this project with some hesitancy. For better or for worse, historians tend to become bound up with their subjects. Writing about court cases or elections understandably brands an author as a legal or a political historian. Having already been linked with the colonial army as a result of my dissertation and first book, I found that many of my academic peers considered the study of Scouting to be another colonial military project (although, apart from a few Scout troops sponsored by military authorities for African soldiers' sons, there was absolutely no connection between Scouting and the colonial army). In fact Scouting was almost entirely an extension of the schools and missions during the colonial era. There is also a broad perception that Scouting is a relatively inconsequential institution that is not worthy of serious academic investigation. Friends and acquaintances often responded with wry chuckles or bemused looks when I explained that my next project was going to be a study of African Boy Scouts during the colonial era.

Ultimately, however, Scouting proved too tempting a target to ignore. As a social historian, I am interested in institutions that illuminate the conflicting values and cross-cultural tensions of colonial society. Indeed, Scouting proved an ideal analytical tool in mapping the social divisions of anglophone colonial Africa. The term *scouting* includes both male members of official Scout organizations around the world and boys who simply believed that they were Scouts. Scout authorities became willing allies of colonial authority and reconfigured the core Scout canon to support the British imperial agenda in Africa. Yet they could not gloss over the Fourth Scout Law, which declared all Scouts to be brothers. This was a contentious assertion in territories practicing de facto racial segregation, and so Africans ranging from nationalist leaders to schoolboys seized upon the movement to challenge the legitimacy of the colonial regime. African opposition to colonialism is an old story, but institutions like scouting provide deeper insights into what it was like for Africans to grow up under British rule. For example, the material culture of Scouting, which includes the Scout Law and Oath, badge tests, rank requirements, and uniforms, exposes key tensions over local administration and governance, Western education, gender, and generational friction between African youth and their elders.

Africanist social historians of the twentieth century seek to understand the lived experience of colonialism. In undertaking this project I assumed that my insider status as an ex-Scout would give me a greater understanding of the world of colonial African Scouting. To some extent this proved to be true. National Scout and Guide associations in Britain and Africa were welcoming, and I was able to answer in the affirmative when my informants asked if I had been a Scout. Yet I missed an opportunity to develop a degree of intimacy with a key African figure in colonial Scouting who went on to hold high political office in postcolonial Kenya when I failed to offer him my left hand in greeting. Many Scout organizations use the "left handshake" as an insider acknowledgment of shared Scout status. My old troop, however, never went in for this sort of thing.

My botched handshake led me to an important insight into the nature of Scouting as a social institution. Almost all local Scout organizations make key alterations to core Scouting beliefs to reflect local values and circumstances. I belonged to a troop in Rochester, New York, that frequently deviated from the official dictates of the Boy Scouts of America. Founded in 1919, just nine years after the establishment of the American Scouts, my troop based its identity on its founder, J. Taylor Howard. Although technically designated Troop 19, it is popularly known as Tay House, which is also the name of the large cabin where it meets, on the grounds of its sponsoring public elementary school. The troop developed institutions and traditions over its ninety-plus years that ultimately took it out of step with mainstream American Scouting. For example, it got around official Scouting's former opposition to Cub Scouting in the 1920s by importing manuals and badges from Canada.

When I joined the troop in the mid-seventies, Tay House acknowledged the authority of the Otetiana Council but essentially followed its own program. At a time when most troops consisted of about ten or so boys in one or two patrols led by a Scoutmaster who was the father of one of the members, Tay House had more than fifty members organized in at least five patrols. We had a committee of five to eight Scoutmasters in their twenties and early thirties, most of whom had been members of the troop themselves. An informal rule banned fathers from serving as Scoutmasters—to create an objective distance between the troop activities and family relationships. Moreover, although they seemed very old to me at the time, I looked up to these younger Scoutmasters because they seemed funnier and hipper than adults who were closer to my parents in age.

Tay House managed to retain older boys by giving them a substantial role in running the troop as junior and senior leaders, positions that do not exist in official American Scouting. Even as a boy, I realized that in Tay House we were a different kind of Scout. American Scouting was in decline as a result of the growing antiestablishment sentiments in the seventies, but our troop never wanted for members. Group pictures from that period show rows of mostly middle-class white boys, many of them with extremely long hair, in uniforms consisting of red and blue scarves, collarless green shirts, rolled shorts, knee socks with garters and green tabs, and hiking boots. This was at a time when the Boy Scouts of America was trying to make Scouting more popular by modernizing its uniforms, and I recall coveting the military-style long pants, shirts with epaulets, and berets that other troops got to wear. Instead we continued to wear our outdated shirts and shorts (even in the dead of the western New York winters) and were dressed down by the older boys if we deviated even slightly from the troop's standard uniform. Conversely, I don't think I ever saw another troop that managed to dress all its members in the newer uniforms. In most cases they wore a mix of blue jeans, sneakers, and whatever bits of the uniform appealed to them. Tay House, on the other hand, presented an even odder picture of long-haired boys dressed smartly in the style of a bygone age.

As a social historian, I now recognize that my old troop demonstrates that official Scouting as defined by national Scout associations is rarely representative of how Scouting is practiced at the local level. At Tay House we began each meeting with the Pledge of Allegiance and a recitation of the Scout Oath, but I was only vaguely aware of the nationalism and social conformity embedded in these key Scout texts. Similarly, although my Scoutmasters were not particularly concerned that my family did not attend church regularly, district Scout officials gave me a rough time over it when I came before them to get my Eagle Scout badge approved. I also now understand the purpose of our slightly silly uniforms. Although they were a serious deviation from official dress, they simultaneously bound us together and made us stand out. We got teased a lot, but we were not just different from regular Scouts; we believed we were better.

In closing, this book is written for multiple audiences. Hopefully general readers interested in Scouting's coming centennial will find this an interesting account that places African Scouting within the broad political and social context of the colonial era. Nostalgia aside, there are also compelling reasons for historians to pay attention to my old troop's eccentricities. Tay House's strong sense of tradition dictated its reinterpretation of the Scout canon, but in other cases individual adaptations to Scouting can just as easily be shaped by local concerns over race, gender, class, or political affiliation.

I also hope that Scouts and Scout leaders will find this investigation of colonial African Scouting useful. I know that the national Scout associations and ex-Scouts in Africa, Britain, and America who assisted me in my research are looking forward to seeing this book in print, but I imagine that some will be quite distressed by my critique of Scouting as a colonial institution. To them I would stress that I am writing as a historian and a former Scout who has no interest in discrediting the movement. I came away from my time in Tay House with a sense of service, tradition, and responsibility. The troop also laid the groundwork for my future career by teaching me how to teach. Facing a classroom for the first time was not very scary after I had learned how to manage thirty or so rowdy boys with very short attention spans.

My account of the failings of Scouting in colonial Africa should be read in part as an appeal to current Scout leaders to learn lessons from that questionable period in Scout history. The colonial Scout authorities' toleration of racial segregation in eastern and southern Africa meant they failed to uphold the Scout Law's admonition to treat all Scouts as brothers. In short, they put their ties to prevailing institutions of political authority and legitimacy ahead of their obligation to the boys in their charge. As a result, official Scouting became an integral part of colonialism and almost collapsed in Africa when the imperial era drew to a close.

There is a lesson here for the current leadership of the Boy Scouts of America. It was with a certain amount of pride that I read an editorial in my hometown newspaper written by one of my old Scoutmasters, now president of the Otetiana Council, criticizing the decision by the U.S. Supreme Court to allow the national organization to exclude gay leaders: "Neither I nor a majority of the Otetiana Council board favors the national policy. . . . No Scout in our local organization has been denied membership because of his sexual orientation and it is my sincere hope that none ever will. . . . We are acutely aware of Rochester's historical contributions to the anti-slavery and women's suffrage movements and their later-day legacy. We want to honor that legacy and help to do our part to fulfill it."[2] Happily, the African case study suggests that there is cause for optimism that this controversy can be resolved successfully. Scouting continues to thrive in contemporary Africa because independent African Scout leaders managed to reinterpret the movement to reflect the values and mores of postcolonial African society. The best chance for the long-term survival of Scouting in the United States would be to follow their example.

Acknowledgments

THE RESEARCH FOR THIS BOOK included field and archival work in three countries on two continents. It would not have been possible to undertake such
a project without considerable support and assistance. David Anderson of
the Five Rivers Scout Council in Horseheads, New York, and Al Morin, director of the Boy Scouts of America's International Division, provided important introductions to Scout authorities in Britain and Africa. In Kenya a
group of old and new friends made my work possible and enjoyable. B. K.
ole Kantai and Peterson Kithuka Nthiwa of the Kenya National Archives fall
into the first category. Ndung'u Kahihu, the Kenya Scout Association's national executive commissioner; Sarah Tum, executive officer of the Kenya
Girl Guides Association; and the late Kiraithe Nyaga, director of the Africa
Regional Office of the World Scout Bureau, generously introduced me to
the world of Kenyan Scouting and Guiding. J. A. Hunneyball, chief executive of the South African Scout Association, and Colin Inglis, a former chief
Scout of the South African Scout Association, were similarly helpful. Kings
and Jean Phiri most generously shared their home with me when I was
working on Scouting in Malawi. Finally, C. E. Bignell and Paul Moynihan
helped me navigate the archives of the British Scout Association.

I also owe a considerable debt to colleagues who helped me contex-
tualize my Scout research. My work is strongly influenced by the thinking of John Lonsdale and Derek Peterson, both of whom gave parts of the
manuscript an invaluable critical reading. Being an East Africanist by primary training, I relied heavily on the assistance and insightful criticism
of Robert Edgar, Carol Summers, Benedict Carton, and Robert Vinson to
situate my work properly in southern African history. Alan Booth merits
a special word of thanks for introducing me to Swaziland and generously
sharing his research on the *emabutfo* experiment. Maggie Garb, Nic Sam-
mond, Mark Pegg, and Andrea Friedman of Washington University's history department provided perceptive feedback and suggestions on various
pieces of the manuscript. Finally, Garret Duncan, my colleague in the
African and Afro-American Studies Program, helped me frame my study
within the context of educational research.

There is also a group of colleagues, old friends, and family members who helped make this book possible. My mentor Richard Davis was characteristically encouraging. Priscilla Stone helped me win outside funding for the project. Adele Tuchler and Raye Riggins of the African and Afro-American Studies Program played their usual key roles in turning my manuscript into a book. Looking backward, I should mention Don Trevoy and Tom Mayne as important old friends from my days as a Scout. Finally, I thank Ann Parsons, Jaime Tomé, Mike Zegans, and Elizabeth Lewandowski for continually encouraging me to write for a wider audience.

This project was funded by grants from the Spencer Foundation and the Fulbright-Hays Faculty Research Abroad Program. The data presented, the statements made, and the views expressed are solely the views of the author. Similarly, if the book fails to reflect the exceptional guidance and criticism I have received from my friends and colleagues, the fault is mine alone.

Race, Resistance, and the Boy Scout Movement
in British Colonial Africa

Eastern and southern Africa, ca. 1950.

1
Introduction

A Scout is a friend to all, and a brother to every other Scout, no matter to what country, class or creed, the other may belong.
—The Fourth Scout Law

ON 25 FEBRUARY 2001 approximately ten thousand Scouts from around the world met in Nyeri, Kenya, at the tomb of Lord Robert Baden-Powell to honor him as the founder of the international Scout movement. From 1939 until his death in 1941, Baden-Powell lived out his waning years in a small cottage he named Paxtu at the base of Mount Kenya. Although Britain reserved a spot for him in Westminster Abbey, his will insisted that he be buried in Kenya. The government of Kenya intended its Founder's Day celebrations to be a national showcase to demonstrate its efficiency and stature in the international Scout movement, but the then State Minister Julius Sunkuli had to contend with a proposal by the South African Scout Association to exhume the founder and rebury him at Mafeking in South Africa, the site of his greatest military victory. The South Africans argued that the Kenyan authorities had allowed the tombstones of Baden-Powell and his wife, Olave, to collapse and become overgrown with grass and weeds. Equally troubling, a five-acre plot on the site that the Kenyan government had set aside for an international Scouting conference and camping center had been "grabbed" by anonymous, but politically connected, individuals.

Baden-Powell's grave in Nyeri is one of the three most important centers of the international Scout movement, along with Mafeking and Gilwell Park in Great Britain. Expecting tens, perhaps hundreds, of thousands of the roughly thirty million registered Scouts from around the world to make a pilgrimage to the site during the movement's centennial in 2007, the Kenyan authorities moved quickly to fend off the South African challenge. Baden-Powell's gravesite and cottage at Paxtu have been restored with funds provided by a local Coca-Cola bottler. The local Nyeri Scout association has undertaken responsibility for improving the town's visitor accommodations, and the new National Rainbow Coalition government that came to power in December 2002 will most certainly move to retrieve the land set aside for the international Scouting center.[1]

At first glance it seems odd that an institution like Scouting, which has its origins in the colonial past, would enjoy so much prestige in modern Kenya. Although Baden-Powell created the movement for British, rather than African, boys, colonial officials, missionaries, and educators introduced Scouting to Africa to discipline younger generations of Africans. African boys became Scouts for a variety of reasons during the colonial era. Jeremiah Nyagah and J. G. Kiano, both cabinet ministers in independent Kenya, credit Scouting with teaching them self-reliance, integrity, and political skills. The late Kiraithe Nyaga, director of the Africa Regional Office of the World Scout Bureau until his death in a plane crash in 2000, enjoyed the prestige associated with the movement.[2] None of them paid much attention to the reality that the colonial regime sponsored Scouting to promote social stability and loyalty to the British Empire. In 1955, Governor Sir Evelyn Baring singled out the movement as a solution to the Mau Mau Emergency in particular and anticolonial nationalism in general: "In Kenya today scouting has a most important role to play. In one part of the country many young Africans had come under the influence of what was really a totalitarian movement. . . . an attempt must be made to encourage them to grow up each with a personality which will resist a second movement that might attempt to overwhelm their powers of individual judgment. For this reason scouting will play an enormous part in training the African school boy not only in basic education, but also in the art of citizenship. It is designed to provide just that training which is not necessarily learnt in the . . . school-room."[3]

Baring's faith in Scouting's ability to shape the "character" of its members is not borne out in the recollections of individual African Scouts from that period. Although Kiraithe Nyaga was an enthusiastic and committed Scout, he also willingly and secretly supported the Mau Mau fighters who caused the Kenyan governor so much worry. British officials hoped the Scout Law's affirmation that a Scout was loyal would convince African boys to support the colonial regime. Yet African Scouts had little difficulty separating their commitment to the movement with their distaste for the discriminatory realities of colonialism. Matthew Kipoin hated serving in the King's African Rifles but as a boy appreciated Scouting's prestige and discipline.[4] Even more problematic from the standpoint of the colonial authorities were the members of Scout troops sponsored by independent African schools and churches and the outright impostors who wore illegally acquired Scout uniforms to trade upon the respectability of the movement.

Yet it was Scouting's vulnerability to appropriation by local actors that has allowed it to thrive in postcolonial Africa. The European Scout authorities were bitter enemies of African nationalism, but the Africans who took control of the colonial Scout associations after the transfer of power easily transformed Scouting into an explicitly nationalist institution. Teachers, parents, and boys throughout the continent value Scouting because it still teaches the same values of integrity, discipline, and self-reliance that made the movement so popular under the British. Now, however, Scouting promotes loyalty to independent nation-states rather than a foreign colonial regime. This explains why the modern Kenyan government values the movement and viewed the South African attempts to exhume and rebury Baden-Powell as a serious threat.

SCOUTING AS AN ANALYTICAL TOOL

The contradictions between official Scouting and the experiences of individual African Scouts expose the fractures in the paternalistic institutions of authority and legitimacy that sustained the colonial enterprise. To British eyes Scouting appeared ideally suited to the task of disciplining educated Africans like Nyaga and Kipoin. Conceived by Gen. Sir Robert Baden-Powell (later Baron Baden-Powell of Gilwell) to reduce Edwardian class tensions and improve the quality of potential military recruits, Scouting evolved into a international youth movement that offered a romantic program of outdoor life as a cure for social disruption caused by industrialization and urbanization. Baden-Powell promised Scouting would remedy declining physical and moral fitness and juvenile delinquency by providing a healthy outlet for youthful rebellion. The Scout movement won governmental support by echoing dominant social values and teaching patriotism and service. Although Scouting captured the imagination of boys around the world, its global spread was due primarily to its success in attaching itself to the institutions of political and social authority.

British administrators, educators, missionaries, and social welfare experts transplanted Scouting to Africa as part of the process of socialization and social control that introduced Africans to Western values and material culture. In essence, they sought to create reliable African functionaries who would assist in the colonial enterprise. The movement held that a Scout was trustworthy, loyal, obedient, and self-reliant. These are relatively universal values, but British authorities interpreted this core Scout canon to mean that African Scouts must be loyal to the colonial regime and its African allies. They worried that Western education fostered social instability by teaching African students to expect political and social equality and question the values and authority of their elders. Colonial youth experts saw the movement as an instrument of "retribalization" that encouraged young Africans to accept their place in colonial society. Working with Scout officials, they sought to reduce generational tensions and promote politically safe conceptions of adolescence and docile masculinity. Scouting never became a mass movement in anglophone Africa, but it targeted the secondary school graduates, juvenile delinquents, and young urban migrants that constituted the greatest threat to the security of the colonial regime.

Yet colonial Scouting proved to be an ineffective instrument of social control. African Scouts embraced the movement because they considered it entertaining, progressive, and useful, but they had their own ideas of what it meant to be loyal and disciplined. It seems that very few of them gave their unqualified allegiance to the British Crown. Membership conferred sophistication, social status, and legitimacy, and demonstrated a mastery of Western cultural norms. Neighbors in Kiraithe Nyaga's Meru community believed that Scouts were mysterious people whose woodcraft skills allowed them to read secret signs. However, the Scouts' "special knowledge" also included a greater understanding of the inner workings of the colonial regime. Uniformed Meru Scouts traveled on specially discounted rail tickets, mixed easily with the police, and appeared to cross institutional racial barriers with relative ease.[5]

Most important, African Scouts and their communities embraced the movement to claim the rights of full citizenship in colonial society. They used the Fourth Scout Law, which declared that a Scout was a brother to every other Scout, to challenge racial discrimination under what was known as the color bar. African independent churches and schools created unauthorized scout troops to appropriate colonial symbols of authority and legitimacy. Rather than papering over the contradictions of colonialism, Scouting offered Africans another means of contesting their subordinate social status. In anglophone Africa, therefore, Scouting was thus both an instrument of colonial authority and a subversive challenge to the legitimacy of the empire.

Scouting became a nearly universal global institution because its core conservative values are sufficiently adaptable to support the established political order in nations around the world. The movement is thus a useful analytical tool for exploring the tensions and fissures in a given society. The strength of official Scouting, as represented by national Scout associations, depends on an alliance with established institutions of legitimacy and authority. Scout officials invariably interpret the Scout canon to reflect prevailing norms and values and rarely, if ever, push the boundaries of social conformity. Conversely, unofficial local interpretations of Scouting have the capacity to express opposition to the dominant social order.

National Scout associations usually prevail in the struggle to define Scout orthodoxy for as long as their alliance with political authority remains in tact. They face problems when the political and social terrain shifts before official Scouting, which tends to be highly conservative, has time to react. In such cases Scout authorities have found themselves embroiled in controversies ranging from the civil rights struggle in the segregated American South, nationalist resistance movements in India and late-colonial Africa, and the debate over gay rights in the contemporary United States. Thus, an analysis of the struggle between colonial authority and African independency to define the "true" nature of Scouting has broad comparative applications. The colonial African Scouting case study provides a guide to map the divisions in any given society that supports a Scout movement.

No society is monolithic and inherently stable, and the tensions surrounding Scouting expose common points of friction generated by unequal relationships of class, gender, and often race and ethnicity. Colonial society in anglophone Africa, however, was particularly fragile and fragmentary. Originating from the autocratic, and often violent, suppression and co-option of local political and social institutions, the colonial regime attempted to transform the African majority into a permanent underclass on the basis of their supposed cultural inferiority. Scouting in this context exposes the efforts of Africans to imagine alternatives to established institutions of political authority, schooling, masculinity, and generational authority that threatened to shatter the brittle colonial social order.

The primary actors in this story are European colonial officials, teachers, and Scoutmasters, and individual African Scouts and Scoutmasters and their local communities. The African group was divided into official and unofficial Scouts. Scouting could be an elite movement based at secondary schools, part of educational experiments in reconciling Western schooling with "native tradition," a social welfare tool for community development, or a grassroots African expression of autonomy and anticolonial resistance. Although formal African Scouts usually belonged to troops sponsored by mission schools, they often used the egalitarianism of the movement to contest Britain's imperial agenda by imagining a more open and inclusive colonial order. Unofficial scouts were largely outside direct colonial control and embraced the movement for a variety of reasons. Some treated Scouting as a business or confidence scheme to enrich themselves, while others reinterpreted the movement to mount a direct challenge to the legitimacy of the colonial regime. This struggle between formal and informal Scouting for control of the movement throws light on the tenuous shape and character of colonial society by exposing larger conflicts over social reproduction and political legitimacy.

GOVERNING THE AFRICAN MAJORITY

Scouting both facilitated and complicated colonial rule. The men who governed Britain's African empire believed Scouting was a useful tool of "native" administration. They had ambitious plans to develop it into a mass movement that would give African youth a greater stake in the colonial enterprise. The short-lived technological and military advantages that allowed Europeans to carve out African empires in the late nineteenth century obscure the relative weakness of the resulting colonial states. British officials worked tirelessly to win at least the tacit support of the subject majority, but ultimately the viability of colonial rule depended on the threat of coercive violence. This "dominance without hegemony," as Ranajit Guha puts it, meant that the colonial authorities could not govern through "universal practices and norms," as they did in metropolitan Britain.[6] Scouting was part of a broader strategy—which included education and Christian evangelism—to win local allies and introduce these Western values into local African communities.

Great Britain became an African power in the late nineteenth century in response to specific economic, strategic, and domestic social needs. The relative ease and rapidity with which it acquired sovereignty over large expanses of territory under the "new imperialism" meant that British politicians, missionaries, businessmen, and adventurers gave little thought as to how they would govern millions of new African subjects. With most colonies and protectorates acquired on the basis of speculation rather than tangible and immediate value, the British treasury insisted that the new territories strive for economic self-sufficiency lest

8

they become a burden on the metropolitan taxpayer. As a result, British colonial policy was largely pragmatic and adaptive.

Territorial governments lacked the financial resources and manpower to govern their African subjects directly. They had to weigh the potential returns of remaking African economies to serve Western commercial interests against the danger of provoking widespread unrest if their intervention was too rapid or unduly invasive. Bruce Berman and John Lonsdale have shown how the colonial state had to balance the demands of metropolitan and settler capitalist interests to mobilize labor and restructure local production with the necessity of maintaining rural stability. Mahmood Mamdani argues that these realities produced a "bifurcated state" where the civil power governed urban areas directly but relied on "tribal authorities" to extend its influence into rural areas. Labeling this system of "native" administration "decentralized despotism," Mamdani rightly makes a distinction between the handful of urban "civilized" Africans who enjoyed the privileges of citizenship and the African majority who became "tribal" subjects.[7]

To be sure, colonialism was authoritarian, exploitive, and often brutal, but it also had its limits. The "thin white line" of the colonial administrative service, to use Anthony Kirk-Greene's term, relied on African intermediaries to govern the countryside. In theory, under the philosophy of "indirect rule" Britain's local administrative partners were "native rulers" who commanded obedience on the basis of their "traditional" status and prerogatives in precolonial times. In practice, these chiefs and headmen derived their authority largely from their participation in the colonial system. In addition to being inexpensive, indirect rule also allowed colonial authorities to claim a measure of legitimacy by posing as African rulers. In the countryside, the colonial regime governed by codifying local traditions and fixing the authority of male elders over women and younger men. The legitimizing ideology of indirect rule therefore had an additional consequence of making the British the self-styled guardians of "native custom," but their interpretation of what constituted African tradition proved highly pragmatic and flexible.[8]

The colonial regime was never powerful enough to simply impose invented customs on unwilling local communities. Indirect rule therefore created opportunities for individuals who depicted themselves successfully as the arbiters of tradition. British colonial doctrine held that every African belonged to a "tribe" and that customary "native law" governed every aspect of a person's political and social life. In other words, British colonial experts believed African identity was corporate rather than individual. In theory, these "tribal" identities were primordial and encapsulated the customary laws that empowered the colonial regime's rural allies. Colonial chiefs and headmen combined judicial, legislative, executive, and administrative power in their narrow parishes, and British officials cited "native tradition" to excuse their despotic behavior. Under the realities of indirect rule, "tribes" rather than people had rights.

Yet the legitimizing ideologies that reconciled Britain's despotic seizure of an African empire with its commitment to humanitarianism and liberal democracy at home placed limits on the authority of the colonial state and its local African allies. Britain needed to depict Africans as primitive to alleviate the guilt of colonial rule. As the chief architect of indirect rule, Frederick Lugard, later Baron Lugard, argued that Britain had a "dual mandate" to foster the material and moral benefit of "backward" peoples while simultaneously exploiting the economic potential of the colonies.[9] In practice, this meant that the colonial governments had to at least appear to show concern for African social welfare and development to demonstrate that they were a paternalistic rather than an opportunistic foreign power. To lend credence to Lugard's highly unrealistic blending of altruism with self-interest, they tried to silence African and metropolitan critics of colonialism by claiming to govern in the best interests of the subject majority. Ideally, this meant allowing "tribal" societies to develop at their own pace.

In reality, the necessity of catering to metropolitan commercial interests, coupled with the fiscal priorities of the territorial governments, significantly undermined the ability of colonial officials to pose as paternalistic custodians of "primitive" peoples. The presence of small but politically influential communities of Europeans in eastern, central, and southern Africa made it impossible to treat Africans as anything more than subjects and "protected persons." Colonial governments in these regions encouraged Western settlement on the assumption that local Europeans would provide a more solid base for agricultural and commercial development than the African farmers and pastoralists, who resisted integration into the colonial economy on subordinate terms. Colonial officials also hoped that these "islands of white" would bring permanence and stability to British rule in Africa.[10]

The settlers invariably forced their needs ahead of African interests. They refused to consider any form of African political participation and protected their dominant social position through rigid racial segregation. In dismissing the qualifications of educated Africans an administrator in Tanganyika sneered, "Does anyone who sees the Europeanised

African believe him to be genuine? Too often he seems only a caricature of a European and an insult to his own race."[11] This racial discrimination exposed the inconsistency of colonial social policy. Although British officials invoked enlightened paternalism to legitimize the colonial regime, there were solid, if not always clear, barriers that prevented Africans from becoming equal partners within the empire.

Britain's reliance on skilled and semiskilled Africans to reduce the cost of developing its African possessions further complicated the dual mandate. Lacking the financial resources to employ large amounts of European manpower, territorial governments, European businessmen, and even racially minded settlers relied on a small class of educated but poorly paid Africans for administrative, coercive, technical, and commercial assistance. As "native labor" expert W. Ormsby-Gore explained, "The economic development of tropical Africa calls increasingly for Africans to man the railways, the motor lorries, to build, to carpenter, and to do a thousand things which are familiar to us and quite new and strange to the African."[12] "Native tradition" was of little use in training African clerks, interpreters, catechists, soldiers, policemen, prison wardens, agricultural demonstrators, medical assistants, artisans, and the like. The forced economy of colonialism led British officials to delegate the responsibility for training these essential African auxiliaries to the Christian missions. Mission schooling followed a "moral" Western curriculum, thereby providing proof that Britain was fulfilling its humanitarian obligations in Africa.

Yet the Western liberal arts curriculum almost always proved incompatible with "native tradition." Mission educators, particularly in the early days of British rule, believed in an ideal of "liberal individualism and universal citizenship" that complicated the colonial regime's intention to accord Africans only communal, rather than individual, rights. Although they were partners in the colonial enterprise, missionaries had their own evangelical agenda that placed a heavy emphasis on literacy and the diffusion of Western religious and secular values. As what Julian Huxley termed the "de facto Third Estate" in most territories, the missions often brushed aside official concerns about the destabilizing consequences of their educational policies. British officials therefore worried that the mission schools were instruments of "detribalization" that inspired educated Africans to reject the authority of their chiefs and headmen. The educated intermediaries produced by these schools were both essential to the economic vitality of the colonial regime and a threat to its very survival. Occupying the uncertain ground between "tribal" subjects and full citizens, they considered themselves outside the bounds of customary law and demanded full access to civil society.[13]

Colonial officials desperately sought to reintegrate mission school graduates into rural society and seized upon Scouting as an instrument of "retribalization." The movement would teach African students to be "tribal" by preserving what colonial authority deemed useful and wholesome in local age grade systems. European Scout leaders sought to incorporate "tribal lore and custom" into their programs to compensate for the detribalizing impact of Western education, wage labor, and urbanization.

Much of the work on indirect rule's inherent contradictions either has tended to overestimate the power of the colonial regime and its rural African allies to stifle dissent or has valorized the educated Africans' oppositional strategies within the larger framework of subaltern resistance. Frederick Cooper is convincing when he notes that this approach has difficulty reconciling colonial subjects' agency and consciousness with their subordinate status. The conflicting official and unauthorized interpretations of African Scouting demonstrate that Africans had the ability to turn the mechanisms of colonialism to their own ends. Colonial institutions like Scouting were authoritarian and occasionally despotic, but they were also vulnerable to subversion and reinterpretation. To categorize the movement solely as a "retribalizing" tool of social control is to miss the larger picture. Scouting shows how middle figures navigated the difficult terrain between cooperation and resistance to achieve mobility within the confines of colonial society. African Scouts used the Fourth Scout Law to contest the color bar and traded upon the colonial regime's assumption that their membership in the movement meant that they could be trusted.[14]

Adaptive resistance often took the form of autonomous Western-style institutions that mirrored, but were independent of, the colonial bases of power and legitimacy. With political participation and social advancement blocked by racial discrimination under the color bar, Africans created their own businesses, churches, schools, and Scout troops to acquire the benefits of Western culture without having to submit to colonial authority. Through this independency they laid claim to the symbols of progress, civics, and faith that legitimized the colonial regime and adapted them to suit local African circumstances. Independency meant creating autonomous Western-style institutions that were free from the taint and influence of colonial authority. Derek Peterson describes these processes as "contracting colonialism." In explaining why the leaders of Kikuyu independent churches and schools went to such great lengths to adopt Western bureaucratic institutions and practices, he argues that "playing by the state's rules of recognition was for Kikuyu organizers a way of claiming entitlement from colonial administrators." By mastering the "grammar and practice of citizenship" the Kikuyu independents demanded full access to civil society.[15] Scouting was unquestionably part of the grammar of citizenship and proved a tempting target for the independents.

Much to the consternation of European Scout officials, independent African scout troops freely modified the Scout canon to reflect their own political and social values. Independent Kikuyu troops substituted "Jomo [Kenyatta]" for "Jesus" in Scout songs and hymns.On an individual level, African boys and men styled themselves Scouts and Scoutmasters by donning variations of the Scout uniform. In some cases, they were simply seeking the status that the colonial regime accorded uniformed African Scouts. In other instances, they were outright impostors who traded on the prestige of the movement to pose as government representatives and engage in illegal fundraising. The behavior of the second group was unquestionably larcenous, but their tactics also represented a challenge to the controlling power of the mundane in colonial culture. John and Jean Comaroff have shown how the authority of the colonial regime depended on its ability to capture the banalities of everyday life. Unauthorized African scouting was part of the larger African contestation of colonial culture that produced "half-caste currencies, playful synthetic styles, and mixed modes of production."[16]

CONTRADICTIONS IN THE COLONIAL SCHOOL

Sanctioned official African Scouting was largely an informal extension of the colonial school system. The movement had a much stronger link with formal educational institutions in Africa than it did in virtually any other part of the world. Baden-Powell was deeply interested in correcting the perceived failures of metropolitan British schools and conceived of Scouting as a supplemental educational tool for teaching the character development and morality that he believed was missing from the conventional curriculum. He called Scouting "a venture for a jolly outdoor recreation which has been found to form also a practical aid to education. . . . It is, in a word, a school of citizenship through woodcraft."[17] It would have been virtually impossible for Scouting to exist in colonial Africa without the support of the education establishment. Mission and government schools sponsored the vast majority of official Scout troops because they had the manpower, financial resources, and official connections needed to reach African boys. Colonial educators imported the movement to Africa to resolve the inherent contradictions in indirect rule by teaching students to give their loyalty to their "tribal rulers" and, by extension, the British Empire. There was no African "citizenship" under British rule, and "character training" in the colonial context meant rejecting the lure of personal enrichment and political activism and subordinating individual interests to the collective needs of the "tribe." Formal Scouting's important auxiliary role in African schools means that the movement must be considered in scholarly debates over the nature and legacy of colonial education.

Generally speaking, historians have not been kind to the colonial schools. Many experts on African education have charged that British colonial education amounted to cultural imperialism that imposed alien values on subject African communities. To some degree, this argument is based on an idealized view of precolonial African society. Critics of colonial schooling have argued that prepartition African communities developed systems of education that were in harmony with their material and social life and made no distinction between physical and intellectual labor. They charge British educators with destroying this educational harmony by teaching individualism rather than the values of a collective society.[18] Yet this was exactly the agenda of the colonial teachers, who tried to modify Western educational practices to create a new curriculum that was specifically "adapted" to the needs of "primitive" pluralistic African communities. This adapted colonial curriculum assumed that "tribal" Africans were incapable of mastering Western cultural norms. Colonial officials worried that Western schooling led to materialism and individualism and turned to Scouting to strengthen the "traditional" communal values that buttressed indirect rule.

Many scholars attribute political and social problems in contemporary Africa to the colonial regime's imposition of an alien Western value system that destroyed the sense of cooperation and community that bound Africans together in precolonial times. They stress that colonial education prepared Africans to be nothing more than "hewers of wood and drawers of water," and indict it for "brainwashing" students into rejecting their heritage and embracing the allegedly superior Western culture. To be sure, colonial schools denigrated local learning practices by projecting an image of backwardness and incompetence on people who remained outside the Western education system. Colonial school certificates and diplomas were of limited value because many employers considered them inferior, and African workers usually learned lucrative vocational skills on the job.[19]

These attacks on colonial education are part of a broader leftist critique of education in Western societies positing the existence of a "hidden curriculum" in state school systems that strengthens and perpetuates divisions of race and class. In this sense British colonial schools were part of the larger Western educational system that sustained capitalist power relationships. They followed an "adapted" curriculum taken from the segregated American South that stressed vocational skills and manual labor over a scholastic liberal arts education. The colonial regime transplanted this adapted education system to Africa in the 1920s to limit the political impact of Western schooling and strengthen the rural social order threatened by colonial demands for labor and commodity production. Under this system only a handful of privileged African students had access to a classic literary education at the secondary level.

This narrow education pyramid that characterized "native education" in anglophone Africa was not unique to the colonial periphery. The metropolitan British education system also made a sharp distinction between vocational training for the masses and higher education for administrative and technical elites. Whether in Africa or in the West, formal schooling reproduced subordinate future generations and acted as an instrument of imperialism by linking subject populations to world markets and teaching capitalist concepts of work. Far from being a universally egalitarian force, it provided real social mobility only for the fortunate few who served the capitalist state as compradors and overseers.[20]

These critiques of colonial African schooling make some telling and damning points, but they run into the subalternist problem of reconciling the subordinate status of subject peoples with their capacity to resist, alter, and adapt colonial policy. Although many Africans were understandably suspicious of the avowed civilizing agenda of the colonial schools, they eagerly sought access to Western education as a means of economic accumulation and social advancement. Even a basic primary education qualified graduates for lucrative clerical and administrative positions, thus allowing an escape from subsistence agriculture and unpleasant manual labor on public works projects, corporate plantations, and settler farms. As products of an elitist and restrictive school system African students had high expectations for social mobility and became embittered upon realizing that the color bar would forever block their progress. Secondary school graduates in particular believed that their mastery of Western culture entitled them to full rights as citizens and rejected the authority of their "tribal rulers." Western schooling produced a class of educated elites with the ambition, political expertise, and social sophistication to challenge the legitimacy of the colonial regime on its own terms. To be sure, they had few ties to the less educated general population, but they were hardly willing tools of the colonial regime.

In the eyes of British officials, education was the cause of, and the solution to, these dangerous contradictions in colonial administration and society. Educators and administrators believed that it was possible to develop new styles of schooling that would be civilizing and humanitarian, provide economically useful technical training, and teach young Africans to seek their fortunes within the safe confines of "tribal" society. They tried to fulfill their educational obligations under the dual mandate but not to the point where their students had the ability or inclination to challenge British rule. Believing that they could remake African society through the schools, colonial educators developed an adapted curriculum to reflect the political and social goals of the colonial regime. As C. T. Loram, a South African authority on "native education," explained, "Reduced to its lowest terms, education is the process by which a human being is changed from what he is to something that those in authority wish him to be."[21] More simply, this meant fitting Africans into the new economic and social realities of colonialism.

The adapted curriculum favored by "native education" experts in the 1920s was weighted heavily toward "practical" vocational skills at the expense of advanced literacy, mathematics, science, and history. On the surface, it appeared relatively uncontroversial in stressing mundane subjects like agricultural science, handicrafts, literacy in African vernaculars, and "native lore and tradition." The conventional literary curriculum was available only at one or two elite secondary schools in each territory. Advocates of adapted education promised to promote rural development, reduce political discontent, and reinforce the sanctioned conceptions of tradition that underpinned indirect rule.

The ability of African students and local communities to reinterpret and subvert these educational efforts demonstrates the limits of colonial authority. They demanded full access to the Western literary curriculum and viewed adapted education as an attempt to institutionalize their inferior status. The colonial educators' efforts to create a class of economically useful but politically compliant graduates failed miserably. Educated Africans, even the products of adapted schools, were some of the most vocal and effective opponents of the colonial regime. Moreover, African communities created their own independent schools to wrest control of the Western literary curriculum from the colonial state. It is significant that most independents did not try to re-create the romanticized precolonial education systems celebrated by leftist critics of the colonial schools.

Nevertheless, Scouting was indeed part of the "hidden curriculum" of colonialism. It promised to counter the politicizing tendencies of Western schooling through "character training." European Scouters and teachers interpreted the Scout canon as an obligation for African Scouts to give their loyalty to the colonial regime. Scouting was to be a form of supplemental education that corrected the flaws of the adapted curriculum. Yet the movement proved as open to reinterpretation as colonial schooling. In reworking the Scout canon within the context of independency, African Scouts challenged their subordinate social status. Far from being the deculturized victims of an alien value system, they demonstrated a strong sense of agency in appropriating the methods and legitimacy of the international Scout movement and local colonial schools.

MAKING THE AFRICAN BOY

Scouting also exposes the uncertain nature of masculinity in colonial society. As was the case with governance and schooling, gender became a key site of contestation between colonial authority and African independency. The security of British rule in the countryside, law and order in the cities, and the reliability and productivity of migrant labor all depended on the capacity of the colonial regime to reorder African family life by promoting specific conceptions of masculinity and femininity. In theory, colonial rule imposed a gendered division of labor where women were responsible for domestic rural agricultural work while men became labor migrants in service of settler and foreign capitalist interests. Properly regulated gender relations were also a key to the viability of indirect rule. Much of the authority of the colonial regime's rural allies depended on their control of the productive and reproductive capacity of young women. The ability to define customary practices regulating adolescence, bride price, and inheritance also gave the chiefs and headmen control over younger generations of men who had to defer to their authority in order to marry. The ability of young men and women to slip the bonds of rural authority by finding alternative means of support and forming new conjugal relationships was a veiled, but direct, challenge to the security of the colonial regime. Scouting was an important tool in addressing this "gender chaos" by promoting sanctioned conceptions of masculinity.[22]

Although patriarchal institutions of authority generally privilege men over women, not all men share this power equally. In other words, there are multiple and often contradictory masculinities. The most accepted conception of masculinity in a given society usually reflects hierarchies of class and racial privilege and enjoys the distinction of being perceived by the general public as natural. Alternate masculinities are often, but not always, challenges to the established political and social order. Although they would have objected strenuously to the suggestion that gender was socially variable, Baden-Powell and the founders of Scouting were consciously aware that they were promoting a specific form of masculinity over a range of less desirable masculine identities. In their eyes, manliness meant physical courage, patriotism, stoicism, chivalry, and sexual continence. They viewed the early feminists' demands for greater social and economic autonomy as a serious threat and sought to confine women to the private domestic sphere.[23] Scouting became a tool for staking out the public arena for middle- and upper-class men. Poor and working-class British boys had little use for Scouting's emphasis on discipline and social conformity. They certainly also aspired to be men, but embraced a decidedly different concept of masculinity that preserved their autonomy. Similarly, African boys frequently rejected the movement's attempt to make them into obedient men who accepted their place in colonial society and sought sexual release solely within the bonds of marriage.

The linkage of homosexual desire and expression with alternate masculinities was a particular concern of Scout authorities in Britain. The ossification of masculine and feminine identities linked to domesticity, patriarchal authority, and aggressive imperialism in late Victorian Britain led to the classification of a preference for emotional and physical same-sex relations as an abnormal psychological state. Homosexually oriented masculinity called key elements of the Scout canon into question by suggesting that there were alternate conceptions of manliness that were not linked to chastity, conformity, and patriarchal privilege. Yet Scouting's all-male environment often attracted men who were sexually drawn to males. Tim Jeal, Baden-Powell's biographer, suggests that the chief Scout himself found men physically attractive and approved of young Scouts swimming and sun bathing in the nude at Gilwell Camp, the British Scout Association's primary training center. Nevertheless, Baden-Powell was appalled when he had to remove two of the first Gilwell Camp chiefs for molesting boys in their charge. He stressed sexual self-control and continence above all else, and wrote privately that the offenders should be flogged for their crimes.[24] The Scout establishment was thus concerned with promoting respectable conceptions of heterosexual masculinity and ensuring that the movement was not tainted by charges of pederasty.

Homosexuality was far less a concern in African Scouting. There is virtually no mention of either specific scandals or official fears about same-sex relations in the archives of the territorial Scout associations. Colonial officials and educators generally believed that homosexuality was an imported Western "perversion" and not part of "traditional" African culture. They considered the sexualized relationships that developed between older and younger men in southern African mines to be aberrations caused by the breakdown of "tribal law." Yet this is not to say that homosexuality was never present in African Scouting; instead, it may be absent from official Scout records because the Scouting authorities never looked for it. They had full control over the movement only at the elite secondary schools and were dimly aware, at best, of what went on in rural African troops. Certainly sexual contacts between African boys and adult European men in positions of authority were not unheard of. Chenjerai Shire recalls that some mission school students who could not pay their tuition shared a house and, by implication, a bed with priests.[25] Colonial officials denied the existence of African homosexualities because they complicated the patriarchal heterosexual conceptions of masculinity that underpinned indirect rule and gendered divisions of African labor.

Scout authorities were much more concerned with making Africans into the right kind of boys and men than they were with the perceived threat of homosexuality. To most European officials and settlers, African men were perpetual boys who lacked the self-control to be accorded adult status. The resident commissioner of Basutoland put it this way: "With the young native the attainment of the years of manhood appears to be accompanied by an arrest of intellectual development, an increased dominance of the appetites." Similarly, a Southern Rhodesian official denied the adulthood of Shona men because they "never learned the value of hard work; indeed, they hardly know what it means." In reality, the colonial regime itself bore primary responsibility for hindering the ability of African males to reach the markers of adulthood by making it difficult for young men to acquire enough cattle or land to marry and support a family. Taxation, land shortages, stock culling and grazing controls, and the destruction of rural economies drove young men to become labor migrants. Denied the opportunity to establish stable families, many formed temporary conjugal relationships with urban women. The fleeting and often overtly commercial nature of these sexual contacts threatened government attempts to create stable family units and seemed to validate colonial stereotypes regarding the unquenchable sexual appetites of African men.[26]

Interestingly, the colonial Scout establishment did not fully subscribe to the stereotype of Africans as permanent children. As in Britain, European Scout leaders genuinely believed they were making African boys into men. In the colonial context this meant reinforcing "tribal" discipline on graduates of government and mission schools. As allies of the missions and the colonial state, the Scout authorities taught that true men were obedient, disciplined, and sexually continent. More specifically, they sought to control the youthful sexuality that led to bride price disputes, illegitimate childbirth, and the spread of venereal disease. These outbreaks of "immorality" threatened colonial authority by undermining African families, the patriarchal authority of the chiefs and headmen, and the coherency of "tribal" life.

From the Scouts' standpoint, a true man controlled his sexual desires. Julian Huxley, once a lecturer in experimental zoology at King's College London and who conducted an educational survey of East Africa for the Colonial Office in 1929, believed that Africans could achieve full adulthood if they mastered the sexual urges that blocked their intellectual maturation. "In the existing state of native culture, sex looms large, and at puberty comes to occupy the focus of life. If you can provide native boys with a different background of thought and practice, their intellectual development can continue through puberty with no more break and disturbance than overtakes the white child, and [they] can continue and mature with us." Scouting was just the vehicle to provide these new "thoughts and practices." African Scouting in South Africa, commonly known as Pathfinding, taught boys to respect girls while avoiding their company until marriage. The Pathfinders could associate with Wayfarers (Girl Guides) only if their leaders gave them "special permission."[27] African Scouting "made men," but these men were to be responsible clerks and teachers. Similarly, the few nonscholastic official troops sought to produce chaste labor migrants and tribally conscious peasant farmers.

The colonial regime was attempting the impossible in trying to fix African gender identities. African opposition to its despotic social and economic policies inevitably produced conflicting conceptions of masculinity. In urban areas migrants could acquire entirely new gender roles. Women adopted male roles by becoming financially independent, and, according to Marc Epprecht, men experimented with alternate masculinities, including homosexuality. The cities also bred more dangerous forms of manliness as the colonial regime's limits on education, employment, and legal residence made poor rootless young men more aggressive. In South Africa, the highly masculine gang culture that developed rejected generational authority and forced women into subordinate roles through violence and intimidation.[28]

Independent African scouts also contested and manipulated colonial gender identities. Their claim to respectability and legitimacy made them rivals of the urban gangs, but their conceptions of manliness were equally, albeit more subtly, subversive. In Kenya, independent Kikuyu scouts agreed that true men were tough, self-reliant, and "loyal," but in the early 1950s they gave their allegiance to the Mau Mau forest fighters. The independents also rejected the colonial regime's insistence on strict gender segregation. Much to the horror of the Scout and Girl Guide leadership, the Kikuyu schools often enrolled females in their scout troops instead of creating separate guide companies.[29] Although the independent school leaders shared the Kenyan government's concerns about sexual immorality, they created a coed scout movement to conserve financial resources. They did not believe that scouting had to be an all-male institution. This was not the norm in most independent troops, but those African scoutmasters who added girls to their troops most likely sought to contest the colonial authorities' attempts to define the proper relationships between pubescent African boys and girls.

YOUTH AND THE CRISIS OF GENERATIONAL AUTHORITY

The colonial regime's attempt to shore up the patriarchal authority of its local African allies was the last of the four main social fault lines that Scouting exposed in anglophone Africa. Each generation worries that the young people who follow will not uphold its values or recognize established patterns of authority and divisions of wealth. In the West these concerns have become more pronounced in the last two centuries with the classification of postpubescent youth as adolescents who were socially and morally undeveloped. Social reformers and youth experts conceived of juvenile delinquency as rebellion stemming from an immature attempt by young people to acquire the autonomy of adulthood before they were ready. In the late nineteenth century, Western social reformers began to worry that formal education could not provide the necessary supervision to guide adolescents to adulthood. Technical advances in transportation and communication gave young people a greater sense of a common identity and a powerful capacity to shape culture. More seriously, youthful demands for autonomy also had the capacity to grow into political activism and open rebellion because young people were less invested in established social norms.[30]

Scouting was the most popular of the organized youth movements that established institutions of authority created to provide structured diversions for the energy and ambitions of younger generations. The success of these movements depended on their ability to make their programs relevant to the lived experience of adolescence. Scouting was particularly popular because adults believed it extended their control over youth while convincing boys that the movement actually increased their autonomy. The Scout canon thus became an effective means of transmitting established norms and values to succeeding generations.[31]

To a large degree, adolescence was an elite category in colonial Africa. Only a fraction of children attended school in each territory, and most of those completed only a few years of schooling before being forced to drop out by high fees, competitive examinations, or the pressure to earn a living. In most cases, only advanced students and young people with semipermanent urban residency could be classified as adolescents in the Western sense. Yet as such they represented one of the most serious threats to the stability of the colonial regime. Intermediate and secondary school graduates demanded social mobility and the rights of full citizenship. Young nonstudents migrated to the cities for work and excitement when rural economies began to collapse. In both cases, they rejected the authority of their elders, who could no longer provide the means for succeeding generations to establish themselves as respectable adults. In southern Africa young men in particular blamed their older relatives for failing to prevent the imposition of colonial rule and saw little reason to defer to seniors who could not give them land and cattle.[32] This rejection of generational authority eroded the foundations of indirect rule and threatened to spark widespread social instability.

Scouting promised to correct this imbalance by teaching "detribalized" students and city boys to respect their elders. The movement implicitly reinforced the Western concept of adolescence by subjecting African teenagers and young men to extended supervision while they theoretically acquired the discipline and deference to authority required for full adulthood in colonial society. Thus, in embracing Scouting, the colonial regime sought to extend its reach into local African communities by exercising power over the smallest units of society, namely families, households, and children. Colonial African Scouting was also part of larger state-sponsored social welfare initiatives that aimed to improve labor discipline and stifle political dissent by structuring African leisure time.[33] Just as metropolitan social reformers worried that unchecked urbanization and class antagonism led to the physical and moral degeneration of Britain's lower classes, colonial officials worried that African resistance to state and generational authority was due to a similar decline in communal "tribal" values brought on by the deleterious introduction of Western materialism. Scouting would "retribalize" individualistic Africans by teaching them to be selflessly "loyal" to their elders and "native rulers."

The Scout uniform played a central role in these processes of social control. Baden-Powell modeled it on the uniform of the South African Constabulary, a paramilitary police force that he raised and commanded after the Anglo–South African War. In adapting an adult military uniform for use by boys he sought to create a potent socializing device that would become an enticing recruiting tool, establish Scouting's elite credentials, and reinforce the Fourth Scout Law by blurring class distinctions within the movement. Although the Scout uniform's martial origins left Baden-Powell open to charges that he was secretly preparing boys for military service, his primary goal was to defuse the potential for intergenerational conflict by creating a structured outlet for youthful rebellion.[34] The uniform marked its wearers as members of an exclusive, tough, but also chivalric youth gang. It tempered boys' energy and aggression with elitist conformity. The Scouts were not the only youth group in Edwardian Britain to wear military-style uniforms, but their successful blending of martial style with woodlore and social egalitarianism made them the most popular.

The Scout uniform had even greater potency in colonial Africa, where Western styles of clothing conveyed gentility, sophistication, and respectability. European employers usually insisted that Africans dress in simple utilitarian work clothes to reinforce their subordinate status, and laborers had to carefully husband their earnings to purchase Western clothing. Most students went barefoot, and colonial armies generally did not issue their African soldiers boots until the Second World War. As a result, even the simplest items of apparel acquired considerable prestige and status. Workers, military men, and young people coveted high-class European-style clothes to wear in their free time. Western clothing became a means of contesting colonial social restrictions by acquiring more sophisticated identities that could be put on and off as the situation allowed.[35]

Most African boys coveted the Scout uniform for many of the same reasons as their British peers, but the uniform had additional meaning in colonial society. The Scout authorities hoped the uniform would inspire African boys to be proud, but also disciplined and obedient, members of the movement. They never expected that it would become a tool for circumventing colonial authority. Uniformed Scouts had more autonomy than the average African boy because the colonial authorities assumed they could be trusted. African Scouts were less likely to be questioned by the security forces and enjoyed greater freedom to travel as well as free admission to public events. Scouts also had considerable prestige in rural communities, where the local people generally assumed that anyone wearing a khaki uniform was some sort of government official. The trust accorded uniformed Scouts by district officers and policemen reinforced this belief. It was therefore not surprising that some Scouts traded on this deference to circumvent colonial authority and exact privileges and tribute from local communities. In other cases, enterprising individuals simply posed as Scouts by wearing illegally acquired parts of the uniform. Their manipulation of the material culture of Scouting is illustrative of the ways in which colonial peoples adapted Western institutions to fashion hybrid colonial cultures that brought greater freedom and autonomy.

Wearing a uniform did not mean that African boys accepted the general principles of British colonialism. Instead they appropriated the Scout uniform to imagine an alternative version of colonial society where Africans had access to positions of authority and legitimacy. Uniforms exposed one of the most fundamental and potentially disruptive contradictions of African Scouting: "To make things uniform means to make them equal. Making individuals equal means abolishing distinctions of class and demographics."[36] Most of the settler colonies in eastern, central, and southern Africa also supported European Scout troops. In theory, their common Scout uniforms conveyed the message that African and European Scouts were equals. Combined with the Fourth Scout Law, which affirmed that all Scouts were brothers, the Scout uniform was a serious challenge to the color bar. Following Baden-Powell's lead in Britain, the territorial Scout associations were committed to maintaining their ties to the institutions of political and social legitimacy. They were therefore unwilling to jeopardize their alliance with the colonial regime by adhering to the spirit of the Scout canon. The Scout authorities' attempts to fashion a distinctly African uniform and, by extension, an adapted form of Scouting that respected the realities of the color bar left the Scout movement open to reinterpretation by African independents who used the Scout canon to challenge colonialisms' inherent racism and social inequality. Scouting was thus both an instrument of social control and an equally potent expression of social protest.

THE SHAPE OF THE STUDY

Scouting comprised a package of values, norms, and rituals that varied considerably in each local culture. In one sense, Scouting can be compared to a secular religion with Baden-Powell as its prophetlike founder whose writings constituted the core of the Scout canon and whose personal example became the guide for model behavior. The territorial Scout associations around the world correspond to national churches with the authority to make alterations to the movement within the limits of Scouting orthodoxy. At the local level, troops are the congregations who put core Scout values into practice. Local applications of Scouting usually result from a syncretic blending of Scouting orthodoxy and community values. In some cases these adaptations have the full blessing of the Scout authorities. Scouting allows religious institutions to create "closed" troops solely for the members of their congregations, and national Scout associations are free to choose their own emblems to symbolize patriotism and loyalty. Some local communities, however, also make alterations to the Scout canon that official Scouting considers unacceptably heretical. This was the case in colonial Africa, where nationalists, independent schools, churches, and outright impostors appropriated the movement for their own purposes.

Understanding the full social implications of colonial African Scouting therefore requires a vertical study of the interplay between manifestations of the movement at the metropolitan, territorial, and local levels. This study traces connections between the orthodoxy of Baden-Powell and the British Scout Association (BSA), the adapted "native" Scouting developed by territorial governments and Scout associations to support colonial policy, and the conflicting attempts by missionaries, teachers, Scoutmasters, and African Scouts to make the movement relevant to local circumstances. In some cases African Scouts and Scoutmasters worked within the confines of orthodox Scouting to claim imperial citizenship by establishing their respectability and mastery of Western values and material culture. In other instances unauthorized scouts reinterpreted the Scout canon and transformed the movement into an expression of social and political dissent.

Historians of late Victorian and Edwardian Britain have paid close attention to the development of uniformed youth movements, and the question of whether early Scouting was militaristic has generated considerable scholarly debate. Education specialists have also explored the movement's pedagogical applications. Finally, in addition to Tim Jeal's comprehensive biography of Baden-Powell, we have the founder's own voluminous publications on virtually every aspect of Scouting. The Scout canon consists of these writings, the Scout Oath and Law (originally referred to in Britain as the Scout Promise), and the national Scout associations' bylaws and Scout handbooks. These core tracts, institutional histories, and official and semiofficial sources outline the development and goals of imperial Scouting, but they show only how the Scout authorities thought troops should be run rather than how the movement played out at the local level.[37]

In colonial Africa, the territorial Scout associations, colonial administrators, and mission educators constituted another layer between official Scouting and its grass roots. In explicitly trying to adapt the movement to African circumstances they created versions of Scouting that were distinctly different from the metropolitan model. Although a few historians of India have addressed Scouting and Guiding under the British Raj, there are no comparable studies of the colonial uses of Scouting in Africa. Girl Guiding in South Africa offers important comparative insights into Scouting, but the two movements developed in markedly different ways in the African context. Histories of colonial African education also pay little attention to the movement on the grounds that it was a relatively narrow extracurricular activity. Social historians have examined Scouting as part of the colonial regime's social welfare programs, but their studies deal with the movement only tangentially. As a result, Scouting's ties to colonial authority have remained largely unexplored.[38]

Colonial Scouting has been largely forgotten in contemporary Africa because membership levels were relatively low. Despite the best efforts of British administrators and educators, Scouting never became a mass movement in the colonial period (see table 1.1). Overall, there were probably about one hundred thousand registered African Boy Scouts in all of anglophone Africa by the 1950s. Admittedly these figures do not account for the hundreds, perhaps thousands, of boys who belonged to informal troops that the territorial Scout associations did not recognize. The colonial governments and territorial Scout associations were deeply concerned with adapting the movement for Africans, but they often had little clue as to what was actually going on individual African troops. In

Table 1.1. African Scouts as a Percentage of the Student Body

Territory	Students Registered	African Scouts	Percentage
South Africa, ca. 1950	747,026	14,885	1.99
Nyasaland, 1950	219,667	750	0.34
Kenya, ca. 1948	262,300	759	0.29

Source: Muriel Horrell, Bantu Education to 1968, 51; Union of South Africa, Report of the Commission on Native Education, 1949-1951, 94; Lord Arthur Hailey, An African Survey, rev. ed., 1165; Extract from CO Report on Nyasaland, 1950, MNA, 17/BSA/1/210; Kenya Colony and Protectorate, African Education in Kenya, 14; Kenya Colony and Protectorate, Annual Report of the Welfare Organization, Kenya Colony, 1949 (Nairobi: Government Printer, n.d.).

essence there were two types of African Scouts. The first belonged to troops sponsored by missions, government schools, or social welfare organizations. These sanctioned groups usually had either a European leader or a supervised, "reliable" African Scoutmaster. Government and Scout archives deal with these Scouts in some detail. They mention the second kind of scouts—independents and impostors—only in disapproving terms. Thus, official sources offer only tangential insights into the experiences of individual African boys in the movement.

Ideally, comprehensive interviews with formal and informal ex-Scouts would provide this information. It is relatively easy to locate members of the sanctioned troops. Most attended elite secondary schools and often occupy positions of prestige and authority in postcolonial society. Not surprisingly, they tend to have warm memories of their Scout experiences. These men have tended to stay in touch with each other and can often be contacted through alumni organizations and old-boy associations. Finding members of the informal unauthorized troops is much harder. Many are poorly educated and are much harder to identify as scouts. Moreover, in both cases there are significant methodological problems in asking old men to recall details from their youth.[39] Interviews with former Scouts from both official and unofficial troops made it clear that older informants often recalled even the most difficult childhoods with a certain degree of nostalgia. Colonial authoritarianism, poverty, and a racist education system were problems they overcame in the remote past, and many men dwelt on warm recollections of friends, parents, and youthful accomplishments. They often scathingly recalled their mistreatment by the colonial authorities but had little negative to say about their Scout experiences. Those who disliked the movement might provide a more balanced picture, but they are much harder to locate because they have little reason to identify themselves as ex-Scouts. As a result, the oral histories of African Scouting are usually romanticized and often frustratingly vague.

The records of the metropolitan and territorial Scout authorities are more detailed but also problematic. The archives of the BSA are well maintained and easily accessible to researchers, but they only provide insights into the official thinking and high policies of Baden-Powell and his successors. For the most part, there are no formal archives of the national African Scout associations. The Kenya Scout Association stored the once voluminous records of its colonial predecessor in a disused latrine building on the grounds of its Rowallan Camp, where they fell victim to rot, mold, and insects. The Kenyan Girl Guide Association kept its colonial archives in the rafters of a building that had lost part of its roof. The semiofficial status of most colonial Scout associations meant that much of their correspondence survives in state archives. Although incomplete, these surviving records provide a fairly comprehensive picture of colonial Scout policy. Unfortunately, the only insights they offer into local and informal African Scouting is through worried and often scathing denunciations by European Scout officials.

This study allows for these problems by taking a vertical approach that integrates metropolitan sources on official Scouting and government and territorial Scout archives with the testimony of former African Scouts. Imperial ideology and colonial policy can be understood only through their application to specific historical circumstances. Official Scouting provides a baseline standard for comparing local adaptations of the movement. Tracing the linkages and tensions between imperial rhetoric and ideals, territorial colonial policy, and local adaptation and resistance provides insights into how the idealistic legitimizing ideologies of colonialism played out in practice at the local level. Local variation makes it impossible to construct a picture of African Scouting that depicts faithfully every African boy's experiences in the movement, but hopefully this book will provide the inspiration and context for future research on the local applications of colonial education and youth movements.

This project focuses on the tensions between formal and informal Scouting through specific regional case studies. Kenya and South Africa had entrenched settler communities that protected their social and political privileges through strict racial segregation. The Fourth Scout Law's insistence on egalitarianism and brotherhood complicated this color bar and brought the inherent contradictions of colonialism into sharp focus. Kenya provides a central point of reference for comparing local Scouting variations in Uganda and Tanganyika, while South Africa serves the same function for Britain's colonies and protectorates in southern Africa. The study also touches on Scouting in anglophone West Africa, French Equatorial Africa, the Belgian Congo, British India, and the segregated American South for additional comparative perspectives. It also pays attention to the Girl Guides and rival male youth groups to shed greater light on how uniformed youth movements developed in segregated and divided societies.

2

Scouting and Schools as Colonial Institutions

IN LATE JULY 1907, Gen. Sir Robert Baden-Powell gathered a mix of twenty-two public school and working-class boys on Brownsea Island, off the coast of Dorset, to conduct the first experiment in Scouting. Baden-Powell, a hero of the South African War, used the expedition to try out ideas for youth work that he developed while adapting for boys his widely read military manual *Aids to Scouting for NCOs and Men*. During the roughly ten-day camp (accounts differ on the exact length), he ran his charges through a program encompassing what has become the standard Scouting fare. The boys slept in tents, cooked their own food, played games, tied knots, and learned tracking and woodcraft. Baden-Powell also taught values reflecting his own upper-class Victorian background. He stressed proper hygiene, daily Christian prayer, patriotism, and his interpretation of the chivalric code of medieval knights.[1]

The Brownsea program also reflected Baden-Powell's experiences as a colonial soldier in Africa. He roused the boys each morning with a kudu horn he had captured during the fighting in Matabeleland. Around the evening campfire he told the new Scouts yarns about the colonial wars and led them in his interpretation of a Zulu call-and-response chant that he called "Een-Gonyama-Gonyama." Yet although Scouting had a strong African flavor, Baden-Powell never expected Africans to become Scouts. His primary aim in including British boys from elite and common backgrounds was to develop Scouting into a force that would paper over the class divisions that he believed undermined the stability of Edwardian society and threatened the coherence of the empire. The Scout movement became a colonial institution in Africa because administrators, missionaries, teachers, and social welfare experts believed that its message of service, responsibility, and social conformity would teach young Africans to be loyal to the empire and to accept their place in colonial society. In other words, British officials looked to Scouting to resolve the inherent contradictions in colonial administration, education, and society as a whole.

BRITAIN'S AFRICAN EMPIRE

Although this is not the place to retell the story of the colonization of Africa, the examination of Scouting in colonial society must begin with an understanding of how Britain acquired and governed its African territories. The character and influence of the Scout movement in a given colony was determined by the political economy of the territory and the strength of its color bar. These factors established patterns of authority and dictated the potential, or lack thereof, for African social mobility. The demand for unskilled labor, the need for educated intermediaries, and the political subordination of Africans as "protected persons" shaped colonial education policy and thus the development of African Scouting.

Britain's colonial possessions in sub-Saharan Africa grew out of nineteenth-century trading enclaves and protectorates in western and southern Africa. In the later case, Britain took control of the Cape Colony from the Dutch after the Napoleonic Wars. Cape Town had considerable strategic value due to its central location on the maritime route to India, but the Afrikaner majority in the colony did not adapt well to the imposition of British rule. Angered by Britain's emancipation of slaves and the anglicization of the government and culture of the Cape, approximately fourteen thousand Afrikaners, known as *voortrekkers*, left in the 1830s for the high veldt of southeastern Africa. Three years later they founded the republics of the Transvaal and the Orange Free State after defeating the forces of the Zulu king Dingane at the Battle of Blood River. The British government blocked their access to the sea by annexing Natal as a Crown Colony in the 1840s. For the remainder of the century, British imperialists sought to further isolate the Transvaal and Orange Free State by claiming neighboring territory under the ruse of "protecting" local African communities. They also encouraged increased British settlement in Natal and the Cape Colony to strengthen their hold on the region.

In West Africa, Britain's formal possessions at mid-century consisted of trading stations that took on strategic value during the British anti-slavery campaign. Although British merchants had extensive commercial interests throughout the region, the metropolitan government opposed acquiring more territory on the grounds that the cost of African colonies did not justify the expense of formal rule. Britain therefore paid little attention to West Africa during the era of informal empire and relied on Westernized English-speaking Africans to run its few coastal possessions.

The British government abandoned its commitment to informal empire in the 1880s under increased economic and strategic competition from its western European rivals. Although there were few lucrative outlets for British trade and investment in late-nineteenth-century Africa, increased industrial production, rising tariffs, and economic depression in Europe led Britain and the other imperial powers to acquire more African territory on the premise that it might have future value. Few African societies were integrated directly into the world economy in the 1880s, but the imperial lobbies considered formal African possessions a long-term investment. Britain also had to defend its tangible economic and strategic interests in Egypt, West Africa, and the Cape from the expanding French and German empires. Concerned it might be shut out of potentially valuable regions, the British government abandoned its distrust of formal empire by claiming extensive territory in central and eastern Africa.

Although the geographical boundaries of British Africa were largely set when Baden-Powell introduced Britain to Scouting in 1908, there was no uniform system of administration to govern the new African empire. Most territories were under the jurisdiction of the secretary of state for the colonies, with a governor and an executive council-cum-cabinet composed of senior administrators and nominated "unofficial" representatives of the local settler community. Most colonies also had a legislative council made up of government officials and councilors drawn from settlers and, depending on the territory, cooperative African, Indian, and Arab representatives. Legislative councils usually had the power to enact laws subject to the governor's veto.

These lines of authority appear logical and robust on paper, but colonial governance was usually tentative and highly improvisational when applied to local African administration. In most territories the colonial state had only a limited capacity to impose its will directly on the African majority. Britain acquired most of its African possessions for speculative and strategic reasons rather than their actual economic value, which meant that colonial administrators usually lacked viable sources of revenue for development and local government. They could expect no help from the metropolitan treasury, which insisted that each territory bear the cost of its own administration. In most cases, colonial states had to generate revenue through forced labor or commodity production. Yet these African sources of funding were extremely limited because officials could not risk widespread unrest by intervening too drastically in local systems of production and governance. Lacking extensive police and military forces, they had to co-opt local African institutions of authority.

Although administrative structures and policies varied from territory to territory, the broad philosophy of governing through local intermediaries was known as indirect rule. British imperialists developed the system originally to control much of India through cooperative princes and local notables. Soldiers and administrators like Frederick Lugard, who began his career in the Indian army, adapted the system to Africa by drawing kings and chiefs into the lower levels of the colonial administration. Indirect rule was ideally suited to African governance because it was economical. It shrank the costs of colonial rule by limiting the need for European manpower and reduced the chances of unrest by limiting the British administrative footprint. Indirect rule lent credence to the legitimizing ideology of colonialism by demonstrating that British officials were acting as the responsible custodians of "primitive" societies. By invoking evolutionary development Lugard and his fellow administrators claimed to fulfill their obligations under the "dual mandate" by tutoring Africans in a form of "modernity" that was compatible with local culture.

Thus, indirect rule made British officials the self-appointed guardians of "native tradition." In theory, Britain's local allies derived their authority from their preeminence in precolonial society. By British colonial thinking, the primary basis of African identity was communal and corporate rather than individual, which made "tribes" the basic building blocks of indirect rule. John Iliffe defines a tribe as a "cultural unit possessing a common language, a single social system, and an established customary law" and basing its political and social systems on conceptions of kinship (either biological or fictive).[2] In other words, British officials conceived of a tribe as a lower political and social order that was less than a nation. Although colonial doctrine held that tribal identities were almost primordial in their rigidity and permanence, in reality African ethnicities were determined largely by specific political, economic, and environmental circumstances. In precolonial times, Africans could acquire new identities via intermarriage, enslavement, adoption, or migration. British administrators limited that fluidity by refusing to recognize African individuality. They considered tribal identity to be inborn, and therefore under indirect rule tribes had rights and standing but people did not.

Yet ethnicity and identity were still open to manipulation and adaptation during the colonial era. Africans could often assume a new tribal identity simply by playing on the ignorance of colonial officials. There were even circumstances when British officials found it expedient to create rules allowing African adults to be "adopted" into a new tribe.[3] Moreover, tradition proved to be equally malleable under the right circumstances. Although colonial officials based political legitimacy on "native tradition," in reality they usually appointed African intermediaries on the basis of their influence and willingness to cooperate in the colonial enterprise. Those Africans able to depict themselves successfully as arbiters of tradition exploited the new political order by interpreting customary rules governing land tenure, inheritance, marriage, and political succession for their own personal enrichment.

Many also recognized the opportunities offered by the British fixation on communalism. In analyzing indirect rule in Tanganyika, Iliffe noted, "The British wrongly believed that Tanganyikans belonged to tribes; Tanganyikans created tribes to function within the colonial framework." To be recognized as a "native authority" by the colonial regime brought not only opportunities for accumulation but significant political power at the local level. British officials conceived of "native courts" as "mouthpieces of local law and custom, only to be interfered with or modified if [they] conflict with certain fundamentals of white justice." African cultural brokers, who were often mission trained, invented or "rediscovered" customs and traditions that reinforced their claims to leadership roles in tribal communities. For the majority of Africans, however, indirect rule was a straitjacket confining them to second-class status as "protected persons" within the empire. The custom and tradition legitimizing the "native authorities" denied most individuals access to local and national governance, commercial entrepreneurship, private land tenure, gender equity, and advanced education.[4]

From the British standpoint, however, tribalism was vital to the success of colonial rule. Fixed ethnic categories imposed order and rationality on alien African societies, thereby allowing British imperialists to exploit Africans on an individual basis by posing as guardians of collective tribal institutions. Colonial officials believed that because African tradition made the interests of the individual subordinate to the tribe, Britain could fulfill its humanitarian obligations by protecting the integrity of tribal values and the legitimacy of the native authorities. So long as the tribe was safe the rights of specific individuals did not matter.

Needless to say, the colonial regime was intensely distrustful of any institution or ideology that weakened African attachments to tribal identity. The threat of "detribalization" loomed large in the minds of local administrators, and most suspected Western education was its primary cause. C. F. F. Dundas, the assistant chief secretary in Tanganyika, told a 1925 conference on education that Western schooling was fundamentally incompatible with indirect rule.[5] Dundas and his contemporaries believed foreign schools complicated British rule by introducing Africans to inassimilable values and aspirations. Colonial officials were certain it would take centuries of cultural evolution for Africans to acquire the sophistication and psychological poise to make proper use of Western education.

These prejudices made life particularly difficult for Africans educated in Western-style mission schools in the nineteenth century. Although these African civil servants, doctors, and brokers virtually ran Britain's West African enclaves, they were swept aside after the partition of Africa and the rise of pseudoscientific racism in the 1880s. British officials justified this blatant discrimination on the grounds that these "imitation Europeans" were illegitimate in the eyes of "traditional" African society. In reality, however, the colonial regime could no longer tolerate Western-educated Africans because they were living proof that the stereotype of African backwardness legitimizing British rule was nonsense.

Large numbers of settlers further complicated matters. Southern Rhodesian officials argued that Africans could not fully grasp the principles of "English citizenship" through "mere book learning." H. E. D. Hammond dismissed Africans as lying in a "trough of degeneracy" and attacked the missions for offering Africans a Western-style education in the Cape Colony. "These were the misguided enthusiasts who believed the black man and white were equal, and the black man could assert and maintain his equality at the word of command which they were called to give. Therefore they hailed him as a brother, and married his women. Blinded by the excess of zeal they led the blind, and fell into the ditch."[6] Educated Africans could do little to refute these attacks directly because unsympathetic colonial officials and racist settlers denigrated them as "trousered Africans." Lacking political representation, they could no longer assert their rights as "civilized" citizens of the empire.

These realities set the scope and character of the Scout movement in Africa by determining the relatively limited opportunities for African education and social advancement in a given colony. African Scouting was most unfettered in West Africa, where a well-developed export economy and an unfavorable climate ruled out permanent European settlement. Nigeria and the Gold Coast in particular supported large and popular Scout associations that grew with the support of government officials, missionaries, Western merchants, and educators.

Scouting was more problematic in East Africa, where the metropolitan British government encouraged European settlement in the East Africa Protectorate (Kenya) in the hope settlers would become paying customers for the Uganda Railway. Local authorities tried to recruit aristocratic immigrants by making large sections of the Kenyan central highlands open to settlement. They attracted over five thousand settlers by 1914 but made room for them by confining large numbers of Africans to tribally based "native reserves." In practice, most of the expropriated land went to waste because few of the new immigrants had any agricultural expertise. They could not compete commercially with African peasant farmers and relied on subsidies, price supports, and coerced low-cost African labor to survive. The settler community therefore guarded its privileges under the color bar jealously and used its political influence to limit the scope and nature of African education not only in Kenya but in Uganda and Tanganyika (after its conquest by Britain during the First World War) as well.

These tensions were even more pronounced in the Rhodesias and, to some extent, Nyasaland, where local settler communities were larger and more influential. Northern and Southern Rhodesia had significant reserves of copper, gold, and coal, but these relatively lucrative mineral deposits were not enough to keep the territorial governments solvent. Local officials therefore followed the East African policy of promoting European settlement. Unlike in Kenya, however, Southern Rhodesia courted middle-class immigrants to balance the large numbers of Afrikaners who moved to the territory after the Anglo–South African War. Although Northern Rhodesia focused mainly on copper mining rather than commercial agriculture, it also drew a small but politically vocal settler community. British settlement in Nyasaland was essentially limited to the southern half of the protectorate, where planters appropriated extensive coffee and cotton estates in the Shire Highlands. In all three territories marginal settler farmers and undercapitalized mining interests depended heavily on cheap African labor. They were therefore adamantly opposed to granting Africans political representation or social equality.

Not surprisingly, racial discrimination had the greatest impact on African education and Scouting in South Africa, where strategic and economic considerations led Britain to reach an accommodation with the Afrikaners at the expense of the African majority. Political expedience and the expense of the South African War led London to allow its former adversaries to settle the "native question" on their own terms when the Cape Colony, Natal, the Transvaal, and the Orange Free State became a self-governing dominion within the British Empire after the fighting was over. Seeking to unify the new dominion's two "white races," British officials allowed a succession of Afrikaner prime ministers to determine the Union of South Africa's treatment of its non-European majority. As a result, the color bar in South Africa was so rigid that the Scout movement remained highly segregated throughout most of the twentieth century. African Scouting in the three High Commission Territories (Bechuanaland, Swaziland, Basutoland) offered a sharp counterpoint to the South African Scout experience. Originating as British protectorates outside the sphere of direct Afrikaner political control, these territories offered Africans a much wider array of educational opportunities and actively challenged the South African application of the color bar to the Scout movement.

THE ORIGINS OF COLONIAL EDUCATION

The fundamental contradictions in the aims and application of Britain's rule in Africa were mirrored in its colonial education policies. Lugard's propagandistic assertion that Britain could fulfill its "dual mandate" by simultaneously developing the economic potential of the colonies while protecting African interests was a pipe dream. Economic necessity and local political pressure forced colonial officials to favor the interests of foreign commercial concerns and European settlers over those of the African majority. Nevertheless, the dual mandate required territorial governments to demonstrate their humanitarian intentions by providing a Christian "civilizing" education. Moreover, fiscal limitations forced cash-strapped administrators, missionaries, and settlers to rely on educated Africans employed as low-salaried clerks, interpreters, nurses, catechists, teachers, and artisans. Western-style schooling was thus an ideological and economic necessity.

British colonial education in Africa had multiple inspirations and origins. Nineteenth-century Britain lacked a centralized educational policy, and formal schooling was primarily for the elite. In 1833 social reformers convinced Parliament to provide limited financial assistance to schools for the lower classes. The Elementary Education Act broadened the scope of education in 1870, but the earlier system of government aid to private schools run by voluntary societies was the model for overseas colonial education. Parliament first voted supplementary funding for mission schools in the West Indies in 1833 and extended this limited financial support to African missions over the next four decades.[7]

Metropolitan educators, social reformers, and evangelical Protestants viewed schooling as an instrument of social transformation. They considered the British laboring classes to be as much in need of salvation, moral uplift, and discipline as colonized Africans. Members of the Church Missionary Society (CMS) prepared for overseas service by practicing their proselytizing skills on the East London poor. The evangelists viewed their schools primarily as instruments of conversion, and many Protestant missions made literacy a precondition for baptism. The official historian of the London Missionary Society declared that education was "an essential way of witnessing the Truth; it is a process by which children may be led into that fullness of life which is part of the Gospel's meaning for mankind. From this standpoint missionaries are under an obligation to educate, just as they are under an obligation to evangelize." This view explains why early mission curricula in Africa emphasized literacy and a classical Western curriculum.[8]

For most of the nineteenth century, British missionaries believed that Africans were fully capable of moral and cultural redemption through conversion to Christianity and the assimilation of Western values. They were confident that Christian education could bring about a social revolution in non-Western societies. Yet metropolitan educators also believed schooling should have economic value and combined Christian morality with training in practical technical skills. In 1847 the Education Committee of the Privy Council to the Colonial Office recommended exporting this technical education to the empire in the hope of creating an industrious "improving" peasantry in the colonies.[9]

In practice, most African missions retained their literary curricula for the rest of the century in spite of official support for a more practical emphasis in imperial schooling. These mission schools usually offered a first-class literary education. The CMS founded Fourah Bay College in Sierra Leone in 1827 to train African clergymen and teachers. Scottish Presbyterians established the Lovedale Missionary Institute for similar reasons in the Cape Colony in the 1820s. By mid-century, Lovedale concentrated on producing assimilated graduates to lead in Westernizing the larger African community. Yet the appeal of Western education was by no means universal. In most cases, Africans became interested in formal schooling only when they lost their sovereignty and their economies became subordinate to Western interests. Precapitalist agrarian and pastoral peoples saw little value in learning Latin in mission schools. Most students came from communities of ex-slaves in West Africa and peoples displaced by colonial wars in southern Africa who had no possibility of returning to their original modes of subsistence.[10]

Imperial authorities took a greater interest in colonial education as an instrument of economic development after the turn of the century. In 1902 the Foreign Office sent a questionnaire to each territorial government asking for a detailed account of its regulations and funding for "native education," the scope of industrial education and its impact on the "character of natives" and their economic usefulness, the possibility of combining an industrial and literary education, and the extent to which local settler communities opposed educating the indigenous population.[11] With the partition of Africa now a reality, the metropolitan government hoped education might help make formal empire pay.

The Foreign Office's questions revealed a growing distrust of Western schooling in imperial circles. Britain's educational experiences in India led many policymakers to question the wisdom of offering a formal literary education to colonized peoples. Early in the nineteenth century British reformers sought to cure India's perceived backwardness and moral stagnation through educational reform and social transformation. Disdaining Indian culture, they set out to create an anglicized elite that, in the words of Thomas Babington Macaulay, would be "a class of persons Indian in blood and colour, but English in taste, in opinions, in morals and intellect."[12] The reformers' English-language universities succeeded in producing an anglicized Indian middle class. Their graduates filled the lower ranks of the civil service and became vocal advocates for reforming Indian society. Yet racial discrimination blocked their advancement in government service. Moreover, Western-educated Indians did not prevent the Indian Mutiny of 1857. British officials of the Raj therefore decided that the Western educational experiment had been a failure. Ridiculing educated Indians as semicivilized "babus," imperial educators concluded that the universities had produced nationalist activists who coveted the material trappings of Western culture before they had the capacity to achieve them on their own.

British administrators carried these prejudices with them to Africa, where the Indian "failure" loomed large in colonial education thinking for decades. As late as 1925, W. B. Mumford, a "native" education expert, invoked the Indian lesson in his assertion that schooling in Tanganyika had to be compatible with African tradition and indirect rule.[13] British educators in Africa concluded that the Indian experiment failed because it secularized the Western literary curriculum to make it more acceptable to Indian Muslims and Hindus. The colonial regime's delegation of responsibility for African education to the missions was thus more than just a financial stopgap; Christian schooling provided a perceived measure of security by teaching students officially sanctioned conceptions of morality, humility, and discipline.

At the metropolitan level, J. H. Oldham, a leading English missionary, was the primary advocate of adapting Western models of schooling to colonial circumstances through a church-state educational alliance. He was the driving force behind the 1910 Edinburgh World Missionary Conference that institutionalized an "adapted" hybrid of Christian, Western, and "native" education as a primary tool of evangelism. Oldham and his fellow missionaries had lost much of their confidence in the classical literary curriculum and instead favored transplanting industrial education modeled on the Tuskegee and Hampton Institutes to Africa. In short, they sought to adapt the African-American industrial curriculum to colonial African circumstances.

British education specialists made regular visits to Hampton and Tuskegee, where they became convinced that industrial education was ideally suited to Africa. Similarly, Booker T. Washington, the African American president of Tuskegee, shared British colonial views of African primitiveness and supported mission efforts to transplant adapted industrial schooling in Africa. He became an inspiration for colonial officials seeking to reduce the disruptive social influences spawned by Western education. J. R. Orr, the first Kenyan director of education, admired Washington for "attempting to divert [his people's] attention from politics to useful industry because he realises the hopelessness of competition between black and white." Washington inspired Orr to open a state technical school for Africans at Machakos in 1914 so he could apply the Tuskegee model directly in Kenya. Comparable government schools were rare in British Africa, but when circumstances dictated their creation colonial authorities were careful to apply the Indian lesson by including Christian religious instruction in the curriculum.[14]

In the United States white experts on African-American education also took an interest in African educational matters. In 1919 the Foreign Missionary Conference of North America secured backing from the

Phelps-Stokes Fund to survey colonial education in Africa. The commission made two tours of Britain and Africa between 1920 and 1924. Its reports criticized the older colonial practice of relying on Western literary education to produce government clerks and Christian converts. Instead, the commissioners advocated educating Africans for their environment, which meant rural agrarian development within a "tribal" context.[15]

The Phelps-Stokes reports became the basis of the colonial regime's adapted industrial education policies in the interwar years. Motivated in part by the advocacy of Oldham's International Missionary Council and the need to demonstrate its humanitarian credentials to the Permanent Mandates Commission, the British government created the Advisory Committee on Native Education in British Tropical Africa in 1924. Five years later it expanded the committee's responsibilities to include the entire empire and renamed it the Advisory Committee on Education in the Colonies. The committee was made up of influential colonial experts including Oldham and Lugard. Using the Phelps-Stokes Reports as their inspiration, the committee members acknowledged that state support for African education was entirely inadequate and in 1925 laid out a plan for territorial governments to work in closer cooperation with the missions in adapting Western education to the African "environment and mentality." The committee issued another report in 1935 that further stressed the necessity of using the schools to reinforce African "tribal" identities by teaching rural agricultural skills and communal values while de-emphasizing elite education.[16]

Clearly, the primary function of adapted education was to buttress indirect rule. This meant shaping the curriculum to conform to what colonial and mission authorities perceived to be "traditional" African cultural values. The 1925 report by the Advisory Committee on Native Education declared, "Education should be adapted to the mentality, aptitudes, occupations and traditions of the various peoples, conserving as far as possible all sound and healthy elements in the fabric of their social life; adapting them where necessary to changed circumstances and progressive ideas, as an agent of natural growth and evolution." Colonial authorities interpreted this pronouncement as a directive to expand the capabilities of peasant farmers and train semi-skilled artisans for villages and settler farms. They hoped their rural focus would convince Africans to remain in the countryside by creating self-sufficient Christian communities that valued the "dignity of labour." The new strategy would limit detribalization by narrowing the gap between the peasantry and educated elites. In theory, primary school graduates who formerly aspired to urban clerical work would become "native leaders" guiding the development of rural societies.[17]

"Native education" experts used a number of arguments to justify their faith in this adapted schooling. Kenyan authorities cited a eugenicist study by H. L. Gordon that found that the "cubic brain capacity" of Africans was less than Europeans, which they interpreted to mean that Africans were unable to process advanced concepts and ideas. The 1926 annual report of the Education Department used this pseudoscientific nonsense to justify refocusing African schooling on handicrafts and manual training. The Advisory Committee on Native Education invoked slightly less odious reasoning in arguing that rural economies could not gainfully employ large numbers of African white-collar graduates.[18]

At the territorial level, British officials embraced adapted education as a powerful tool of colonial administration. Indirect rule rested on the assumption that all Africans belonged to "tribes" and that the schools were ideal places to teach and reinforce "tribal" identities. Ethnographers, anthropologists, and district officers assumed that Africans lived in a bounded and unchanging rural world where the interests of the tribe were paramount. As liberal South African educator C. T. Loram put it, "The African is much more conscious of his community than is the individualistic European. . . . in African society the group is everything, the individual little or nothing." Loram's American missionary colleague Ray Philips argued that "African tribal society provided for youth a training adequate to its needs. . . . Unquestioning obedience to the chief, headman, father and older brothers, was demanded."[19]

These stereotypes allowed colonial officials and their African allies to claim authoritarian powers under indirect rule by depicting themselves as traditional authorities. They relied on the colonial schools to teach the "native traditions" that legitimized this system of "native" governance. As would-be social engineers, colonial educators sought to strengthen what they found useful in "native tradition" while replacing customs they deemed backward or immoral. In the 1920s the Anglican bishop of Masasi in Tanganyika tried to create Christian versions of unacceptable "obscene" initiation ceremonies marking the transition to adulthood. The willingness of local converts and clergymen to embrace the male initiation rites (female versions were far more problematic) suggested that Africans might accept adapted forms of education if they found them valuable.[20]

Yet colonial schooling also had the potential to undermine British rule. Oblivious to the artificial nature of state-sanctioned "tribal" identities, British officials believed that Western education joined labor migration, urbanization, and rural economic dislocation in causing a rising tide of individualism and materialism that threatened to destroy "traditional" African society. The symptoms of this social decay included juvenile delinquency, petty crime, and sexual immorality. A mission educator in Nyasaland worried that detribalization led to the breakdown of generational authority: "Tribal restraint, submissively borne in the past, is chafing the coming generation; respect for elders is giving way to self-assertion; the sacred is often profaned; tribal discipline is often scorned, taboos sniffed at."[21]

Many colonial officials blamed this social unrest on educated Africans who had become dissatisfied with their social station. In criticizing the lack of practical manual training at the Church of Scotland Mission (CSM) school at Tumu Tumu, a Kenyan school inspector wrote: "The danger is that the village youth who receives no hand eye training and does not get his mind opened at school to the joy of creative work, leaves school at Standard II, considers himself an educated man, is disappointed in his hopes of clerical work, falls into the hands of malcontents and becomes a nuisance to himself and everyone else in the Reserve."[22] Education critics worried that detribalized graduates who were psychologically unequipped for rural life would drift into towns to look for white-collar jobs for which they were not qualified and thus fall under the sway of political agitators. Colonial educators hoped that the right kind of schooling would become an instrument of "retribalization," but there was very little that was useful in adapted education at the local level. Acting on the recommendations of the Phelps-Stokes Reports, and with $100,000 in funding from the American Carnegie Foundation, colonial education officials set up a series of rural demonstration institutions, known as Jeanes Schools, in Kenya, Zanzibar, Nyasaland, and the Rhodesias. They were modeled on similar schools financed by the Anna T. Jeanes Fund in the American South, which trained visiting teachers and their wives to instruct rural African American communities in "scientific" agriculture, hygiene, and domesticity. Colonial educators added training in tribal culture and tradition to this curriculum.[23]

In more conventional schools, adapted education meant an increased emphasis on manual training, vernacular literacy, and religious instruction. In practice, this "practical" training included clay modeling, mat making, basketry, woodcarving, brick making, blacksmithing, and leatherwork. Students usually did not begin to study English until Standard V (roughly the equivalent of American junior high school) to ensure that they did not lose touch with their "tribal communities."[24] The colonial authorities expected to fill their need for skilled English-speaking graduates by limiting exposure to potentially detribalizing Western-style secondary and higher education to only a handful of the most intellectually promising students. Adapted education therefore consigned most Africans to social stagnation in the rural agricultural sphere.

Not surprisingly, African parents and students rejected these adapted versions of Western education. It was unrealistic and hypocritical for colonial authorities to insist African schools focus on agricultural training when there were limited markets for African produce and colonial restrictions on private land tenure limited opportunities for personal accumulation. Widespread land shortages and a ban on African cultivation of lucrative plantation crops, like coffee and tea in settler-dominated societies, made farming an even less appealing vocation in eastern and southern Africa. Conversely, a formal academic education offered African students the greatest chance for social mobility by escaping the agricultural sector into white-collar employment. In spite of official hand-wringing over detribalization and social instability caused by Western-style schooling, the demand for skilled and literate African workers by private commercial concerns and territorial administrations continued to grow throughout the interwar era. Fluency and literacy in English brought social prestige, and government attempts to require schooling in local vernaculars sparked protests from South Africa to Uganda. Official reassurances that adapted education was not inferior just because it differed from European models carried little weight when employers demanded conventional school certificates and peasant farmers outperformed "scientific" school demonstration farms.[25] Moreover, Western education and fluency in English gave Africans the means to challenge local colonial authority by appealing directly to the centers of imperial power in metropolitan Britain through lawsuits, letters, and petitions.

Africans therefore had strong incentives to oppose adapted education. They avoided mission schools that placed too heavy an emphasis on manual training and subverted the adapted curriculum by neglecting nonacademic courses. Students at the Nyabururu Roman Catholic mission in western Kenya demanded payment for work undertaken in school workshops and gardens. In 1931 mass withdrawals by Maasai students forced the government school at Kajiado to close after school officials tried to introduce a new curriculum focusing on the production of ghee. A sister school at Narok survived only by modifying its course of study to place a greater emphasis on literary education. Moreover, colonial officials could do little to force African students to make use of adapted skills after they left school. Tanganyikan educators deemed their "rural industries" courses a failure because most graduates became clerks in government departments instead of village handymen or efficient peasant farmers. Similarly, most of the students leaving agricultural schools in South Africa used the literary component of their training to qualify for white-collar jobs.[26]

Adapted education became even more unworkable after the Second World War, when dissatisfaction with the social and economic inequities of British rule inspired a growing African nationalist movement. As chiefs and headmen proved unable to tamp down this unrest through sheer authoritarianism, British officials realized they needed to give educated Africans a greater stake in the colonial enterprise. De-emphasizing indirect rule also appealed to the postwar metropolitan Labour government that hoped expanded political opportunities at the local level and intense social development would validate the paternalistic ideology of colonialism and head off African demands for independence. In 1947 the Labourite colonial secretary, Arthur Creech Jones, directed the African territorial governments to develop democratic systems of local governance to train a new generation of enlightened African leaders.[27] British officials hoped that expanding the scope of African political participation would defuse mounting international criticism of imperialism and strengthen the colonial regime by creating a new class of popular progressive African intermediaries.

These ambitious plans to broaden African political participation in the postwar era came to naught because the adapted colonial schools were unsuited to preparing Africans for an active role in Western-style local government. Agricultural training, handicrafts, and tribal lore were of little use in producing progressive African councilors. Colonial educators therefore had to place greater emphasis on expanding and improving African secondary education. Using funds from the 1940 Colonial Development and Welfare Act, they made a classical literary education more widely available and laid the groundwork for regional African university colleges. This shift away from adapted education came at a price. Although the act expanded the financial resources of the territorial governments, most devoted only a small fraction of their budgets to African education. Even more troubling, they paid for the improvements in secondary education by limiting African access to schooling beyond the primary level.

Moreover, colonial educators never really abandoned their distrust of the classic literary curriculum. British administrators remained convinced that the security of the colonial regime was in peril if African graduates became alienated from tribal society. They therefore tried to broaden the consciousness of the entire community through mass education. In other words, they sought to educate parents and elders to the level of their children. Postwar social welfare experts used a variety of strategies, including Scouting, to provide a simple program of basic literacy, civics, hygiene, and manual training for illiterate adults, urban dropouts, and children who failed to qualify for secondary school.[28] In practice, these supplementary programs did little to raise community standards of education and drew resources away from conventional schooling, which remained largely in the hands of the missions. As a result, the numbers of students who completed an advanced degree still remained quite small and African education scarcely improved after the war.

These broader metropolitan and territorial shifts in colonial education policy over the first half of the twentieth century had surprisingly little impact on African schooling at the local level. In most areas the missions relied on a network of rudimentary village, "bush," and "kraal" schools to reach the rural population. One or two poorly trained African teachers, who often doubled as catechists, staffed most of these simple institutions. In addition to religious conversion, the primary purpose of these "outschools" was "community development" rather than the production of advanced students. According to the Ugandan Education Department, "The aim is not to give an academic education in these schools, but to raise the standard of living conditions, to inculcate the first principles of hygiene, to increase production by demonstrating better methods of agriculture, and in general to give a simple but sound education, which will result in the evolution of better citizens." Community education provided ideological cover for the fact that only a small fraction of Africans had access to conventional Western schooling. The percentage of children receiving a formal elementary education varied from 19 percent in Nyasaland to less than 5 percent in Uganda. From these figures colonial educators predicted it would take a thousand years to bring universal literacy to East Africa.[29]

Mission authorities tried to maintain a degree of control over the outschools through irregular visits by school inspectors, and territorial governments withheld financial support and official recognition from institutions that did not meet minimum standards for organization, curriculum, and quality.[30] Colonial officials were particularly worried about what African teachers did with their de facto autonomy. These worries about "efficiency" had as much to do with fears that Africans would teach subversive ideas as they did with a commitment to maintaining educational standards.

Most African students never advanced beyond the village schools, but promising students with parental support and sufficient money for tuition moved on to central primary schools that were usually based at a mission station. These schools still followed an elementary curriculum, but they often offered a higher caliber of instruction because they were better funded and staffed by European mission teachers. Curricula at central schools varied considerably, but adapted education was the common theme. In Tanganyika the government-mandated Standard IV curriculum called for seven hours of instruction per week in reading and literacy (in either English or a vernacular language), five hours for arithmetic, five hours for religious instruction, and an additional twelve hours for subjects including geography, nature study, hygiene, singing, physical education, and handcrafts. The civics portion of the curriculum required students to learn the "dignity of agricultural work," the structure of local tribal government, and the merits of thrift.[31]

Although these curricula focused on "adapted" subjects, most central schools still produced academically proficient graduates. Yet settler political opposition and budgetary constraints restricted drastically the scope of African secondary education. As in Britain, educators used highly competitive selection exams to limit the number of primary school graduates who would have the privilege of continuing their education. Ironically, most territories based these exams on classical metropolitan models in spite of their formal commitment to adapted education. In interwar Kenya 90 percent of all African students failed the primary school exam, and there were only 193 Africans in South Africa enrolled in Standards IX and X (the equivalent of eleventh and twelfth grade in the United States) in 1935.[32] Students who completed secondary school successfully had to achieve a top score on the rigorous Cambridge Local Exam, jump huge financial hurdles, and gain permission and a passport from suspicious colonial administrators to attend a university in Africa, Great Britain, or the United States.

Taken as a whole, African education in the British colonies resembled a pyramid with a huge mass of poorly qualified primary students at the bottom, a tighter middle stratum of slightly better prepared primary students, and a tiny pinnacle representing the privileged few with access to higher education. Territorial governments with larger settler populations rigidly applied the color bar to education and devoted most of their financial resources to European schools. These circumstances made education a demanding and ultimately frustrating experience for most African students. Nevertheless, the schools were a powerful draw in colonial society, where a simple primary diploma was a ticket to lucrative white-collar employment and students and parents went to great lengths to gain access to a Western-style education.

Yet many African students found it quite hard to stay in school. High tuition costs, competitive entrance exams, and harassment by colonial authorities made it extremely difficult for African students to earn even a primary school certificate. Yearly school fees in Kiambu, Kenya, in the 1940s averaged twenty-two shillings, which was roughly 15 percent of the annual wage for unskilled Africans. Uniforms and other required items, like Bibles, were extra. Many students dropped in and out of school as time and funding permitted, often forcing them to repeat the same grade level for several years in a row. In Kenya some students who had been enrolled for six years had completed the equivalent of only a single year of school.[33]

Colonial schools were also often harsh and difficult places to live and learn. Limited funding meant that food and housing were usually quite poor. Colonial educators also believed that too many "luxuries" would teach individualism and materialism, thereby detribalizing the students. Economic necessity and adapted curricula also required students to spend long hours at manual labor in school farms and workshops. Discipline was harsh as teachers and headmasters tried to prevent students from developing a sense of superiority toward their fellow Africans and social equality with Europeans. In Kenya, school officials could beat male students for playing, hitting, stealing, "grave neglect of work, lying, bullying, gross insubordination, or truancy." Regulations permitted them to use a cane on the buttocks or a strap on the palm of the hand. These were just the official rules; in practice, hazing by older students and beatings by teachers (both African and European) could be far more brutal.[34]

African parents and students had few options in challenging the restrictions and inequities of "native education." A common form of protest, particularly among advanced students, was the school strike. As a rule, African students tended to be older than their Western peers.[35] They understood the status conferred by a Western education and were highly sensitive to slights, both real and perceived, by school officials. Kenyan students struck at the CMS School at Maseno to oppose manual training and at Alliance High School to protest the replacement of ground maize with cassava.[36] Although the causes of these incidents often seemed trivial, there were real risks in challenging school authority directly. Colonial educators took collective protests as evidence of detribalization and expelled disruptive students who became too "big-headed."

In reality, most school strikes were an indirect challenge to the limitations on social mobility. Rebellious African students challenged the legitimizing stereotype of African backwardness by using their Western educational credentials to demand the rights and status of "civilized" people.

Yet school strikes were inevitably doomed to failure. African students had no right to an education and could do nothing to protect themselves from disciplinary action or expulsion. Faced with the limitations of the colonial school system, parents and community leaders began their own independent schools to gain access to the privilege and status of Western education. In most cases these schools were offshoots of independent churches developed around the turn of the twentieth century by Africans seeking access to Christianity outside the bounds of mission control. Independent churches and schools essentially turned the colonial concept of adaptation on its head by co-opting the Western symbols of progress and legitimacy and reinterpreting them in an African context. British officials were fully aware of the political potential of this movement, and worried that the independents would teach "subversive" religious ideologies in African elementary and primary schools. Seeking to bind educated Africans more closely to the colonial regime, they looked to Scouting to reduce the threat of independency and help resolve the contradictions created by liberal Western education in a colonial context.

SCOUTING'S ORIGINS AND ORGANIZATION

Although Scouting was partially inspired by Robert Baden-Powell's experiences in the South African War, it developed initially in response to political and social tensions in Edwardian Britain. To some extent, elite fears that industrialization had undermined traditional conceptions of deference and contributed to the physical and moral decay of the lower classes presaged colonial concerns about the breakdown of "tribal" African society under the pressure of Western materialism and rapid economic change. Convinced that the schools were unequipped to promote moral values, Baden-Powell and his supporters conceived of Scouting as a form of supplemental education that would teach initiative, character, and useful life skills in a popular and exciting format. The success of the movement and its rapid global expansion was due to its ability to address generational fears about juvenile delinquency and its usefulness in reinforcing the established political and social order. Baden-Powell was careful to keep the Scouts above divisive questions of politics and religion, but his emphasis on discipline and loyalty gave the movement a strongly conservative focus. He enhanced Scouting's universal appeal by establishing a core set of beliefs while allowing national Scout associations a great deal of leeway in interpreting them in local contexts.

Baden-Powell was not the first social reformer to apply the principles of military discipline and organization to a popular youth organization. He was inspired in part by the success of the Boy's Brigade movement founded by William Smith, a Glasgow businessman, in 1883. Responding to concerns about social unrest in the city's overcrowded working-class slums, Smith introduced military uniforms and drill into the Sunday school classes he taught for the Free Church of Scotland. These military trappings appealed to the boys and made them easier to control. Smith responded to the growing popularity of the classes by creating a formal command structure for the movement and expanding it throughout Scotland and England. Individual churches sponsored companies under the leadership of adult volunteers with the ranks of captain and lieutenant. Older boys holding the ranks of noncommissioned officers led squads, and the entire company met regularly for drill, work on proficiency badges, and Bible study in uniforms that included military pillbox hats, white knapsacks, belts, and dummy rifles. Six companies formed a battalion for competitions and parades, and the combined battalions constituted the Boy's Brigade under the jurisdiction of an executive council with Smith as brigade president.[37]

Smith's movement touched a popular chord and grew to approximately eighteen thousand members by 1891. The overseas exploits of evangelical soldiers like Gen. Charles Gordon and Sir Henry Havelock captured the imagination of the late Victorian public and made it socially acceptable to link militarism and Christianity. The constitution of the Boy's Brigade explicitly stated, "The Object of the Brigade shall be the advancement of Christ's Kingdom among Boys, and the promotion of habits of Obedience, Reverence, Discipline, Self-Respect, and all that tends towards a true Christian Manliness." Yet the brigade remained largely Scottish Presbyterian in character in spite of its commitment to a universal Christianity. The Anglicans founded their own Church Lads' Brigade, and nonconformist Protestants rejected the overt militarism of the other organizations by creating the Boys' Life Brigade, which replaced military drill with life-saving exercises. There was even a Jewish Lads' Brigade begun by Col. A. E. Goldsmid and the Maccabean Society to "iron out the ghetto bend" in foreign-born working-class Jewish boys in London by transforming them into proper Englishmen.[38]

The popularity of the various incarnations of the numerous youth brigades at the turn of the twentieth century stemmed primarily from widespread fears that urbanization and social friction threatened the security of Britain and the empire. Alarmed by the British army's rejection of large numbers of lower-class urban recruits as physically unfit for the South African War, a 1904 Parliamentary Commission on Physical Deterioration determined that the problem sprang from pollution, slum housing, long working hours, bad diet, alcoholism, and juvenile delinquency. These concerns were part of a larger national anxiety that union unrest, falling birthrates, unhealthy children, and disrespect for authority made Britain unprepared to fight a European war.[39] Political elites and social reformers concluded that drastic reforms were needed to save Britain from following the great historical empires into decline.

Baden-Powell's career as an Indian army officer, African adventurer, and decorated war hero gave him a strong interest in imperial defense and national reform. In his early career he fought in a series of colonial wars in the Gold Coast, Southern Rhodesia, and Natal. Although he would later emphasize the importance of discipline and sportsmanship in the Scout canon, Baden-Powell could be quite ruthless in campaigning against non-European foes. During the 1896 Ndebele rebellion he justified the slaughter of two hundred African combatants on the grounds that his forces were outnumbered and needed to bring the revolt to a swift conclusion. "Any hesitation or softness is construed by [the Ndebele] as a sign of weakness, and at once restores their confidence and courage. . . . Don't think me a nigger-hater for I am not. I have met lots of good friends among them—especially among the Zulus. But, however good they may be, they must, as a people, be ruled with a hand of iron in a velvet glove."[40] Baden-Powell was particularly incensed by murder of "little white children" and subsequently faced a court martial for his summary trial and execution of Chief Uwini, one of the leaders of the revolt. Although his superiors in the Cape Colony admitted he had acted illegally by failing to turn the Ndebele leader over to a civil court, they excused his actions on the grounds that Uwini's execution helped end the rebellion.[41]

Baden-Powell became a national celebrity for his successful defense of the frontier town of Mafeking against a much larger Afrikaner force during the South African War. Uncertain of what to make of Baden-Powell's new fame, the War Office gave him command of the South African Constabulary, which became a testing ground for his theories on the potential of military institutions to promote individual self-improvement. The constabulary's Stetson hats, khaki shirts and shorts, gold-and-green colors, and "Be Prepared" motto became models for the Boy Scout movement.[42]

Baden-Powell applied his experience with "frontier scouting" to the national youth problem when he returned to Britain in 1903 to become inspector general of the cavalry. Inspired by the huge juvenile readership of his *Aids to Scouting for NCOs and Men* (written in 1898 as an army scouting manual) Baden-Powell reasoned that he could use his personal fame to inspire the nation's youth to self-improvement. He was influenced by Ernest Thompson Seton's plan for adapting American Indian lore for organized wilderness training for boys and the British public's fascination with the popular ideal of the independent imperial frontiersmen. Although in the *Eton College Chronicle* he laid out a plan for public school boys to become "knights" providing moral and practical training for lower-class village "retainers," the more direct inspiration for the Boy Scouts came when William Smith asked him to rewrite *Aids to Scouting* for the Boy's Brigade. Baden-Powell became one of Smith's vice presidents and created a scouting proficiency badge for the brigade.[43]

Baden-Powell put his views on wilderness training and moral development into practice at the demonstration camp on Brownsea Island in July 1907, and scouting took on a life of its own after an ambitious publisher brought out a serialized version of *Aids to Scouting* six months later. It acquired a huge popular readership and inspired Baden-Powell to bring out a new edition entitled *Scouting for Boys*. When Smith refused to give scouting a greater role in his movement, Baden-Powell parted company with the Boy's Brigade and created a national advisory committee to take control of the independent "scout" groups that sprang up in response to the new scout manual. Smith turned down his offer to merge the two movements, and Baden-Powell justified the split on the grounds that he needed to reach boys who were not regular churchgoers. The YMCA provided institutional support for the project in the hope that scouting would direct young men into its adult organization. Baden-Powell's publisher provided funding for a paid organizer to expand the movement and broaden the market for the newly rewritten handbook.[44]

Baden-Powell's greatest priority was maintaining close personal control of the movement. Throughout the country inspired adults and enthusiastic groups of boys founded their own troops to put *Scouting for Boys* into practice. Yet Baden-Powell was concerned that his strongly held ideals, which were at the heart of the movement, would become diluted if local leaders had too much autonomy. In 1909 he called together respected public figures to select an executive council that would direct the development of scouting under his close leadership as national chief Scout. The council, composed largely of sympathetic former army officers, appointed county commissioners for the main regions in Britain, who in turn appointed district commissioners. The district commissioners recruited influential community leaders to serve on local associations, which were responsible for selecting Scoutmasters, conducting proficiency badge examinations, and fundraising. Individual Scoutmasters had a fair amount of leeway in running their troops so long as they held to the core Scout canon as laid down in *Scouting for Boys*.[45]

As Scouting became more established, Baden-Powell tried to broaden its appeal by creating specialized branches of the movement for different ages and interest groups. These included Wolf Cubs for pre-teens and Rover Scouts for young men. The "group system" integrated a Cub pack, Scout troop, and Rover crew under the direction of a group Scoutmaster. Ideally, a young man would progress through the various branches as he grew up and would never have to leave Scouting until he became a mature adult, when he could become a Scoutmaster. Scouting's program of adventure and national service also appealed to British girls. Baden-Powell was caught by surprise when a group of girls turned up in Scout uniforms at a public rally in 1908. He allowed eight thousand to register temporarily as Scouts until he created the Girl Guides for them under the leadership of his sister, Agnes. He ran the Guides through Agnes from 1910 to 1918, when he replaced her with his wife, Olave.[46]

Class circumscribed the movement's appeal in its early years. Baden-Powell conceived of Scouting initially to improve poor boys, but before the First World War the movement drew mostly from the upper-working and middle classes. Where the poor tended to view Baden-Powell's message as patronizing and elitist, Scouting offered boys from strict, respectable middle-class families an escape from the restrictions of class and social conformity through outdoor adventure and patriotic national service. Conversely, the young upper-class "knights" whom Baden-Powell had hoped would serve as role models for their more common brothers were put off by the classless ideology of the movement.[47]

Nevertheless, Scouting grew rapidly in Britain in the first two decades of the twentieth century. Its success was due to Baden-Powell's ability to ally his movement with prevailing social and political attitudes. Forty percent of British males were members of either the Scouts or one of the religious brigades between 1901 and 1920. The extent to which the Scouts were an instrument of prewar militarism has been the subject of considerable historical debate. In 1909, R. B. Haldane, the secretary of state for war, pushed the uniformed youth movements to become part of the County Territorial Force Associations, and the War Office denied groups that refused access to campgrounds, training, and financial assistance. Baden-Powell declined to affiliate the Scouts with the Cadets or Territorial Forces, and banned Scout troops from marching in military parades. His main goal was to reassure worried parents, particularly those belonging to northern nonconformist churches, that his organization was not militaristic. Although the Scouts wore military-style uniforms, he did not sanction drill as an approved activity on the grounds that it dampened individuality and initiative. Nevertheless, a number of academic critics have argued that Baden-Powell purposely de-emphasized Scouting's martial aspects to reassure pacifist critics, and that he had a hidden agenda to quietly improve the military readiness of British youth.[48] The colonial supporters of the movement expected it to inspire imperial loyalty in educated African boys even if these sentiments ran counter to their allegiance to their parents and local communities. Just as British educators would find that Scouting could not paper over popular African hostility to the colonial regime, Baden-Powell's underlying motives are largely irrelevant because it is doubtful that Scouting had enough influence to teach boys values and ideals that ran against those of their parents.

Moreover, Baden-Powell's sensitivity to prevailing social and political attitudes led him to embrace a much more pacifist brand of internationalism in the interwar era. As the British public recoiled from the horrors of the First World War, he emphasized that the movement contributed to world peace by creating a brotherhood of all Scouts. Scouting's training in service and altruism was the cure for the selfishness that lay at the root of the nationalist aggression that had driven Europe to war. In Britain, Baden-Powell refused to ally the Scouts with the nationalist Society of St. George, and his wife did not allow Young Imperialist Clubs to sponsor Girl Guide companies. Under Scouting's postwar internationalism, his followers were "Peace" Scouts who joined North American fur trappers, Central American hunters, Australian bush rangers, Western missionaries in Asia, and his own South African Constabulary as agents of Western civilization. Scouting thus became a universal movement theoretically open to peoples from all nations and creeds. Baden-Powell was a vocal supporter of the League of Nations and was proud that it officially embraced Scouting as an instrument of world peace.[49]

These changes helped Scouting expand at a time when the public considered rival Cadet organizations too militaristic and the popularity of the religious brigades was limited by confessionalism. The Scout movement was officially nondenominational but it successfully combined the popular appeal of self-discipline, educational improvement, and religious idealism. Baden-Powell's ability to redefine his movement in more universalistic terms allowed it to expand beyond its prewar lower-middle-class roots to attract youth from more diverse backgrounds. Some working-class boys remained suspicious of the Scouts because of the cost of the uniforms, their emphasis on religion, and Baden-Powell's opposition to trade unions. Scouting developed a Bob-a-Job program to help poorer Scouts raise money for their troops by doing simple tasks about the community in return for a shilling. This made it easier for poor boys, who were drawn to Scouting because of its opportunity for increased education, adventure, and social interaction with wealthier boys, to join the movement. These qualities also drew large numbers of British girls to Guiding, and the combined membership of the two movements topped one million children during the interwar era.[50]

Scouting owed much of its success to Baden-Powell's passion for innovation, organization, and centralization. He ensured that all Scouts would adhere to his personal commitment to patriotism, service, discipline, and social conformity by enshrining these values in the Scout Law (see appendix). Scouts took an oath to adhere to these laws in the form of the Scout Promise (known as the Oath in the United States). Throughout the world, no youth group could call itself a Scout group unless members promised to uphold the Scout Law and Promise.

These ideals were almost entirely unobjectionable. They called for obedience and respect for authority, but defined that authority in the broadest terms possible. Few adults could take issue with the admonition to respect country, parents, and employers. Foreign Scout associations simply replaced the word King with country in the promise. Similarly, the promise's intentionally vague reference to God allowed the members of any religion or denomination to become Scouts. These factors made Scouting a natural ally of established institutions of political and social authority and explain how national Scout associations easily secured official recognition from governments throughout the world.

Baden-Powell and his allies maintained influence over the overall character of the movement through a training program for Scoutmasters at Gilwell Park. Acquired in 1919 by the British Scout Association (BSA) with donated funds, Gilwell became a place where adult Scouters played the role of boys in learning how to run a troop. Using a syllabus originally

2.1 Woodbadge Training Course, Lexden, South Africa, 1954. Courtesy of University of Cape Town Libraries, Special Collections. Reproduced with permission of the South African Scout Association.

developed by Baden-Powell, they worked under senior Scout officials on the camp staff to earn the Woodcraft badge by demonstrating knowledge of the theory, practice, and administration of Scouting.[51] The Woodbadge was not required, but conveyed considerable status and prestige within the movement. Scoutmasters therefore had a direct incentive to follow Baden-Powell's lead in running their troops.

Scouting's system of ranks and proficiency badges ensured an additional degree of consistency. The specific terms of these requirements varied from nation to nation, but the general order of ranks remained relatively constant. New recruits in imperial associations earned the Tenderfoot badge (which consisted of the basic fleur-de-lis design), signifying full Scout membership by learning the Scout Law and Promise, salutes, the cleaning and dressing of wounds, basic knots, woodcraft, and the composition of the Union Jack. They advanced to second- and then first-class ranks by undertaking public service and mastering more advanced skills in first aid, tracking, orienteering, pioneering, nature study, and camping. Advanced Scouts earned proficiency badges, which Baden-Powell expected to provide a basic grounding in skills and hobbies that would form the basis of a future career. Those who earned a sufficient

2.2 Kenyan Scouts learning their knots, ca. 1949. *Kenya Scout Bulletin*, September 1949. Reproduced by permission of Kenya National Archives.

number of required badges and demonstrated mastery of advanced wildness skills could become a King's or Queen's Scout (depending on the era), the highest rank attainable in British imperial Scouting.[52]

In addition to the Scout canon enshrined in the law, promise, ranks, proficiency badges, and Woodbadge courses, Baden-Powell also exercised considerable influence on the character and interpretation of Scouting through his extensive published writings and personal example. Knighted for his service in the South African War, he became a baronet in 1922 and a baron in 1929. More significantly, the Scouting community accorded him iconic status in 1920 when it declared him Chief Scout of the World at the first international Boy Scout jamboree. Thus, Baden-Powell became nothing less than the ideal Scout whose opinions and pronouncements carried the weight of orthodoxy. Scouting was an international institution by the interwar era, but Baden-Powell served as its primary interpreter until his death. Although he made Scouting a universal movement by keeping it above divisive questions of politics and religion, his personal views on the virtues of the frontier, politics, faith, class, education, sex, and race shaped the development of the movement in Britain, the empire, and, to a large degree, the entire world.

Scouting's primary emphasis on adventure and wilderness training stemmed directly from Baden-Powell's service in India and Africa. Reacting to social changes in metropolitan Britain, he blamed industrialization and urbanization for the moral and physical decline of the empire. Just as the imperial frontier taught virility, resourcefulness, and self-discipline, Scouting was a "school of the woods" that would save the empire by instilling these same ideals in British youth.[53] Although he did not want to imitate these "primitive" peoples, Baden-Powell looked to non-Western "tribal" peoples of the frontier to rediscover the resourceful martial qualities that materialism had expunged from "civilized" Western society.

Baden-Powell's thinking along these lines was influenced in part by Ernest Thompson Seton's writings on Native American lore, but his romantic interpretation of "savage" African "tradition" was the primary inspiration for Scouting's outdoor culture. Africa loomed large in Baden-Powell's imagination. He made his reputation in Africa's colonial wars and eventually retired to Kenya, where he died and was buried in 1941. Having served extensively in South Africa, he was particularly taken with the Zulu. King Cetshwayo's crushing defeat of the regular British Army at Isandhlawana in 1879 fixed their reputation as a "martial tribe" in the imagination of the British public. Baden-Powell romanticized the Zulus' discipline and courage, and he adapted many of their cultural institutions to Scouting. These included the Zulu praise song "Een-Gonyama" and the Nguni age tests that became the model for the solo Scout "journey" required for the First Class badge. More significant, Baden-Powell used beads from a twelve-foot-long Zulu necklace as the centerpiece of the badges, signifying successful completion of the Woodbadge course. He claimed to have captured the necklace from King Dinizulu during the Zulu Wars, but biographer Tim Jeal argues that he took the necklace from a dying Zulu girl. Regardless of which version is true, "Dinizulu's necklace" became an established part of Scout lore, and the South African Boy Scout Association further legitimized the story by investing Dinizulu's grandson Cyrian Bhekuzulu Nyangayizwe as a Scout in 1965.[54]

Baden-Powell stressed national unity and social stability over allegiance to a specific political party or doctrine. He insisted that scouting was "non-military, non-political, non-sectarian, non-class" and told Scouts to listen to both sides of an issue and not to automatically join their parents' parties. Nevertheless, Baden-Powell's emphasis on social conformity and stability reflected a commitment to protecting the interests of the upper

2.3 Baden Powell's illustration of Scouting's egalitarianism. *The Scouter*, August 1914. Reproduced with permission of British Scout Association Archives.

classes. Having no patience for labor unions or working-class activism, he worried that class tensions led to national weakness. He wrote in *Scouting for Boys*: "A Scout must never be a SNOB. A snob is one who looks down upon another because he is poorer, or who is poor and resents another because he is rich. . . . We are very much like bricks in a wall, we have each our place, though it may seem a small one in so big a wall. But if one brick gets rotten, or slips out of place, it begins to throw undue strain on others, cracks appear, and the wall totters." Although the Scout Law declared all Scouts to be brothers, Baden-Powell believed that Scouts should be treated as figurative equals rather than as actual social equals. He considered Scouting a venue for elites to exercise their paternalistic obligation to improve society, and he expected the movement to foster national unity by promoting mutual understanding among the various classes.[55] He never intended Scouting to be a mechanism of social mobility.

Baden-Powell was a pious Christian, but in practice his religious views were rather unconventional. He voiced no preference for a particular faith so long as it worked toward "God's kingdom" on earth, which he defined as "the prevalence of love in the world in place of dominance of selfish interest and rivalry such as at present exists." Baden-Powell told a conference of Guiders in 1920 that Scouting and Guiding contributed to world brotherhood and peace by bridging denominational divisions within the churches. The official Scout stance on religion left it up to parents to select a faith for their sons. Six years after Baden-Powell's death the Religious Advisory Panel of the BSA issued a directive that it was "desirable that every unattached Scout be brought into touch with a religious denomination." Although many British Scout officials believed that secular humanists and agnostics could not be Scouts, a meeting of the Scout World Conference in 1949 allowed men who did not belong to a recognized church but continued to "search for the truth" to take the Scout Promise and serve as Scoutmasters. Ultimately, Scouting was highly flexible on religious matters, and Baden-Powell won the support of church leaders by allowing them to sponsor "closed" troops that included explicit religious instruction as part of the Scout program. This also allowed devout Jews, Muslims, and Hindus to become Scouts.[56]

Although relatively circumspect in matters of politics and religion, Baden-Powell was openly critical of conventional Western schooling. He had no patience for rote learning and believed that true education should inspire boys to learn for themselves. He was particularly concerned that lower-class schools failed to provide a moral education and let students drop out before they had the chance to learn a viable trade. Baden-Powell therefore conceived of Scouting as supplementary education, a "school of citizenship through woodcraft," that would use adventure training to teach the character and discipline that the schools could not. It would counter the selfishness and materialism embedded in the classic liberal arts curriculum. By following the Montessori philosophy of learning through doing, capturing the boys' imagination though their love of adventure, and harnessing the appeal of the "gang spirit," Scouting would produce moral, self-reliant, and disciplined citizens. Baden-Powell took great pride in the fact that educators accepted his criticisms and recognized the value of Scouting as an extracurricular activity. School officials could support Scouting because it did not challenge their primacy in the classroom and it imposed a higher degree of discipline on unruly students.[57]

Finally, the unofficial ideology of the Scout movement reflected Baden-Powell's conceptions of sex and gender. Although he married and fathered several children, Baden-Powell's sexual orientation has been the subject of considerable debate. He generally avoided women until late in life and maintained an intensely emotional friendship with a fellow army officer, Kenneth McLaren, whom he nicknamed "the boy." Some historians have used the fact that Baden-Powell, McLaren, and their families burned most of their letters to suggest that there was a physical dimension to this relationship. However, Tim Jeal argues that Baden-Powell was essentially asexual and that strong emotional attachments between men were relatively common in late Victorian society. What is certain is that Baden-Powell believed that sex was primarily for reproduction, and his respect for women was based on their role in procreation: "It is a sign of manliness when a man shows courtesy and consideration for woman because she is a woman—a person to be protected for the sake of the race." He warned boys that girls should be avoided until marriage because unrestrained sexuality led to weakness, selfishness, and venereal disease. Masturbation was almost as problematic because it was enervating and, in his opinion, broke the common male trust on which Scouting depended. Baden-Powell therefore preached total abstinence as a way of building moral strength and self-control.[58]

On an organizational level, Baden-Powell's views on sex influenced the movement's institutionalization of late Victorian and Edwardian gender roles. He expected Scouting to instill a proper conception of masculinity in the youth of the empire. Baden-Powell believed the key to producing "manly men" lay in the strict segregation of boys and girls to ensure that the former were not corrupted by sexual attraction to the latter. He did not consider the rough game of Scouting suited to girls and disapproved of their participation in the early Scout troops. Girl Guiding preserved Scouting as an all-male institution by giving girls access to adventure training in an environment where they would also learn the domestic skills that would prepare them to be, as Baden-Powell put it, "mothers of the future generation of boys."[59] These views were entirely in keeping with prevailing British concepts of gender in the early twentieth century and built the popularity of the movement by tapping into popular fears about blurred gender identities in the industrial age.

SCOUTING IN THE COLONIES

Although Baden-Powell conceived of Scouting initially as an institution for metropolitan British boys, he quickly realized its value to the empire as the movement expanded overseas. Scouting would provide excellent preparation for careers in the colonial military and civil service and bind imperial subjects more closely together through the brotherhood of Scouting. Baden-Powell particularly hoped that Scouting might strengthen Britain's hold on South Africa by uniting English and Afrikaans-speaking whites. Yet he also held that Scouting should be opened to non-Europeans. Believing in the humanitarian mission of British imperialism, he envisioned

Scouting as a tool of "civilization" that would persuade African youth to "see things from the white man's point of view."[60] Similarly, the Boy's Brigade also participated in the colonial enterprise. Although the Glasgow headquarters of the brigade did not follow Baden-Powell's lead in promoting its expansion overseas, the missions founded companies in West Africa, China, India, and the South Seas to reinforce their Christian teaching and attract potential converts.

The spread of Scouting throughout the empire was a natural consequence of Baden-Powell's commitment to internationalism. Before the First World War, independent scout troops sprang up around the globe as enterprising individuals read and applied *Scouting for Boys*. Baden-Powell gave most of them his blessing, and in 1917 he created an Imperial Headquarters within the BSA to register and supervise the thirty or so existing colonial Scout organizations as overseas branches of the metropolitan association. The overseas branches had their own constitutions and chief commissioners with a representative of the Crown, usually the governor, serving as the local ceremonial chief Scout. Imperial Headquarters provided further support for the imperial cause by creating a Migration Department in 1922 to encourage former Scouts to settle in suitable overseas territories.

In 1920, Baden-Powell and the BSA used the gathering of international Scout officials in London for the first world jamboree to establish an International Bureau to oversee associations in independent countries. The bureau ensured that these non-British groups adhered to the Scout canon by conferring official Scout status on only one organization per country. Independent associations could set their own badge and rank requirements, but the overseas imperial branches needed permission from Imperial Headquarters to deviate from the metropolitan British model. Representatives of the national associations and colonial branches met during the London jamboree for the first biannual meeting of what became known as the World Scout Conference.[61] Although this international group served as the deliberative body of international Scouting, Baden-Powell exercised enormous authority over the movement in his role as chief Scout of the world. After he died in 1941, succeeding British chief Scouts, who also served as chief Scouts of the empire and commonwealth, retained much of this influence through their role as the leader of the founding Scout association.

From an ideological standpoint, exporting Scouting to other Western societies posed few problems. Baden-Powell was more concerned with class than race in his original conceptualization of the movement and had little difficulty envisioning other Europeans as brother Scouts. Offering Scouting to Africans and Asians in a colonial context was another matter. Baden-Powell's academic critics have drawn attention to a series of disparaging statements he made about Africans to suggest that he was a racist. Frustrated with problems recruiting African auxiliaries for the Asante Campaign in 1874, he wrote: "The stupid inertness of the puzzled negro is duller than that of an ox; a dog would grasp your meaning in one half the time. 'Men and brothers'! They may be brothers but they certainly are not men." He also used "nigger" relatively freely, and incorporated it into a cartoon mnemonic device of "Nimble Nig" being chased by a crocodile to represent the letter "N" (dot-dash) in Morse Code.[62]

Yet Baden-Powell was certain that Africans could become Scouts. Although he considered that their skulls were not "constructed for the reception of modern Western school methods," he believed that formal education provided non-Westerners with the capacity to take part in Scouting. "Boys up to a certain age are much the same as boys in other parts of the world, and if one can only reach them while they are still young and train them in the right way I am convinced that a very large number of them would grow up into . . . white men with black skins."[63] His deep commitment to internationalism during the interwar era led him to formally declare that Scouting was open to all boys. "In this Movement there is no barrier of race, no barrier of class, no barrier of religion. The Indian boy and the British boy, the public school boy and the slum boy and boys of every religion, are all equal partners in this wonderful brotherhood."[64] In other words, Baden-Powell had a nineteenth-century cultural rather than a biological conception of race. He believed that character and discipline were the true measure of civilization and bestowed the status of having a "white character" on African individuals and groups (like the Zulu) who exhibited characteristics he admired. Nevertheless, Baden-Powell was never ready to accord educated Africans equal status with Europeans.

More significantly, the Scout Law's declaration that all Scouts were brothers created serious complications in societies with legalized and institutionalized segregation. This was particularly true in the southern United States, where the National Association for the Advancement of Colored People (NAACP) used Scouting to challenge legal and social discrimination against Americans of African descent. Although James West, chief executive of the Boy Scouts of America, explicitly left out race in his declaration that the movement was open to "all classes, all creeds," African Americans used the Fourth Scout Law to demand their full rights as Scouts, and, by extension, citizens.[65] Neither West nor the Boy Scouts of America were overt racists. The Scout movement's policy of building legitimacy by reinforcing prevailing political and social values obligated them to cater to dominant racial prejudices in American society.

The American Boy Scouts tried to skirt the issue of race by allowing individual troops to set their own membership policies. Thus, multiracial troops existed in some northern towns between the two world wars. Southern troops, however, were strictly segregated, and white Scout officials had the power to prevent African Americans from starting Scout troops in their communities. Black Scouts in the South had to demonstrate their ability to live by the Scout Law and Oath, which in practice meant accepting segregation, before local Scout officials allowed them to even put on a Scout uniform. Some southern Scouters tried to deny African Americans membership in the movement altogether, and in 1919 white Scout leaders in Atlanta and Chattanooga threatened to march on city hall to burn their uniforms if black troops began in their cities. West tried to defuse the problem by making supportive but purposefully vague statements about his commitment to black Scouting. His declaration that he was "sincerely sympathetic to the negro boy" did not nothing to placate African American critics of the movement.[66]

The NAACP in particular recognized the political value in forcing the Scouts to follow their own Scout Law. Their struggle to integrate the movement continued well into the 1930s, when Roy Wilkins, assistant secretary of the NAACP, used a controversy over segregation at the 1937 national jamboree in Washington's northern Virginia suburbs to further embarrass West. "It is a mystery to this association how the Boy Scouts of America could hope to train their youngsters in rural American citizenship . . . when at the outset they cater to the lowest and meanest forms of pettiness and prejudice."[67] Thus, although Scouting attached itself to institutions of political authority, disenfranchised peoples could use the movement's commitment to universal brotherhood to contest their subordinate political and social status.

Similar problems existed in the British Empire, where racial, sectarian, and nationalist tensions complicated the universalistic message of Scouting. The movement's emphasis on patriotism, social conformity, and loyalty to the established political order, which worked so well in metropolitan Britain, was far more problematic in heterogeneous colonial societies that institutionalized ethnic and social inequality. In 1911, Irish nationalists took over the Irish National Boy Scouts Association to advance the Republican cause, and one year later Barbados commissioners tried to prevent nonwhites from becoming Scouts. In interwar Palestine, where the British army introduced Scouting, Zionist Scouts refused to share a territorial association with their "brother" Arab Scouts.[68]

The greatest problems, however, lay in India, where British officials tried to restrict membership in Scouting to Britons. Army officers founded the original European Scout troops in 1908. During that same year, a British missionary convinced the BSA to recognize an all-Indian troop, but government fears that Indians might turn Scouting into a political organization dominated by the militaristic nationalist movements led to its demise. British viceroys in the 1910s denied Scouting official recognition, and the commander-in-chief of the Indian army barred his officers from serving as Scoutmasters in both European and Indian Scout troops. Yet the government lost control of the movement by refusing the Indian Scouts official status. Missionaries, the YMCA, progressive British businessmen, and Indian politicians, activists, and religious leaders all started their own unauthorized troops for Indian boys. The unofficial Indian Boy Scouts Association, founded by Fabian socialist Annie Besant, was the most popular, with roughly twenty thousand members by 1920.[69]

The Raj denied Indians access to Scouting at its own peril. Although Baden-Powell and the Imperial Headquarters refused to recognize the Indian groups, they could not prevent Indians from creating uniformed youth organizations that used Scouting as a model. In addition to the appeal of outdoor adventure and international brotherhood, Scouting in the colonial context conferred political legitimacy on the Indian nationalists. The growth of unauthorized scouting forced the Raj to create a sanctioned Indian Scout organization to bring the movement back under official control. Edwin Montagu, secretary of state for India, also recognized that Scouting taught loyalty to the empire. He therefore pushed Viceroy Lord Chelmsford to create an official Scout association for India that would include both Europeans and Indians.[70]

Baden-Powell was initially against this amalgamation, but the YMCA's decision to challenge the authority of Imperial Headquarters by starting its own Indian troops forced him to support a single Indian Scout Association. In 1920 he visited India to guide the leaders of the various Indian factions in creating an all-Indian Scout Council. Although Indian Scouting remained segregated at the troop level, the council recognized the authority of the viceroy as chief Scout for all Indians and Europeans. This provision, along with the Scout Promise's pledge of loyalty to the British king as emperor of India, led more nationalist-minded groups like the Seva Samiti Boy Scouts Association to refuse to join the new national association. Indian Scouting became even more divided in 1937, when additional Indian troops left the movement over Baden-Powell's refusal to apologize for his foolish declaration that Indians would benefit from Scouting's character training because Hindus, in his view, did not have a word for "honor." His obstinacy strengthened the hand of the nationalists, and the Seva Samiti organized the defectors into an unauthorized Hindustan scout association that proved more popular than official Scouting.[71] In hindsight, the lesson of this split was that although Scouting had its uses as an instrument of social control, the movement could be a destabilizing force in societies riven by political and ethnic discord.

As with conventional education, British officials tried to learn from the Indian example in introducing Scouting to Africa. As in India, Scouting began in the African colonies in 1908. These were almost entirely all-European troops, and most territories did not offer Scouting to Africans until after the First World War. Taking note of the movement's African origins, the Advisory Committee on Education in the Colonies gave Scouting official sanction in its 1925 report on African education. Each territorial Scout association was an official branch of the BSA, and thus enjoyed the protection of its royal charter.

On the surface, the movement seemed ideally suited to solving some of the key contradictions in the colonial system. Baden-Powell's admonition to individual Scouts to "be a brick" suggested that educated Africans should accept their place in colonial society. As supplementary education, Scouting provided an added measure of control over African students by teaching loyalty and obedience in an appealing and exciting environment. Daniel McKinnon Malcolm, chief inspector of native education in Natal, spoke for many colonial school officials when he urged education departments throughout the Union and southern Africa to make Pathfinding (the South African version of Scouting) an official part of their African curricula. Nevertheless, Scout officials were careful to remind headmasters that Scouting was a voluntary movement and could never be a required part of the curriculum.

African students embraced Scouting as an extracurricular activity because it was an entertaining break from the strict discipline and dryness of the colonial school system. However, it also taught the colonial regime's notions of deference, hygiene, and morality. Northern Rhodesian educators hoped Scouting would defuse labor unrest on the Copperbelt by giving young African townsmen a wholesome and disciplined use for their leisure time. Nigerian Scouts fulfilled their community service obligations by teaching villagers to dig latrines, and the South African

Scout Association required African Cub Scouts to explain the benefits of clean hands and feet, trimmed fingernails, breathing through the nose, and proper posture. J. W. C. Dougall, a mission expert on sex education, believed that Scouting was a cure for the perceived rash of promiscuity and illegitimate pregnancy that threatened the stability of "tribal" society because it taught young Africans to control their sexual impulses. Pathfinding urged boys to steer clear of complications with girls. In 1935 the *Pathfinder* magazine published a song that it claimed was written by an African who found sufficient sexual release in the movement:

> I want to be a Pathfinder until I'm 73
> Pathfinding is a glorious life
> I never want to take a wife
> So all you girls please keep your eyes off me until I'm 30, 40, 50, 60, 73.

The movement strengthened institutions of indirect rule by fixing useful colonial gender roles that emphasized responsibility, self-control, and respect for patriarchal authority.[72]

Missionaries constituted much of the senior Scout leadership in most colonies and did not share Baden-Powell's support for religious pluralism in the movement. A high school teacher and Scoutmaster considered Scouting to be "religion in practice," and the Rhodesian Scout Association declared that "Duty to God" was the most important part of the Scout Promise. The missions used Scouting for evangelism by sponsoring closed troops for their adherents that incorporated religious instruction into the Scout training program. Dougall recommended that Scouting be part of the official curriculum at teacher-training colleges because it was a particularly effective form of religious instruction. Not surprisingly, non-Christians often found the Christian emphasis of African Scouting to be oppressive. In 1960 there were only three Scout groups sponsored by non-Christian bodies in Kenya, and South African Indian troops sometimes accused their national association of using Scouting to promote Christianity.[73]

Finally, colonial administrators embraced Scouting as an instrument of retribalization. The key qualification in the Advisory Committee on Education's support for the movement was that, like the classical literary curriculum, it had to be adapted to the African context. Just as Anglican missionaries experimented with Christian initiation ceremonies in Masasi, Scouting could be adapted to preserve worthy African traditions that reinforced morality, communal identity, and respect for authority. Territorial governments feared that Western education broke down "tribal" identities

2.4 The Kenyan Scouts who performed for Queen Elizabeth II in ceremonial "tribal" dress, 1957. *Batian* 1957, Kenya National Archives. Reproduced with permission of Kenya National Archives.

and turned to adapted Scouting to teach respect for their African allies. Believing that unchecked individualism threatened the coherence of "native society," colonial authorities hoped the movement's emphasis on service and selflessness would inspire a new sense of community spirit among African youth and their parents. They also hoped that "adapted Scouting" in the countryside would stem the tide of urban migration by making rural life more appealing and exciting.[74]

Senior Scout officials were more than willing to adapt the movement to serve the needs of the colonial state. Baden-Powell actively promoted Scouting as the cure for detribalization and corrosive Western materialism in South Africa. In Baden-Powell's eyes, Scouting could discipline African youth because it preserved the best of what had been lost from "tribal" society. Lord Rowallan, his successor as chief Scout of the empire and commonwealth, urged the African overseas branches to adapt their rank and proficiency badge requirements to local African conditions to help reinforce "tribal" identities. Scouting became an integral part of adapted education and played an explicitly political role in buttressing colonial institutions of authority.[75]

As was the case with formal schooling, the realities of African Scouting often diverged considerably from official prescriptions for adapting the movement to African conditions. Rather than reinforcing communalism, Scouting gave Africans considerable prestige and privilege in colonial society. African boys were drawn to the movement not because it preserved "tribal" traditions but because it was entertaining and offered a degree of social mobility by helping them navigate the colonial school system. Colonial officials considered African Scouts to be trustworthier than their non-Scout peers and gave them preferential treatment in terms of scholarships and employment. Uniformed Scouts received free rail tickets in South Africa and enjoyed a degree of protection from rigid pass laws in the settler colonies of eastern and southern Africa. Moreover, national and world jamborees provided relief from the color bar by allowing a few African boys to mix with Scouts from other communities and nations on near equal terms.[76]

The movement's semiofficial status also gave African Scouts considerable prestige in local communities. They helped the police with crowd control at public meetings (where they got in free), and provided uniformed honor guards for visiting dignitaries. Most rural Africans had only the vaguest understanding of the nature of the movement, and often believed that Scouts were people with special knowledge and skills. In addition to their mastery of Western culture, their woodlore training allowed them to track and read signs that other people could not. One of the key differences between African and European Scouting lay in the power and prestige of the Scout uniform. European boys certainly enjoyed the sense of belonging and the quasi-military status that came with wearing the uniform, but for Africans it conferred a much greater measure of status on the wearer. Possessing a full uniform was a sign of affluence, and Scout belts were particularly popular because they were similar to army belts and could be used to open bottles or swung as a weapon.[77]

The only way of knowing if an African was a Scout was by the uniform (which often consisted of nothing more than a Scout badge pinned to a school shirt), and thus any African wearing a uniform could claim the privileges of the movement. The uniform could also be put to larcenous purposes because many rural communities assumed that anyone in uniform had the authority of a government servant. As a result, colonial officials had considerable problems with rogue Scouts or impostors who acquired a uniform by unapproved means. Most territories gave their Scout associations sole legal claim to their uniforms and badges, and the Ugandan government passed a specific ordinance barring Scouts from posing as government agents. Nevertheless, it was relatively easy to acquire parts of the uniform by buying them from poorly run Scout shops or unauthorized Indian businessmen or by simple theft. Even registered Scouts often skirted regulations by buying rank and proficiency badges instead of earning them.[78]

Scout officials grew extremely frustrated by their inability to stamp out this practice and attributed their problems with impostors and unauthorized scouts to the African public's inability to grasp the aims and methods of the movement. In reality, however, these tensions reflected a conflict over the method and nature of adapted Scouting. African boys vehemently opposed the South African attempt to consign them to the adulterated Pathfinder version of Scouting, and, as was the case with education, believed that adapted Scouting was inherently inferior to European Scouting.[79]

Africans generally agreed that the movement should be modified to fit African needs; they simply differed over who would have the privilege of making these adaptations. European Scoutmasters usually adhered to the official version of Scouting in running their African troops. However, just as African clergymen and teachers laid claim to Christianity and Western education by founding independent churches and schools, individual African Scoutmasters often took advantage of limited oversight by Scout officials to modify the movement as they saw fit. The BSA maintained control over individual troops by requiring potential Scoutmasters to hold a warrant from their local associations, but Scoutmasters running troops at remote rural schools could generally do as they pleased.[80]

Britain acquired an African empire largely out of speculation that its new colonies would have future economic value. In reality, most territories could barely cover the costs of their own administration. Seeking viable sources of revenue, colonial administrators privileged settler and foreign commercial interests over those of the African majority. These fiscal realities clashed with the humanitarian rhetoric that legitimized British rule in Africa. Under the terms of the dual mandate, colonial administrators had a duty to promote the civilization and development of "primitive" peoples. Western education and Christian evangelism met this obligation, but made it difficult for colonial administrators to govern through African intermediaries. Under indirect rule, British imperialism masqueraded as an indigenous African institution by co-opting local institutions of authority. Colonial doctrine held that the "tribe" was the main basis of African identity and that legitimate African interests were communal rather than individual. Western-style schools provided cash-strapped colonial interests with inexpensive skilled African labor but undermined the authority of the colonial regime's "traditional" allies by inspiring Africans to slip the bonds of "tribal" society. Faced with the realities of the color bar, educated Africans would eventually seek social mobility through political means. Thus British rule in Africa contained the seeds of its own destruction.

Colonial administrators supported African Scouting because they hoped it would resolve these fundamental contradictions by giving educated Africans a stake in the empire. The movement's emphasis on obedience, self-sacrifice, and community service suggested that African students should accept their place in colonial society. British officials hoped that adapted Scouting would strengthen the legitimacy of indirect rule by using tradition to teach sanctioned "tribal" identities. Yet the movement was not an effective instrument of retribalization. Rather than promoting discipline and service, it actually conferred considerable status and privilege. The Scout Law and Promise stressed restraint and social conformity, but Scouting's close links with Western education in Africa made it an elite movement. Moreover, Africans used the power of independency to claim the symbols of progress and legitimacy that were imbedded in the Scout movement. By reinterpreting Scouting in a local context they appropriated the privilege of adaptation for themselves. Thus Scouting was a key, if unrecognized, site of contestation. Colonial officials vied with educated Africans to define the true nature of African Scouting because control of the movement conferred political and social legitimacy.

3

Pathfinding in Southern Africa, 1908–45

FORMAL AFRICAN SCOUTING in the Union of South Africa began at Grace Dieu Diocesan College in the early 1920s. Located roughly eighteen miles from Pietersburg in the northern Transvaal, the Anglican school trained African teachers. Informal European Scout troops in South Africa predated the official establishment of the movement in Britain in 1908 by several years. As Baden-Powell's fame spread, mission educators like Canon W. A. Palmer, Grace Dieu's principal, recognized that Scouting could also be a useful extracurricular activity in African schools. In 1911, Palmer asked the newly formed Transvaal Scout Council for permission to start an African troop at the college. The Transvaal Scouters were determined to reserve Scouting for white boys and instead offered to help Palmer create a separate "native" scout-type movement. Palmer declined on the grounds that the universalism and brotherhood embodied in the Fourth Scout Law were the most valuable aspects of the movement. He saw Scouting as a "civilizing" tool that would prepare his African students for their place in South African society by teaching responsibility and service while promoting mutual understanding between Africans and Europeans. Palmer therefore repetitioned the Transvaal council in 1922, after S. P. Woodfield, a veteran Scoutmaster from Britain, joined his staff.[1]

The Transvaal Scout establishment was resistant but grudgingly allowed liberal proponents of African Scouting to create the Pathfinders, an African organization that used the aims and methods of the movement without enjoying official recognition as Scouts. Palmer and his liberal allies accepted the Pathfinders because they hoped to use the principles of adapted education to create a distinctly African movement that would gradually transform Africans into "civilized" men. Although they wanted their students to have official Scout status, they worried that formal Scouting was too European to be relevant to African circumstances. The Pathfinders' sponsors hoped their adapted Scout hybrid would reduce the contradictions in African schooling and limit African political activism, intergenerational tension, and juvenile delinquency by teaching African youth self-discipline, loyalty, and interracial "understanding."

The 1st Pietersburg Pathfinders came into being at Grace Dieu in September 1922. The company was popular, but it quickly became apparent that students at the college had their own ideas of what it meant to be a Scout. The hypocrisy of institutionalizing racial discrimination in a purportedly universalistic movement undermined the conformist ideology of the new organization. The Grace Dieu Pathfinders aspired to be full Scouts because they wanted to demonstrate that they were as capable, sophisticated, and prepared as European boys. The minutes of the Grace Dieu troop show that Woodfield had to constantly explain why the Pathfinders could not wear the same uniforms as the Union's European Scouts. The Grace Dieu students' concern over their uniform reflected their attempts to make Pathfinding an elite movement. A complete uniform was not a prerequisite for membership, but it conveyed considerable status at the school. Pathfinders had to pay the fairly considerable dues of one shilling per term, but there were always more applicants than the troop could accommodate. Patrol Leader Isaac (troop minutes never mention Africans by their last names) told Canon Woodfield that most students believed that the Pathfinders were exempt from Grace Dieu's strict disciplinary codes.[2]

The Grace Dieu archives are frustratingly vague on the exact motives of the first Pathfinders, but it is clear that the students saw Scouting as a means of breaching the color bar. Adapted education was an empty promise because it was pointless to prepare Africans to be progressive farmers or simple tradesmen when legalized segregation limited their access to land and gainful employment. African frustration with this educational hypocrisy drove the independent school movement and sparked widespread student strikes in African schools by the 1940s. Pathfinding floundered over these contradictions. Politically conscious Africans rejected Palmer's arrangement with the Scout authorities and invoked the Fourth Scout Law to demand equal status in the official Scout movement and, by extension, South African society. They rejected the European Pathfinder leadership's adulteration of Scouting and exploited the South African Scout authorities' limited capacity for supervision and their poor understanding of African society to adapt the movement on their own terms. Scouting's claims to legitimacy and authenticity therefore made it a site of conflict in southern Africa rather than an instrument of social control and conformity.

THE DIVIDED ORIGINS OF SOUTH AFRICAN SCOUTING

In justifying the differences between Scouting and Pathfinding to the Grace Dieu students, Woodfield and his colleagues tried to defend the indefensible. South African Scout officials made a mockery of their own Scout Law by claiming white parents would withdraw their sons en masse if they admitted Africans and Coloureds.[3] They were adamant that Scouting could not get ahead of white public opinion on racial issues. More to the point, the Scouts valued their ties to political and social legitimacy above all else and would not jeopardize their intimate relationship with the South African state by weakening the color bar.

Scouting was controversial in southern Africa because the political and cultural character of the Union of South Africa was unresolved. Metropolitan British Scouting thrived because it linked itself successfully to established institutions of authority. Divisions in southern African Scouting sprang from the political compromise that Britain struck with the Afrikaners following the South African War. Faced with war in Europe and the demands of defending a global empire, Britain could not spare the manpower or resources to maintain a large standing army in the region. Under the terms of the 1902 Treaty of Vereeniging, Afrikaners reluctantly acknowledged the British monarch as their sovereign. In return, Britain promised them considerable local autonomy, including representative self-government and control over their public schools.

The metropolitan government hoped that increased immigration and a generous postwar reconstruction program would ensure a pro-imperial political majority in a single union of the British and Afrikaner territories. However, many poor, English-speaking whites voted with the Afrikaners to defend their racial prerogatives under the color bar. The expected postwar wave of British immigration never materialized, and the Afrikaners remained in the majority when Britain created the Union of South Africa in 1910. Afrikaner political discourse emphasized republicanism, linguistic and cultural autonomy, and the defense of the privileged racial position of poor whites. British attempts at postwar reconciliation were futile, and most Afrikaners detested the Empire. South Africa's "white races," to use one of Baden-Powell's favorite terms, remained divided along linguistic and class lines because, although Afrikaners controlled the new government, English-speakers held most of the skilled and managerial positions in the Union.[4]

The African majority was almost entirely disenfranchised. South Africa's constitution preserved the Cape Colony's color-blind voting system for a few wealthy Africans and Coloureds, but the vast majority of Africans had no direct political representation. They were powerless to block the 1913 Natives Land Act, which made race the primary criterion for land ownership. The act confined Africans to "native reserves," which constituted only 7 percent (a figure eventually raised to 13 percent) of the Union.[5] Politically sophisticated African elites created the African National Congress (ANC) to contest these racist laws. Similarly, the non-European Industrial and Commercial Workers' Union (ICU) fought the alliance between capital and segregation in South Africa. Yet these movements were largely unsuccessful because white South Africans denied them political legitimacy. Depicting African politicians and labor activists as detribalized malcontents, the Union government stifled the political activism of the ANC and turned its security forces on trade unionists and the ICU.

Britain's attempt to reconcile with the Afrikaners also greatly eroded educational opportunities for Africans. The 1910 constitution extended the segregationist education policies of the Transvaal and Orange Free State to the entire nation. This meant that the Transvaal director of education's pronouncement that the "ultimate social place of the Native [is] that of an efficient worker" became the basis of South African school policy. This was not a particularly controversial statement as the Union government and the Christian missions largely agreed on the need for adaptation and manual instruction in African schooling. The economic and political development of South Africa accelerated the disintegration of rural African society and drew growing numbers of migrants to the cities in search of work. Faced with increased detribalization and urbanization, mission educators became more concerned with ensuring African social stability than promoting development and Westernization through a classical literary curriculum. James Steward, principal of the Lovedale Missionary Institute, advocated adopting the Tuskegee Institute's industrial curriculum in South Africa. C. T. Loram, a liberal "native education" expert, also favored the Tuskegee model on the grounds that Africans made the greatest contribution to the Union through manual labor.[6]

This official embrace of racial segregation complicated the introduction of organized youth movements in southern Africa. As in Britain, the Boy's Brigade preceded the Scouts in the region. The first companies dated from 1889 and placed Christian brotherhood ahead of the color bar by admitting boys from all races. Nevertheless, brigade leaders had to cater to European sensibilities by allowing white boys to form their own segregated companies. Racial tensions led to the brigade's demise in the Transvaal and Orange Free State by the First World War, but it remained popular among the Cape Coloured community. The missions also retained the movement as an evangelical tool. Racial integration was a nonissue in the African countryside, and John Muir started the first company for Zulu boys at the Gordon Memorial Mission in 1891.[7]

The Boy's Brigade's willingness to admit Africans and Coloureds cost it support among whites and contributed to the English-speaking community's interest in Baden-Powell's early experiments with Scouting. Baden-Powell was already a celebrity in the English-speaking community due to his exploits during the South African War. Many local boys clubs invited him to be their patron even before he returned to Britain to become inspector general of the cavalry. In 1901 the director of education for Johannesburg invited him to address local teachers on adventure training as a supplement to the official literary curriculum. Driven by this growing interest, formal Scout troops sprang up quickly in the Transvaal and Cape Colony following the publication of Scouting for Boys in Great Britain in 1908.[8]

The membership of these early European troops was almost entirely English speaking. The Anglo–South African War had created a sharp emotional divide between English and Afrikaans speakers. The two groups grudgingly shared power within the Union government and supported formal racial segregation out of a common fear of being dispossessed by the colonized African majority. They disagreed profoundly and bitterly, however, over the political and cultural future of white South Africa. The fissures in South African Scouting grew from these tensions. The decision by European Scout officials to deny African boys official Scout status stemmed from the uncertain nature of political legitimacy in the Union. Lacking clearly established lines of political authority, Scout leaders promoted unity between the dominion's "white races" at the expense of would-be African Scouts. The Scout authorities protected the color bar by forcing African boys into adapted pseudo-Scout organizations, thereby politicizing the movement in a way that Baden-Powell never intended.

South African Scout authorities cited the demise of the Boy's Brigade as a European movement in the Union as an excuse for their exclusionary policies. Four years after the birth of Scouting in the Cape, Baden-Powell brushed aside a Coloured clergyman's questions about the possibility of Africans and Coloureds joining the movement by fudging his commitment to the brotherhood of Scouting: "[This] is a matter for your local people here to deal with. I can only refer you to the Fourth Scout Law but local conditions must govern."[9] This seemingly offhand remark became the basis of official Scout policy in the Union for the next forty years.

The "local people" to whom Baden-Powell referred were the leaders of the four provincial Scout councils. The South African Boy Scout Association (SABSA) came into being in 1910 with the establishment of the Union. The British governor-general became South Africa's ceremonial chief Scout, but provincial Scout commissioners remained largely autonomous. The Transvaal Scout Council, which began as the Transvaal League of Boy Scouts in 1909, was the most conservative on questions of race. Forever hoping to lure Afrikaner youth into the movement, the Transvaal Scouters argued that Scouting had to be reserved for whites. Based in Pretoria, Chief Scoutmaster P. F. F. White insisted that the Fourth Scout Law did not apply to race and referred only to brotherhood between social classes and different national groups of Europeans. Conversely, the Natal Association was more open to the idea of African Scouting but envisioned strictly segregated adapted troops in keeping with prevailing racial attitudes. Each provincial association was affiliated directly with the BSA's Imperial Headquarters until 1921, when, at Baden-Powell's urging, they formed a unified governing council. Although the provincial bodies retained a great deal of autonomy, they were now divisions rather than associations.[10]

Baden-Powell essentially gave the South Africans a free hand in interpreting the Fourth Scout Law, but this did not stop African boys and community leaders from demanding admission to the movement on equal terms. In 1915 a group of senior Lovedale students asked school officials for permission to start a Scout troop. The Lovedale authorities were supportive, but Union Scout leaders turned them down. Denied official recognition, the students created the Lovedale Braves to learn Scouting on their own. Although the only Europeans in the group were teachers, the Braves remained true to Scouting's universalist ideals by including Coloured and Indian members. Similarly, a Coloured troop in the Cape Colony requested official Scout status one year later, but Scout authorities again refused them formal recognition. They offered support and advice to the Coloured boys, but forbade them to use Scout regulations or wear the Scout uniform. Baden-Powell supported this position on the grounds that Scouting had to conform to local standards.[11]

Transvaal Scout officials used Prime Minister Louis Botha's opposition to African Scouting to postpone the entire issue until the conclusion of the First World War. Once the conflict was over, Canon Palmer of Grace Dieu joined other liberal and mission supporters of African Scouting in renewing their request to admit Africans to the movement. In 1919 the Transvaal Scout Council tried to appease them by creating the Trackers as an African alternative to Scouting. African students and their elders again refused to go along, and their hostility doomed the experiment from the start. Faced with this official obstruction, individual missions continued to innovate on their own. A Congregational minister created an adapted troop for African boys in the Johannesburg slums, and in 1921 Coloured leaders on the Cape organized the Paladins as an alternative to Scouting.[12]

LIBERALISM AND ADAPTED EDUCATION

The South African Scout establishment's opposition to granting Africans formal Scout status grew even stronger as the Union's commitment to formal segregation deepened after the First World War. A political alliance of relatively moderate Afrikaners controlled the South African government until Prime Minister Jan Christian Smuts's South African Party lost popular support after using force to put down a white miners' strike in 1921. B. M. Hertzog, leader of the more conservative Nationalist Party, allied with the Labour Party to defeat Smuts on a platform promoting Afrikaner nationalism and white working-class interests. Hertzog and his right-wing allies justified the color bar in moral and religious terms. Using the Dutch Reform Church's teaching that segregation protected lesser peoples, the Nationalists depicted their racial exclusivity as Christian trusteeship that allowed Africans to develop separately and without contamination from the "superior" white culture.[13]

In reality, racial segregation served the region's industrial and mining interests. The native reserves destroyed rural African economies and generated cheap migrant labor. South African mine owners and industrialists paid higher wages to privileged white workers in return for state support in keeping their African labor costs down through police harassment, anti-union legislation, and pass laws limiting labor mobility.[14]

Thus Afrikaner intellectuals and major capitalists, who were often English speakers, found common cause in their support for subordinating the African majority.

European Scout leaders generally agreed with the Afrikaners on the need for strict racial segregation. Conversely, the founders of the Pathfinders were mostly missionaries and white liberals who accepted the reality of the color bar but hoped to use the movement to create a cadre of Westernized elites who would assist in uplifting the greater African population. Liberalism had specific connotations in South Africa. Liberals in the Union, many of whom had close ties to business and mining interests, believed in the strict rule of law and the protection of colonized minorities. Yet they would not challenge the political and economic subordination of the African majority directly. South African liberals believed in gradually "civilizing" Africans to the point where they imbibed enough Western values to warrant full political rights in the Union. This widespread social transformation was always in the comfortably distant future.

In the short term the liberals advocated promoting social harmony and stability by improving African living conditions, pressing the government to repeal its more oppressive "native policies," and conducting a rigidly structured "inter-racial dialogue" with educated Africans. In 1929, J. D. Rheinallt Jones, the secretary of the Witerwatersrand Council of Education and the chief Pathfinder, joined with Loram and other prominent liberals and progressive missionaries in founding the South African Institute of Race Relations (SAIRR). Funded by grants from the American Phelps-Stokes and Carnegie Foundations, the institute promoted interracial understanding by bringing African moderates together with socially conscious whites. These same liberals were also active in the Joint Council movement, a social organization which sought to wean middle-class Africans away from radicalism and independency by giving them an opportunity to meet socially with sympathetic Europeans to discuss "native issues." Interwar South African liberalism was thus an elite movement that tacitly accepted the necessity of racial exclusivity.[15]

South Africa's political, economic, and psychological commitment to racial segregation gave it a vested interest in exporting the color bar to its neighbors. The South Africans worried that African political and social gains abroad would inspire their own subjects to seek similar rights. Northern and Southern Rhodesia willingly embraced the South African segregationist model. Where roughly 11 percent of all South Africans were of European ancestry, whites constituted 5 percent of the Southern Rhodesian populace and just 2 percent in Northern Rhodesia. Europeans in these territories felt even more threatened than their southern neighbors and clung tightly to the color bar to protect their political and social privileges. Yet the Afrikaners' hostility to the empire led the mostly English-speaking settlers to refuse to join the Union of South Africa when the Rhodesias attained self-government in the early 1920s. Nevertheless, the Rhodesians shared South African views on race. Most Rhodesian whites were farmers, but mining interests were also influential in both colonies. As in South Africa, mine owners reserved skilled jobs for well-paid whites in return for state support in securing cheap African labor. Taxation and the disruption of rural economies drove Africans into migrant labor. Thus, the Rhodesians' stake in segregation led them to embrace the Pathfinder model for African Scouting.[16]

The color bar was less of a factor in Nyasaland and the High Commission Territories. There were only two thousand settlers in Nyasaland in 1940, and settlers were virtually nonexistent in Basutoland and Bechuanaland. Swaziland had a tiny European population but did not support a formal color bar. South Africa's constitution contained a provision for incorporating the three High Commission Territories into the Union, but institutionalized racial discrimination in South Africa made it politically impossible for Britain to sanction the transfer. Yet economic necessity and the political power of southern capitalist concerns forced colonial administrators to run Nyasaland and the High Commission Territories as labor reserves for South Africa and the Rhodesias. The limited opportunities for reasonably paid work in Nyasaland forced many men in the protectorate to seek employment in the south.[17]

In practice, the color bar was extremely difficult to enforce. The security forces in South Africa and the neighboring colonies did not have the resources or cultural knowledge to intervene effectively in African daily life. This enabled average people to find ways around racially discriminatory laws and regulations. Although pass laws mandated that most migrants could enter European areas only as temporary workers, African laborers often became permanent urban residents. Opportunities for more lucrative employment, the amusements of city life, and the disintegration of rural economies created powerful incentives to abandon the countryside. Many workers lived illegally in white areas, and the police could do little to stem the tide of urban migration because the southern economies depended on cheap African labor.[18] With formal avenues of resistance closed to them, Africans created their own churches, schools, and social organizations to circumvent day-to-day oppression and challenge the dominant racial order in southern Africa. In seeking to appropriate Western symbols of legitimacy the independents became primary sponsors of unauthorized, and eventually illegal, informal African Scout troops.

Despite their deep philosophical differences, Afrikaner nationalists, South African liberals, missionaries, and British colonial administrators all viewed these developments with alarm. They worried that rapid urbanization and the increasing autonomy of women would lead to the breakdown of rural "tribal" society. Colonial officials feared that the countryside would become ungovernable without the cooperation of "traditional" patriarchal authorities. White South Africans and Rhodesian settlers were equally alarmed by the growth of urban African communities. Believing that African males were unable to control their sexual urges, the more hysterical observers worried about the safety of European women.

The southern African governments looked to legislation, policing, and the courts to deal with these problems, but the missions and their liberal allies believed that social problems were best addressed through education and youth work. They sought to reduce the tensions caused by the destruction of rural African economies, extensive labor migration, and the breakdown of generational authority by adapting Western schooling to colonial circumstances. Liberals and missionaries saw education as a tool for gradually developing African societies along Western lines, while Afrikaner chauvinists, Rhodesian settlers, and capitalists viewed it as a tool for exploiting the economic potential of rural African communities. In practice, however, it was impossible to do both.

Experts on native schooling worried that African graduates would put their knowledge and skills to subversive purposes and hoped adapted Scouting would resolve the conflict over African education by teaching advanced students to aspire to self-advancement within the confines of colonial society. Liberal welfare activists therefore worked closely with mission educators as the primary proponents of adapted Scouting in southern Africa. Most were relatively comfortable with the color bar. C. T. Loram believed that Africans were not yet ready to play an equal role in white society and was a self-described segregationist. Loram and his allies sought to create a small class of educated elites that would assist in the gradual Westernization of the rest of African society by bridging the cultural gap between the "modern" and "traditional" African worlds.[19]

Settlers dictated African education policy in the Rhodesias. They viewed African schooling at best as a tool of economic exploitation and at worst as potentially subversive. As a "kindly and just employer of over two thousand Natives" told a 1925 government commission: "If you want to spoil a good nigger send him to a mission. He is casual and approaches you as an equal."[20] These biases stemmed in part from the Rhodesian whites' fear that educated Africans would compete with European children for jobs. On the whole, the settler community was not very well educated because it was difficult for farming families to send their children to secondary school. Lacking the educational qualifications to justify their political and social prestige in terms of merit, they used racial stereotypes to paint Africans as inherently unable to function in European society.[21]

Not surprisingly, the Southern Rhodesian government turned to adapted industrial education to resolve these social tensions. Beginning in the 1920s, the Native Affairs Department's Domboshawa and Tjolotjo industrial schools gave rural Africans agricultural and manual training. Government officials tried to ensure that African graduates would not compete with white Rhodesians by barring the schools from offering advanced technical courses. Although mission educators in the colony retained their autonomy, the Southern Rhodesian government would provide financial assistance only to schools that followed an industrially focused curriculum. Most African students attended rudimentary rural "kraal" schools, and the colony did not have an African secondary school until 1939. Similarly, Northern Rhodesia did not have an elite African secondary school until the Rev. David Maxwell Robertson, who was a primary proponent of African Scouting, incorporated advanced studies into the curriculum at the Lubwa Teacher Training School in the 1930s.[22]

Nyasaland's much smaller settler population did not have sufficient political influence to dictate education policy to the missions. The protectorate government gave church schools an annual grant of one thousand pounds beginning in 1908 but did not assume direct oversight of them until 1926. The Scottish Presbyterian Livingstonia and Blantyre Missions ran some of the best secondary schools in southern Africa, and the protectorate was a primary exporter of skilled and educated African labor. Nevertheless, even by the 1930s, most students attended unassisted village primary schools that received no state aid because they did not meet government standards.[23]

Although economically subordinate to South Africa, the High Commission Territories followed education policies that were much closer to the Nyasaland model. Each of the three protectorate governments was woefully underfunded, but there were hardly any European children to compete for educational resources. Lower primary schooling was relatively cheap, if not free, but most advanced students had to attend South African secondary schools if they wanted to continue their education. Seeking to end this reliance on the Union and the missions, Swaziland's Paramount Chief (later iNgwenyama, King) Sobhuza II created the Swazi National School in 1931, and the Bechuanaland government opened the Khama Memorial School four years later.[24]

Economic considerations were equally significant in shaping African education in South Africa. Limited state support for African and Coloured schooling ensured that the missions bore primary responsibility for "native education" before 1948. At the close of the Second World War the Union and provincial governments gave the missions an average of just R7.78 per African student as compared to the R76.58 they spent on each white student. Only Natal supported state-run African schools, but in 1937 they served only 19 percent of the province's 68,000 enrolled African students. These funding problems limited the scope and quality of African and Coloured education. By 1946, just 30 percent of African children between the ages of seven and sixteen were in school. Less than 3 percent of these approximately 580,000 students were in secondary school, and only a very small handful of elite mission secondary schools produced top-quality African graduates. This meant that very few boys actually had the chance to become Pathfinders.[25]

The common denominator in African schooling throughout southern Africa was that each territory supported an extremely narrow educational pyramid. Most students attended underfunded and largely unsupervised rural lower primary schools. Only the most able and fortunate had access to advanced primary and secondary schooling. This helped make Pathfinding an elite institution. Most government and mission educators favored this arrangement out of economic necessity and a fear of exposing Africans to advanced Western education. Nevertheless, each territory supported one or more elite secondary schools that catered to a few advanced students. In spite of their varying commitments to adapted education, Christian humanitarianism and the necessity of training African clergymen and teachers compelled the missions to offer Western education on a limited scale. Not surprisingly, it was institutions like Lovedale and Grace Dieu in South Africa, Lubwa in Northern Rhodesia, and Livingstonia in Nyasaland that became the centers of African Scouting. Yet there was no papering over the fundamental contradictions of African education in southern Africa. Widespread land alienation, racial discrimination in employment, and the destruction of rural African society rendered adapted industrial education self-serving, irrelevant, and hypocritical. Pious

European pronouncements about the virtues of country life and manual work meant little when collapsing rural economies forced large numbers of poorly educated Africans into exploitive wage labor.

Educated Africans hoped to escape this labor trap and achieve full citizenship by proving their ability to master Western culture. They used boycotts to force Cape Province and Southern Rhodesian agricultural and technical schools to adopt a more literary focus. School strikes became common in the interwar era, and students at elite institutions formed social organizations like the Transvaal Student Organization to quietly pursue their political aims. The American School Movement in South Africa's Transkei and independent church schools in Nyasaland were even more troubling to European educational authorities because they constituted a direct challenge to the colonial school system.[26]

Western education opened the door to political activism and social mobility when the color bar turned agrarian and technical education into a dead end. African students understandably rejected adapted schooling as inferior and oppressive. Their clergymen, teachers, and parents turned to independency to provide the trappings of Western civilization without the restrictions of colonial control. Yet even the most formal and carefully structured mission education could be equally subversive. Once a student acquired the ability to think critically and a basic command of English there was no effective way to control what he or she read or thought. Given these realities, partisans of the color bar argued against giving Africans any access to Western education. Yet denying Africans the "fruits" of Western civilization would have exposed the hypocrisy of Lugard's dual mandate. Moreover, African education was largely in the hands of missionaries, who used Western schooling as a primary tool of conversion. It was only when the missions became more dependent on government subsidies that South African segregationists and Rhodesian settlers could force them to curtail their educational initiatives. Nevertheless, international political pressure and economic expedience prevented the politicians from forcing the missions to close their Western-style schools.

THE PATHFINDERS

Pathfinding began as part of a broad liberal strategy to resolve the educational crisis in southern Africa that exposed the failings of colonial schools, undermined "traditional" authority in the countryside, and fed urban juvenile delinquency. These problems were ultimately unsolvable because they stemmed from the economic exploitation and political subordination of the African majority. Adapted African Scouting was one of many stopgap measures that addressed the symptoms rather than the underlying causes of social unrest in the region. Liberal welfare experts and mission teachers considered the formal Scout movement's egalitarianism unsuitable for Africans. Instead they applied the principles of adaptation to Scouting in an effort to discipline educated Africans and supplement overtaxed colonial schools by socializing African youth. Adapted Scouting promoted rural stability and retribalization by reinforcing the "traditional authorities" that were the cornerstone of indirect rule. It addressed urban juvenile delinquency by offering young men "constructive recreation" during their free time while teaching them to respect local elders and government officials. Pathfinding was thus part of a broad liberal attempt to convince educated Africans to accept narrow social development as an alternative to political activism.

Yet African students were the real instigators behind the birth of the Pathfinder movement. They dismissed the watered-down versions of Scouting offered by the Scout establishment and renewed their appeal for official Scout status in the early 1920s. Faced with growing interest in Scouting among his student body, Canon Palmer renewed pressure on the Transvaal Scout Council to sanction a Scout troop at Grace Dieu in 1922. When the Transvaal authorities refused, he convinced Union Scout leaders to meet with missionaries and liberal youth workers to discuss the matter. After considerable debate, the conference decided (by a single vote) to allow Palmer and his allies to create a formal African youth organization that would be modeled on the Scout movement.[27]

The conferees dropped the discredited Tracker designation in favor of Pathfinder, a name they claimed was based on the African tradition of sending a youth ahead of a group of travelers as a "dew-breaker" to mark out a path in the long grass. They also created a junior branch of the Pathfinders modeled on the Cub Scouts that was originally to be called the Klipspringers (a small antelope) until opposition from urban Africans forced them to adopt the more prosaic name Junior Pathfinders. The conference chose first J. B. Young and then J. D. Rheinallt Jones, cofounder of the liberal SAIRR, to serve as chief Pathfinder. By the end of 1924, there were twenty-eight mission-sponsored Pathfinder troops within the Union.[28]

Although the European founders of Pathfinding were harshly critical of the most abusive aspects of the color bar, they were also certain that

European Scouting was unsuitable for Africans. During the Pathfinder negotiations, Ray Phillips raised doubts about the wisdom of using Scouting as a template for an African youth movement. Young assured him that Imperial Headquarters would allow them to make any necessary alterations so long as they did not "clash with the actual interests of the European boy."[29] Thus, even though the Pathfinder Council fought hard for full recognition as Scouts, they did not intend for their African troops to be run along European lines.

The seemingly satisfactory resolution of the Pathfinder controversy set a precedent for adapting Guiding for African girls. Faced with the South African Guides' refusal to admit Africans and Coloureds in the early 1920s, mission leaders and educators founded the Lightfinders in Transvaal, the Girl Pathfinders at the Marion Institute for Coloured Girls in Cape Town, and the Lovedale Sunshine Girls for African girls. An African Methodist Episcopal church in Cape Town went one step further and created an African Guides company. In 1925 prominent female missionaries and liberal activists, including the wives of Rheinallt Jones and Phillips of the American Missionary Board, followed the lead of the Pathfinders by forming the Girl Wayfarers Association as a supervised movement for African and Coloured girls. The Wayfarers adopted the Pathfinders' segregationist polices, and South African Guide officials convinced Lady Olave Baden-Powell, chief Guide of the British Association, not to wear her Guide uniform while inspecting the Wayfarers during her 1927 tour of the Union.[30]

Liberals and missionaries sought to use the Pathfinder/Wayfarer compromise to reassure Africans that they were indeed equal members of the British Empire. Yet the Pathfinders' status remained unsettled. The SABSA grudgingly dropped its objections to a uniformed African youth movement, but the powerful provincial Scout divisions refused to acknowledge the Pathfinders as Scouts. Palmer was incensed when he read a statement by Imperial Headquarters in the March 1923 issue of *The Scouter*, the British Scout Association's semiofficial publication, disavowing responsibility for the Pathfinders. Believing Scout officials had tricked him into accepting a watered-down version of the movement, Palmer accused the Transvaal Scout Council of blatant racism. He pointed out that his students read newspaper accounts of Asian and African Scouts in other countries and reminded metropolitan Scout officials that Britain would need African support if the Afrikaner nationalists tried to take the Union out of the empire.[31]

Imperial Headquarters claimed to sympathize with the Pathfinders but tried to avoid Palmer's challenge by citing the need to "recognise local prejudice" in South Africa. Palmer and Canon Woodfield, the Pietersburg

FORWARD

3.1. Pathfinder badge, interwar era. Courtesy of University of Cape Town Libraries, Special Collections. Reproduced with permission of the South African Scout Association.

Pathfindermaster, finally captured official Scouting's attention by warning that failure to support the Pathfinders would lead to the growth of unsanctioned uniformed African youth movements that would be beyond the control of the Scouts. The steady growth of independent and unregistered Scout-type organizations in Cape Province and the Transvaal during the second half of 1923 finally convinced South African Scout officials that embracing the Pathfinders was a necessary evil.[32] If these unauthorized scout groups became linked with the overtly political activities of the ANC or ICU, official South African Scouting faced public embarrassment and the potential loss of government support.

Recognizing that granting the Pathfinders semiofficial status would provide a greater measure of control over African Scouting, the SABSA issued a constitution for the Pathfinders in February 1925 that explicitly placed the movement under the control of Union Scout authorities. The constitution addressed the threat of independent African scouting by empowering the Pathfinders to reject "undesirable" applicants and declared explicitly that "politics may not be discussed or participated in by any members of a Troop in uniform." It also forced the Pathfinders to wear a uniform that was visibly different from that worn by European Scouts. Although Woodfield managed to defeat the SABSA's proposal that Africans wear red rather than khaki shirts and shorts, he had to accept a Pathfinder uniform that omitted the Scout belt and consisted of a tie instead of a scarf and a military-style peaked cap instead of Baden-Powell's broad Stetson. Instead of the European fleur-de-lis Scout badge, the Pathfinder badge consisted of a triangle—whose sides represented purity, clarity, and obedience—surrounding a P that stood for Pathfinder, Progress, Peace, and Prosperity. Mission troop leaders added that the triangle also stood for the Christian trinity. The Grace Dieu Pathfinders deeply resented these obvious deviations from official Scouting.[33]

In terms of organization, the new movement was to be a Union-wide organization consisting of seven divisions under the supervision of a divisional Pathfinder and an executive council consisting of local liberals and missionaries. In reality, the Pathfinders were concentrated in the Transvaal, and the segregationist Transvaal Scout Division insisted on taking responsibility for their supervision. The other three provincial divisions followed the Transvaal model in adapting Scouting for Africans. The Transvaal authorities recognized Rheinallt Jones's Pathfinder Council in 1928 but appointed Kenneth Fleischer, a leading Johannesburg Scoutmaster, to represent European interests on the governing body. The rest of the Pathfinder Council consisted of liberals, missionaries, and Job Rathebe and T. P. Mathabathe as the sole African representatives. The Pathfinders still did not have full Scout status, but their constitution gave the SABSA the power to veto any action by the Pathfinder leadership.[34]

The SABSA was certain it had resolved the thorny question of African Scouting and set out to spread the Pathfinder movement throughout the Union and beyond. Their main goal was to reconcile Scouting's commitment to egalitarianism with the political realities of southern Africa. Worried that the adoption of unsegregated Scouting by South Africa's neighbors would reopen the controversy over the Fourth Scout Law at home, the council made a concerted effort to export the Pathfinder/Wayfarer model abroad. Their task was made easier by the fact that most missionaries and colonial governments in the region looked to South Africa for leadership and guidance on African education and the "native question."

The High Commission Territories introduced Pathfinders and Wayfarers in the 1920s. With no significant European populations, the territories should have been more open to Scouting. However, mission educators believed that adapted Scouting would be a more useful evangelical tool because it theoretically had greater relevance in local circumstances. Unlike Scouting, which was officially nondenominational, Pathfinding was an explicitly Christian movement. In practice, African teachers and parents were largely indifferent to Pathfinding. Faced with this apathy, Bechuanaland used part of its Native Fund to hire a professional organizing commissioner from South Africa to promote and supervise the movement. The Boy's Brigade was also active in Bechuanaland, and in the

1930s the two movements pitted their first aid, drill, and signaling skills against each other in a competition for a commemorative shield provided by the protectorate's resident commissioner.[35]

Nyasaland, further removed from the racial tensions of South Africa, never found it necessary to force Africans into Pathfinding. Maxwell Robertson, a teacher at the Church of Scotland's Livingstonia mission and the future patron of African Scouting in Northern Rhodesia, started a Scout troop for Africans in the 1920s. Although some of the other missions joined the European planters in favoring the Pathfinder model, the Scottish missionaries refused to bring the segregation of the South African movement into Nyasaland. But as in Bechuanaland, there was a division between the European partisans of Scouting and the Boy's Brigade, with the CSM's Blantyre mission and the Dutch Reform Church favoring the latter. The three European troops in the territory did not oppose African Scouting but also had little to do with the Livingstonia Scouts. Guiding remained a European movement until Livingstonia established an African company in 1941.[36]

Pathfinding received much greater support in the Rhodesias, where government and Scout officials were more preoccupied with ensuring that the Fourth Scout Law did not undermine the color bar. European Scouting in Southern Rhodesia dated from 1909, but the colony did not acquire its own independent territorial association until white voters decided not to join South Africa in 1923. As in South Africa, Scouting was for whites only, and the Southern Rhodesian Pathfinders were affiliated directly with their Union counterparts.

The movement was far less established in Northern Rhodesia. It took the intervention of Governor Sir Herbert Stanley to give it a foothold in the colony in 1924. Worried that reliance on African servants made European youths soft, Stanley believed segregated Scouting on the Transvaal model was an absolute necessity. It fell to Maxwell Robertson, now principal of the Church of Scotland's Lubwa teacher-training college, to bring the Pathfinders to Northern Rhodesia in 1929. Although he had supported African Scouting in Nyasaland, he quickly learned the futility of trying to force the pace of interracial cooperation in Northern Rhodesia. Reverend George Fraser built on Robertson's efforts by expanding the movement to the Copperbelt in 1935 as part of an effort to reduce social and racial tensions in the mining compounds.[37]

The 1930 Northern Rhodesian Scout Ordinance put the Pathfinders under the control of European Scouting, but the European association's open neglect of the movement forced the Northern Rhodesian troops to remain affiliated with the South African Pathfinder Council. Maxwell Robertson bitterly opposed segregated Scouting and begged the Northern Rhodesian Scout Council to allow the Lubwa troop to use the three-finger Scout salute and for permission to add to the Pathfinder Law: "A Pathfinder is a friend to all, and a brother to every other Pathfinder and Scout, no matter [to what] class or tribe he belongs." When the NRSC refused he sought help from the Imperial Headquarters but met with the same indifference that confronted the supporters of African Scouting in the Union. Harold Legat, commissioner for overseas Scouting, responded: "How can a Pathfinder be a friend to every Scout when the latter will not allow the Pathfinders to be Scouts?"[38]

In hindsight, it seems strange that a relatively simple youth movement like the Boy Scouts would generate so much controversy. The actual programs followed by individual European and African Scout troops were quite similar and consisted largely of patriotic displays, camping, knot tying, marching, first aid training, and acts of public service. Yet the idea that African and European youth could use the same curriculum and engage in the same recreational activities was indeed highly controversial because it made Scouting a potential bridge across the color bar. Moreover, it offered the opportunity for African boys to demonstrate that they were as resourceful, reliable, and prepared as European boys. Government officials, mission educators, liberal welfare experts, and European Pathfinder leaders therefore went to great lengths to fashion an adapted form of African Scouting that embodied the ideals of the movement but was safely distinct from the European version of Scouting.

The true struggle for Scouting took place at the local level, where African innovators vied with European Scout authorities to adapt the movement to African circumstances. The stakes of the contest over the character of African Scouting were nothing less than the viability of the colonial regime and the ability of Africans to claim the rights and privileges of full citizenship within the empire. Scouting represented political and social legitimacy, and African versions of the movement had the potential to lend respectability to opposition groups like the ANC and the ICU. Unfortunately, it is difficult to gauge the full extent of early African experiments with unauthorized scouting because it is difficult to find surviving African Scouts from this era. European observers spoke of independent scouting as a threat but offered little detail on how the rogue troops were founded or run.

It seems certain, however, that the Grace Dieu Pathfinders spoke for most African boys and community leaders when they insisted that adaptation could not lead to lower standards. Canon Woodfield was incensed when the Transvaal Scout Association suggested using European Cub Scout regulations as the basis for Pathfinder proficiency badges. The Grace Dieu missionaries and their allies convinced the Pathfinder Council to adopt the Scout Law and Promise verbatim, with the sole exception being that the word "Scout" was replaced with "Pathfinder." The Pathfinder regulations used virtually the same rank tests for Tenderfoot through First Class Scout but made no mention of requirements for a Pathfinder King's Scout. At the official level, the only other main divergence between the regulations for Pathfinding and Scouting was that the Pathfinder Council translated the Pathfinder Prayer, Promise, Law, and enrollment ceremony into Secwana, Zulu, Xhosa, Venda, Thonga, and Southern Sesotho. At the troop level, Pathfinder meetings tended to place more emphasis on marching, drill, and band competitions than on the skills and badge training European Pathfinder leaders considered so important.[39]

SCHOOL CRISES, JUVENILE DELINQUENCY, AND THE PATHFINDER COMPROMISE

Pathfinding nearly collapsed in the 1930s when state repression and the failing African school system exposed the inherent racial hypocrisy of adapted Scouting. The debate over the Pathfinders' status as Scouts took place against the backdrop of the South African government's decision to codify and strengthen racial segregation in the Union. In 1934 the Depression forced Prime Minister J. B. M. Hertzog to ally with Smuts to form the United Party. Together they negotiated the Status of Union Act with Britain, affirming that legislation enacted by the metropolitan parliament was valid in the Union only if it was also passed by the South African parliament. Similarly, the act also established that Britain's governor-general could act only on the advice of his local South African ministers. The act gave the South African government de facto political autonomy and free reign to embed the color bar even more deeply in the Union's legal code. New laws segregated cities and towns by restricting African residence to specific urban "locations" and abolished what was left of the Cape franchise.[40]

Nevertheless, hardcore Afrikaner nationalists were not satisfied. Although their hold on power was secure by the 1930s, they felt threatened by African urban migration and political activity and still rejected all ties with Britain. Angered by the United Party's alliance with Smuts, the right-wingers broke with Hertzog to form the Purified National Party.

The new party worked closely with a secret society known as the Broeder-bond to push for more robust segregationist legislation and to raise Afrikaner chauvinism to new heights.[41]

White South Africa's mounting anxiety in the decade before the Second World War stemmed in part from a crisis of generational authority in rural and urban African communities. Education officials worried that rural schools promoted detribalization by failing to reintegrate students back into community life. Lacking viable opportunities for social mobility in the reserves, graduates, dropouts, and children who never made it to school grew disenchanted with their elders and left to seek work in the cities and towns, threatening to overwhelm the poorly funded and disorganized urban school system. By the late 1930s, Johannesburg had spaces for only 38 percent of the roughly forty thousand school-age African children the municipal authorities acknowledged as city residents. Even though school fees depressed enrollments, urban African teachers faced classes of up to one hundred children.[42]

By the 1930s, young townsmen who had difficulty competing with rural migrants for jobs often turned to petty crime and gangsterism. Johannesburg alone experienced a 64 percent increase in juvenile court cases between 1937 and 1938. Liberal welfare experts blamed this rise in juvenile delinquency on detribalization and the erosion of African family life by uncontrolled urbanization. By pretending that African migrants were only temporary sojourners in European areas, the South African government hindered workers from establishing stable families in the cities. Instead, male migrants formed temporary relationships with the relatively few women who lived illegally in urban areas. The children of these often ephemeral unions grew up unsupervised in households where adult men were largely absent.[43]

The neighboring colonies and protectorates experienced similar problems in their urban centers. In Northern Rhodesia rootless young men joined protests by African copper miners against taxation and racial disparities in employment that turned violent in 1935 and 1940. Concluding that Copperbelt children needed discipline and direction, the Northern Rhodesian Education Department worked with the United Missions in the Copperbelt to provide compulsory schooling in the mine compounds. Copperbelt schools followed a more conventional literary curriculum than other African institutions in the colony and provided the roughly forty-five hundred school-age children in the compounds with free tuition and books. Copperbelt educators were more concerned with discipline than the potentially detribalizing influence of Western education, and many schools employed former African drill instructors to main-tain order among the student body.[44]

European observers blamed the increasing lawlessness of urban youth on the breakdown of "tribal sanctions" that underpinned rural genera-tional authority. Many parents shared these concerns as their children grew up with little hope for the future. The Reverend A. M. Sikakana spoke for the older generations when he worried about the failure of urban schools to deal with the problem. "The future is most dangerous to our nation. Children are growing up without the full control of their parents. Boys and girls do whatever they like during the day. There is no school for man and no care after school. A ruinous future!"[45] Young men in particular saw no reason to defer to elders who had been powerless to stand up to the racist South African state. Many rejected the values and traditions of their parents by joining violent street gangs, the Scouts' main rivals in South African cities, that embraced an urban lifestyle based on aggression and the reworking of Western material culture.[46]

Coupled with the inadequacies of the colonial schools, these urban tensions convinced government officials, missionary educators, and lib-eral welfare experts that the new generation of interwar African youth posed a threat to the security of European rule in southern Africa. They sponsored Pathfinder troops at schools and youth centers as part of a vain attempt to impose order on urban African society. These problems con-tributed to a growing sense of unease in white communities throughout southern Africa. The erosion of rural society, steady urbanization, and the strength of African trade unionism and political activism made the privi-leged white minority feel vulnerable. Government officials, missionar-ies, and liberal social welfare experts were certain they were facing a moral crisis threatening the future of Western civilization in the region. Adapted Scouting offered the possibility of imposing order and disci-pline on the increasingly restless younger African generation. Yet the Pathfinder model could not paper over the fundamental inequalities in South African society.

Hoping to protect themselves from charges of hypocrisy in their ap-plication of the Scout canon, Union Scout officials tried to reconcile their racial prejudices with the Fourth Scout Law by funneling all African and Coloured boys into the Pathfinders. This was not to be. Representatives of the Coloured community attended the conference that gave birth to the Pathfinders but refused to join a movement that institutionalized the color bar. Indian groups were even more strident on the question of segregated Scouting. As Hindus and Muslims, they found the explicitly

Christian character of Pathfinding intolerable. Linking official Scouting with full political and commercial rights, they refused the Transvaal Scout Division's invitation to join the Pathfinders and formed a troop of "Indian Boy Scouts" in 1928. The Natal Scout Division actually backed the appeal by the Natal Indian Congress to admit an Indian troop to the Durban Local Scout Association, but the SABSA overruled the Natal Scouters. Led by the Transvaal Division, European Scout authorities worried that accommodating the Indians would drive Afrikaners out of the movement and destroy the Pathfinder compromise by inspiring Africans and Coloureds to demand equal treatment. Baden-Powell again rejected the South African Indian community's appeals to intervene.[47]

The Scout leadership went to such great lengths to exclude Africans and Coloureds because they still sought to convince the Afrikaner community to embrace Scouting. Building on Baden-Powell's stated goal of unifying the Union's two "white races," the SABSA hoped Scouting would strengthen European minority rule and keep South Africa in the empire by reducing the mutual acrimony that lingered after the South African War. Afrikaner intellectuals, however, remained profoundly suspicious of Scouting's imperialist origins and character. Recalling Sir Alfred Milner's failed anglicization campaign following the Treaty of Vereeniging, they championed a highly nationalistic vision of Afrikaner culture that they expected would eventually absorb the English-speaking community. Not surprisingly, the Afrikaner chauvinists viewed Scouting as a threat and never forgot that Baden-Powell made his reputation as a British general in the South African War.[48]

Led by prominent educational authorities like Nico van der Merwe, C. F. Visser, and J. V. Hesse, the nationalists compiled a lengthy list of criticisms of the movement that included the SABSA's subordination to Imperial Headquarters and the Scout Promise's declaration of allegiance to the Crown and the Union Jack. Above all else, the English-speaking political establishment and the Scout leadership hoped to prevent Visser and Hesse's Afrikaans Educationalist Committee from founding its own competing youth movement. The South African Scout authorities therefore sought to appease the nationalists. They translated all their Scout literature into Afrikaans and declared in 1930 that Scouting "should foster . . . international brotherhood, but should not aim at social equality between European and Coloured Races." Yet the SABSA refused to abandon the Union Jack or replace the declaration of loyalty to the king in the Scout Promise with the words "my country," as the Afrikaners demanded. As a result, negotiations between the two groups collapsed. Taking the pioneers

CHAPTER 3

of the Great Trek as their inspiration, the Afrikaner nationalists created the Voortrekkers in 1931 as a uniformed youth movement for Afrikaner boys and girls.[49]

Although the South African Scout authorities were dismayed by the Voortrekkers, they never gave up hope that the Afrikaners might eventually embrace their movement. Throughout the 1930s the SABSA continued to promote white racial solidarity at the expense of their obligations to Africans, Coloureds, and Indians under the Fourth Scout Law. The council's negotiations with Habonim ("the builders"), a Jewish youth group modeled on the Scouts, exposed the contradictions of this policy. Although a company of the Jewish Lads' Brigade existed briefly in Johannesburg from 1898 to 1903, the South African Jewish community did not have a viable youth movement until Norman Lourie brought Habonim to the Union in 1931. Wellesley Aron, a Zionist British Jew, created Habonim to use Scouting methods in helping Jewish youth in the British Empire retain their identity and resist anti-Semitism. By the late 1930s Habonim claimed roughly five thousand members in South Africa, 40 percent of whom were girls.[50]

Ironically, where Africans and Coloureds in South Africa wanted nothing more than to achieve full recognition as Scouts, Habonim petitioned the South African Boy Scout Association for the very affiliated status that African members of the Pathfinders found so demeaning. Lourie sought this quasi-official relationship because he wanted access to the prestige and universalism of Scouting without sacrificing the Jewish character of his organization. Yet race trumped religion in the eyes of South African Scouting, and the SABSA rejected his appeal on the grounds that, according to Sir William Campbell of the Orange Free State Scout Division, there was "room in the Boy Scout Movement for all European sections of the community." The Scout authorities offered the Habonim a seat on the Scout Council and the privilege of maintaining their own closed troops where they could follow a special Jewish curriculum. It made these concessions over the objections of several prominent Jewish Scouters who opposed the Habonim movement on the grounds that it fostered self-segregation and produced only an incomplete knowledge of Judaism. Nevertheless, the Habonim politely rejected the Scout authorities' offer.[51]

The inconsistencies of the SABSA's policies on who qualified for full Scout status was not lost on African community leaders. In 1931, African members of the Witwatersrand District Pathfinder Committee leaked a resolution to the press condemning the color bar as a "denial of Scout Spirit" and threatened to withdraw forty-four Pathfinder troops from the movement if they did not receive full recognition as Scouts. Chafing under the enforced "tutelage" of the Transvaal Scout Council, at the very least the Pathfinder leadership wanted direct representation on the governing South African Scout Council and the right to appoint their own chief Pathfinder. The Union Scout authorities did not help matters when they barred the Pathfinder Council from asking the governor-general to be their president in 1931 on the grounds that the Pathfinders were already "a branch of the Boy Scout Association."[52] Clearly Scout status was something that the SABSA could extend and withdraw to serve its own interests.

Frustrated by the Scout leadership's self-serving manipulation of their status, the Pathfinders appealed to Imperial Headquarters to intervene on their behalf. Yet Baden-Powell had already made it clear that he was not prepared to jeopardize the Scouts' institutional ties with the South African government by breaking the color bar, lest "the white boys . . . be withdrawn en masse from the Movement." Privately, he assured Rheinallt Jones that integration would come eventually. But in the meantime Scouting had to follow a policy of "softlee, softlee, catchee monkey." Baden-Powell raised serious doubts about his commitment to African Scouting, however, when during a tour of South Africa he urged white Scouts to "buck up" and "not let the rising generation of Natives beat [them] in the race."[53]

The situation grew even tenser in 1933 when the Scout authorities declined to help three Pathfinders attend the World Scout Jamboree in Hungary. The South African government denied them passports, and the SABSA refused to intervene on their behalf when the Union Castle Steamship Company made their passage conditional on the Scouts' assuming responsibility for them. To make matters worse, the South African papers carried an account of the European contingent's performance of a "Kaffir war dance" at the jamboree. The backlash in the African community was swift and intense. Pathfinder troops disbanded throughout the Transvaal, and African teachers and youth leaders resorted to the technically illegal strategy of founding their own unauthorized scout groups. One such troop was sponsored by a "Bantu Social Club" in Natal and openly wore complete Scout uniforms and undertook public fund raising campaigns to support its activities. For Rheinallt Jones and his allies the last straw came in 1935 when the Transvaal Scout Council turned down an invitation from Lord Clarendon, the governor-general and chief Scout of the Union, to attend a joint rally with the Girl Guides, Pathfinders, and Wayfarers in Cape Town. Faced with such an overt repudiation of the Fourth Scout Law, he invited the governor-general to chair a meeting of the Pathfinder Council that would discuss freeing the Pathfinders from the authority of the SABSA and their transformation into an independent Scout association.[54]

Rheinallt Jones's rebellion came at time when the collapse of negotiations with the Voortrekkers led some senior Scout officials to rethink their opposition to African Scouting. In 1935 the relatively liberal Natal Scout Division introduced a motion in the Scout Council to admit Indians on the grounds that there was a fully recognized Scout association in India. The Natal Scouters argued that public opinion in the province would no longer tolerate segregated Scouting and suggested that if the Afrikaners could not accept the Scouts' commitment to universal brotherhood then it was better that they did not join at all. However the Natal authorities were not proposing full social integration within the movement. They remained committed to segregated Scouting at the troop level and reassured the council that "there is no social equality now between Europeans and non-Europeans in matters of church, school, or sport, nor would there be in Scouting." The Natal division cited Frederick Lugard's doctrine of separate African development within the confines of "native tradition" to justify local segregation in the movement but proposed to finally grant the Pathfinders full Scout status.[55]

These suggestions did not sit well with the Scout leadership. Rather than recognizing Africans as Scouts, they planned to answer Rheinallt Jones by creating an autonomous all-white national South African Scout association. In seeking independence from the British Scout Association, the Union Scout authorities sought to show Afrikaner politicians and Voortrekker leaders that the movement was free of imperial entanglements and that the Scouts would respect Afrikaner racial sensitivities. In mid-1935 hardliners led by the Transvaal and Orange Free State divisional commissioners proposed revising the SABSA's new national constitution to explicitly exclude Africans and Coloureds.

This was a declaration of war to the African community and its liberal allies. Pathfinder leaders in Northern and Southern Rhodesia threatened to break away if the color bar became an official part of the Scout constitution. Sir Charles Rey, resident commissioner of Bechuanaland, demanded that Bechuana Pathfinders be granted Scout status "just like all other natives are all over the world." Rheinallt Jones took the white hardliners' proposed constitutional revisions as a violation of the implicit understanding that Africans and Coloureds would eventually become full Scouts. He and his allies threatened to set up a rival association that would challenge the European monopoly on Scouting. Initially, the Scout Council was unmoved. One council member argued that the Fourth Scout Law required African and Coloured Scouts not to impose on their "white brothers" by hindering reconciliation between the "white races." Percival Whitely, a Transvaal commissioner, argued that "racial mixing would encourage European children to adopt undesirable African habits, manners and customs." The hard-liners blamed opposition to the new constitution on "extremist" members of the Transvaal Pathfinder Council and were confident that they could run the Pathfinders by themselves if Rheinallt Jones and his allies went through with their threat to secede.[56]

Yet the Scout authorities overplayed their hand in trying to make segregation a formal part of the Scout canon in South Africa. Although Baden-Powell ruled out recognizing the Pathfinders as an independent association, he could not afford to let the South Africans flout the Fourth Scout Law so openly. He therefore brokered a compromise in February 1936 granting the European, African, and Asian communities "parallel" self-governing Scout associations linked together under the broad supervisory umbrella of an autonomous "national" South African Boy Scout Association. The agreement called originally for Coloured Scouts to be part of the African association, but Coloured leaders refused to be lumped together with "natives" and lobbied successfully for the privilege of having their own separate section.[57]

The Pathfinders became the Pathfinder Scout Association and finally achieved technical Scout status. However, the compromise required each organization to have its own distinctive emblem, and although it finally allowed Africans and Coloureds to wear the trademark Stetson, it required them to wear a different hatband. The SABSA also convinced the Union government to grant them sole legal ownership of the Scout badge and uniform to prevent their use by unauthorized African and Coloured groups. In return for dropping their demands for formal segregation, the hardliners gained an even greater measure of control over African and Coloured Scouting. Although a technically self-governing council ran each new association, the European faction became the de facto South African Boy Scout Association. It retained the power to review and block resolutions or actions by the other sections. If one of the African and Coloured associations refused to abide by its rulings, the SABSA had the authority to suspend or withdraw their constitution, thereby expelling them from the movement. Conversely, the 1936 compromise kept the funding of the four associations entirely separate, and in 1940 the European section refused the Pathfinder Council's appeal to share the funding it received from the Abe Bailey Trust and direct government grants.[58]

Baden-Powell and the Union Scout authorities pronounced themselves entirely pleased with the new arrangement. It gave the SABSA the authority to move against unauthorized African and Coloured scout organizations but still left the door open for Afrikaners to join the movement by segregating Africans and Coloureds in separate federated associations. Scout leaders also naively hoped that granting Africans full Scout status would put an end to their attempts to use the Fourth Scout Law to challenge the wider color bar. Borrowing directly from Lugard's *Dual Mandate*, they offered the following public explanation for the new constitution: "Here then is the true conception of the inter-relation of colour. Complete uniformity in ideals; absolute equality in paths of knowledge and culture, equal opportunity for those who strive; equal admiration for those who achieve; in methods social and racial a separate path, each pursuing his own race purity and race pride; equality in things spiritual, agreed divergence in things physical and material." Lest there be any doubt about the Scouts' commitment to social segregation, the SABSA issued a public declaration promising that there would be no interracial Scouting activities at any level. Baden-Powell affirmed this by telling the London press that the main purpose of South African Scouting was to teach Britons and Boers to be "comrades."[59]

The apparent resolution of the Pathfinder controversy seemed to pave the way for the movement to become part of the Union's official African school curriculum. In 1938 the Pathfinder Council sent a circular letter to "all institutions and high schools" in South Africa asking them to support the Pathfinder initiative. They also asked representatives from the Native Affairs Department and provincial education officials to serve on the Pathfinders' divisional councils. The Union government rejected the invitation, but mission and provincial government schools continued to make Pathfinding an official extracurricular activity. Many teacher-training colleges covered the fundamentals of the movement, and local school authorities and principals often made Scout experience a requirement for employment. By 1950 roughly 49 percent of all African teachers were somehow involved with the Pathfinders or Wayfarers.[60]

The 1936 constitution also facilitated the amalgamation of the Wayfarers and the Girl Guides. Led by Edith Rheinallt Jones, the Transvaal Wayfarers Association petitioned the World Guide Headquarters for official recognition in 1930, but the Guide authorities rebuffed them by telling them to apply through the South African Girl Guides Association.[61] By comparison, the Wayfarers had a much more sympathetic ally in Olave Baden-Powell than the Pathfinders had in her husband. Lady Baden-Powell was far less willing to tolerate segregated Guiding, and her support helped the Wayfarers negotiate a slightly better accommodation with the Guides than the Pathfinders won from the Scouts. There is no easy explanation for why Guiding was slightly more open to Africans and Coloureds than Scouting. In South Africa it seems that the overall subordinate status of women made the closer integration of the two female movements less controversial. Furthermore, the narrower domestically focused Guide program created far fewer opportunities for girls from different ethnic communities to interact. Thus, it was easier for them to embrace integration.

In early 1936 the Guides and Wayfarers agreed on a union that made the president of the Wayfarers the vice president of the South African Girl Guides Association. The Wayfarers received a "branch membership" as Wayfarer Guides and seven seats on the South African Girl Guides Headquarters Council. The Scout authorities were certain their sister organization had gone too far and appealed to Lord Baden-Powell to convince the Guides to adopt their federated segregated constitution. In reality the Scouts had little to complain about. The Wayfarers retained separate rules and uniforms, and the Guide leadership publicly declared: "There will be no question of joint companies or camps." Nevertheless, these arrangements did not go down well in the Transvaal, where European Guiders refused to ratify the new constitution because it admitted Africans and Coloureds to the movement. Conversely, Edith Rheinallt Jones complained that it did not go far enough and broke with her European counterparts by nominating an African as a Wayfarer representative on the Union Headquarters Council. Lady Baden-Powell and most provincial Guide leaders accepted this choice and tried to keep the controversy private. However, the Transvaal Guides leaked their complaints to the press, and several Dutch Reformed Church congregations threatened to shut down their Wayfarer companies. European opposition to amalgamation, coupled with a preference among many missionaries for a more adapted African form of Guiding, meant that most Wayfarer companies in the Transvaal did not join the new amalgamated association. They remained part of a separate Wayfarer organization based almost entirely at non-Anglican churches and missions in the province.[62]

Conversely, South African Scout authorities were confident that the 1936 constitution finally resolved the debate over African and Coloured Scouting. The rising popularity of Pathfinding in the late 1930s seemed to bear them out. The numbers of Africans in the Union that the SABSA recognized as officially enrolled Pathfinder Scouts (it is impossible to know the numbers of unauthorized scouts) rose from 5,267 in 1931 to 11,575 in 1939. The Scout authorities tried to build on this success by exporting the new Pathfinder model to their neighbors and wrote a provision into the 1936 constitution that provided for its extension to adjoining territories. Rheinallt Jones was entirely supportive of these efforts and asked Imperial Headquarters to appoint him chief Pathfinder Scout of the High Commission Territories. Believing that most Africans were not ready to mix with Europeans on equal terms, he saw Pathfinding as an adapted form of Scouting that was best suited to gradually remaking African societies along Western lines. Having won official Scout status for the Pathfinders, Rheinallt Jones and his liberal allies agreed on the need to keep African and European Scouts strictly segregated at the troop level.[63]

Popular reaction to the de facto segregation enshrined in the 1936 South African Scout constitution in the rest of southern Africa was decidedly mixed. With 1,156 registered Pathfinder Scouts, Bechuanaland had the largest and most active Pathfinder organization. However, its resident commissioner, Charles Rey, voiced the grievances of African leaders in the protectorate when he condemned it as a "thoroughly bad and vicious proposal born by colour-bar prejudice out of expediency." In a bitter protest to Imperial Headquarters, he declared that Bechuanaland would never accept the South African brand of federated Scouting. Although technically divisions of the SABSA, the Bechuana Scouts joined Basutoland and Swaziland in rebuffing the South African Scouts' efforts to expand into their territories by taking direct control of local Pathfinder companies. Popular opposition to segregated Scouting in Bechuanaland was a key factor in the London Missionary Society's decision to continue to favor the Boy's Brigade over Baden-Powell's movement. In 1940 the two groups reached an agreement dividing the protectorate into spheres of influence. This meant that the Bangwato and Batwana territories became closed to Scouting.[64]

Conversely, Southern Rhodesian Scout leaders readily embraced the segregated South African model. With just 237 registered Pathfinders in the entire colony in 1933, they faced little pressure to adhere to the letter of the Fourth Scout Law. Governor-General Herbert Stanley told Baden-Powell in 1937 that local politics made it totally impossible to consider desegregating Scouting, and he embraced the 1936 Pathfinder compromise as a convenient way of creating a fictitious bridge between the separate European and African movements.[65] Political friction between the

3.2. Bechuana Wayfarers, 1930s. Courtesy of the Botswana Society.

Rhodesian settlers and Afrikaner nationalists ruled out the possibility of direct ties between Southern Rhodesian Pathfinders and the new South African Pathfinder Scout Association, but the mission teachers who served as Pathfindermasters in the colony followed the lead of Rheinallt Jones's organization.

The Pathfinder leadership in Northern Rhodesia was far less certain of how to respond to the developments in South Africa. Pathfinding in the colony was still largely unestablished in the 1930s because a succession of governors procrastinated in recognizing African Scouting. The Northern Rhodesian Pathfinder troops were technically under the supervision of the South African Pathfinders until 1938, when Maxwell Robertson convinced the government to grant a constitution to the Pathfinder Scout Movement. European Scout leaders initially refused to consider any links with the Pathfinders, but in 1940 grudgingly recognized the African troops as the Native Section of the Boy Scout Association of Northern Rhodesia. As African Scouting expanded beyond the Lubwa Mission and the Copperbelt mining compounds, this semiofficial status became increasingly intolerable to African Pathfinder leaders. Their efforts to win full recognition as Scouts sparked a racial backlash in the colony's settler community. The two movements remained segregated right up to the council level, and there was a steady decline in the popularity of Scouting among European youth in the colony due to the Scout movement's limited African connections.[66]

EXPERIMENTS IN ADAPTED SCOUTING

J. D. Rheinallt Jones and the Europeans on the Pathfinder Council were highly dissatisfied with the state of Pathfinding in the neighboring colonies and protectorates and were particularly critical of the colonial associations' cursory efforts at adaptation. Their commitment to creating a more comprehensive version of adapted Scouting gained momentum during the heyday of indirect rule in the 1930s. Concluding that the various state, religious, and voluntary organizations engaged in African youth needed to cooperate more closely, Rheinallt Jones called a meeting of colonial youth workers in Salisbury, Southern Rhodesia, following the 1935 Jeanes School Conference. The agenda of this Conference on Youth Movements covered adapting youth work to village conditions, "sex hygiene and purity teaching in view of the breakdown of [tribal] sanctions," and making use of African age grades and "native crafts."[67] Imperial Headquarters declined Rheinallt Jones's invitation to send an observer, but the conferees included government officials, colonial education experts, anthropologists, missionaries, and European representatives of the Boy Scouts, Girl Guides, and Boy's Brigades from territories throughout eastern, central, and southern Africa.

Rheinallt Jones's primary goal was to convince colonial youth workers to embrace the South African principles of adaptation that were the foundation of the Pathfinder model. He believed it was particularly important to incorporate "native tradition" into youth movements to cloth their "civilizing" message in African garb. For the South African Pathfinder leadership, adaptation meant using African emblems in Scout badges, basing badge tests on African "village life," incorporating "native singing and dancing" into troop programs, and possibly replacing the Scout system of ranks with African age grades. Rheinallt Jones and the European Pathfinder leaders considered Scouting a progressive force but believed that Africans could grasp its core principles only if they were framed in familiar terms. Moreover, adapted Scouting paid an additional political bonus in South Africa by departing visibly from the European version of the movement.

Yet Pathfinding was much harder to defend outside of the Union, and the delegates to the Salisbury conference voiced considerable doubts about its institutionalized segregation. The SABSA sent a representative to explain its racial policies, but many of the delegates remained highly critical of the South Africans' interpretation of the Fourth Scout Law. Ian Orchardson, a Kenya-based anthropologist, warned that segregation led to racial friction. Most conferees agreed that a generational crisis threatened the stability of rural African societies but had markedly different opinions on the capacity of adaptation to solve the problem. The Boy's Brigade representatives argued that Christianity rather than adapted "indigenous arts and customs" was the best foundation for youth work in Africa. They also stressed that the brigade "gladly welcomes boys of all races."[68]

Thus, Rheinallt Jones failed to get the conference to accept Pathfinding as the blueprint for African youth work when the delegates resolved that youth movements should serve both Europeans and "natives." However, they agreed that full membership in a movement did not necessarily mean full "uniformity of methods" at the local level and accepted that where equal membership was not politically feasible for all races it "would be advisable for there to be concurrent organisations within the same movement." This grudging acceptance of Pathfinding was all Rheinallt Jones would get from the conference, and his attempt to convince the delegates to sanction the adaptation of African "crafts, musical instruments, rhythmic dances and music, traditional history, folklore and dramatised stories" for use in organized youth movements generated only mixed support.[69]

The failure of the Salisbury Conference to produce a universally accepted youth work curriculum left it to individual missionaries, teachers, and Scout leaders throughout anglophone Africa to modify Scouting as they saw fit. One of the most interesting experiments with adapted Scouting took place in Swaziland during the mid-1930s when Paramount Chief Sobhuza II reconstituted the Swazi regimental age grade system to bolster his legitimacy. Having been rebuffed in his legal suit to reclaim large tracts of land from European speculators, Sobhuza remade himself as a "traditionalist" by reviving and reconceptualizing local institutions of authority. He sought to exploit the opportunities presented by indirect rule to compensate for his defeat in the British courts by building popular and aristocratic support for the Swazi monarchy.[70]

More specifically, he endeavored to reassert control over Swazi youth and limit mission influence in the territory by reviving the regimental *emabutfo* ("regiment"; colonial texts usually used the Zulu term *ibuto*) system as the official youth organization at the new Swazi National School. In precolonial times Swazi kings raised these militarized age grades for war, cattle raiding, and communal labor. Under British rule they were demilitarized and weakened as young men migrated to the mines and farms of South Africa. In seeking popular and aristocratic support for his royalist version of Swazi nationalism, Sobhuza proposed to make the emabutfo system a required extracurricular activity at the national school. The paramount chief was deeply suspicious of the Christian missions in the protectorate because they undermined his political base. In reintroducing the strict social controls of the old regimental system, he sought to exert greater influence over Swazi society by bridging divisions between Christian and non-Christian Swazis and addressing the crisis of generational authority in the countryside. He also envisioned that the emabutfo youth movement would teach "pride of race" and deal with the perceived problem of growing sexual immorality by reintroducing peer sanctions against full premarital intercourse. The program would eventually expand to include all Swazi children. Sobhuza assured the colonial authorities that the new organization would not be militaristic but would instead follow the lead of the Scouts in adapting drill and discipline to youth work.[71]

Swaziland's mission community, led by Anglican archdeacon C. E. Cary Brenton, adamantly opposed Sobhuza's plan on the grounds that it was immoral. Although they refused to offer specific criticisms, they were essentially unwilling to surrender their monopoly on the formal education and socialization of Swazi youth. The charge of immorality stemmed from their fear that the new youth movement would sanction the revival of the Swazi institution of ukujama, a form of sexual education and release that encouraged adolescent boys and girls to engage in supervised interfemoral intercourse as a substitute for full coitus and its inherent risk of pregnancy.[72]

Alan Marwick, deputy resident commissioner for Swaziland in the early 1930s, sided with Sobhuza against the missionaries. As a firm believer in indirect rule and adapted education, he accepted the paramount chief's assurances that the new movement would not be immoral. Marwick invited the noted South African anthropologists Isaac Schapera and A. W. Hoernle to study the emabutfo system and judge whether it was a suitable basis for a government-sanctioned youth movement. Schapera and Hoernle gave Sobhuza their unqualified backing and drew colleagues W. W. M. Eiselen and Bronislaw Malinowski into the debate. Faced with the powerful testimony of these "native experts," the missions changed tactics and offered a compromise proposal to create a hybrid Emabutfo-Pathfinder movement. There were already a handful of Pathfinder troops at mission schools in the territory, and one missionary suggested that the Pathfinder Law and Promise would provide a safeguard against the emabutfo experiment becoming too immoral or militaristic. Sobhuza had little use for the Pathfinders, and he called on his anthropologist allies to argue against establishing the movement at the National School. Malinowski helpfully dismissed the Pathfinders' claim that their movement was modeled on African age grade systems.[73]

Rheinallt Jones, however, jumped at the chance to entrench the Pathfinder movement in Swaziland. Citing the Colonial Office Advisory Committee's support for adapted Scouting, he offered to let the Swazis alter the Scout uniform and curriculum to better reflect their cultural values. He was also willing to let Sobhuza serve as honorary president of the Emabutfo-Pathfinders but was adamant that the movement had to be controlled by the South African Pathfinder Council. Moreover, he considered that "fundamental" differences between Christian and non-Christian Swazis made it necessary for the missions to have their own closed troops and a separate Pathfinder Promise swearing allegiance to a Christian God.[74]

Marwick had little sympathy for Rheinallt Jones's position. He believed closed Christian troops would divide the Swazis and worried direct European control of the movement would undercut the authority of Sobhuza and the "traditional authorities." Yet Marwick was only the deputy resident commissioner and he did not have the stature to stand up to the Swaziland missions. In 1935 the Board of Advice on Native Education approved the mixed Emabutfo-Pathfinder model. Funding came from the Swazi National Fund and a personal contribution from W. B. Mumford, a lecturer on native education at the University of London and an enthusiastic advocate of adapted Scouting. The Swazi National School was to be a working laboratory for adaptation, and the supporters of the Emabutfo-Pathfinder compromise hoped that it would become the model for similar youth movements throughout anglophone Africa.[75]

The emabutfo experiment began in late 1935 when the principal of the Swazi National School appointed T. Kuhne as his "Pathfinder expert." Kuhne divided the students into four groups of twenty, with each choosing its own leader. Sobhuza sent representatives to explain the origins, philosophy, and duties of the emabutfo and to appoint an indvuna (regimental leader). The representatives also declared the national school uniform to be the official emabutfo uniform. As part of the school day the groups played soccer, drilled, and learned signaling, first aid, and Pathfinder games. On Fridays they undertook community service projects under the direction of their group leaders. To promote unity among

Swazi youth the Emabutfo-Pathfinders invited thirty-four nonschool boys to join them on a three-day camping trip near Sobhuza's royal kraal. The local boys wore Swazi ceremonial costumes as part of a special temporary Pathfinder group under the direction of younger members of the royal family. Sobhuza met with the Emabutfo-Pathfinders personally to explain their duties, and the camp program consisted primarily of the paramount chief sending orders via semaphore to the various groups.[76]

Although the national school authorities were initially pleased that the program improved school discipline and spirit, problems quickly arose. Integrating the schoolboys, who enjoyed considerable prestige for winning positions at the highly competitive institution, with youth from local communities proved quite difficult. The young Swazi scholars guarded their status jealously and did not embrace the emabutfo experiment's emphasis on egalitarianism. The local boys ignored the school schedule by coming and going at irregular hours and frequently missing meetings. School officials also groused that Mfudza Sukati, the regimental indvuna, had a weakness for beer. Moreover, Sobhuza had his own reservations about the emabutfo experiment. He dragged his heels in selecting thirty candidates for a Pathfinder training course in the Union and worried that expanding the program to the mission schools would give the missionaries greater influence in the Swazi National School. His indifference meant that the entire experiment was dead by 1939. The missions reintroduced Pathfinding in 1944, and the territorial government reconstituted the emabutfo age grades as a recruiting device for the African Auxiliary Pioneer Corps during the Second World War.[77]

Clearly, the emabutfo experiment was too ambitious in its attempt to reach all Swazi youth, and experiments in adapting Scouting on a smaller local scale generally proved more viable. In Northern Rhodesia, Maxwell Robertson had more success in introducing Pathfinding into the Lubwa teacher training curriculum in the early 1930s. He divided the boys at the school into seven troops consisting of two patrols each. Each patrol had a separate dorm and constructed its own dinning hall of thatch and "bush timber." This system approximated the residential houses of British boarding schools, with patrols competing against each other in tests of Scout skills and community service projects.[78]

The Pathfinder Court of Honour, consisting of senior schoolboys, provided discipline. It had the authority to award two weeks of hard labor or six strokes with a cane for various infractions. One staff member claimed this arrangement got around the problem of Europeans beating Africans because "they did it themselves." The Court of Honour once

3.3. The Lubwa Pathfinders, 1930. From At Ipenburg, *"All Good Men": The Development of Lubwa Mission, Chinsali, Zambia, 1905–1967* (Frankfurt: Peter Lang, 1992). Reproduced by permission of the author.

saved a boy from expulsion for impregnating a girl by convincing the school authorities to let the court punish him instead. Maxwell Robertson also used adapted Scouting to teach religion, sex education, and hygiene. He held a Pathfinder Initiation Camp at Chipoma Falls, a sacred site in precolonial times, where the school staff and senior Pathfinders provided students with "secret" information reflecting Western notions of propriety and sexual continence dressed up in the form of "native tradition." The Pathfinders also openly taught Christianity and marched in uniform with the school's Wayfarers at a regular Thursday prayer service. On the whole, the Pathfinding program was relatively popular with the Lubwa student body. Although many Africans in Northern Rhodesia distrusted Scouting as a military movement, Lubwa produced some highly dedicated Scouts. Kenneth Kaunda, the first president of Zambia, was a member of the original Pathfinder troop and returned to Lubwa as a teacher. He ran the school Tracker (Cub) Pack and recalled in his autobiography that Pathfinding broke down ethnic barriers and maintained school discipline.[79]

In South Africa, Rheinallt Jones and the European Pathfinder leadership embraced adaptation on a territorial scale. Much of their funding came from missions and large mining companies in the Transvaal. Although church and business interests often disagreed on African social policy, they approved of the Pathfinders' attempts to use "native tradition" to teach young Africans discipline, loyalty, thrift, hygiene, and sexual continence. These were values that addressed problems in the labor force and the mounting generational crisis in local African societies. African Pathfindermasters attending a 1933 training course in Natal thus learned that trustworthiness meant following orders without question.

This South African interpretation of the Scout canon enhanced the Pathfinder movement's utility as an instrument of social control. The Pathfinder Council used adaptation to give their social agenda humanitarian credibility and to make it more acceptable to African public opinion. Nowhere was this more evident than in their efforts to strengthen indirect rule by using Pathfinding as an instrument of retribalization. Seeking to buttress the legitimacy of rural chiefs and headmen, the Pathfinders emphasized respect for generational authority as a primary obligation of the movement by framing their curriculum as part of "native tradition." They promised African community leaders that the Pathfinder movement would "never forget their good customs of old and only develop them and refine them in their Christian lives." Instead of being insulted by this blatant effort to exploit their ethnic identity, it is likely that the Pathfinders' appeal to Zulu pride played into the hands of the Zulu cultural brokers who founded Inkatha kaZulu (the Zulu National Congress) in the 1920s. As with Sobhuza's Swazi neotraditionalism, they sought to reinterpret Zulu ethnic identity and culture to build popular support for the Zulu royal family. In this light, the Natal Pathfinders probably enhanced Inkatha's credibility.[80]

South African liberals also tried to use adapted Scouting to address the growing problem of urban juvenile delinquency. They naively hoped that if they made rural Pathfinding appealing enough it would dissuade African boys from going to the cities to look for work and excitement. The Pathfinder Council directed local leaders to assist municipal governments in repatriating African boys to the countryside by keeping records of their members who became labor migrants. Yet the Pathfinder leadership also accepted the inevitability of African urbanization and promoted adapted Scouting as a wholesome recreational activity for township youth that would keep them in touch with their rural culture and heritage. By 1936, there were roughly fifteen hundred Pathfinders on the Rand in thirty-seven troops. Missions and youth clubs sponsored most of these Pathfinder groups as an alternative to drinking, gambling, and crime. Yet the discipline of Pathfinding was acceptable only to schoolboys who had reasonable aspirations of social mobility. The Pathfinders' celebration of tribal culture and woodlore had very little relevancy for most urbanized South African youth, who faced a future of unemployment, marginalization, and harassment.[81]

Conversely, Pathfinding won considerable support from older, more established Africans. Many African religious and educational authorities in the interwar era were more than willing to use the Pathfinder movement to strengthen their control over young men. Canon James Arthur Calata, an Anglican African clergyman, used Pathfinding to address the problem of sexual immorality and juvenile delinquency among the youth of the small Western Cape town of Cradock. As Commissioner for the Cape Midlands Division, one of the highest supervisory positions held by an African in the interwar Pathfinder movement, Calata established African Pathfinder Scout troops at schools and churches throughout the region. He worked with white liberals on the Cradock Joint Council to use Pathfinding to improve race relations in the town and to draw African Scouts and their parents into the Anglican Church. Yet Calata was also president of the Cape African Congress and chaplain of the ANC in the 1930s. Although he thoroughly approved of the Pathfinders' efforts to impose greater social discipline on African youth, he also used the Scout movement's egalitarian ideals to challenge the color bar by adopting a literal interpretation of the Fourth Scout Law.[82]

Moreover, many African community leaders and students refused to accept the Pathfinder Council's version of adapted Scouting. The Scout leadership tried to maintain control over the Pathfinder Scouts by requiring troops to submit a yearly statement of their sponsoring authority and total membership or face deregistration. The Transvaal Pathfinder authorities sought an additional measure of influence over African Scouting by hiring two full-time organizing Scout commissioners to visit, inspect, and supervise individual troops. It also made their organizers available to the other provincial Pathfinder divisions for several weeks out of the year. The primary mission of these professional African Pathfindermasters was to ensure that individual leaders and troops did not modify or reinterpret the movement's core values.[83]

AFRICAN EXPERIENCES IN PATHFINDING

The threat of independency in southern African Scouting was quite real. European Pathfinder leaders lacked the manpower and the cultural understanding to supervise remote African troops. The best they could do was try to ensure that only the most reliable African men became troop

3.4. Pathfinder warrant certificate, interwar era. Courtesy of University of Cape Town Libraries, Special Collections. Reproduced with permission of the South African Scout Association.

leaders. Using a model first established by Baden-Powell in Great Britain, they required all Pathfindermasters to hold a "warrant" from the SABSA. Any evidence of personal transgressions or deviance from the official version of Pathfinding would result in withdrawal of the warrant and expulsion from the movement. In theory, candidates had to demonstrate a basic understanding of *Scouting for Boys* and a familiarity with the regulations of the SABSA. In practice, many educated Africans became Pathfindermasters to secure teaching jobs and were only dimly aware of the ideals of the movement. Nevertheless, some teachers became passionately committed to the ideals of Scouting.

Moreover, Scouting was widely respected throughout rural South Africa. Although there was a brief drop in membership during the 1933 jamboree controversy and again at the outbreak of the Second World War, when parents worried that the movement was part of a secret plot to conscript their children, many Africans aspired to the status and prestige of being a uniformed Scout. As P. M. Kondlo, a founding member of a Pathfinder school troop, explained: "We used to close the door of our meeting room but many boys flocked outside in great eagerness to come in. We did not drive them away, but we spoke to them kindly asking them to wait for some time. We got the best boys for our troop and we then began to pick out the three leaders: namely two section leaders and a Troop-Leader. The door was now opened for anyone to join."[84] Pathfinder troops became elite organizations within schools, and successful members enjoyed considerably more autonomy and status than their non-Pathfinder peers because they held the trust of teachers and school authorities.

There were real barriers, though, to becoming a Scout. The movement was based almost exclusively in schools and was largely inaccessible to the average boy in the countryside or the township. Regulations required each troop to pay a substantial subscription fee to the SABSA. In most cases it fell to individual Scouts to find this money through strictly regulated fundraising activities. Few boys had the resources to pay their dues from their own pockets. Similarly, the simple Pathfinder uniform was still too expensive for most African families, who had to struggle to pay school fees. Poorer troops tried to get by with a scarf and badge pinned to a school uniform, but this was a poor substitute for the full uniform coveted by so many boys.[85] Thus it is not surprising that many local communities founded their own independent troops. In addition to claiming the right to adapt Scouting for political purposes, they sought to make the movement more accessible and relevant to the difficult day-to-day realities of life under the colonial regime.

4

Scouting and the School in East Africa, 1910–45

ALTHOUGH THERE WERE several significant experiments in adapted Scouting in East Africa in the interwar era, the 6th Nairobi troop at Kenya's Alliance High School (AHS) was one of the most accomplished formal Scout groups, African or otherwise, in the region. In 1928 school authorities established a class to introduce students to the movement. Official Scout status for Africans in the colony was less of an issue than in South Africa, and European Scout leaders at the school convinced the Kenya Boy Scout Association (KBSA) to recognize the troop two years later, after the boys had demonstrated sufficient understanding of the Scout canon.[1] Although the Kenyan settlers guarded the color bar jealously, they paid little attention to African Scouting because there were very few African schools that had the capacity to support fully active troops. Therefore the expansion of the movement to non-Europeans was not a significant political issue in East Africa in the 1920s and 1930s.

In 1941 the Alliance Scouts won an interracial competition among Nairobi troops. The 6th Nairobi's score of 723 for "general efficiency" was substantially higher than the 464 posted by its closest European rival. With Scouting a sanctioned extracurricular activity at AHS, the troop met on Mondays after school at 5:00 P.M. and on Thursday mornings before school at 7:00 A.M. Scoutmaster Stephen Smith, a missionary and Alliance teacher, de-emphasized Scout ranks and badges because he worried Scouting at the school would "degenerate into academic competition for badges." Instead the schoolboys focused on "open-air work" during weekend camping trips. The troop's bugle band was popular, and uniformed Alliance Scouts put on Scouting displays at Government House and provided a guard of honor for Armistice Day ceremonies.[2]

Not surprisingly, Scouting became one of the most prestigious extracurricular activities at the school. The original troop included future leaders like Eliud Mathu, an AHS Scoutmaster and the first African representative on the Kenyan legislative council; Magugu Waweru, an influential chief; the Reverends Obadiah Kariuki and Festus Olang, the first African Anglican bishops; and James and Walter Mbotela, noted authors. Julius Gikonyo Kiano, the first Kenyan African to earn a Ph.D. and a future minister in the postindependence Kenyan government, joined the Alliance troop in 1942. Drawn by the troop's dedication to excellence, he considered Scouting a worthwhile activity for boys who aspired to push the boundaries of colonial society. As a Scout, Kiano ran the school library and conducted religious classes at local Christian churches. The Alliance High School troop's success lay in its ability to draw the most ambitious and academically gifted students in interwar Kenya.[3]

Clearly, East African Scouting differed substantially from the southern Pathfinder model. The development of African Scouting in Uganda, Kenya, and Tanganyika followed the political and social realities of British colonial rule in the region. There were virtually no permanent European residents in Uganda other than missionaries. British plans to develop Kenya as a "white man's country" came to naught, and its small but vocal settler community failed to dissuade the Colonial Office from declaring African interests paramount in the colony. Similarly, when Britain seized Tanganyika following the First World War, it expelled most of the German residents of the territory. British colonial administrators adapted variations of the Lugardian system of indirect rule to govern the African majority in all three territories through "native authorities."

Yet as in South Africa, Western education undercut the legitimacy of these chiefs and headmen. The East African governments relied on educated Africans to offset the high cost of colonial rule, and schools provided tangible proof that Britain was fulfilling its obligation to promote African development. These schools produced highly individualistic graduates who rejected the premise that the interests of African individuals should be subordinate to their "tribe" and challenged the collectivist "traditional" authority of the chiefs and headmen. In seeking to reconcile these contradictions through adapted education, colonial officials and teachers looked to Scouting to discipline and socialize this potentially dangerous class of educated "detribalized" Africans. Almost every authorized African Scout troop in pre–Second World War East Africa was attached to a mission or government school. Colonial educators hoped Scouting would support adaptation by teaching African students to accept their place in colonial society.

The Scout movement did not have to cope with uncertain lines of political legitimacy in East Africa. Although the Kenyan settlers faintly echoed white South African opposition to opening the movement to Africans, administrators in all three colonies could support African Scouting because they did not have to defend the color bar as closely. There was also no East African equivalent of J. D. Rheinallt Jones and his South African Institute of Race Relations. Responsibility for social welfare before the Second World War remained entirely in the hands of missionaries and a few government officials. These "native experts" shared the South African liberals' conviction that most Africans were still too backward to assimilate Western culture, but they had a freer hand in defending African interests because the small European community in Kenya lacked the political influence of South African and Rhodesian whites.

Government and mission educators therefore faced little resistance in promoting African Scouting. Most were also strong supporters of adapted education and considered European-style Scouting suitable for only the most Westernized African boys, like the Alliance High School students. They had serious doubts about the movement's compatibility with "native tradition" and created adapted versions of Scouting to reconcile the social aspirations of African students with the realities of indirect rule. As in South Africa, they sought to modify the movement to fit local African circumstances by infusing it with wholesome "tribal" customs, particularly those they perceived to buttress African collectivism. As a result, the interwar experiments with adapted education in Tanganyika and Kenya had strong Scouting components.

Yet adapted Scouting was no more palatable to East African students than Pathfinding was to their southern African counterparts. The high standards of the Alliance troop demonstrate that African schoolboys saw Scouting as an opportunity to prove their sophistication, respectability, and excellence. Yet formal Scout status came with a great many strings attached. As in the south, African independent churches and schools sponsored their own unauthorized troops to resist adaptation and claim the ideals and legitimacy of the movement. In Kenya many Kikuyu independent schools sponsored scout organizations without the knowledge of the KBSA. In other cases, individuals turned themselves into Scouts by dressing in illegally acquired Scout uniforms. Colonial officials viewed

African modifications of the movement with alarm. The misappropriation of the institutions of political and social legitimacy that were an integral part of Scouting had the potential to undermine the viability of the colonial regime.

The threat of African autonomy in education and Scouting in the early 1930s was a key factor in convincing colonial officials to support full Scout status for Africans. The colonial governments tried to deal with the problem of unauthorized scouting by giving the territorial branches of the British Scout Association sole legal title to the Scout badge and uniform. Despite their reservations about granting Africans official status under the Fourth Scout Law, European Scouters, mission educators, and colonial officials found that according Africans the legitimacy of full membership in the movement was the best defense against independency.

SCOUTING COMES TO EAST AFRICA

East African Scouting was shaped by the relatively limited scope of Western influence in the region in comparison to southern Africa. The absence of a large European expatriate community made it easier for British officials to use the movement as a tool of colonial administration. The East African model of indirect rule depended far more on African intermediaries than southern systems of colonial administration. The British East Africa Company conquered Uganda and Kenya (known as the East Africa Protectorate until 1920) in the late nineteenth century. The territories passed to direct British rule when bankruptcy forced Sir William MacKinnon to surrender his royal charter in the 1890s. The British treasury kept both protectorates under tight financial reign, and administrators had to rely extensively on African military and administrative assistance. This was also the case when Britain took over Tanganyika (formerly German East Africa) at the close of the First World War.

In the Uganda Protectorate, the Bugandan *kabaka* (king) and the Lukiko (consultative assembly) retained a measure of local autonomy when colonial authorities transformed the kingdom into a self-governing province. British officials maintained the fiction that they governed through "traditional" institutions, but in reality they transformed Gandan elites into an extension of the colonial bureaucracy. Although African "tradition" provided the legitimizing ideology for this system of indirect rule, in practice the chiefs essentially served at the pleasure of their colonial supervisors.

The Kenyan settlers adamantly opposed the Ugandan model of "native" administration on the grounds that it granted Africans too much authority. Led by Lord Delemere, they influenced legislation through their "unofficial" representatives on the legislative council. Nevertheless, the settlers' efforts to make Kenya a "white man's country" suffered a fatal blow when the Colonial Office's 1923 Devonshire White Paper declared that "primarily Kenya is an African territory, and . . . the interests of the African natives must be paramount."[4] This definitive statement ended the settlers' dream of developing Kenya into an independent white nation but did little to undermine their dominant position in the colony.

Although only a few Kenyan laws explicitly discriminated against Africans on the basis of race, the settlers guarded their privileges rigorously through a rigid de facto social and economic color bar. The Kenyan government ensured them a steady supply of cheap labor by confining Africans to South African-style "tribal reserves" through restrictive labor passes (kipande). Colonial officials claimed segregation protected fragile "tribal" cultures from European land speculators, but the reserve system ultimately made it impossible for many Africans to practice subsistence agriculture or pastoralism. By the 1930s, 86 percent of Kenya's African population lived in reserves comprising only 22 percent of the arable land in the colony.[5] Aggressive hut and poll taxes provided additional incentives to seek paid employment.

These economic realities clashed with the colonial regime's obligation to educate its African subjects under the dual mandate. The humanitarian legitimizing ideology of colonialism required British officials to make Western schooling available, but only select Christian missions had any real enthusiasm for developing a comprehensive African education system. Revenue shortfalls and competing budgetary obligations forced colonial governments to delegate responsibility for "native" schooling to the church. The East Africa Protectorate (Kenya) created a department of education in 1911, but it was concerned almost exclusively with European, Arab, and Indian students. Uganda and Tanganyika did not establish education departments until after the First World War. Although the missions had virtual autonomy in curricular matters during this early period, financial constraints greatly limited their ability to accommodate a significant number of students. Yet even these rudimentary educational efforts were too much for Kenyan settlers, who charged the mission schools with teaching political subversion and failing to train Africans in economically useful skills.

Church leaders guarded their monopoly on African education jealously. In Kenya they fought settler demands for the state to take a direct role in producing semiskilled African artisans. Mission educators grudgingly accepted state intervention, but lobbied for Christian instruction in the curriculum. Marion Stevenson told a government education commission that "secular teaching would be disastrous because it would destroy the natives' superstitions which help to keep them straight without replacing it with something else."[6] Most government officials agreed, but African students and parents complained that the missions placed too much emphasis on religious instruction at the expense of the rest of the curriculum. Colonial administrators came to view organized youth work as Stevenson's "something else" that would teach values and morality in a supervised extracurricular setting.

Given the missions' early dominance of East African education, it is not surprising that the Boy's Brigade was the first uniformed youth movement in the region. Unlike in South Africa, there was little controversy over the creation of African companies at mission schools because there were no European members of the movement in Uganda, Kenya, or Tanganyika. The Church of Scotland Mission station at Kikuyu began the first Boy's Brigade company in the region in 1909 for their "black boys who require so much to learn the great lesson self-control."[7] Within a year, the movement expanded to the CSM's Limuru and Kenia stations, but it did not gain a foothold in Uganda or Tanganyika until the 1930s.

These early companies followed a program that was neither innovative nor elaborate. Funded by donations from the Scottish branch of the movement, the 1st Kikuyu Company consisted of thirty-five boys, who spent most of their time marching, drilling, and playing soccer. Although the original boys were not particularly enthusiastic about this overly martial program, many were won over by the promise of a smart military-style uniform. As Charles Muhoro Kareri, one of the first members of the company, recalled: "To be in the Boys Brigade was an astonishing sight, because one was in a shirt and shorts, on the top of that he had a bag, then he girded himself with a belt. On the head he wore a cap with white and black colour, therefore becoming a very beautiful soldier. . . . There were strict rules, tougher than those followed by the police or soldiers in the battlefront." Kareri's last observation is telling in that when the First World War broke out the CSM missionaries led their Boy's Brigade company into the army labor corps as the Kikuyu Mission Volunteers.[8]

By the early 1920s the company had grown to 130 boys. Its leadership still consisted entirely of CSM teachers and doctors. The company also still spent a good deal of time playing soccer and drilling (often under the direction of African ex-servicemen), but its formal program expanded to include Bible study, bugle band, and signaling. The Boy's Brigade enjoyed prestige as the only formal African youth group in the colony, and the 1st Kikuyu received its colors (flag) directly from the governor at a public ceremony. Yet the overtly Presbyterian character of the movement limited its growth and overall appeal. By the 1930s it was overshadowed by the spread of African Scouting in East Africa. Only the original 1st Kikuyu Company remained active in Kenya after the Second World War.[9]

Unlike the Boy's Brigade, Scouting came to East Africa as a European institution. In 1910, two years after the birth of the movement in Britain, the Anglican Men's Society sponsored the 1st Nairobi Troop at St. John's Church. During the First World War, the troop provided messengers for the military in Nairobi and helped guard Government House. As Scouting became more popular many European boys in other parts of the colony began independent troops and recruited leaders on their own. In 1917 the Nairobi Boy Scout Association formed a general committee to bring these scattered groups under central control. Four years later Scout leaders convened the Kenya Scout Council and convinced Governor Sir Edward Northey to serve as the ceremonial chief Scout.[10]

Formal African Scouting began in Zanzibar and Uganda in the 1910s. The movement was short-lived on Zanzibar because its close ties to Christianity on the largely Muslim island offset its early start. The Anglican Universities' Mission to Central Africa (UMCA) brought the movement to Zanzibar by forming a troop for African boarders at Kiungani High School. Most of the forty-five boys in the 1st Zanzibar were Christian ex-slaves or migrants from the mainland. Arab leaders initially shunned the movement on the suspicion that it was anti-Muslim. By the 1920s, however, African Scouting had essentially died out because the UMCA decided that the boys no longer needed it. The mission's withdrawal from the Scouting field made the movement more accessible to Muslims, and by the 1930s Arabs and Indians were the only active Scouts on Zanzibar.[11]

African Scouting in Uganda was more viable. The movement owed its start in the protectorate to the work of Canon H. M. Grace, an educator and Anglican missionary. Grace began the first African troop at Mbarara High School in Ankole in 1916. As headmaster of Mengo High School in

Buganda five years later, he tried to introduce Scouting into the school to improve student morale. The Lukiko initially refused because they suspected the movement was a plot to teach schoolboys to favor King George V over the Bugandan government. The Gandan chiefs pointed out that Gandan-English dictionaries translated Scout as "spy" and alleged that Scouting's emphasis on service without payment was a veiled plot to exploit African labor. However, Ham Mukasa, the *katikiro* (prime minister) and regent, having encountered Scouting when he attended King George's coronation, reassured the Gandans that the "true" aims of the movement were benign.[12]

Farther south, Scouting in Tanganyika began when Britain captured the territory from Germany in 1917. Tanganyikan Scouting started initially as an offshoot of the UMCA's Scout work on Zanzibar. Bishop Frank Weston founded the first African troop at St. Martin's School at Magila. From there UMCA missionaries spread the movement to their schools in Tanga, Pangani, and Lindi Districts. In the west a Catholic priest introduced Scouting in the White Fathers' mission schools in Bukoba District. The colonial administration was almost entirely unaware of these early African troops. In 1921 the Tanganyikan Secretariat erroneously reported to the Colonial Office that there was no active Scout organization in the territory because the African education system was too underdeveloped. Nevertheless, government officials welcomed the introduction of Scouting to Tanganyika to provide "moral training" that was lacking in African schooling. The director of education became chief Scout commissioner even though he had no firsthand experience with the movement.[13]

African Guiding began in Uganda, where a Miss Foster Smith introduced an informal version of the movement in the CMS school at Kabarole in 1920. She had no formal training but took a course in Guiding while on home leave in Britain. When Foster Smith returned to Uganda she became captain of the 1st Toro Guides, the first formal African company in East Africa. She also became the organizing commissioner for the Uganda Girl Guides Association, and upon graduation the members of her Toro company became Guide leaders throughout the protectorate. In Kenya, however, Guiding was initially limited to European and Indian girls. In Tanganyika African Guiding remained almost entirely a private endeavor in the hands of the Anglicans. In Kenya the movement did not expand to include Africans until the mid-1930s.[14]

East African education policy in the interwar era focused primarily on reconciling Western schooling with indirect rule. European settlers were of no use in governing the African majority. They were thin on the ground in Tanganyika and nonexistent in Uganda. Direct British rule in Kenya was limited to urban areas and settler farms in the "white highlands." As in southern Africa, the Kenyan government relied on indirect rule to extend its authority to the countryside. District officers needed cooperative chiefs and headmen to collect taxes and maintain order in the reserves, and native courts and tribunals transformed customary "tribal" law into a colonial civil code. Theoretically, these local authorities drew their legitimacy from "native tradition," but in reality they owed their positions to their ability to execute colonial policy. Many became wealthy by using their authority to acquire land, commercial licenses, and additional wives, which helped offset the social alienation that came with serving as the coercive agents of the colonial state.[15]

Lacking a significant settler community, Tanganyikan officials were the most committed to indirect rule. Under the terms of its League of Nations mandate, Britain acknowledged that Tanganyika would be a "black man's country" and accepted the development of the subject majority as a "sacred trust." Governor Sir Donald Cameron, who had spent sixteen years in Lugard's Nigerian colonial service, oversaw the adaptation of the "west coast" model of indirect rule to Tanganyika in 1924. During Cameron's tenure, district officers delegated responsibility for local government, tax collection, and rural law and order to "native authorities." Although the proponents of this system claimed it embodied the traditions and customary laws of discrete African communities, many "tribal units" were colonially engineered conglomerations of smaller and more loosely defined ethnicities. Nevertheless, the privileges and patronage that came with being recognized as a native authority by the colonial regime created a powerful incentive for African cultural brokers to embrace and expand these tribal identities.[16]

Indirect rule in all three East African territories allowed territorial governments to extend their influence into rural African communities at a minimal cost in manpower and resources. Ruling through "traditional" institutions of authority also brought the colonial regime a measure of legitimacy and appeared to fulfill Britain's obligations under the dual mandate. Yet indirect rule was not an effective engine of economic development. The "traditional" authorities did not have the power to or-ganize African labor on a broad scale, and African peasant producers did not constitute a sufficient tax base to support more ambitious colonial development plans. As a result, East African administrators supported in-vasive economic strategies that undermined the legitimacy and author-ity of their local African allies.

African communities often contested unpopular policies through peti-tions, tax revolts, and political organizing. Colonial officials responded by building up "tribal assemblies" and "local native councils" as sanctioned outlets for African political expression. District officers usually chaired these largely consultative bodies and had veto power over all resolutions. Educated Africans understandably sought alternative platforms for their political views. In Kenya groups like the Kavirondo Taxpayers Association and the East Africa Association tried to organize colonywide opposition to colonial land, labor, and education policies, but government pressure forced them to evolve into ethnically based movements with much nar-rower regional and local agendas. In Uganda organized African political activity was largely concentrated in the Kingdom of Buganda, where the Bataka Association challenged the right of Gandan elites to monopolize common land in the 1920s. There were no comparable movements in interwar Tanganyika, but African civil servants formed the Tanganyika African Association in 1929 to lobby the territorial government for more equitable terms of service.[17]

Although none of the early African political organizations challenged the legitimacy of the colonial regime directly, their refusal to air their grievances through tribal councils and assemblies worried colonial offi-cials. Concluding that the African leadership of these associations clashed with native administration because they had become detribalized through Western-style schooling, government educators sought to develop an edu-cation system that reconciled "native development" with the necessity of stifling African political dissent.

Inspired by the African American model of industrial schooling in the southern United States, colonial administrators looked to adapted educa-tion to "retribalize" educated Africans by teaching them to seek their po-litical and economic fortunes within the collective context of the "tribe." When the Phelps-Stokes Commission visited East Africa in the early 1920s it criticized the missions for following a conventional Western cur-riculum that was not relevant to the educational needs of rural African communities. Recognizing the fiscal, organizational, and philosophical limits of mission education, all three territories followed the commission's recommendations by requiring private schools accepting state aid to submit to regular inspections and follow an approved adapted curriculum. In theory, native councils and tribal assemblies were responsible for funding and overseeing African schools, but in practice local communities had little influence over education policy. Government inspectors could close schools that did not meet minimum standards for "efficiency," which in practice referred to fiscal transparency, accurate record keeping, and an adapted industrial primary syllabus.[18]

Many missions became more willing to accept adapted education after developing doubts about the efficacy of their literary focus. In western Kenya, the Quaker Friends African Mission shifted to an adapted curriculum to gain greater control over their converts. Faced with land protests, strikes by African teachers, and increased political activity among their adherents, they were enticed by the commission's promise that adaptation would produce a stable Christian peasantry.[19] The affirmation by the Advisory Committee on Education in the Colonies that Christianity would have an integral role in African education allayed mission concerns about the potentially secular nature of the new initiatives and strengthened the church-state partnership in adapted education.

Interwar colonial educators worked out a division of labor in African schooling. The missions retained their monopoly on primary education and generally left technical education to the state. Most missionaries were willing to let the government set overall education policy because the civil authorities accepted the necessity of giving adapted schooling a strong religious character. In 1925 in the Nairobi suburb of Kabete, Kenyan officials used a £7,500 grant from the Carnegie Foundation to establish a Jeanes School that, like its southern African counterparts, promoted rural development within the context of indirect rule by training African village teachers in hygiene, agriculture, handicrafts, "tribal folklore," and basic pedagogy. J. W. C. Dougall, a member of the Phelps-Stokes Commission and a Presbyterian missionary, was its first principal. Dougall created an adapted version of Scouting to strengthen these educational initiatives and gradually educate Africans in the proper aims and purposes of Baden-Powell's movement. He taught his African Jeanes teachers to begin village Helpers' Clubs, where boys and young men would wear distinctive "tribal" dress, earn badges, and, most important, counter the trend toward individualism and detribalization by providing service to the community. The clubs would constitute a village elite with young helpers using special "praise names" taken from local "tribal tradition." In explaining his idea to the Jeanes teachers Dougall emphasized that they did not need conventional Western Scouting because Baden-Powell had borrowed the idea for the movement from Africans.[20]

Several of the original Jeanes teachers were sufficiently inspired by Dougall to begin "native Scout troops" in their village postings. In 1928, Jeremiah Segero founded one of these groups for Luhya boys near the Friends African Mission station at Kaimosi in western Kenya. Echoing Dougall, he claimed to have revived a distinctly African type of Scouting that predated the colonial era:

> These ideas appeared long ago in our country before even the first European came. The natives of the district where these items were known say that there used to be many people who behaved as true Vagosi in the past, but that when civilisation was introduced they forgot these practices and discarded them. They also say that these customs were lost because men began to go out to work and to earn a monthly-wage, and thus they lost sight of the fact that the habit of giving service freely and without reward is a fine one. . . . Among the natives some thought that when they learnt to be Christians and could read and were baptized it was right to discard their old habits entirely.[21]

According to Segero, the Vagosi offered help without payment, respected their parents and elders, shared their food, and were truthful, brave, and merciful. Community service for the Vagosi also included support for colonial policy. When villagers balked at taking antiplague vaccinations because they suspected the hypodermic needles were dirty, the Vagosi helpers set an example by being the first to get the shots.[22]

In the short term Segero succeeded in giving his movement a measure of prestige in western Kenya. The Vagosi uniform consisted of black shirts and khaki shorts with bracelets and anklets of colobus monkey skins. Invoking the folklore that underlay Scouting's outdoor rhetoric, Segero made the colobus monkey, a medium-size primate indigenous to the forests of Kenya, a special totem of his movement, "for this monkey is a leader." Stefano Atsinwa, a fellow Jeanes teacher, was sufficiently impressed by Segero's movement to start his own troop of "helpers," which also adopted the colobus monkey uniform. The Friends African Mission supported the Vagosi and helped Segero write a letter to Baden-Powell outlining the principles of the organization. The chief scout of the world was not interested, and the Vagosi could not compete with mainstream Scouting. They were absorbed into the Kenya Boy Scout Association in the late 1930s, when the movement expanded to include Africans.[23]

Another Jeanes teacher, Justin Itotia, tried to put Dougall's native Scout program into practice in central Kenya. Invoking Kikuyu culture, Itotia called his movement Endwo ni Iri na Iriri, which he defined as "blessings obtained by actions and good character." Having read a Swahili-language introduction to Scouting entitled Mashujaa wa Afrika (Heroes of Africa), he concluded that valuable elements of Kikuyu custom were "exactly parallel to the Scout law." According to Itotia, his Kikuyu helpers obeyed their parents, respected their elders, helped cripples and the less fortunate, cared for trees, found and returned lost things, and were truthful, industrious, and cheerful. In lauding the "native troops" the Jeanes authorities claimed that groups like the Vagosi and the Endwo ni Iri na Iriri not only taught character to village youth but also preserved useful but vanishing "tribal lore." Dougall was particularly interested in bolstering indirect rule by teaching African boys to subordinate their individual interests to those of their "tribe." Itotia's success as a Kikuyu cultural broker and informal ethnographer made him a willing ally in much of this endeavor.[24]

Tanganyikan educators were even more committed to adapted education. Taking the 1925 report by the Colonial Office's Advisory Committee on Education as his blueprint, Governor Cameron pushed government and mission schools in the territory to work more closely together in creating an adapted agriculturally focused curriculum. The 1927 Tanganyika Native Education Ordinance placed all African schools under state supervision and provided financial support to mission schools that met minimal curricular standards.[25] Eight government provincial central boarding schools training clerks, artisans, and civil servants for service in the native administrations were at the top of the education pyramid. They were based on the English public school model but embraced adapted education by organizing students into "tribes" rather than residential houses.

W. B. Mumford, the University of London lecturer who helped fund the emabutfo experiment at the Swazi National School, was the driving force behind the Tanganyikan program of adapted education. In the mid-1920s he organized the central schools in Bukoba and Malangali as "replicas of native organization." At Bukoba, Mumford created four "tribal" houses, each with twenty-four boys grouped together on the basis of "taste, hereditary alliances, and geographical proximity." The institution was essentially a school for teaching elite Africans to accept the ethnic administrative units underpinning indirect rule. Under Mumford's guidance as "headmaster and great chief," the school's four "tribes" elected sultans and waziris, local terms for chiefs and subchiefs, to serve as student leaders. These student chiefs met as an executive council to handle disciplinary matters and assign maintenance and housekeeping duties to the four houses.

Mumford also created a special "native" Scout troop to reinforce Bukoba's adapted curriculum. He argued that the movement was inherently "African" in its character and provided an ideal code of conduct to develop admirable collectivist qualities lost by the decline of the "warrior tradition" under colonial rule. In other words, Scout training was an antidote to the dangerous individualism that led to detribalization. Although he admitted to have little direct knowledge of Scouting, Mumford had strong ideas about how it should be adapted for African boys. "The wholesale adoption of Western organisation, titles, uniforms and codes would . . . defeat our fundamental aim." For example, he felt "the boys should be called 'Mashujaa' [heroes] not Scouts." Under Mumford's direction the Bukoba Scouts wore simple homemade uniforms and fezzes. He replaced the moralizing Western fables that were at the heart of the European movement's curriculum with tales of African heroes.[26]

Compared to their East African neighbors, mission authorities in Uganda had more doubts about employing "native tradition" in African schooling and retained more faith in a Western-style literary education. The Ugandan government was generally more tolerant of this view than its counterparts in Kenya and Tanganyika. Although they worried that Westernized graduates would be difficult to absorb into the colonial economy, Ugandan officials saw high-quality secondary schooling as a useful tool in co-opting "native elites." The missions were willing allies in this endeavor. Viewing Ganda, Nyoro, Nkole, and Teso aristocrats as ideal allies in the conversion of the greater African population, mission educators established several elite secondary schools for the "sons of chiefs." These included the Church Missionary Society's Mengo High School and King's College, Budo.

The elite Uganda institutions were nothing like Mumford's adapted secondary schools. The CMS ran Budo along the direct lines of a formal English public school and followed a rigorous literary curriculum. In 1920 the Uganda Development Commission tried to introduce a more vocationally oriented curriculum, but African and mission resistance successfully defeated the official push for adaptation. When Julian Huxley visited Budo in the late 1920s he deemed it the best school he had seen in all of Africa. He was particularly impressed with the Englishness of the student body."[27]

Not surprisingly, Budo ran one of the most accomplished African Scout troops in Uganda. Canon H. M. Grace, the founder of Scouting at Mengo High School, was a strong proponent of formal African Scouting after becoming the Budo headmaster. Huxley judged Budo Scouting to be equal to the full standards of the metropolitan BSA. Yet it was not easy to expand the movement beyond the limited confines of the elite Ugandan high schools. Imperial Headquarters registered the Uganda Boy Scout Association in 1922, but the Catholic missions in the protectorate were wary of Scouting because they initially regarded it as an Anglican movement. It fell to African teachers who had been members of the Budo and Mengo troops to bring Scouting to the countryside. By the Second World War, all but two of the southern districts in the protectorate had their own Scout commissioners.[28]

Literary schooling and, by extension, formal African Scouting were far more controversial in Kenya. The settlers had strong doubts about opening advanced Western education to Africans. Nevertheless, the Protestant missions wanted an elite secondary school to produce Christian leaders and recognized Scouting's value in providing "character training." Alliance High School grew out of an aborted plan to use the East Africa War Relief Fund to establish a mission-run African medical college in Kenya. Using £5,600 of government money and a £10,000 donation from a Nairobi businessman, the Kenya Missionary Council created the first African secondary school in the colony in 1926.[29] While weak primary training meant the first cohort of students struggled with the school's demanding literary curriculum, Alliance quickly established a reputation for academic excellence as one of only two African secondary schools in interwar Kenya.

The 6th Nairobi, the Alliance High School troop, represented a competing interpretation of African Scouting. Although the Kenyan government was reluctant to sanction formal Scouting for Africans, Alliance officials won permission to start a "class in Scouting" in 1928. In what constituted a two-year probationary trial, the students had to demonstrate sufficient desire and understanding of the movement before qualifying for official Scout status in 1930. Stephen Smith, an Alliance agriculture instructor, Presbyterian missionary, and former Glasgow Scout, was Scoutmaster of the troop, which by the late 1930s consisted of forty boys in eight patrols. Most were Second Class Scouts working toward their First Class badges. This was at a time when few European and Asian Scouts in the colony progressed beyond the Tenderfoot stage. Smith took great personal pride in the success of his troop and in bringing Africans into Scouting.[30]

The 6th Nairobi was a special case, and formal Scouting remained a European movement in Kenya in the 1920s. Having successfully allied themselves with the government, European Scouts enjoyed considerable prestige in the colony. They joined African soldiers of the King's African Rifles in mounting honor guards for the governor, which reflected their semiofficial status as an informal arm of the government. Yet they did not feel the need to defend the color bar as zealously as their South African peers. Scouting in Kenya was sufficiently decentralized to allow for the creation of an Indian troop (the 3rd Nairobi) without much European opposition. When Imperial Headquarters sanctioned the Kenya Boy Scout Association's constitution in 1929 as an overseas branch of the British Scout Association, it recognized Indians as a formal part of the movement in the colony. African Scouts were another matter. A senior district administrator proposed using Scouting to recruit and train African soldiers (despite the Scouts' adamant declaration that they were not militaristic), but the Kenyan government refused to sanction regular African troops beyond the AHS troop on the grounds that Africans could not yet grasp the full meaning of the movement.[31]

THE CHALLENGE OF INDEPENDENCE AND THE GROWTH OF FORMAL AFRICAN SCOUTING

In the 1930s approximately 12 percent of African school-age children in Kenya were attending school, in Uganda 6 percent, and in Tanganyika just 1 percent. Settler hostility to educated Africans, government doubts about Western schooling, and fiscal realities restricted African educational opportunities sharply. In 1924, Kenya devoted roughly 50 percent of its £75,000 education budget to Africans in comparison to the 32 percent it spent on a few European schools. In practice, this broke down to twelve pounds per capita for European students and roughly ten shillings for each African pupil. African schooling was an equally low priority for Ugandan and Tanganyikan administrators. From 1931 to 1935 government spending on education in Tanganyika dropped 30 percent even though the inflow of revenue increased by nearly 40 percent. Similarly, the Kenyan government barred local native councils from spending more money on education on the grounds that nonscholastic municipal services were more important.[32]

Official support for adapted education remained strong in the decade before the Second World War. Prodded by the Phelps-Stokes Committee and the Colonial Office White Paper on education, government educators from Uganda, Kenya, Tanganyika, and Zanzibar began to meet regularly in the late 1920s to draw up common policies for school organization, language, and curricula. In 1933 the Inter-Territorial Education Conference resolved that governments throughout the region should promote an agriculturally focused primary curriculum taught in local vernaculars. The conviction that elementary schooling should be conducted in "tribal" languages was a central focus of adapted education. Brushing aside African complaints that English was the key to social mobility, the East African governments mandated that African schools could teach English only at the intermediate level. Since most African students never finished primary school, this meant that few students would ever learn the language. Language policy thus became one of the most controversial aspects of adapted education. Given that English was a prerequisite for higher education and professional employment, African communities rejected vernacular and Swahili instruction. This debate had the unplanned consequence of increasing the appeal of Scouting because most troops conducted their programs in English.[33]

East African students and parents were understandably frustrated with the narrow and underdeveloped colonial education system. Primary schooling was scarce and almost prohibitively expensive. The undermanned and poorly funded rural "bush" schools offered a decidedly inferior education that made it extremely difficult for students to progress to the intermediary and secondary levels. Those fortunate to reach one of the elite mission schools complained that the curriculum stressed religious indoctrination at the expense of academic subjects covered by government exams. From the African standpoint, the adapted curriculum's focus on agricultural training, simple industrial work, and "native tradition" was designed to keep them politically subordinate. It is not surprising that Africans sought alternatives to the colonial school system.

Many community leaders initially hoped to convince colonial officials to offer Western-style literary education in state schools. Yet government institutions followed a highly simplistic industrial curriculum intended to produce low-cost semiskilled labor. For most Africans, industrial education was a dead end because it did not provide sufficient training to compete with Indian or European artisans. Adapted agrarian education in Kenya was particularly hypocritical, since there was little land available in the overcrowded reserves. Colonial educators expected primary education to lead directly to farm or simple artisanal work, but on average a Kenyan student leaving primary school in the interwar era was just ten years old.[34] Faced with the prospect of becoming landless squatters or unskilled wage laborers, African students worked desperately to remain in school for as long as possible.

The structural and pedagogical limits of colonial schooling led community leaders and parents to favor educational autonomy. In 1922 a member of the Young Kavirondo Association declared: "We want to teach ourselves. We don't want to be taught by the Missions alone: we want our own schools. The missions don't teach us *safi* [pure] teaching. We want our own schools. Our own teachers are able to manage them."[35] Although nascent political organizations like the Young Kavirondo Association wanted to run their own schools, it was the independent churches that were the main sponsors of autonomous literary education in East Africa. In many cases, the initial stimulus for clerical autonomy came from conflicts between literate Africans and missionaries over the translation and interpretation of the Bible.[36] By the 1920s these tensions gave rise to independent branches of established churches and entirely new African Christian denominations. Taking the missions as their model, the new religious bodies often founded their own schools. In other cases, educationally minded independents founded churches primarily to legitimize their autonomous schools. Many of these independent schools also sponsored scout troops without the knowledge and sanction of the East African Scout authorities.

Independent education in Uganda began in 1902 when Apolo Kagwa started a private school in Kampala as an alternative to the missions. This early experiment failed because the Church Missionary Society discouraged its followers from teaching in the school. Uganda did not develop a viable independent school movement until 1926, when Reuben Spartas opened the Anonya Private School under the auspices of the African Orthodox Church (AOC). Spartas eventually become an ordained Orthodox priest, but most of the students at Anonya were not members of his church. Instead, the school tended to draw pupils who could not find a place in the Ugandan mission schools.[37] Its program of English language instruction and its literary curriculum were much more powerful draws than the AOC's religious message.

Most Kenyan independents also emphasized education over religious doctrine. Although African-run schools in central and western Kenya grew out of independent churches, their founders were inspired as much by dissatisfaction with colonial education policy as they were by religious controversies with the missions. Their grievances included the inadequacies of the government's technical curriculum, the missions' focus on religious instruction and rejection of over-age students, general discrimination against African teachers, and the colonial administration's unwillingness to let local native councils build intermediate and secondary schools.[38] The first independent schools in the Kikuyu districts dated from the early 1920s and were largely the work of mission outcasts and prosperous local businessmen. They were Christian in character, but their primary purpose was to circumvent the missions' monopoly on African education.

The Kikuyu push for educational independency coalesced into the Kikuyu Independent School Association (KISA) by the mid-1930s. Although KISA had close ties to the Kikuyu Central Association, its leaders denied that they were a political movement. One of the founders put it this way: "KISA wanted to prepare pupils for the time when the whites would leave. It was not their aim to produce politically active people. Knowledge was first; political action would come to a knowledgeable people."[39] Nevertheless, the founders of the Kikuyu schools did have an implicitly political agenda. Recalling the promise of nineteenth-century prophet Mugo wa Kibiru that the Europeans would leave once the Kikuyu had learned their secrets, the KISA founders believed they were laying the foundation for a new autonomous Kikuyu society. In the meantime, the Kikuyu independents staked a claim to full imperial citizenship by appropriating the church and school as proof of their respectability.[40] In colonial Kenya, respectable schools had a strong Christian focus and, by the late 1930s, Scout troops.

The African Orthodox Church originally sponsored KISA. After failing to get help from the established missions, the independents asked Daniel William Alexander, the South Africa–born archbishop of the AOC, to ordain their clergymen. In 1931, Alexander, the son of a Martiniquan father and a Cuban-Javanese mother, was visiting Uganda to ordain Reuben Spartas. He was more than willing to stop in Kenya and charged two to five shillings for each baptism. The colonial government suspected that he was secretly raising money for KISA and its schools. It is more likely that Alexander was building personal power. His demand that all newly ordained priests accept his discipline under a branch of the AOC of South Africa exacerbated a rift among the Kikuyu independents over the direction of the independent school movement. Alexander sided with a faction that became known as the Karing'a (pure) Kikuyu Educational Association (KKEA). The KKEA styled itself as the defender of Kikuyu culture and refused to cooperate with colonial authorities on educational matters. KISA, on the other hand, sought a broader territorial movement that would appeal to all African communities. It was also willing to work with the colonial government in return for financial assistance for its schools. Alexander's support for the KKEA when he left Kenya in the mid-1930s forced KISA to form the African Independent Pentecostal Church to oversee its schools.[41]

These larger doctrinal and organizational disputes had little impact on the actual operations of the Kikuyu schools. The independents were concerned primarily with expanding the scope of literary education in central Kenya. Most schools were funded by contributions from local communities and were usually run by African teachers who had left the mission and Jeanes schools in search of better pay. By 1935 the Kenyan government estimated that there were nearly four thousand children attending independent schools, just under 5 percent of the African primary students in the colony. This figure almost exactly matched African enrollment in the state-run schools.[42] The Kikuyu independents became a viable alternative to colonial and government schools because they offered an escape from the adapted curriculum and captured the political imagination of the Kikuyu community.

The strength of Kikuyu educational independency was most evident in the debate over language instruction. Where colonial educators restricted English to the intermediary level, the independents taught English in their primary schools and Kikuyu parents accepted the higher tuition to improve their children's employment chances. Mastering English also served a political function by demonstrating that Africans were respectable citizens of the empire. Johana Kunyiha, one of the founders of KISA, dismissed government criticism of the independent curriculum on the grounds that "I am one of the subjects of [King Edward VIII] and I am bound to teach his tongue in our schools."[43] Colonial officials had to pay greater attention to petitions and appeals in English, and the language also helped politically minded Kikuyu find allies with the anticolonial lobby in Britain.

Yet relations between the independents and government and mission educators were actually relatively cordial in the 1930s. Colonial officials worried that the Kikuyu Central Association secretly controlled the new schools, but they lacked the legal authority to shut them down. In 1936 the director of education therefore convened a meeting of missionaries, colonial officials, Kikuyu chiefs, and KISA representatives to discuss the status of the independent schools. The KKEA refused to attend. The centerpiece of the conference was the government's offer of financial assistance to schools that followed an approved curriculum, limited English instruction to grades Standard III and above, segregated students by age, and submitted to regular inspections. Kunyiha and his allies fudged on the question of English but declared themselves willing to follow government policy.[44]

By 1940 the Education Department was inspecting fifty independent schools a year, and KISA representatives sat on education boards in all three Kikuyu districts. Yet only a handful of schools ever received a direct grant from the central government. In most cases language was the key sticking point. Although Kunyiha promised not to teach English in the lower primary levels, most of the Kikuyu independent schools continued to offer English classes for the entire student body. The independents put the state school inspectors off through false promises of future compliance with government policy.[45] Their obstinacy stemmed from the fact that English was at the heart of the independent school movement in Kenya. Scouting's use of English thus made it particularly appealing to the independents.

Colonial officials were also troubled by Kikuyu efforts to expand independency beyond the primary level. Frustrated by the government's insistence that they divert tax revenues to mission schools, the Kiambu Local Native Council lent its support to the independent school movement. The Kikuyu leaders originally planned a teacher-training college, but their school at Githunguri grew to offer instruction at the primary, intermediate, secondary, and adult levels in addition to teacher training. Mbiu Peter Koinange, a holder of a master's degree in education from Columbia University and the first African to qualify for the Kenyan civil service, became Githunguri's headmaster. The colonial authorities tried to co-opt him by offering to make him an assistant master at Alliance High School or a vice principal at the Machakos Government African School, but he turned them down to lead Githunguri.[46] The salaries of the Alliance and Machakos jobs were considerably less than what the European staff earned, but Koinange was motivated more by the hope and enthusiasm that the community had for Githunguri than anger over discriminatory pay scales.

Although colonial officials viewed Githunguri as an explicitly political institution that threatened their monopoly on African education (and the Kenya police kept it under surveillance), the school was not a particularly subversive place. Seeking government recognition, it followed a curriculum built around agricultural and technical education. Although Koinange taught an anthropology course and Jomo Kenyatta, a central figure in the Kikuyu Central Association, lectured on current affairs when he returned from Britain in 1946, Githunguri still had to give its students the credentials to pass government exams and impress colonial officials and potential employers.[47] The independents may have rejected the premise of adapted education, but they could not escape the fact that it constituted respectability and legitimacy in interwar East Africa.

Nevertheless, the strength of African educational independency helped doom the experiments in adapted schooling and Scouting. By 1931 the Kenyan Jeanes School had produced seventy-one teachers who were supervising 349 village schools. Although the Kenyan government considered the Jeanes experiment a great success because it addressed the criticisms of the Phelps-Stokes Commission, the African student body was frustrated with its overt focus on adaptation. They resented being taught in vernaculars instead of English, and most aspired to be more than simple village teachers. Jeremiah Segero supplemented his meager teaching salary by illegally growing coffee, which the colonial government reserved for the settlers, with the tacit permission of his district commissioner. Dougall's "native" youth movements did not catch on either. Although Segero had some success in western Kenya, Justin Itotia's group never seems to have attracted any members. T. G. Benson, a former English public school headmaster, replaced Dougall in 1931 and became a strong advocate of formal African Scouting in Kenya. In the mid-1930s the Kenyan government stepped in to assume full financial responsibility for the Jeanes School, but this support failed to revive the school. Only one in five Jeanes graduates accepted teaching positions in the countryside by the close of the decade, where they supervised just one quarter of the approximately three thousand village schools in rural Kenya.[48]

The success and status of Alliance High School further undermined the credibility of adapted education. To gain admission to Alliance, students had to score at the top of the primary school exam, have a fluency in English sufficient for advanced study, and muster the financial resources to pay roughly one hundred shillings per year in tuition. By comparison, an unskilled African laborer earned eight to twelve shillings a month in the late 1930s. The Kenyan government pressed the Kenya Missionary Council to give Alliance an adapted industrial focus, but by 1938 the school was following a full Western-style secondary curriculum. When a government soil conservation expert inspected Alliance two years later he found the school gardens had fallen into neglect. Dismayed that agricultural training was offered only one period per week, he sniffed that Alliance was becoming "merely a training place of white collared natives, who inevitably must tend to despise anything to do with agriculture, and it is said, of political agitators."[49]

In Tanganyika even government officials were beginning to doubt the effectiveness of adapted education and adapted Scouting. W. B. Mumford initially considered the Bukoba experiment an unqualified success. In reality, things did not run so smoothly. Mumford originally tried to institute an adapted curriculum that stressed "learning by doing." In practice this meant the students studied agricultural techniques, animal husbandry, "native handicrafts," and hygiene. The student body protested that they already could do most of these things, and the Bukoba-Bahaya Union complained to the government that the school was becoming an agricultural training center. Mumford eventually had to back down and allow formal instruction in reading, writing, and mathematics in a conventional classroom setting.[50]

Mumford's experiments in adapted Scouting also proved a total failure. The students insisted on being called Scouts instead of Mashujaa because they wanted the status and prestige that came with full membership in the movement. Mumford blamed their resistance on the incompatibility of Scouting with the "educational ends of the tribe," and ruefully concluded that although Scouting's origins were in Africa, it was not African in "moving spirit."[51] Even Cameron had his doubts about Mumford's attempts to teach "native tradition." Cameron's successor was even more critical, and in the early 1930s the Bukoba and Malangali schools shifted to more conventional Western curricula and their Scout troops collapsed. The Tanganyika Education Department still supported adapted education in rural primary schools, but Mumford moved on to his lectureship in native education at the University of London.

African opposition to adapted education and the demise of "native" Scouting created problems for the East African Scout authorities. Inspired by the success of independent schools, many African teachers and community leaders took it upon themselves to create their own troops. In some cases they explicitly rejected adapted versions of Scouting, but in others they were simply trying to bring the benefits of the movement to their children. The colonial authorities paid little attention to these informal troops in the 1920s (if they were aware of them at all) but had to take action when African dance societies in Mombasa began to use Scout uniforms in the early 1930s. B. S. Mohindra, the secretary of the mostly Indian Mombasa Scout Association, complained that during Sunday dance competitions "self-styled [African] Scouts often get drunk at the finish of the Ngoma and do all sorts of things." By 1934 Kenyan Scout leaders began to worry that these unauthorized groups threatened the reputation of the movement and asked the colonial government to enact legislation giving them sole legal title to the Scout uniform and badge. Otherwise, the Kenyan police could not act against the dancers because at the time there were no laws against the unauthorized use of Scout materials.[52]

It is difficult to be certain why the Mombasa dancers were dressing as Scouts, but the most likely answer is that the *ngomas* (dances) were Beni dance competitions. The Beni dance tradition grew up in Swahili communities on the East African coast in the early decades of the twentieth century. Rival societies dressed in Western clothing and competed with each other in drilling and dancing to the music of brass bands. Many seemed to satirize symbols of colonial authority by dressing as members of the army, police, civil administration, and, apparently, Boy Scouts. Whatever the actual motives of the dancers, colonial officials were certain they were being mocked and undermined by the Beni societies. European Scout authorities therefore had little difficulty in convincing Kenya and Tanganyika (which also had active Beni groups) to draft legislation reserving the symbols of Scout legitimacy for the territorial associations. These laws barred Africans from impersonating Scouts or forming unauthorized troops. They also made it illegal for legitimate African Scouts to masquerade as policemen or government agents. Violators faced a fine of two hundred shillings or one month at hard labor. The Kenyan and Ugandan governments enacted virtually identical legislation.[53]

Although the new laws provided some protection against unauthorized scouting, East African Scout officials soon realized that bringing Africans into the movement with full Scout status was the best defense against independency. Having been exposed to the South African version of Pathfinding through his Jeanes School work, Benson was adamant that there would be no racial division of the movement in Kenya. Imperial Headquarters reassured the East African Scouters that it fully supported African Scouting and considered racially separate organizations to be a last resort. As a result, the Kenya Scout Council voted unanimously in March 1934 to include Africans and created a standing subcommittee to deal specifically with African Scouts. Many European Scout leaders were unwilling to parade in public with Africans, but Baden-Powell declared himself thoroughly pleased with the integration of Kenyan Scouting but warned that colonial officials would have to be careful in selecting just the right "type" of Africans to be Scoutmasters. The absence of intense local European opposition to full African membership allowed the chief Scout of the empire to uphold the universalistic ideals of his movement without jeopardizing Scouting's alliance with the colonial authority.[54]

Armed with the open support of Baden-Powell and Imperial Head-quarters, East African Scout officials met at the Nairobi home of the Kenyan Scout commissioner in January 1935 and affirmed their support for African Scouting and agreed to circulate copies of Scout Council minutes and annual reports between the territorial associations of Kenya, Uganda, Tanganyika, and Zanzibar. Although they were committed in principle to the goals of adaptation, the territorial representatives decided there was not enough interest to warrant publishing translations of Scout materials in Swahili and local vernaculars. As a result, English remained the default language of African Scouting.[55] The commissioners thus created a powerful incentive for African students to join the movement. The use of English in Scout literature and weekly troop meetings made Scouting a potent symbol of sophistication for African boys that meshed neatly with the political agenda of the Kikuyu independents.

By comparison, formal African Scouting in anglophone West Africa was considerably more advanced and uncontroversial. During the 1920s, the colonial governments of Nigeria and the Gold Coast gave their Scout associations money to hire paid organizers, acquire land, and construct buildings. By the 1930s both colonies supported associations that were almost entirely African, with Europeans controlling the territorial headquarters and serving primarily as district and provincial Scout commissioners.[56] There was no need for a color bar in West Africa and thus no barrier to making the movement widely available to Africans. Even though the East African authorities gradually came to accept the value of Scouting, they still considered it an entirely voluntary movement. Formal state support for Scouting in East Africa would have to wait until after the Second World War.

The Uganda Boy Scout Association was the most viable of the new territorial associations because it relied extensively on African leaders trained at King's College, Budo. Tanganyika, by comparison, developed a relatively weak and decentralized territorial Scout association. It was mostly dormant in the 1930s and remained confined almost entirely to the elite central schools. It often fell to enterprising African students to start troops on their own. In 1937, Emmanuel Kibira and Julius Nyerere took the lead in introducing Scouting to the Tabora Central School. Nyerere, who would go on to be the first prime minister of independent Tanganyika, read *Scouting for Boys* on his own and convinced his headmaster to assign a pair of teachers to serve as Scoutmasters. Nyerere easily mastered the Scouting curriculum and became the senior patrol leader of the troop.[57]

In Kenya, Scout authorities wrestled with the problem of reconciling official Scout status for Africans with the informal color bar. The KBSA's governing council reorganized itself in 1939 to better represent its multi-ethnic membership and asked the colonial administration to find them an African member with a sufficient command of English to serve along with Europeans. The council briefly considered Peter Mbiu Koinange but eventually put off naming an African representative until after the Second World War. It was money, however, that proved to be the biggest hurdle in the KBSA's efforts to create more structured Scouting opportunities for Africans. In 1939 the association's financial reserves amounted to only several hundred shillings, and its effort to raise funds from African local native councils faltered when the African councilors insisted that their contributions be used at the local rather than the territorial level. Kenya Scout authorities and their Girl Guide counterparts therefore relied on limited government funding and a grant from the King George Memorial Fund to expand their African operations.[58]

This semiofficial support for Baden-Powell's organization left the Boy's Brigade out in the cold. Even the Church of Scotland Mission had doubts about the viability of the brigade in East Africa once the colonial governments threw their weight behind Scouting. The metropolitan Boy's Brigade tried to arrest this decline by approaching the Church Missionary Society to start Boy's Brigade companies at its East African mission stations. Although Anglican officials in London were open to the idea, CMS missionaries in Kenya rejected the proposal because they did not have the resources to support two youth movements, and most schools were commited to the Scouts. As a result, the original 1st Kikuyu Company was the only Kenyan Boy's Brigade group to survive the interwar period. Yet Baden-Powell even managed to crack this CSM bastion because the Boy's Brigade could not offer a viable movement for African girls. The Scottish missionaries began one of the first African Girl Guide companies in Kenya in 1938, and the 1st Kikuyu group became one of the premier African companies in the colony.[59]

African Scouting in Kenya grew rapidly once the Boy's Brigade was out of the picture. In 1935 the KBSA's annual census listed 510 officially enrolled Scouts of all races in thirteen troops. Three years later, there were 1,636 Scouts and Rovers in the colony. The vast majority of these new Scouts were Africans. The KBSA held its first integrated general camp at Nyali Beach, near Mombasa, in 1937, and within the year many district Scout associations started their own local camps. The Machakos District camp alone drew 140 African Scouts in 1938. The colonial administration played a direct role in this expansion. In 1937 the colony's provincial commissioners affirmed their support for the movement and issued a circular urging district officers to promote African Scouting and Guiding. Despite this encouragement, most of the credit for the growth of African Scouting in Kenya belonged to the 6th Nairobi Alliance troop. Its members fanned out across the colony to begin their own troops after receiving their degrees. They were responsible for introducing Scouting to the engineering department in Nairobi, the Government African School at Kagumo, and the CMS's Maseno primary school in western Kenya.[60]

The Jeanes School also became a center of formal African Scouting under T. G. Benson, who formed a conventional troop, and later a Rover crew, for African teachers in the mid-1930s. As an unofficial and voluntary part of the school curriculum the 2nd Kabete troop trained teachers as Scoutmasters and cubmasters. School officials also hoped the movement would make African teachers more obedient by teaching them "character." The troop planted trees, earned money for uniforms by digging latrines, and mounted an honor guard for the governor when he visited the school. Benson expected the Jeanes Scouts to help run existing troops or form new ones in villages and remote primary schools after they graduated. By 1936 he counted 122 conventional African Scout groups throughout the colony. Most of the older adapted village groups died out by the end of the decade because the Jeanes graduates serving as Scoutmasters were either too overworked or had difficulty running a troop on their own. Lacking institutional support, the "native troops" tended to collapse when their founders lost interest or moved to new academic postings.[61]

The most viable African troops were affiliated with a well-run primary or secondary school. This was partially due to the fact that these were the only African institutions with the infrastructure and funding to sponsor a troop, but the educational focus of Kenyan Scouting was also due to Baden-Powell's personal push to anchor the movement in schools. Having retired to Kenya in 1940, he took a semiactive interest in the affairs of the KBSA. Through Imperial Headquarters he constantly reminded Kenyan authorities that Scouting could make a substantial contribution to African schooling, though not through the conventional curriculum.

Although Baden-Powell complained that the Kenyan authorities were slow to recognize the educational value of Scouting, by the mid-1930s the Education Department included updates on Scout and Guide activities in its annual reports. Educators believed that the movement improved school discipline but were not willing to make Scouting a part of the formal curriculum. Their reports show that most troops operated outside regular school hours. At the CMS's Maseno School the Scouts met Thursday evenings and Saturday mornings. Nevertheless, most Scoutmasters were African teachers who embraced the movement as it acquired greater official sanction. Many saw Scout work as a means of furthering their careers and took the lead in expanding Scouting beyond the elite mission schools.[62]

The scholastic focus of Scouting in Kenya and the rest of anglophone East Africa proved a weakness as well as a strength of the movement. Although the schools were the most effective sponsors of African troops, Scouting was almost entirely inaccessible to the majority of African boys who remained outside the colonial school system. Tanganyikan officials hoped to expand the movement to rural villages, with African clerks and artisans serving as Scoutmasters and considered linking Scouting with Young Farmers' Clubs and cooperative societies. The KBSA tried to tackle the same problem by affiliating European-run troops at central schools with simple troops at rural "bush" schools. Neither plan met with much success. It took constant supervision by Europeans or highly educated Africans to keep the movement on track. Left to their own devices, most remote troops either collapsed or had to be closed because they made unacceptable revisions to the Scout canon.[63]

The Second World War further limited the expansion of Scouting in East Africa. Many local Scout associations shut down when the colonial administrators, missionaries, European and African educators, and sympathetic settlers who supplied most of their leadership joined the army. The Kenyan and Tanganyikan associations suffered the most. The smaller and better-organized Ugandan Boy Scout Association, which made more effective use of African leadership, managed to hold regular training courses and territorial camps throughout the war. In Kenya most Scout activities outside Nairobi ground to a halt as the armed forces took over campgrounds, and African Scouts suffered from wartime food shortages. At the territorial level, the KBSA stopped taking its annual census and provided almost no guidance for individual troops. Although the details are sketchy, this supervisory vacuum appears to have allowed independency to flourish in the countryside as African leaders were free to reinterpret the goals and methods of the movement for themselves.[64]

Not surprisingly, the Second World War had far less of an impact on African Guiding, which continued to expand from CMS and CSM Kenyan mission stations during the early 1940s. The Boy's Brigade also made an effort to revive its East African operations in 1944 by offering a grant of two hundred pounds for youth work in Kenya. Ultimately, though, the movement faced the same manpower shortages and organizational problems that beset the Scouts, and their initiatives in East Africa came to naught. Nevertheless, the virtual collapse of Scouting at the territorial level did not prevent African Scouts from contributing to the war effort. Although the Ugandan government conscripted Scouts with signaling training, most Scout activities during the war were nonmartial. African Scouts guarded truck parks in Uganda, served as coast watchers in Mombasa, and helped with the fire brigade in Nairobi and Nyanza Province. Scouting may have become moribund at the territorial level, but individual troops of boys remained committed to the movement throughout the war.[65]

EAST AFRICAN EXPERIENCES WITH SCOUTING

The viability of local African Scouting while the territorial associations fell dormant during the Second World War underscores the distinction that must be made between official versions of Scouting and how the movement played out in specific African communities. As in southern Africa, it is difficult to fully document African experiences with Scouting during this period because it is difficult to locate surviving members of the original troops. Moreover, the European Scout officials who produced Scouting's institutional memory were only dimly aware of what was going on in rural African troops. Nevertheless, it is still possible to draw conclusions about how individual Africans made sense of the movement. Coupling the recollections of surviving ex-Scouts with a close reading of official Scout records produces an interesting picture of African Scouting in the interwar era. Although African Scouts enjoyed considerable prestige for their uniforms, respectability, and mastery of Western culture, they also faced suspicion and ridicule from members of their local communities, who resented their status and apparent subservience to the colonial power.

Only a handful of African boys had the opportunity or resources to join the Scouts, and only boys from comparatively wealthy families attending elite schools could participate fully in the movement. Matthew Kipoin, a student at the Government African School in Narok, used a one-hundred-shilling wartime remittance from his brother in the army to become the only boy in his troop to have a full uniform.[66] Within the privileged confines of elite schools Scouts enjoyed special status because most scholastic troops could accommodate only twenty to thirty boys. J. G. Kiano, Mathew Kipoin, and B. K. ole Kantai all recall being attracted to the movement because Scouting at their schools stood for excellence, self-discipline, and sophistication. It was much harder to be a Scout outside the safe boundaries of the school. Gilbert Lewa, a member of the Alliance 6th Nairobi, faced heckling by African boys at home for following the Third Scout Law ("A Scout's duty is to be useful and helpful to others") by carrying wood for his grandmother. The local boys laughed at him for doing "women's work." In addition to being guilty of elitism, Scouts could face social discipline for blurring local gender lines.[67]

However, the perquisites of Scouting were usually more than sufficient to compensate for criticism and heckling by other boys. Unlike in South Africa, East African Scouting actually did offer the prospect of limited socializing with European and Indian Scouts. Although individual troops remained tightly segregated (reflecting racial divisions in the colonial school system), Scouts from various communities had the opportunity to interact at territorial camps. The Uganda Boy Scout Association, for instance, held annual interracial gatherings of Scouts at its Kazi Camp.[68] Nevertheless, few European Scouts attended the camp, and the color bar loomed large over Kenyan Scouting. Benson was a strong advocate of interracial Scouting and despaired when only four Europeans attended a general camp at the Kabete Jeanes School. For most European Scout leaders in East Africa, brotherhood meant a handshake with African and Indian Scouts at ceremonial functions and little else. Most former African Scouts recall that they rarely, if ever, spoke with non-African Scouts. Although few were aware of the overt hypocrisy of the European Scouts' fudging on the Scout Law, racial segregation in Kenyan Scouting (the Ugandan and Tanganyikan associations were almost entirely African) undercut the legitimacy and status that Africans expected to come with full membership in the movement.

Independency seemed an obvious solution to official Scouting's racial policies. By forming troops outside the authority of the KBSA, Africans were free to interpret the movement on their own terms. The lack of surviving records from the independents and the difficulty in locating former members of these often remote rural troops makes it much more difficult to explore the implications of this type of African scouting. However, it is possible to gain insights into the nature of interwar independent scouting by looking at official attempts to control it.

As in Britain, the East African territorial associations tried to vet and register all potential asters to be sure they were of the right "character." In Uganda, new African troops had to have a European Scoutmaster (or at least a European district Scoutmaster nearby), and potential African troop leaders served a probationary period where they were regularly inspected by Scout authorities before receiving a warrant to expand their troops as fully recognized Scoutmasters.[69] The KBSA followed the same policy, and pro-African European Scouters complained that its strict guidelines for warranting Africans prevented the growth of the movement in Kenya. The Kenya Girl Guides Association did not even begin to warrant African Guide leaders until the mid-1940s. In theory Africans could rise to responsible leadership positions in the territorial Scout associations if they passed the Woodbadge Course, but few educated African ex-Scouts had the free time or the inclination to complete the program. Ugandan Scout officials complained that former Mengo and Budo Scouts were not willing to accept the extra work involved in running a proper troop. Kenya did not have an African Woodbadge holder until J. M. Mogwanja, a product of the 6th Nairobi troop, successfully completed the course in 1945.[70]

For many Africans interested in scouting it was simply easier to start their own unauthorized groups. In the late 1930s the KBSA was alarmed to discover that many of the Kikuyu independent schools had their own scout troops. Most of these groups had been active for several years before they applied to the KBSA for official recognition in 1938. One such troop was the 1st Limuru (Kikuyu Karinga) Rironi School. It was run by Bewes Francis, who had been a First Class Scout at the CMS school at Kabete. After observing the Rironi Troop, a government school inspector was forced to admit that it was a "good type and is very keen." The troop consisted of nine patrols and spent its meetings parading and learning semaphore, Morse code, knots, first aid, and drumming and bugling. The European inspector had no choice but to recommend that the KBSA register the troop if it dropped "Kikuyu Karinga" from its name.[71] Githunguri also had scout and guide groups. The Githunguri guides were under the direction of Martha Koinange, most likely a relative of the headmaster, who was a former teacher and member of the 2nd Fort Hall Company at the CMS Kahuhia mission. The Kenya Girl Guides Association refused to grant her a warrant to lead the Githunguri company on the grounds that she challenged the authority of the CMS missionaries by leaving Kahuhia without their permission.[72] The Kikuyu independents did not try to conceal their scouting and guiding activities and sought official recognition from the territorial associations because they wanted to use the movement to legitimize their efforts to create a viable alternative to the colonial education system. However, there were also less conventional African experiments with unauthorized scouting during the interwar era. The movement's trappings of

4.1. The Scout belt. Photo by and courtesy of the Scout Association UK Archives.

authority and quasi-military hierarchy had the potential to be turned to other uses. When the Kenya police arrested Samuel Muindi for organizing a nonviolent collective protest against government efforts to destock the Kamba Reserve in the late 1930s, they found Scout literature in his car.[73] There are no surviving records of how Muindi became involved in Scouting, but it is possible, if not likely, that he either posed as a Scout to bolster his authority in the Kamba community or that he was actually a former Scout who used the skills he learned in the movement to organize the large-scale protest challenging government authority.

It certainly was easy for an enterprising African with enough money to pose as a Scout. Indian merchants throughout the colony sold parts of the Scout uniform and made little, if any, effort to determine whether their customers were legitimate Scouts. Scout belts, which were similar in design to army belts, were particularly popular.[74] Although the Scout uniform was protected by law throughout East Africa, the police did not have the resources to check the identity of every Scout they encountered. They could shut down Beni dance societies that appropriated Scout uniforms, but rural Africans were relatively free to pose as Scouts if they could buy or steal parts of a uniform. The colonial archives and official Scout records make only passing reference to such imposters during the interwar era, but this was probably due either to the fact that Scouting was still relatively new in the East African countryside or to the fact that official Scouting was largely unaware of unauthorized African interpretations of the movement.

The slow but steady expansion of formal African Scouting reflected the political and educational realities of pre–Second World War East Africa. Where white South Africans and Rhodesian settlers forced southern African Scout leaders to keep their territorial associations segregated by race, the Kenyan settlers were not strong enough to influence colonial social policy on a grand scale. They had considerable influence in the Kenyan government, but they could not prevent the Colonial Office from affirming the paramountcy of African interests in the colony. The color bar was unnecessary in Uganda and Tanganyika, but in Kenya the settlers protected their privileged position by informal social means rather than explicit legislation on the South African model. Given that the lines of political authority in East Africa were much clearer than they were in the south, it was much easier for territorial Scout leaders to admit Africans to the movement as full members without jeopardizing their alliance with the colonial regime.

5
Scouting and Independency in East Africa, 1946–64

AS FORMAL AFRICAN SCOUTING grew in popularity and scope in postwar Kenya a number of troops approached the standards of Alliance High School's 6th Nairobi troop. The 2nd Fort Hall at the Church Missionary Society's Kahuhia mission station was one of the most active and successful groups in Central Province. Kahuhia was a CMS center in the Kikuyu districts and consisted of a mother church, medical dispensary, normal school (teacher-training college), technical primary school, elementary school, girls' boarding school, and adult day school. Although the CMS school was one of the better mission institutions in Kenya, it faced mounting disciplinary problems by the late 1930s. The staff often expelled students for insubordination, delinquent tuition, and theft of school uniforms and property. Kahuhia was one of the first mission stations to sponsor formal Scouting in the colony, but its troop lapsed into dormancy by the beginning of the Second World War. Kahuhia's principal blamed his disciplinary problems on a lack of wholesome extracurricular activities, and he sought to revive the troop to give students a more "constructive" outlet for their free time.[1]

The task of reinvigorating Scouting at Kahuhia fell to a young teacher named Cyril Hooper, the son of one of the original founders of the mission. Hooper worked with Solomon Adagola, a Kahuhia teacher and an ex-Scout from Makerere University College, to make the 2nd Fort Hall an integral part of school life. The two Scoutmasters used the movement to promote closer ties between students and faculty, with

Hooper volunteering his own living room as the troop's clubroom. They enlisted over fifty boys from across the spectrum of Kahuhia's component schools. By 1944 the 2nd Fort Hall consisted of four patrols of eight Scouts each, a senior troop leader, three assistant Scoutmasters, and Hooper as senior Scoutmaster. Jason Minae, one of Hooper's most able assistants, convinced his father to provide land in the neighborhood for camping. Four years later, Kahuhia's annual report listed Scouting as the normal school's most important and popular extracurricular activity. The 2nd Fort Hall was the best organized and most active troop in central Kenya, and Francis Mbugua recalls that the Kahuhia Scouts took pride in their many victories in district competitions and jamborees.[2]

To school authorities and visiting Scout officials it appeared that the movement had brought stability, discipline, and harmony to Kahuhia. Yet the 2nd Fort Hall crumbled in the early 1950s when its African Scoutmasters and Scouts became embroiled in the Mau Mau Emergency. At its core Mau Mau was a conflict between poor landless Kikuyu and the Kikuyu allies of the colonial government. The CMS station at Kahuhia became a refuge for Christian "loyalists" targeted by the guerillas for refusing to take an oath in support of the rebellion. Police interrogation revealed that Kahuhia's senior prefect had taken such an oath, and further investigation found that Jason Minae, whom the Kenya Boy Scout Association (KBSA) rated an outstanding Scoutmaster, was also a Mau Mau oath taker. In the eyes of the Kahuhia missionaries and the Kenyan Scout authorities Minae's "betrayal" raised serious doubts about the troop's commitment to the Scout canon. They closed it down temporarily as the KBSA reorganized African Scouting to combat the spreading Mau Mau "infection" of its Kikuyu troops.[3]

The apparent defection of the 2nd Fort Hall arose from the inherent tensions and contradictions that characterized East African Scouting after the Second World War. As graduates of the colonial schools came of age they expected positions of responsibility and affluence in colonial society. As products of a highly competitive and elitist education system, they sought employment that fulfilled their aspirations for social mobility. Yet the de facto East African color bar disqualified them from all but the lowest levels of the civil service, commerce, and the professions. Although there were no formal laws against employing Africans in responsible positions, colonial officials and settlers argued that African graduates lacked the requisite education and cultural sophistication to win the jobs they desired. European Scout officials were willing to let Africans join separate troops, but most were not ready to interact closely with Africans as peers at the professional or social level.

These political, social, and vocational barriers exposed the hypocrisy of Lugard's dual mandate and led many educated Africans to conclude that they could realize their ambitions only through independence. In embracing African nationalism they built alliances with struggling farmers and the growing urban unemployed, who blamed their problems on the colonial regime. These coalitions exposed the failings of indirect rule. Popular opposition to invasive and discriminatory colonial policies bridged ethnic and class differences among the African majority. British administrators expected chiefs and headmen to use their "traditional authority" to maintain social stability and stifle political dissent. In practice, the alliance of the "native rulers" with the colonial regime undermined what little influence they actually had. Moreover, rural chiefs were of little use in controlling the "detribalized" urban poor who had fled to the cities seeking alternatives to subsistence agriculture. The colonial authorities therefore retreated from indirect rule and sought an accord with more Westernized Africans. They did not abandon their rural allies entirely but sought to co-opt younger educated elites by drawing them into local government in the countryside. By diverting African nationalists into rural politics, British officials tried to avoid sharing real power at the territorial level. They sought to buy time by promoting gradual constitutional evolution where it would take decades for Africans to come into their political inheritance.

The colonial regime's political and social problems proved a boon for postwar East African Scouting. Having abandoned their attempts to reconcile Scouting with African "tradition," British officials now looked to the movement to co-opt educated Africans through "civics," which in practice meant loyalty to the empire and colonial authority. Postwar African Scouting became a school for citizenship that promoted multiracialism, a political system that granted collective and proportional representation to ethnic communities on the basis of "civilization" rather than the direct franchise and prepared African students to participate in local politics. The East African governments also turned to the movement to remedy their growing juvenile delinquency problems by becoming a partial substitute for formal education in providing primary school dropouts with character training and useful vocational skills. These new official roles allowed the territorial Scout associations to grow considerably as colonial governments poured manpower and money into the movement.

Yet Scouting remained open to reinterpretation and adaptation by Africans at the local level. Although Kenyan Scout leaders vastly overstated the degree to which Kikuyu groups like the 2nd Fort Hall had become active agents of the Mau Mau, many African Scoutmasters did use their troops to teach African nationalism. This should hardly be surprising given that one of most appealing aspects of the movement was its claim to political legitimacy. Just as Scouting could promote imperial citizenship, it could also teach African self-determination. The struggle between the official version of the movement and African adaptations amounted to nothing less than a contest for political legitimacy in the waning decades of British rule in East Africa.

REFORMING COLONIALISM: COMMUNITY DEVELOPMENT AND SOCIAL WELFARE

Much of the inspiration for reforming indirect rule came from the British government's increased attention to its African colonies on the eve of the Second World War. Realizing that propaganda attacks on Nazi racism might leave the empire open to similar charges, colonial experts redefined Lugard's conception of colonial trusteeship to promote economic prosperity through greater metropolitan intervention in local economies. In 1940 the British government passed the Colonial Development and Welfare Act, which allocated five million pounds per year over the next nineteen years for "schemes for any purpose likely to promote the development of the resources of any colony or the welfare of its people." Although the treasury maintained that Britain could not afford such a substantial commitment of wealth, the act's supporters argued successfully that it would counter Axis propaganda, answer American critics of imperialism, develop new markets for British exports, promote African commodity production, and, most important from the standpoint of education and Scouting, generate new wealth that could be used for social welfare in the colonies.[4]

The act received a boost when a new socialist-minded Labour government came to power in Britain after the close of the war. With Indian independence looming, Prime Minister Clement Attlee looked to Africa to bolster what was left of the empire. Seeking increased revenue to rebuild war-ravaged Britain, pay down war debts, and fund the welfare state, the Labourite Colonial Office sought to make the African colonies more profitable by stimulating the production of agricultural commodities for export. These plans led to a "second colonial occupation," in

Table 5.1. Percentage of African Children Completing Specific Grade Levels, ca. 1953

Territory	4th Year	8th Year	12th Year
Nyasaland	10.4	1.4	0.02
Northern Rhodesia	38.9	2.9	0.05
Tanganyika	16.4	1.0	0.04
Uganda	19.7	1.2	0.14
Kenya	31.2	3.7	0.08

Source: Nuffield Foundation and Colonial Office, African Education.

which the imperial government expanded territorial bureaucracies to restructure rural African economies.[5] As a result, Africans faced greater interference in their daily lives from a host of colonial experts in social welfare, agriculture, soil reconditioning, veterinary science, home economics and women's issues, and labor relations.

Colonial administrators hoped to smooth over the social disruption caused by the second colonial occupation by broadening opportunities for African participation in local politics and improving local standards of living. Arthur Creech Jones, Labour's secretary of state for the colonies, was a former member of the Fabian Colonial Bureau and a onetime critic of British imperial policy. In his new role, he brought the Fabians' socialist ideals to the Colonial Office by promoting progressive social engineering in the empire. Creech Jones and his allies envisioned that the African colonies would gradually evolve to the point where they would be ready for democratic self-government within the Commonwealth. This slow evolution would take place from below as representative village councils absorbed the "native authorities." At some point in the comfortably distant future these local democrats would share executive power with European settlers and colonial officials at the territorial level. Labourite colonial experts believed that the success of citizenship training depended on showing Africans that British rule could improve their daily lives. Their more organized, and ultimately more invasive, social welfare strategy focused on cooperation with voluntary agencies (like the Boy Scouts) to address the needs of the community rather than the individual. By raising agricultural yields, expanding medical care and public health, promoting better home life, and improving adult education, colonial welfare experts sought to raise African standards of living on a broad scale.[6]

This ambitious agenda depended on improving and expanding African education at every level. Although local officials still argued that it was dangerous to produce more secondary school graduates than colonial economies could absorb, experts in London blamed underdevelopment on the limited scope of African education. Table 5.1. shows that the education pyramid remained narrow and restrictive in the postwar era. Educationalists in the Colonial Office planned to drastically increase the number of students reaching the intermediate level with the ultimate goal of providing eight years of education for every child. By broadening the education pyramid they sought to create a more sophisticated African citizenry that would contribute to postwar economic development and have a greater stake in colonial policy.[7]

In practice, budgetary constraints and settler resistance made it extremely difficult to expand the scope of African education. Colonial administrators also feared that granting educated Africans a greater political role would allow them to undermine, or even block, the ambitious postwar development plans. Moreover, many colonial education experts still clung to adapted schooling. Although the independent schools drew students by making English a key part of their curriculum, most local educators still insisted that vernaculars had to be the primary medium of instruction in African schools in the postwar era. Although the Colonial Office's Advisory Council on African Education recommended replacing Swahili with English in the East African primary syllabus, most schools did not begin teaching English as a second language until the fifth primary year. These lingering limitations on English strengthened the independents but also enhanced Scouting's prestige because most African troops conducted their meetings in English.[8]

The metropolitan British government's loss of faith in interwar education models forced the East African authorities to reluctantly abandon their commitment to adaptation. Yet colonial educators remained deeply concerned about the potentially disruptive impact of Western education. A 1948 Colonial Office report, *Education for Citizenship*, maintained that African schooling had to be based on "local cultural foundations," although it acknowledged that Africans were suspicious of deviations from the classic literary curriculum.[9] The report warned that formal schooling disrupted social harmony by promoting "detribalization," urban migration, and generational tensions. Colonial administrators tried to solve these problems by narrowing the distance between students and their parents by educating entire communities. In practical terms, this meant opening reading rooms and recreational centers,

5.1. Chief Scout of the Empire and Commonwealth Lord Rowallan greeting Scouts in Kenya, ca. 1950. Reproduced with permission of the Trustees of the National Library of Scotland.

establishing adult literacy programs, and sponsoring African women's organizations. The report singled out Scouting and Guiding as institutions that could contribute to community education by teaching citizenship to children who remained outside the colonial school system. Instruction in "civics" would compensate for the structural and political limits of postwar schooling by buttressing the colonial social order against the rising tide of African nationalism. A 1949 report by the Kenyan Education Department complained that African parents had failed to address the decline in "moral standards" in African society. It therefore fell to the government and mission schools to provide instruction in civics, which the Kenyan deputy governor defined as teaching loyalty to the Crown. The formal school curriculum was not well suited to teaching loyalty and sentiment. The colonial regime's increased emphasis on civics therefore created new opportunities for the Boy Scout movement to expand its role as an extracurricular tool for promoting imperial virtue.

British officials also hoped community education would reduce social friction between Europeans and Africans. Concluding that racial mistrust was a major barrier to economic development, the Colonial Office's 1947 administrative "summer school" recommended that territorial governments support youth organizations that fostered volunteerism and "interracial understanding." Colonial educators admitted that formal schooling would be the best means of reducing racial tension if they could get white parents to accept an end to segregation. This remained a virtual impossibility in postwar East Africa. Scouting and Guiding, however, seemed ideally suited to improving race relations within a colonial context. The two voluntary movements bridged the color bar in a nonthreatening manner. Not only would they provide opportunities for African boys and girls to interact with Europeans in a positive environment, colonial officials hoped that the Scouts and Guides might also wean European children away from the extreme racial views of their elders.[10]

Yet Scouting by itself was hardly a remedy for the institutional failings of the colonial schools and the legacy of the color bar. During the final years of the Second World War, the Colonial Office directed individual territories to draw up development plans for the funding from the Colonial Development and Welfare Act. All three East African colonies promised to increase primary enrollments and improve secondary schooling. Yet their plans envisioned that only 20 percent of primary school graduates would advance to secondary school. Although this was an improvement over the highly limited interwar school system, the proposals angered African parents and students by focusing on raising the "standards" of existing schools instead of making education more widely available. The education plans essentially diverted funds from primary schooling to improve the quality of a few secondary schools.[11]

In the late 1940s the Kenyan government convened a committee of missionaries, settlers, and education experts to draft a new education program that would provide low-cost answers to these criticisms. Eliud Mathu was the sole African member. The committee's report, which took its name from its chairman, Archdeacon Leonard Beecher, recommended that the government fund all approved African schools by 1951. Rejecting African appeals to make education more accessible, the Beecher Report restricted primary schooling to four years, imposed school fees at all grade levels, and retained competitive exams to limit access to upper-primary and secondary schools. It also stressed practical agricultural training over literacy at the primary level and reaffirmed the role of religious instruction in countering the detribalizing influence of education by teaching morality and communal responsibility.[12]

Not surprisingly, the Beecher Report provoked a storm of popular protest. It left the missions in control of most schools and recommended a four-year primary syllabus that was too short to achieve basic literacy. Parents were not placated by the promise of increased funding for existing schools when their children stood little chance of acquiring the skills needed to reach the intermediate and secondary levels. African opposition to these educational "reforms" was so intense that the British House of Commons debated the report's merits. Forced to defend its education policies, the Kenyan government argued that giving in to African demands would create a politically unstable elite class and was thus ultimately against the interests of the African majority. In practice, Kenyan officials lacked the funding and the administrative capabilities to implement even the limited recommendations of the Beecher Report. The government could not produce enough trained African teachers and could not fund, much less expand, the existing primary school system.[13]

The main financial burden for African schooling fell on individual students and their families. By the early 1950s the average primary school tuition was fifteen shillings, while intermediate and secondary schooling cost forty-five and one hundred shillings per year, respectively. The fees had to be paid in full at the beginning of each academic term. These were heavy burdens at a time when wages failed to keep pace with inflation. As a result, most children entered school at age seven and left when they were eleven, and only 1 percent of all students completed more than eight years of education. In the late 1940s only Alliance High School and the Catholic Holy Ghost College at Mangu taught up to the secondary school certificate level in Kenya. The situation was much the same in Tanganyika, where exclusionary exams limited access to the four secondary schools in the territory.[14]

It is easy to see how African students and parents lost what little faith they had in the colonial school system. In 1945 every Tanganyikan candidate failed the Makerere University College entrance exam, which contributed to the Colonial Office's conclusion that the Tanganyikan Education Department was "rotten bad." Some Kenyan parents used bribery to circumvent the exam system and get their children a place in an intermediate school. Most students who lost the chance to continue their education had no interest in the agricultural work promoted by the colonial government and coveted well-paying white-collar jobs in the cities and towns.[15]

In Kenya, the Kikuyu continued to be the most vocal critics of colonial education policy. Faced with the increasing nonviability of subsistence agriculture, Kikuyu families usually viewed education as their best hope for social mobility. The inability of many parents to secure advanced schooling for their children contributed to growing generational tensions in the Kikuyu community. These sentiments were at the root of the continued growth of independency in the late 1940s. By 1951, Jomo Kenyatta estimated there were 342 independent Kikuyu schools throughout the colony. The Kenyan government still hoped to co-opt these schools. The Beecher Report renewed the offer of financial aid to institutions that accepted inspection, but most still refused to submit to state supervision. More troubling from the government's standpoint, KISA's sponsoring churches began to take over established mission schools by winning over African teachers and forming rival school committees. The independents won followers by promising to dispense with qualifying exams and admit all interested students.[16]

Ugandan parents and community leaders were also dissatisfied with their government's education policies. In the 1940s student strikes and arson became more common at government and mission schools. The Ugandan independents vastly expanded their reach in the postwar era by offering English at the primary level and making the ability to pay tuition their only requirement for admission. These schools were concentrated in the Kingdom of Buganda, but non-Ganda students accounted for up to 70 percent of the student body at some institutions. Some schools drew students from Kenya, Tanganyika, Nyasaland, and even the Rhodesias by offering what was often a reasonably priced, high-quality literary education. The Aggrey Memorial School followed the government's official curriculum and boasted a total enrollment of six hundred primary students and four hundred secondary students.[17]

INSTITUTIONALIZING EAST AFRICAN SCOUTING

These educational tensions created an opportunity for the Scout authorities to expand their operations in postwar East Africa. The failings of the colonial governments' educational reforms contributed to a growing juvenile delinquency problem as rootless children drifted to urban areas in search of work and excitement. Tanganyikan authorities estimated that the numbers of young vagrants in Dar es Salaam jumped from two to ten thousand between 1943 and 1952. Once in the city they joined the "smart guys of the town," and survived through casual labor, street vending, petty thievery, and brothel touting.[18] Major cities and towns throughout East Africa experienced similar problems, and settlers, missionaries, and colonial officials worried that unsupervised adolescents were a threat to the moral and political order.

Colonial educators and social welfare experts tried a number of solutions for juvenile delinquency before turning to Scouting. Several Kenyan missionaries proposed to cater to non-school-going children in church-run rural training schools, but these were just another version of adaptation and were simply unrealistic in the tense postwar era. Patrick Williams, an ex-teacher and the director of the Kenyan government's ex-servicemen's training program, proposed that the government conscript sixteen-year-old nonschool boys when they registered to pay their taxes. He envisioned that the young men would gather at retribalizing youth camps twice a year to take part in a rigorous program of physical training, agricultural instruction, basic literacy, and community service. Williams hoped to interest the other eastern and central African territories in his plan, but Kenyan parents and community leaders argued that all available funds should go to formal education and vowed not to let their children be grabbed for a quasi-military venture. In early 1946 the Kenyan government finally dismissed the plan as too expensive and unworkable.[19]

Williams's proposal represented the last gasp of the colonial education establishment's interwar flirtation with adapted youth movements. Jury-rigged experiments in adaptation had little hope of resolving the inherent contradictions in colonial rule. Postwar youth problems created a windfall opportunity for the East African Scout associations to recover from their wartime decline by allying themselves more closely with the colonial state. With adaptation discredited, Scout leaders promoted the movement successfully as a "school" for African citizenship. Yet the Scouts first had to overcome considerable organizational problems left over from the Second World War. Having lost most of its European leadership to the military, the KBSA lacked the personnel and financial resources to extend its supervisory reach beyond Nairobi and its environs. The Uganda association came through the war in better shape, but it was largely concentrated in the most populous southern regions of the protectorate. The Tanganyika association was in much more dire straits. Lacking a formal constitution, an active Scout Council, and a source of regular income, it exercised little control over the few remaining active troops in the territory. Imperial Headquarters labeled Tanganyikan Scouting a "headless wonder" because the governor declined to become the territorial chief Scout and fobbed off the ceremonial position on a succession of underlings in the Education Department.[20]

East African Scout authorities promised they could help the postwar social welfare efforts succeed if government subsidies gave them the means to reach significant numbers of African boys. In West Africa the Gold Coast and Nigerian governments had been providing this kind of assistance to their local Scout associations since the interwar era. However, the real inspiration for government supported Scouting in East Africa came from Imperial Headquarters when Lord Rowallan, Baden-Powell's successor as chief Scout of the commonwealth and empire, secured permission from the Colonial Office to ask colonial governors around the globe to take an active role in expanding their territorial Scout associations. In most African colonies, the Scout establishment had already linked itself successfully to the government by convincing the governors to serve as local chief Scouts. Rowallan could therefore address them as peers and fellow Scouters. He promised that Imperial Headquarters would provide trained organizing commissioners from the ranks of ex–colonial army officers with experience "handling natives" if local governments paid their salaries.[21]

The East African governors responded to Lord Rowallan's request (and a matching appeal from the Girl Guides) with varying degrees of enthusiasm. Tanganyika pleaded poverty and claimed it had little public revenue to spare for Scouting or Guiding. Conversely, Uganda's postwar development committee deemed the two uniformed youth movements a worthwhile investment and had recommended that the government hire paid commissioners almost a full year before Rowallan raised the subject in the fall of 1945. The Kenyan government was initially unsympathetic to the Scouts' request. Governor Sir Philip Mitchell rejected Rowallan's appeal on the grounds that pubic funding would turn the movement into a "government sub-department," thereby robbing it of its spirit of volunteerism, "vitality, and enthusiasm."[22]

The KBSA, however, refused to let the matter drop. Mitchell was their territorial chief Scout, and the KBSA made some headway by convincing him to make the government's new social welfare advisor responsible for supervising African Scouting. The Scout authorities further warned that they risked losing control of the movement to the numerous unauthorized

African troops that had emerged during the war. In early 1946 Stephen Smith, the Alliance High School Scoutmaster, worried that the "startling mushroom growth" of these troops "under inexperienced Leaders" would lead to "the lowering of Scouting standards." His warning not only won over the colonial administration but also convinced settler leaders to support African Scouting. The European Electors Union, a settler political interest group, issued a pamphlet on African development in 1945 that advocated increasing the "moral" element in African education through the churches, Young Farmers' Clubs, and the Scouts and Guides. Three years later, Sir Alfred Vincent, a settler leader on the legislative council, told the Imperial Headquarters' overseas traveling commissioner that he favored expanding Scouting in the reserves to distract Africans from politics.[23]

The movement's value as a social welfare and development tool, coupled with the threat of unauthorized African scouting, eventually won over the East African governments. Uganda's Scout and Guide commissioners arrived in 1946 and quickly set to work visiting troops and companies and setting up training courses for African Scouters and Guiders. One year later, the Kenyan government provided a yearly grant of five hundred pounds to hire Frank Evans, one of Kenya's first European Scouts and the leader of an active African troop in Nairobi, as the colony's first organizing commissioner. Even the Tanganyikan government eventually came around in 1948 by directing its Provincial Commissioners and native authorities to "integrate the advancement of scouting in the proposals for the general development of the Territory." In 1948, Tanganyikan officials allocated the Scouts seventeen hundred pounds per year, but it took the Tanganyika Boy Scout Association three more years to fill their paid organizer position.[24]

This official support opened the way for Scouting to play a more direct role in colonial administration. In 1948, Kenya's Chief Native Commissioner (CNC) issued a circular to the field administration directing district commissioners to promote the movement in "native areas" by becoming chairmen of their local Scout associations. The circular also ordered district officers to encourage local native councils to allocate at least fifty pounds per year to their local Scout and Guide organizations. The media lent its support through a regular column on Scouting in the Swahili-language newspaper *Baraza* and weekly radio programs about the movement on civilian and military radio networks. In some areas of the colony this official patronage was unnecessary. The DC for Central Nyanza assured his superiors that the CNC's circular was "preaching to the converted" because he was the chair of the Nyanza Province Scout association and his local native council was already making regular financial contributions to the movement.[25]

Much of this new official enthusiasm for Scouting came from the Scout leadership's success in linking the movement to social welfare. In 1948 the Colonial Office explicitly endorsed "character-forming" youth movements as a remedy for the decline in "traditional morality," child vagrancy, prostitution, and juvenile delinquency. In Uganda the entire African student body of the Social Welfare Training School attended a preliminary training course for Scoutmasters at the Uganda association's Kazi Camp, and Ugandan Scouts raised money for village social welfare centers. The social welfare course at the Ex-Servicemen's Training Centre at the Kenyan Jeanes School included instruction on the life of Baden-Powell, the history of Scouting, and the option of joining a Rover crew. African welfare officers trained at these Kenyan and Ugandan institutions spread the movement throughout the countryside as they moved from posting to posting. They distributed Scout literature to interested adults and began their own troops when they had the opportunity. Their European superiors hoped these community troops would draw nonschool boys into the movement.[26]

The education establishment also embraced Scouting after the war. In Uganda the Education Department endorsed the movement as a tool for "the teaching of resourcefulness" and for promoting school discipline. Looking to Scouting to control African students studying in Britain, the Ugandan government ordered its students to attend the International Woodbadge Course (for training Scoutmasters) at Gilwell Park as a condition of their scholarship. Concerned that young Africans might fall into the "wrong hands" of socialists and prostitutes, the Ugandan authorities viewed Scouting as a wholesome extracurricular activity that offered moral comradeship and a constructive outlet for their free time. In 1948 the Kenyan director of education matched the CNC's circular on Scouting with a similar directive ordering senior education officers to support the movement. The officers in turn asked school principals to begin Scout troops at their schools. Although some education authorities complained that this violated the voluntary spirit of the movement, most schools had no objection to adding Scouting as an extracurricular activity. The troop at the Government African School at Kisii boasted sixty members and held monthly camps throughout the district to support less-established satellite troops at rural outschools. By the 1950s even the Tanganyikan educational authorities gave their tacit support to the movement on the condition that teachers and students at government and native authority schools conducted their Scout work after the close of the school day.[27]

Scouting's semiofficial status in the late 1940s encouraged ambitious East African Scout leaders to seek even higher levels of government aid. The Scout associations complained that they could barely cover the salaries of their professional organizers, much less fund their travels throughout the countryside. Arguing that they had the resources to reach only a small percentage of African youth, they asked for more money to expand their headquarters, hire additional organizing commissioners, run Scoutmaster training courses, and purchase land for camping. In Kenya, Frank Evans resigned his commissionership on the grounds of financial hardship in early 1949. The KBSA asserted that its yearly grant of five hundred pounds was not enough to hire a qualified replacement and appealed to the government to quadruple its aid to scouting. Kenya's member for finance flatly refused on the grounds of fiscal responsibility. In response, the Scout authorities joined the Guides in again warning that unauthorized African scouting might turn subversive if rural troops remained unsupervised, and they threatened to appeal directly to the governor and the secretary of state for the colonies if the matter was not resolved.[28]

The Scouts were also motivated by a renewed threat from the Boy's Brigade to its monopoly on government-sanctioned youth work in Kenya. In the late 1940s the brigade's overseas secretary asked the Kenyan Anglican and Presbyterian missions to sponsor Boy's Brigade companies. He promised that, unlike Scouting, his movement would bind their young converts more closely to the church by promoting social welfare within a strong Christian environment. The KBSA weathered this challenge because the Boy's Brigade lacked a territorial association, and individual missions did not have the manpower or financial responses to run independent companies. The KBSA's victory was short lived, however, because the Kenyan government lost much of its enthusiasm for social welfare in the early 1950s. With the demobilization of the wartime African soldiery complete, Kenyan officials dismissed the pro-Scouting African community development officers. The Kenyan Treasury now claimed that it could spare no further resources for African Scouting. Having failed to secure increased state funding, the KBSA began the decade with an operating deficit of eight hundred pounds. Donations from the Baden-Powell and King George V Memorial Funds and annual subscriptions paid by each Scout were not enough to close the gap. The Scout Council therefore curtailed its training program, froze hiring, and rented rooms in its headquarters building to the Education Department.[29]

Kenyan scouting's difficulty in attracting greater official support stemmed in part from its ties to the failed postwar social welfare and community development programs. From the African perspective, maternity wards, community reading rooms, and civic lessons were poor substitutes for genuine political and economic change. Rising inflation and failed school reforms produced real economic hardship that put many Africans in direct conflict with the colonial regime. Local native councils were hardly viable outlets for African political expression, and as a result the East African governments faced mounting anticolonial resistance by the early 1950s. In Uganda social pressures in the Kingdom of Buganda came to a head when small- and medium-scale farmers challenged the Gandan elite's dominance of land and agricultural production. They opposed Kabaka Mutesa II's (and by extension the colonial regime's) policies on cotton production and marketing. In 1949 these tensions led to rioting, prompting the colonial officials to arrest the ringleaders, including independent African Orthodox Church leader Reuben Spartas, for conspiring to overthrow the Bugandan government. Similarly, the Tanganyikan government's attempt to intervene in rural economies also sparked widespread unrest as local communities resisted increased taxation, soil erosion control, forced cotton cultivation, and restrictive grazing reserves. The government provoked even greater resentment by setting aside roughly five million acres for European use in the fertile Moshi and Arusha districts under the guise of rationalizing the boundaries of former German estates. Tanganyikan officials tried to legitimize these policies under a multiracial constitution that assigned disproportional political rights to communities on the basis of their "civilization."[30]

The situation was considerably more serious in Kenya, where the settlers made it harder for the colonial regime to reach even a limited accommodation with the African majority. The Kenyan government faced the same labor unrest, tax resistance, and challenges to chiefly authority as its Ugandan and Tanganyikan counterparts. Yet the rate of political change in the colony was much slower because the settlers refused to share power on even a communal "multi-racial" basis. Colonial officials treated Jomo Kenyatta's Kenya African Union, a Kikuyu-dominated political organization with the potential to achieve a broad territorial following, as subversive and subjected its leaders to police surveillance and harassment. Although the Kenyan government appointed Eliud

Mathu, the former Alliance teacher and Scoutmaster, to be the first African representative on the legislative council in 1944, there was no opportunity for real African political participation beyond the local native councils.

In the early 1950s frustration with discriminatory colonial policies turned violent in the central Kenyan highlands, where longstanding Kikuyu grievances over landlessness led to the Mau Mau Emergency. Kikuyu chiefs and government allies made the settlers' land grab worse by appropriating much of the remaining land in the reserves. As a result, many Kikuyu had to seek their fortunes in urban areas or become squatters on European farms. In 1951 the Kenya African Union estimated that 250,000 landless Kikuyu had become squatters. As the ex-Alliance Scout and Anglican cleric Obadiah Kariuki explained: "The plots [of land] that they have are not sufficient, and indeed, many have no land at all. . . . It doesn't matter to me for I am engaged in God's service, but just think of the trouble to a man who has not got the kind of treasure in his heart that I have, and has no plot of his own but is simply a servant of another day and night, and has no one who cares about his troubles and those of his children." Although these impoverished Kikuyu held the colonial regime responsible for their predicament, they took out their aggression on its local proxies in the reserves. They blamed chiefs, businessmen, and devout mission adherents for unfairly acquiring extra land. The urban unemployed, dispossessed squatters, and poor peasants who lost land to politically connected members of their lineages bound themselves together with powerful oaths that swore their commitment to restoring social justice in Kikuyuland. Thus, Mau Mau was ultimately a protest against social differentiation in the Kikuyu reserves.[31]

The Kenyan government failed to appreciate the scope of this threat until a few isolated settler families fell victim to lethal attacks. Matters came to a head in 1952, when the Mau Mau hard men assassinated Senior Chief Waruhiu, one of the regime's most influential Kikuyu allies. In response the Kenyan government declared a state of emergency that empowered its security forces to detain suspects without trial. Faced with martial law, the rebels retreated to the forests in the central highlands and waged an intense guerilla war against the settlers, police, and Kikuyu loyalists. The revolt also spread to the neighboring Embu and Meru communities. In assessing the causes of the revolt, Kenyan officials were certain that the independent churches and schools were deeply involved in Mau Mau. The leaders of the Kikuyu independent school movement had become open and committed opponents of the colonial regime, and the managers, teachers, and students at these schools were actively involved in administering and taking oaths. Mission leaders were incensed when they learned that the independents had "blasphemously" modified Christian hymns for political purposes. For example:

> Kenyatta shall reign where're the sun
> Doth his successive journeys run;
> His Kingdoms stretch from shore to shore
> Till moons shall wax and wane no more.

These songs are doubly significant given that the independent scout troops edited the Scout canon in a similar manner.[32]

The KBSA's near collapse during the Second World War had allowed the independents to expand their scout troops without official interference. When the Scouting authorities renewed their effort to bring rural African troops under central control in 1946, they discovered that the independents already had an extensive presence in central Kenya. The Scout leadership sought to co-opt these unauthorized troops by drawing them into the KBSA, and there were so many Kikuyu groups in Kiambu District that they formed a new local association just to supervise them. Most of these independent scouts had ragged or incomplete uniforms, but otherwise European observers were often impressed with their campcraft, discipline, and enthusiasm. Nevertheless, the Scout authorities distrusted the independents profoundly. The KBSA grudgingly acknowledged the Kiambu troops' high standards but worried about what was going on in troops sponsored by rural outschools and squatter schools on remote settler farms. By the early 1950s many of the more established independent groups had spun off large numbers of "satellite troops" in the surrounding countryside that were usually run by untrained African scoutmasters with little direct knowledge of the movement. The KBSA's financial problems in the early 1950s made it difficult to keep track of these highly informal groups. Stephen Smith counted twelve such troops that emerged in the Nairobi suburbs while he was away on home leave. There was little the KBSA could do to supervise them because even the Kiambu Local Association was largely defunct by 1951.[33]

Independent scout leaders therefore had considerable freedom to modify the Scout program to suit local circumstances. A European school inspector was particularly distressed by a satellite troop of the 16th Nairobi (a formal group run by the Church Missionary Society): "At one school I found a heterogeneous collection of boys and girls mixed together, of all shapes and sizes, doing some crude antics under the direction of a

Standard IV boy. I was told these were the Scouts and Guides." Mission Scout leaders generally used the movement to promote conceptions of Christian masculinity where educated African boys learned to become responsible heads of households and abstained from intimate relations (sexual and otherwise) with girls until adulthood. From the KBSA's standpoint, mixing the genders in a single group violated one of the central tenets of Baden-Powell's vision for Scouting. The independents, on the other hand, saw no reason to deny female African students the legitimacy and respectability that came with membership in the movement. As Jimmy Wambugu recalled, "Our teachers could only spare the time for one [youth group], so they chose the Scouts. Everyone at the school [boys or girls] had to belong." Scout leaders and government school inspectors tried to crack down on unauthorized alterations in the Scout canon by sending trained African Scoutmasters to take over the offending satellite troops. Even though they worried that the independent troops were spreading anticolonial propaganda, Scout officials hoped to regain control of rural African scouting through proper supervision.[34]

The Kenya Girl Guide Association (KGGA) adopted a similar strategy when it discovered the existence of unauthorized guide companies at KISA schools in Kiambu and Nyeri Districts. Leaders trained by Martha Koinange at Githunguri led many of these companies. The Guide leadership was largely unaware of the scope of the Kikuyu independent school movement and turned to the KBSA for advice on how to cope with independent guiding. In 1950 the Guide commissioners resolved not to close independent companies that might do good work under proper supervision. They formally asked the Scouts, who had a slightly stronger presence in the reserves, to help them block the creation of any more unauthorized groups. This was wishful thinking. Neither the Scouts nor the Guides had the resources or cultural understanding to grasp the nature and scope of Kikuyu independency. Moreover, most of the trained African Scoutmasters that the KBSA counted on to bring the satellite troops under control were also teachers who abandoned their adopted troops when the Education Department sent them to new postings.[35]

Although the Kenyan Scout authorities understood that their influence over Kikuyu scouting was tenuous at best, they were still shocked to discover the extent of the independents' involvement in Mau Mau. David Hemphill, a settler farmer and the assistant Scout area commissioner for the Rift Valley, recalls a profound sense of unease about the Kikuyu troops: "[One was] made conscious that one was an outsider in a way that was never felt when visiting Scout troops at 'normal' times, whatever the race of that troop might be. There was tension—quite tangible tension that was uncomfortable to meet so starkly."[36] Abandoning even the most rudimentary pretence of deference, the Kikuyu scouts gave Scout songs and oaths a new African nationalist dimension by replacing references to Jesus with the now detained "Jomo [Kenyatta]." In doing so they were following the example of the independent church hymns.

Nevertheless, it is difficult to determine the full extent of the independent troops' involvement in Mau Mau. The Kenyan government's official report on the Emergency singled out the Kikuyu independent schools as "breeding grounds" for nationalism and subversion. The report also took the Scouts to task for failing to supervise independent scouting. In hindsight, however, we can be certain only that most Kikuyu scouts took at least one Mau Mau oath. Some took up arms and went into the forest with their fathers, uncles, and older brothers, but it is more likely that most scouts did what they were trained to do in times of widespread unrest. As during the Second World War, they did their best to support what they considered to be the legitimate symbols of political authority. The fact that many young Kikuyu had transferred their loyalty to the forest fighters was indicative of the growing isolation of the colonial regime. The Kenyan authorities understood the implications of this threat and shut down all groups without European Scoutmasters when they took over the Kikuyu schools in 1953.[37]

The government ruled that the independent schools were a threat to "peace and good government" under terms of the 1931 Education Ordinance and closed over fifty independent troops. Administrators in the Kikuyu districts gave parents a choice between closing their schools or turning them over to the missions or local district education boards. In Kiambu the task of reorganizing these schools fell in part to young assistant education officers like Jeremiah Nyagah, who was also one of the most influential African Scoutmasters in the colony.[38]

Although these measures temporarily solved the problem of independent scouting, many Kikuyu Scouts in troops run by government and mission schools were also passive, if not active, Mau Mau supporters. The late Kiraithe Nyaga, a Meru Scout who rose to become the director of the Africa Regional Office of the World Scout Bureau in the 1990s, recalled admiring the guerillas. With his father in detention, he helped his mother smuggle food to the men in the forests. Nyaga considered colonial Scouting to be a scholastic activity and saw no contradiction in supporting the Mau Mau when he was at home.[39] Children, particularly Scouts, were more likely to escape detection by the security forces, and Nyaga was never detained for his activities. The same could not be said for African Scoutmasters. Kenya Police Reserve officers in Lumbwa arrested a uniformed Scoutmaster for assisting the guerillas, and Scout authorities often had to suspend African leaders who confessed to having taken an oath. Even Festus Kinua, a Scouter whom the KBSA decorated for his role in capturing a Mau Mau guerilla, admitted to being an oath taker.[40] Nevertheless, official government and Scout reports cannot be taken as an accurate measure of the degree to which African Scouts sympathized with the revolt. The arrests and confessions of oath taking could have also been products of government coercion or local conflicts between the Scouts and the government's "loyalist" Kikuyu allies.

Although the government moved aggressively to shut down the Kikuyu independent schools, education remained a site of intense conflict throughout the Emergency. Mau Mau fighters targeted mission schools because they served the more privileged segments of Kikuyu society, which appeared to remain loyal to the colonial regime. The guerrillas and their sympathizers burned approximately fifty schools in the Kikuyu and Embu districts during 1953 and attacked teachers and their families who refused to take a Mau Mau oath. Some Kikuyu mission teachers secretly supported the rebellion and administered oaths to their students. Others took an oath to protect themselves from the rebels. Cyril Hooper blamed the spread of oathing at Kahuhia on an ex-KISA student who pressured his peers to join the revolt and in turn recruit their friends. Hooper concluded that only the most devout Christians at the Kahuhia station remained true. Few Kikuyu students at Alliance High School took an oath when school was in session, but some did so when home on break.[41]

The colonial authorities fortified rural schools with military garrisons and barbed wire and arrested any teacher or student whom they even remotely suspected of taking an oath. Conditions grew so tense by 1954 that some missionaries concluded any teacher who went about his or her daily business without fear must have been an oath taker. African teachers were some of the most influential figures in colonial society, and district officers considered them the key to stopping the spread of subversion. Government screening teams of loyalist Kikuyu elders interviewed teaching staffs to root out Mau Mau sympathizers. In a McCarthyist twist, those who "confessed" had to demonstrate the conviction of their remorse and repentance by naming anyone else they knew who had also taken an oath. This system was obviously open to abuse and allowed individuals to act on petty grievances by informing on rivals and enemies. These conditions put Kikuyu students and teachers under tremendous strain. Caught between violent opposing forces, they faced arrest if they sided with the rebels and murder if they did not take an oath. It was of course easier to blame the spread of Mau Mau on fear rather than on legitimate Kikuyu grievances. Kikuyu students faced great psychological stress and continued their education at great risk.[42]

Kikuyu Scouts faced even greater pressure during the Emergency as both students and members of a government-sponsored youth movement. Some remained genuinely true to the formal interpretation of the Scout Promise; many were devout Christians who refused to take what they considered to be pagan and blasphemous oaths. Their overt alliance with the government made them open targets for Mau Mau fighters. This was particularly true in 1952 and 1953, when several African Scoutmasters in Fort Hall and Embu districts were murdered. In Nairobi the KBSA had to suspend meetings at its suburban Rowallan Camp for fear of Mau Mau attacks. Instead, they camped behind fences on the grounds of the Kabete Jeanes School. Similarly, uniformed Kikuyu Scouts in the reserves needed Home Guard escorts to take them to and from meetings.[43]

The KBSA shut down African troops it suspected of being "infected" with Mau Mau sympathies. While they were shaken by the apparent disloyalty of their African members, the Scout authorities blamed their problems on the total collapse of the "moral life" of the Kikuyu, Embu, and Meru communities. European Scoutmasters at boarding schools blamed problems in their troops on mothers who forced their sons to take an oath during school breaks. The KBSA also took pride in the apparent willingness of African Scout leaders to stand with the government during the Emergency. Some African Scoutmasters served on local screening teams. Others joined the loyalist Kikuyu Home Guard units that the government raised to garrison its strategic villages in central Kenya.[44]

Ironically, the KBSA's fiscal problems would have probably stagnated African Scouting in Kenya were it not for the Emergency. The unexpected outbreak of violence, much of it seemingly linked with the Kikuyu independent schools, appeared to confirm the Scouts' warning about the dangers of independency. As the scope of the unrest became apparent, the KBSA renewed its appeal for increased state support by promising to help the government win the hearts and minds of Kikuyu youth. In March 1953 the Scout authorities gathered fifteen hundred Kikuyu Scouts from all over central Kenya to Rowallan Camp to swear an oath of loyalty to the territorial government and the empire. With the camp safely surrounded by the police, Brig. Gen. Sir Geoffrey Rhodes, Kenya's chief Scout commissioner, told the boys, "each one of you [is] part of the forces for good

5.2. Organizers of Kikuyu rally at Rowallan Camp, 1953. From Colony and Protectorate of Kenya, *Community Development Organization Annual Report 1953* (Nairobi: Government Printer, 1954). Reproduced with permission of Her Majesty's Stationery Office.

will during this Emergency." Rhodes made no secret that the rally was intended to demonstrate Scouting's utility to the government. He wrote to Sir Evelyn Baring, the governor and chief Scout, to remind him that the movement had helped contain the communist insurgency in Malaya. Baring was entirely receptive and asked the Scout leadership to consider how they might help in the "mental reclamation of boys under Mau Mau influence." He praised the movement as a force for good in teaching morality and countering the "totalitarianism" of the Mau Mau.[45]

The Boy's Brigade also tried to use Mau Mau to regain an official presence in Kenya. Brigade leaders asked mission leaders to help them secure a share of government funding for youth work on the grounds their "special methods" would be useful in disciplining Kikuyu boys. Although they promised not to interfere with the Scouts, the Christian Council of Kenya was unmoved. It warned them that they should concentrate their efforts in Nigeria, where the Boy's Brigade was well established, rather than in "an area where they were not particularly welcomed."[46]

The KBSA was much more successful in using Baring's official embrace to acquire more government aid. The Scout authorities particularly wanted to hire additional organizing commissioners who would travel throughout the countryside inspecting and advising African troops. They also hoped to expand the role of the movement in the African locations of Nairobi. However, the Kenyan treasury was still adamantly opposed to raising the Scouts' annual allowance. Baring's public embrace of Scouting made this resistance futile. The KBSA got enough to cover the cost of the Kikuyu rally, and in early 1954 the Kenyan government raised its yearly grant to the Scouts to ten thousand pounds. The Guides won an additional three thousand pounds with a similar appeal. The KBSA used its financial windfall to fund three traveling organizing commissioners and a full-time warden for Rowallan Camp. Three years later, the revived Kiambu Local Scout Association hired an additional commissioner with its own funds. These professional Scouters operated primarily in the reserves with the charge of ensuring that African troops did not become a "cover for Mau Mau, etc." The KBSA also considered hiring qualified African Scoutmasters to run the most at-risk troops in the reserves and urban locations on a full-time basis but dropped the plan when it realized that all African Scouters would demand similar payments.[47]

In practice, Scout officials had difficulty finding the "right kind of men" to be Scout commissioners. They hired Ronald Tyers, a former merchant seaman who joined the movement as an adult in wartime Britain, to supervise Central Province and R. F. Powell to assume responsibility for Nyanza Province. L. S. (Linzee) Colchester became the headquarters commissioner and secretary to the Kenya Scout Council. Colchester was essentially an administrator and had little direct impact on African Scouting. Tyers and Powell were more effective. The third traveling commissioner post went unfilled for several years because Scout officials could not find a qualified candidate who would work for the KBSA's comparatively low wages.[48] Nevertheless, the traveling commissioners played a key role in shutting down Kikuyu troops "infected" by Mau Mau. Their success was also due in part to the colonial forces' military supremacy over the rebels. The uprising forced the British government to commit an entire army brigade to augment Kenya's police forces and King's African Rifles battalions. These units ultimately defeated the guerrillas by turning the forests into free-fire zones. The civil security forces isolated the forest fighters from the largely sympathetic general population by forcibly resettling over one million rural Kikuyu and Embu in 854 heavily guarded strategic villages.

Faced with the reality that the vast majority of Kikuyu had either voluntarily taken or been intimidated into taking at least one Mau Mau oath, the colonial regime resorted to mass detentions. It essentially judged the entire Kikuyu population guilty until proven innocent. Screening teams made up of district officers and politically reliable "loyalists" systematically worked their way through schools, churches, villages, and African locations in Nairobi to root out Mau Mau's "passive wing." The colonial authorities arrested anyone even suspected of taking an oath and often punished the detainees by turning their land over to Kikuyu who appeared to remain true to government.[49]

Their success produced the daunting problem of what to do with the million or so Kikuyu in strategic villages and the roughly twelve thousand Mau Mau suspects in detention. Government experts in "native psychology" were certain the Emergency stemmed from the Kikuyu's inability to cope with "modernity" because Christianity and Western education had stripped them of their "traditional" values and left them mentally unequipped to cope with the breakdown of "tribal" culture. Conversely, the missions blamed the Emergency on a "demonic upsurge" of primitive heathen beliefs.[50] Both theories agreed that Mau Mau stemmed ultimately from the failure of adapted education to reconcile Western values with African culture.

With the collapse of resistance in the forests by 1955, colonial administrators, missionaries, and colonial educators came to see the Emergency as a social welfare problem. Recognizing that most of the guerrillas and their supporters were young men and women, these officials believed they could "rehabilitate" Mau Mau fighters and sympathizers by teaching them "moral Christian values." Their plans relied on voluntary organizations to work in the detention camps and strategic villages. Detainees could win release by renouncing their oaths and accepting manual labor. Government rehabilitation experts, many of whom were from the missions, sought to remake Kikuyu society through Christian proselytizing, vocational education, supervised family life, and community development. Many of the "hardcore" Mau Mau fighters refused to cooperate, but the rehabilitation program was a broad experiment in social engineering that provided less ideologically committed detainees a way to win their freedom.[51]

The KBSA offered Scouting as a means of "rehabilitating" the youngest detainees. In 1956 the commissioner of prisons counted 877 unattached boys between the ages of eight and sixteen in the camps. In addition, there were 571 seventeen- and eighteen-year-old detainees and 207 more children who were imprisoned with their parents. The community development officers and missionaries who ran the detention camps were certain that most of these boys were "redeemable" because they had committed their crimes under "misguided enthusiasm." Some of the detainees were one-time Scouts, but Chief Commissioner Rhodes was adamant that any Scout who broke the Scout Promise by siding with the Mau Mau had to serve a "period of repentance" before rejoining the movement. He was more willing to accommodate detainees with no formal Scouting experience.[52]

The young prisoners posed a special problem. The Kenyan government was embarrassed publicly by Red Cross reports that boys in the main detention camps were often handcuffed and beaten by camp guards. Mission leaders also worried that Kikuyu youth would be corrupted if they remained with "hardcore" adult Mau Mau fighters. The Ministry of Community Development therefore segregated young Mau Mau suspects in thirteen special camps in the Nyeri, Fort Hall, Embu, and Meru Districts. These camps taught the boys basic agriculture, civics, simple carpentry, and Christian theology before discharging them to their families. In 1956 community development officials created the Wamumu Approved School in Embu District for teenage detainees charged with crimes deemed too serious to warrant an early release. One year later they opened a similar school at Mukurweini for younger boys.[53]

Even though rehabilitation officials sent their most incorrigible boys to Wamumu, the reform school developed two of the most successful Kenyan Scout troops. This was largely due to the efforts of Geoffrey Griffin, the school's founder and director. Griffin had been a King's Scout at the Prince of Wales School in Nairobi in the late 1940s and had run several African troops in the locations on his own during the weekends. When Mau Mau broke out he joined the all-settler Kenya Regiment before transferring to the King's African Rifles to lead African troops. Disgusted with the military's conduct during the Emergency, he took his discharge in 1954 and applied for a position with the Ministry of Community Development. Even though he was just twenty-two, Griffin's Scouting background and his kindness made him the ideal person to run the Wamumu school. As Ngugi Kabiro, a former Wamumu inmate, recalled: "Though the warders and askari were frequently brutal in their treatment of the detainees, the European rehabilitation officer was a kind and considerate man who earned the respect of everyone in the camp. The young men would always willingly go to him with their problems or when they'd encountered some difficulty with the warders." Griffin believed passionately that the Scout movement's ideals of universal brotherhood could be used to uplift the boys at Wamumu. The Kenyan Special Branch was adamantly opposed to releasing its most hardcore young suspects, sixty of whom were convicted murderers, to a reform school. Griffin was undeterred and convinced Governor Baring to pardon every Wamumu boy to ensure that the police could not arrest them after they were "reformed" and discharged.[54]

The notorious background of Wamumu's student body did not prevent Griffin from transforming the school into a first-rate educational institution. Although barbed wire and hostile armed guards originally surrounded the camp, he gradually remade the institution into an English-style boarding school. Griffin slowly demilitarized Wamumu and reduced the number of warders from two hundred to forty. The original group of 139 boys lived in unlocked dorms grouped into four residential houses under the supervision of older prefects drawn from the student body. Wamumu's curriculum mixed technical training with a basic literary education. Missionaries on the camp staff baptized willing students and conducted "cleansing ceremonials" to speed the "spiritual decontamination" of the Mau Mau infection. Not one of the over one thousand boys who passed through Wamumu by the end of 1957 was reconvicted of a significant criminal offense after his release. Griffin went out of his way to help them find jobs, and a Wamumu "diploma" became such a powerful testimonial to the discipline and reliability of ex-students that European employers favored them over the graduates of conventional intermediate schools.[55]

Scouting played a central role in the Wamumu curriculum and helped establish the exemplary reputation of the school's graduates. The troop began with forty-eight Scouts under four African assistant Scoutmasters, three of whom were detainees themselves. Griffin made Scouting an explicit instrument of "rehabilitation" by incorporating a renunciation of Mau Mau oaths into the Scout investiture ceremony. The Wamumu Scouts enjoyed special privileges on the assumption that their Scout Promise made them more trustworthy and were free to leave the school to camp and undertake the "journey" required for the First Class Scout badge. They even sold programs and collected money at the 1957 Royal Show. Not surprisingly, Scouting became the most popular extracurricular activity at Wamumu, and Griffin created a second troop at the end of 1956 to accommodate more boys.[56]

The Wamumu troops' standards were some of the highest in Kenya, rivaling Alliance High School's 6th Nairobi troop in terms of progression through the Scout ranks. Most Wamumu Scouts became Second Class Scouts, and, with few demands on their spare time, a considerable percentage advanced to the First Class level. It was very rare to find a First Class African Scout outside Alliance in the late 1950s, and the Wamumu troops would probably have produced several Queen's Scouts (the highest rank in Scouting) if they were not discharged so quickly. Joseph Kamira Gikubu was one of the leaders of the Wamumu Scouts. An intermediate school dropout and a convicted oath administrator, he was considered by the security forces to be part of the Mau Mau's hardcore. Griffin identified him as a natural leader and recruited him into the Wamumu Scouts, where he became one of the troop leaders. Gikubu remained active in Scouting after leaving Wamumu and joined Griffin on the staff the Starehe Boy's School.[57]

Another unique aspect of the Wamumu Scout experience was Griffin's strong personal commitment to following the Fourth Scout Law to the letter, even if it meant flouting the conventions of colonial society. His Scouts wore green uniforms, the only African group in Kenya to wear the same colors as the original European 1st Nairobi troop. More significant, Griffin began a series of interracial "bush camps" to bring European and African Scouts together at close quarters. Griffin's camp at Thiba River in early 1958 included seventy African and twenty-six European Scouts, plus members of Kikuyu youth clubs in Fort Hall District. He divided them into four mixed patrols. They had segregated latrines but cooked together and chose to share tents. A few Europeans used racial slurs, and a white Scout had to apologize for being "insolent" to an African Scoutmaster. Griffin smoothed over most of these bumps and even convinced the widow of a government officer who had been killed by the Mau Mau guerrillas to let her son attend the camp. Yet he received no support from the KBSA, and local Scout officials reprimanded him for not following proper camping regulations.[58] Even though formal Kenyan independence was only five years away, neither the Scouting establishment nor the settler community at large was ready to allow Scouting to break down the social divisions between the colony's European and African communities.

The academic and Scouting successes of the Wamumu boys are relatively easy to explain. Even though Wamumu was a reform school for convicted criminals, it became a premier African educational institution because it offered its graduates the genuine chance to earn relatively good jobs once they were free. Ironically, in the late colonial era, European employers considered the most trustworthy Africans to be reformed criminals. A mission instructor at a Nairobi community center observed:

"Some boys have been known to go to Wamumu and ask to be accepted, or have wanted to know what they have to do in order to be sure that they would be sent there." Many African parents realized that the right kind of juvenile delinquency could be the ticket to free high quality education for their children. One community development officer was appalled when a seemingly affluent African parent drove up to Wamumu in a Peugeot sedan with a gift of bananas for his "delinquent" son. Administrative officers in Embu District, where Wamumu was located, noted that although there were no significant juvenile delinquency problems in the area, there were 280 Embu boys at the school. Wamumu embarrassed Kenyan officials by providing the free quality education that African parents had long demanded. The government did not have the inclination or resources to bring its regular schools up to the same standards. Grousing that Wamumu had become an unfair burden on Kenyan taxpayers, the colonial government closed the school in late 1958 and kept only the three hundred boys who were true orphans on state support. Griffin left to serve full time as the colony youth organizer. He eventually founded the Starehe Boy's Centre as a home for African boys whose fathers had been killed during the Emergency. He did not distinguish between those who had been Mau Mau and those who had been loyalists.[59]

SCOUTING IN THE LATE COLONIAL ERA

Outside the camps and strategic villages, the military phase of Mau Mau was largely over by 1956. Having crushed the Kikuyu insurgency, the Kenyan government sought to regain its credibility by fashioning a new political system that would give Africans a greater political voice without undermining the privileged position of the settlers. The Kenyan authorities pursued a policy of gradual "multi-racial" constitutional reform that denied Africans political representation as individuals. They reserved legislative council seats for set quotas of Africans, Indians, Arabs, and Europeans that failed to reflect African numerical superiority. The Kenyan government intended the new constitutional changes to co-opt African elites by giving them a greater stake in British colonial rule. Yet most politically conscious Africans would settle for nothing less than independence by the late 1950s. The failure of the postwar social and economic reforms and the brutal tactics of the Kenyan government during Mau Mau had thoroughly undermined the legitimacy of the colonial regime.

In Uganda the kabaka ran afoul of the colonial government in 1954 when he insisted that Britain set a timetable for Gandan independence. Colonial officials tried to force him to withdraw his demands by sending him into exile. Yet the British courts ruled that the deportation violated the 1900 treaty that made Buganda a protectorate, and the territorial government had to accommodate Mutesa by guaranteeing Buganda's autonomy in a postcolonial Ugandan state. From the standpoint of African Scouting, these intense political controversies politicized many Gandan Scout troops and made it difficult for the UBSA to claim equal loyalty to Mutesa and the Crown. Similarly, the Tanganyikan government's highly unpopular multiracial constitution generated support for Nyerere's Tanganyika Africa National Union. Popular opposition to British rule grew so strong that it was virtually impossible for Tanganyikan authorities to collect taxes in the countryside by the end of the decade. Governor Sir Edward Twining tried to regain a measure of influence by allying with African elites, but this was pointless, as most of the unrest in the territory came from below rather than above.[60]

The strength of the anticolonial movements created significant problems for East African Scouting because the Scout authorities had vastly expanded their operations in the postwar era by forging a close alliance with the colonial regime against African nationalism. In the short term, African Scouting in Kenya largely recovered from the trauma of Mau Mau by the mid-1950s. The KBSA's official 1954 census listed 7,242 Scouts (the vast majority of them African) in 267 groups. These figures did not account for the unauthorized and satellite African troops that still existed in the non-Kikuyu areas of the colony. They do, however, demonstrate that Scouting remained a viable African institution during the Emergency. Much of the movement's recovery stemmed from the unprecedented levels of official support it received from the Kenyan government as colonial officials relied on Scouting to promote imperial citizenship. The colonial army sponsored Scout troops as part of its social welfare program for soldiers' children living in military camps. The head of the East Africa Command sat on the Kenyan Scout Council and provided money from the Army Benevolent Fund to support barracks Scout troops and Guide companies.[61]

Kenyan education officials also increasingly looked to the movement to compensate for the failings of the colonial school system. They hoped Scouting might occupy the growing numbers of students who left school in early adolescence due to poverty or because they failed the entrance exam for intermediate school. Teacher-training colleges incorporated Scouting into their curriculum to train Scout leaders and reduce the numbers of teacher candidates dismissed for "sexual immorality." These measures were only partially successful at best. Including Scouting in the teacher-training curriculum led many teachers to conclude that the supposedly voluntary movement was part of the Education Department. Moreover, it was virtually impossible for dropouts and nonstudents to belong to school troops. In most cases Scouting remained an extension of the formal school system throughout the 1950s.[62]

Yet the closure of Wamumu and the winding down of the Mau Mau rehabilitation program also marked a downturn in Scouting's official relationship with the Kenyan government. The KBSA relied on state funding for 80 percent of its operating budget by the end of the 1950s, but the Kenyan treasury could not sustain this support after the Emergency was over. The government cut the Scouts' annual grant from ten to four thousand pounds in 1960. Although intense lobbying by Rhodes restored some of the funding, the KBSA had to discharge some of its field organizing commissioners. A visitor from Imperial Headquarters found that African Scouting in Kenya almost entirely dependent on these commissioners and observed that the Kenyan Scout leadership was living in a fool's paradise for becoming so reliant on state support.[63]

The Kenyan government's decision to trim the Scouts' allowance stemmed from budgetary constraints and a growing sense that the movement was not the solution to the colony's youth problem. Wamumu notwithstanding, African Scouting in Kenya was almost entirely based at schools and had little relevance for nonstudents. A sharp demographic jump in the African school-age population in the late 1950s swamped the colonial school system. Children who could not pay tuition or pass the intermediate school entrance exam had few prospects other than subsistence agricultural or unskilled wage labor. Faced with severe overcrowding in the African reserves, they gravitated in ever greater numbers to urban areas, where colonial officials worried they might become the willing tools of political agitators.

In Tanganyika, African youth in Dar es Salaam adopted a cowboy culture from American movies; they affected a tough demeanor and wore wide hats, neckerchiefs, jeans, and multicolored shirts. These urban delinquents were essentially "anti-Scouts" who personified official fears of rootless, defiant, amoral African youth. They demonstrated the failure of the movement to reform nonschool boys. Kenyan officials also warned that rootless urban children would develop into "spiv and criminal types." Worried that young Africans were "ripe for undesirable political agitation," they hoped to develop nonscholastic youth programs that would keep them in the rural areas by providing recreation and limited vocational training. In Nairobi the Protestant missions addressed the urban youth problem by building five community centers in the African slums. In place of formal schooling they offered children supervised recreation, literacy courses, and vocational training. Scout officials supported their efforts by creating a new local association to oversee Scouting in the African slum locations in the city. They began active Scout groups at four of the five community centers to provide wholesome alternatives to urban vices. By 1958 there were roughly 350 active African Scouts in the new Nairobi East association.[64]

Yet the KBSA actually had very little to contribute to the new government initiatives against juvenile delinquency. Kenyan Scouting was an elite school-based movement ill-suited to cater to the needs of poor uneducated boys, who could not understand its written texts, afford its uniforms, or accept its fairly rigid code of conduct. The Girl Guides had the same weaknesses, and colonial officials began to believe that the gender division between the two movements diluted valuable social welfare resources. As the colony youth organizer, Geoffrey Griffin convinced the government to put its money into rural youth clubs. Colonial administrators hoped the clubs would buy them at least five years to reform the school system and improve the carrying capacity of the rural economy through land reform. In the meantime, African children, particularly Kikuyu boys and girls, would learn useful trades and character training to keep them busy during their turbulent adolescent years.[65]

Griffin chose Mathira Division in Nyeri District as the site for his pilot camp. Under youth leaders trained at Wamumu he taught simple hygiene, small-scale agriculture, handicrafts, athletics, current affairs, and character training to approximately one hundred Kikuyu boys and girls. They met three mornings a week and wore a simple uniform of conventional shirt and shorts decorated with a rudimentary crossed-spear-and-hoe badge. Those who mastered specific skills earned proficiency badges worn on a special sash. The clubs were voluntary, but some offered a token stipend to attract members. Griffin's program essentially borrowed the most useful elements of Scouting and made them more accessible to African boys and girls in a less structured format. By 1958 there were ninety-eight such clubs with 11,223 members (6,139 of them paid) scattered throughout the Central, Southern, and Nyanza Provinces.[66] These figures were almost twice the African membership in formal Scout groups.

Although Scout officials and their supporters argued that they could expand their operations to serve nonschool boys, community development

officials concluded that the movement was too restrictive in its membership and too academically focused to do the job. They went to great pains
to reassure the KBSA that the youth clubs were not competing with Scouting, but in reality the Kenyan government cut the Scouts' budget to devote
more social welfare resources to the clubs. Rhodes bitterly protested these
funding cuts but realistically chose not to oppose the youth clubs. He
staked out the schools for the Scouts and convinced several youth clubs in
the Kikuyu districts to sponsor Scout troops. As an active Scouter, Griffin
was entirely receptive to including Scouting in the youth leader-training
program, but most of the club troops failed because the boys could not
afford uniforms and club leaders did not have the time to run their groups
properly.[67]

Thus, Kenyan Scouting faced considerable problems as the colonial era
drew to a close. Although rising membership figures suggested that the
KBSA had recovered from the trauma of Mau Mau, in reality the movement was beginning to pay the price for linking itself so closely to the
colonial regime. Ron Tyers, organizing commissioner for Central Province,
was surprisingly pessimistic about the effectiveness of his five-year tenure
in the Kikuyu districts. Tyers had successfully rebuilt Kikuyu Scouting
after the Emergency but worried that most Africans could not grasp the
underlying meaning of the movement. He warned that Kikuyu Scouts interpreted loyalty to mean "doing what the government says" and that
"the word Loyalty does not exist in the Kikuyu language." Obviously Tyers
never really learned much about Kikuyu society and culture, but his
warning about the tenuousness of official Scouting in rural African communities was well taken. The movement's close ties with colonial authority were a growing liability as Kenyan independence drew nearer.[68]

Although the neighboring East African Scout movements expanded
their African membership in the 1950s, they faced similar problems as
the decade came to a close. As in Kenya, Ugandan and Tanganyikan
Scouting were almost entirely academically based movements with little
capacity to reach nonschool boys. Their operations were also overly dependent on state funding, and both associations had to curtail their activities as their governments shifted social welfare resources to more
pressing priorities. Moreover, Ugandan and Tanganyikan Scouting faced
mounting criticism from nationally minded Africans. In Uganda political tensions in the southern kingdoms weakened the movement as young
Africans came to equate Scouting with colonial authority. Similarly, the
Tanganyika African National Union Youth League drew students away
from Scouting. Yet the Tanganyikan and Ugandan associations were bet-

ter equipped to adjust to the changing political climate of the late colonial era than their Kenyan counterpart. Free from the complications of an
entrenched settler community, they found it much easier to "Africanize"
their organizations in preparation for independence. The Ugandan Girl
Guides began working to co-opt influential Africans in the late 1940s
and convinced the wives of the Gandan kabaka and the Nyoro omugo to
join their national council. The Ugandan Scouts were initially not as progressive, but they began to promote Africans to senior leadership positions the mid-1950s. As a result, the protectorate government could ask
the Scouts to increase their membership to help with the youth problems that complicated the transfer of power without risking an anticolonial backlash.[69]

Tanganyikan Scouting also prospered by Africanizing its leadership.
Julius Nyerere had been an enthusiastic Scout, and he was genuinely
committed to the ideals of the movement even though he became the
primary spokesman for African political opposition in Tanganyika. Tanganyikan Scouting was thus able to achieve a measure of distance from
the colonial regime. As a result, membership levels shifted course radi-
cally in the late 1950s. By 1960 the TBSA enjoyed widespread popularity
and counted approximately ten thousand active Scouts in troops that
were largely run by Africans. Although these new Scout groups probably
deviated from the Scouting canon, Tanganyikan Scouting achieved its
highest membership levels on the eve of independence.[70]

AFRICAN EXPERIENCES IN POSTWAR SCOUTING

It is much easier to explore what it meant for individual Africans to become Scouts after the Second World War than it is to assess African experiences in Scouting in the 1920s and 1930s. Scouting was far more
bureaucratic after the war, and ex-Scouts who recall their experiences in
the movement are comparatively more common. These oral and archival
sources provide a diverse picture of East African Scouting where there
was considerable regional and local variation in what it meant to be a
Scout. Moreover, with a few exceptions, our detailed knowledge of African
Scouting comes almost exclusively from formal troops run by government and mission schools. Firsthand information on the day-to-day operations of the unauthorized troops sponsored by African independent
schools and churches is much more difficult to come by. Independent
Kikuyu scouts are hard to locate because most were swept up into the

Mau Mau Emergency, and they are less likely to identify with the movement today than are their counterparts who belonged to more formal troops and often recall their Scout experiences fondly.

It is still possible to paint a general picture of the full scope of the postwar East African Scout experience. The broad focus on civics and social discipline that so consumed the territorial Scout associations rarely filtered down to the local level. B. K. ole Kantai enjoyed being a Scout, but was disciplined by his district commissioner for refusing to stand during "God Save the King." He disagreed entirely that the Second Scout Law required him to give his loyalty to the colonial regime.[71] Teenaged African schoolboys embraced Scouting because it was an elite movement that enhanced their prestige and respectability. With adaptation largely a thing of the past, Scouts in the formal troops followed a conventional Scout program. This was the main appeal of Scouting for many boys. Not only did the Scout curriculum offer a welcome diversion from school life, it also demonstrated that African boys were as capable, resourceful, and prepared as their European and Indian counterparts.

In postwar Kenya roughly 75 percent of African Scouts were between the ages of fourteen and eighteen. The vast majority were schoolboys. In addition to purchasing their own uniforms, they paid between twenty-five and fifty cents as an annual "subscription." Roughly 20 percent of these dues went to their troops, with the remainder going to the KBSA. Scouts funded their activities through the annual Bob-a-Job program, where they raised money by doing odd jobs around their home communities. Most troops met once or twice a week on school grounds, usually before and after classes. These meetings were more likely to focus on conventional Scout skills and badge work than the drumming, marching, and bugling that usually characterized prewar African Scouting. "Good turns" were also important and demonstrated the Scouts' commitment to their local communities. These might include tree planting, crowd control at public gatherings, building furniture for the elderly, digging latrines, donating blood, and evangelical preaching. Scouts usually went camping once a month and joined with other African troops in district jamborees generally once per year. Wealthier troops with connections to the Scout establishment sometimes had the opportunity to mix with non-African Scouts at territorial jamborees.[72]

In theory, Scouting was a nondenominational movement that required its members to believe in God but did not specify a particular religion—although Muslim religious authorities could run "closed" troops exclusively for Muslim boys. In reality, non-Christian religious bodies sponsored only three Kenyan troops in 1960. The vast majority of East African Scouts were Christians, and mission authorities made extensive use of Scouting as a tool for Christian instruction. They freely admitted non-Christian boys to their troops with the expectation that the movement's emphasis on faith and piety would lead to their conversion. Mission Scouts were often committed Christians who considered evangelism part of their duties as a Scout.[73]

Alliance High School's 6th Nairobi troop remained the premier Kenyan troop, African or otherwise, after the war. J. M. Mogwanja, the first Kenyan African Scoutmaster to complete the Woodbadge Course, took over day-to-day operations from Stephen Smith and led the troop to the 1946 East African Jamboree in Uganda. This set the pattern for the 1950s in which African schoolmasters ran the troop under Smith's supervision. The Scouts received no money from the Alliance administration and ran the school canteen to fund their activities. The troop regularly won the interracial trophy competition between the Nairobi Scout groups. Almost every Alliance Scout also mastered enough first aid to qualify for the demanding Senior St. John's Ambulance Certificate.[74] The 6th Nairobi was hardly the norm for African Scouting, but it was a powerful testimonial to what African Scouts could accomplish if given the proper encouragement and resources.

With the exception of the Alliance and Wamumu troops, most Kenyan Scouts wore a simplified uniform consisting of a clean shirt and shorts (often a school uniform), a clip-on badge, and a monotone Scout scarf. These deviations from the more elaborate and ornate European uniforms stemmed mostly from the need for economy rather than an effort to reinforce the color bar. Nevertheless, many African Scouts coveted a full Scout uniform. The KBSA's Scout Shop was the sole legal supplier of Scout paraphernalia after the Second World War. Many poorer boys made great sacrifices to buy these badges and uniform accessories to demonstrate their authenticity as Scouts. Kiraithe Nyaga shared his uniform and equipment with his three brothers so they could take turns enjoying the social prestige that came with being a properly dressed Scout.[75]

East African Scouts also took pride in their command of English. Although the territorial Scout and Guide associations translated their laws and regulations into Swahili and "tribal" languages, African troops and companies usually conducted their meetings in English. European Scouters complained that most African boys had an uncertain command of the language and did not fully understand the English versions of the Scout Law and Promise. Tanganyikan officials encountered a Scout who defined a good turn as "when the Scouter told you to turn and face the other way and you did it properly." Similarly, Kenyan Scouts sometimes read the Sixth Scout Law, "A Scout is kind to animals," as "A Scout is a kind of animal." These mistakes could have just as easily been misinterpretations of the Scout canon by young Africans who did not necessarily grasp or accept European notions of manners or animal welfare. Fluent or not, most African Scouts considered English part of the "authentic" Scout program. In 1953 an African member of the Kenyan Scout Council tried unsuccessfully to block the KBSA's plan to issue Kikuyu-language versions of Scout materials. Yet Scout officials had trouble coming up with accurate translations of their law and promise. With the exception of missionary leaders, their knowledge of their Scouts' home languages was usually even sketchier than the average African Scout's command of English. Tanganyikan Guide officials tried to stop the East African Literature Bureau from translating *magaidi*, the word they used for "Girl Guide," as "terrorist" or "bandit." When the Literature Bureau refused to change its policies, the Tanganyikan Guiders had to switch to *maguide*, an obvious "Swahilization" of the English word.[76] These tensions underscore the cross-cultural complications of importing a foreign ideology like Scouting into rural African societies, and the resulting translation problems probably also account for much of the local adaptation of the movement that Scout officials found so troubling.

East African Scouting also had problems with the Fourth Scout Law. At the official level, the territorial governments' commitment to "multi-racialism" meshed neatly with the Scouts' conception of proper race relations. In the mid-1950s, Chief Commissioner Geoffrey Rhodes proudly declared that Kenyan Scouting was entirely "inter-racial." Mixed patrols of European and African Scouts greeted visiting dignitaries at Government House and occasionally camped together at carefully supervised interracial jamborees. Young European and African Scoutmasters also formed an integrated Rover crew in Thika, and in 1956 a mixed party of twenty-four African and European Scouts and Guides climbed Mount Kilimanjaro. On the surface, it appeared that the KBSA was making progress towards true integration. Yet these very public displays of interracial cooperation were mostly for show. Multiracialism delegated political power to the various East African ethnic groups on a disproportional communal rather than an equal individual basis. Europeans, Indians, and Arabs retained a greater measure of political and social privilege on account of their purportedly more "advanced" stage of development. Thus, Kenyan schools remained segregated, and African and European

5.3 Members of the "inter-racial" Kenyan delegation to the 1957 World Scout Jamboree. *Batian* 1957, Kenya National Archives. Reproduced with permission of Kenya National Archives.

Scouts rarely encountered each other at the local level. Griffin's interracial camps were an anomaly, and Kiraithe Nyaga recalled that the extent of his interaction with white Scouts was a quick handshake after a public rally. Jeremiah Nyagah, the future chief commissioner of the postwar Kenyan Scout Association, similarly had little contact with European or Asians in the movement outside of the KBSA's Woodbadge courses.[77]

There were hardcore settlers in the movement who still refused to even consider applying the Fourth Scout Law to Kenya. Even as the KBSA became a vocal proponent of multiracialism in the 1950s, some European Scouters remained open about their prejudices. In 1956 the leader of the Kenyan contingent to the Festival of Britain Jamboree argued against efforts to create a more tolerant public image of Kenyan Scouting by sending an interracial patrol. The violence of Mau Mau and the entrenched minority interests of the settlers made truly integrated Scouting an unworkable dream. Although Kenyan Scout leaders might have preferred to be more progressive on racial matters, they were absolutely unwilling to alienate their European constituency by pushing the bounds of social convention.

Not surprisingly, Ugandan and Tanganyikan Scouting did a better job of adhering to the Fourth Scout Law. It was easier for officials in these territories to foresee African independence, and they urged their Scout associations to expand their operations to bind educated Africans and nationalist leaders more closely to the emerging British Commonwealth. In Tanganyika, the 2nd Dar es Salaam troop included Goan, Indian, European, and even Chinese boys. The TBSA was the strongest proponent of mixed Scouting of the three territorial associations and refused to send a delegation to the 1951 all-European South African Rover Scout Indaba because of its commitment to "inter-racialism."[78] Most Tanganyikan and Ugandan Scouts rarely interacted with Scouts from other communities, but they also never faced the entrenched racial discrimination experienced by their Kenyan counterparts.

Yet the KBSA's failure to abide by the spirit of the Fourth Scout Law was not something that particularly troubled the average African Scout at the local level. Although they were highly sensitive to discrimination under the color bar, most never encountered European Scouts and generally considered Scouting to be an African movement. The substantial advantages that came with being a Scout in colonial Kenya helped compensate for distant racial slights by the European Scout establishment. Uniformed African Scouts had considerably more autonomy than their peers because school officials and the security forces assumed they were trustworthier. Scouting thus gave young Africans greater freedom of movement in colonial society. Although Imperial Headquarters forbade Scouts to hitchhike, the KBSA waived the ban for rural African members who had no other means of transport.[79]

The territorial governments gave African Scouts and Guides preferential treatment in schooling and employment. Colonial officials and educators tried to restrict the number of African students who went overseas for advanced schooling because they worried they would be "got at" and politicized by socialists, African Americans, and other critics of colonialism. The authorities were more willing to grant Scouts and Guides passports and scholarships to study in Britain on the grounds that they were politically reliable and that the British Scout and Guide associations would look after them. African Scouts exploited these assumptions, and often covered the cost of overseas travel for schooling by convincing their territorial associations to pay their passage to conveniently timed British jamborees.[80]

European employers in Kenya considered a Scout badge to be a testimonial that an African candidate was trustworthy and hardworking. By the late 1950s the badge became even more important when mounting unemployment diluted the value and prestige of a primary or intermediate school certificate. These educational and vocational advantages propelled the careers of many ex-Scouts. In 1966 the Uganda Scout Association estimated that one-third of all ministers in the postcolonial government were ex-Scouts. In Kenya former members of Alliance High School's 6th Nairobi troop did particularly well. J. G. Kiano, Jeremiah Nyagah, and Ronald Ngala all became government ministers. Kenneth Matiba, a former Alliance Queen's Scout, went on to a lucrative business career and a less successful venture into opposition politics. Much of their success was obviously due to their Alliance academic credentials, but membership in the movement gave former Scouts additional access to state patronage in late-colonial society.[81]

These privileges enhanced the status of Scouting within local African communities. Yet many students and adults had a limited understanding of the movement and often had their own conceptions of the benefits that were due a Scout. Peter Leo Omurunga, a member of a troop in western Kenya, urged his fellow Scouts to support the Bob-a-Job program, where Scouts undertook simple chores to raise money for their troops and the KBSA. However, he believed these funds were a form of salary and urged his comrades to throw themselves into fundraising because "a good fraction [of the money] is yours to use in any way. It is good for the more you bring in, the more you receive. So you see how self-supporting you can be in this movement." Rural Scouts like Omurunga clearly did not understand the voluntary nature of Scouting and looked to the movement for employment. The KBSA archived countless letters from desperate young men hoping to support themselves through Scouting as joblessness mounted in the late colonial era. Eliphaz Mputhia Manene applied for a vacancy in the "Scout business." John Wakhunga assumed that the movement was part of the Kenyan government and asked to join the "Scout Department." Boys who had to leave school early hoped that the movement would give them a chance to continue their education. Geoffrey Kariuki requested admission to the Scouts' "training school." Stephan Tomasi Muliro asked to enroll in the Scouts' "correspondence course," and David Kiami desperately pleaded for a scholarship to continue his studies. Horrified Scout officials pointed to these appeals as evidence that most Africans could not grasp Scouting's core values and ideals. In reality, young Africans recognized that Scouting was linked to the colonial schools and enjoyed official support from the Kenyan government, and it was logical from their perspective to look to the movement for patronage and assistance.[82]

Conversely, Scouting's exclusivity and official status also sparked some negative misconceptions in local communities. The Uganda Boy Scout Association warned its European leaders not to carry canes because of the popular belief that they were used to beat Scouts. Some communities in coastal Kenya suspected that the Scouts were a government-sponsored secret society with a malicious agenda. Kikuyu leaders in central Kenya viewed the Scouts' tree planting program as a plot to seize the land for the government. Many parents worried that Scout training was preparation for military conscription. Others viewed the movement as simple labor exploitation that required Scouts to undertake menial tasks without compensation under the Bob-a-Job program.[83]

Popular impressions of colonial Scouting as a powerful and lucrative organization were at the root of African attempts to capture the movement through independency and local adaptation. As with Christianity, Scouting had a universalistic set of core principals that could be read in a variety of ways. African adults in rural communities began their own troops and interpreted the Scout canon as they saw fit. Moreover, one did not have to be a registered Scout to enjoy the advantages of membership. In many cases, any young African male wearing part of the Scout uniform could claim the privileges and perquisites of Scouting. Even in the late colonial era, rural Africans tended to assume that a person in uniform was to be obeyed and respected.

Colonial Scout officials therefore went to great lengths to strengthen their control of African Scouting in the postwar period. They ran Wood-badge courses in all three territories to indoctrinate African leaders in proper Scouting methods and tried to regulate who could be a Scoutmaster through the warrant system. Although virtually any adult African could start a troop in the countryside, if they wanted official status they had to provide sufficient character references and demonstrate their command of the Scout canon to secure a warrant. Scout officials kept a blacklist of socially and politically undesirable candidates and would revoke a warrant if a Scoutmaster failed to uphold their requirements for Scout standards or personal conduct. Similarly, the Scout associations conducted a yearly census in an attempt to register every troop in their territories. Traveling commissioners inspected accessible groups and deregistered troops they deemed inefficient. In theory, Scoutmasters who failed to register their troops or continued on after their warrants had been withdrawn faced arrest and prosecution under the Boy Scout ordinances.[84]

In practice, official Scouting's reach rarely extended beyond urban areas, secondary schools, and mission stations. Rural Africans often had considerable leeway in adapting the movement to local contexts. The Guides also experienced problems with local innovators and spent much of their time trying to prevent male Scout leaders from starting companies or adding girls to their troops. As Mungai Nganga, who tried to buy Guide uniforms for three of his "Girl Scouts," explained: "I as a Scout Master found it to be unwise to refuse them from learning together with boys."[85] European officials were generally unable to stamp out these unauthorized local adaptations of Scouting and Guiding. As a result, scouting at the local level often actually was a truly African institution.

Many boys and young men also concluded that they did not need to belong to an official troop to appropriate the formal benefits of Scouting. In the 1950s rising unemployment, coupled with the movement's closer ties to the colonial regime, created a strong incentive for enterprising Africans to get involved in the "Scout business" by using the Scout uniform to raise funds and claim special privileges. To most Europeans, a uniformed African Scout was someone who could be trusted. To many rural Africans, the Scout uniform marked the wearer as sophisticated, educated, and most likely a government servant.

Individual Africans in all three East African territories donned Scout uniforms, not to satirize the movement as the Beni dancers had in the 1930s, but to exploit its privileged position in colonial society. Sometimes these impostors genuinely believed that they were living up to Scout ideals as they defined them. In the late 1940s, Kenyan Scout officials began to notice boys in partial uniforms turning up at public events to offer assistance. These "unofficial" scouts most likely felt that they were justified in collecting money for their service. In another case, Ugandan Scout officials discovered a young man "festooned with badges" claiming to belong to a Mombasa troop and trying to collect "official stamps" from police stations, district headquarters, and other government offices. This may have been an innocent hobby, but the stamps were certainly useful to forgers. The colonial police frequently detained impostors caught soliciting donations for Scout hikes and expeditions to finance their travels throughout East Africa. Their motives might have been a simple sense of adventure or an attempt to find a legitimate front for smuggling. Sometimes there were pragmatic reasons to impersonate a Scout. Boys desperate to find work masqueraded as Scouts to impress potential employers. These pseudo-Scouts usually claimed membership in another territorial Scout association on the assumption it would be harder for local authorities to check their credentials.[86]

In other instances, the impostors were basically larcenous conmen. The yearly Bob-a-Job programs and other Scout fundraising initiatives were tempting targets. In Kenya, the situation became so serious that Chief Commissioner Rhodes wrote the *East Africa Standard*, warning potential Bob-a-Job employers to be careful not to let thieves disguised as Scouts into their homes. In 1950 the Kenyan Police arrested Philip Maina, a onetime Scout, for illegally collecting money and selling raffle books. As a repeat offender, he was convicted and sentenced to nine months in jail. Nine years later, Christopher Mutingi was arrested for collecting money from Nairobi shopkeepers to supposedly fund a Scout hike from Dar es Salaam to Kampala. Mutingi explained to the authorities that he wore the Scout uniform because "people [were] kinder to him." An ex-Scout named Joseph Orawo became notorious in Uganda for using a forged Scout membership card to collect money in Kampala. The Ugandan police arrested him several times for illegally using ornate Scout uniforms, complete with epaulettes, to add credibility to his activities.[87]

Adults also posed as Scoutmasters. One particularly brazen impostor claimed to be a touring area commissioner from Zanzibar and managed to charge a large tea party at the Queen's Hotel in Nairobi to the Zanzibar Scout Association. In 1958 the Kenyan Police caught James Kamau with a forged Scoutmaster's warrant and found that he was meeting with local troops in Kiambu without permission. Kamau wore an elaborate uniform with badges covering both arms and claimed to be in command of a hundred and one Scout troops. From a local standpoint, he probably appeared to be one of the KBSA's traveling Scout commissioners. Kamau collected money for badges and demanded absolute obedience from the boys. The colonial authorities suspected he was administering Mau Mau oaths and prosecuted him for embezzlement and impersonating a Scout.[88] Pretending to be a Scoutmaster fed the egos of pompous and grandiose individuals like Kamau and offered the more successful impersonators the prospect of a decent living.

The East African Scout authorities tried to reign in unauthorized scouting by tightening control over Scout uniforms and documents. Yet even though the police and courts were sympathetic to the Scouts' plight, there was little that the territorial associations could do to limit the adaptation of their movement. Some legitimate African Scoutmasters augmented their incomes by ordering extra Scout badges for resale. Individual

Scouts often did the same by claiming to have lost their badges and selling the duplicates. In other cases, the impostors simply forged the necessary credentials to buy Scout materials. Scout officials in Uganda discovered that a number of false Scouts in Kampala were using identical fake documents purporting to be issued by the Tanganyika Scout Association. The uniformity of these warrants and membership cards suggests that they came from some central source.[89]

Scout belts were a special problem. Hugely popular with Scouts and non-Scouts alike, their smart appearance and utility conferred considerable status on the wearer. As a result, there was a steady flow of Scout belts into the hands of impostors in all three East African territories. The situation became so bad in central Kenya in the mid-1950s that the police detained every African wearing a Scout belt until he could produce proof that he was an authentic Scout or Scoutmaster. The Education Department also encouraged teachers to check their students for unauthorized belts. The crackdown was so draconian that Kenyan Scout officials had to issue African Scouts special membership cards to prevent the police from confiscating their uniforms. The KBSA tried to require Africans who wished to purchase Scout materials to produce a letter from their area commissioners, but the belts had such a high resale value that legitimate Scouts often sold them to raise money for living expenses and school fees.[90] Clearly, some Scouts were more than willing to blur the line between official and unofficial Scouting.

Ultimately, the colonial authorities' hopes of using Scouting to defuse rising social tensions in postwar East Africa came to naught. The failings of political multiracialism, the narrow and underfunded African school system, and the neomercantilist colonial economy could not be corrected by winning over select groups of young Africans through an elite uniformed youth movement. Colonial officials hoped to use the movement as a school for citizenship to win allies among the increasingly politicized class of educated Africans but were sabotaged by their inability to weaken the informal social color bar and share real power at the territorial level. The East African Scout associations were unwilling to challenge the social status quo by living up to the spirit, if not the letter, of the Fourth Scout Law.

Nevertheless, the movement still exercised a powerful attraction for many African men and boys. Scouting's ties to political authority made it a tempting target for independent African churches and schools. The Kenyan independents sought to mobilize African youth by reinterpreting the movement to contest the legitimacy of British rule. Similarly, Scout status conferred a measure of privilege and prestige that was considerably more significant than that which Scouts enjoyed in more open Western societies. A Scout uniform testified that the African wearer was trustworthy and possessed special knowledge and authority. Uniformed African Scouts had the power to collect money and the freedom to move about without molestation by the police. They usually commanded considerable respect in less sophisticated rural communities.

6

Scouting and Apartheid
in Southern Africa, 1945–80

IT BECAME MUCH HARDER to be an African Scout in South Africa after the Nationalist Party came to power in 1948. Disdained by the right-wing Afrikaner regime for its ties to the British Empire, Scouting also faced condemnation from Africans for its refusal to challenge the Nationalists' policies of strict legal and social racial segregation under what came to be known as apartheid. These opposing forces buffeted African and Coloured Scouts in the segregated communities on the Cape Flats, on the southern outskirts of Cape Town. In 1953 white liberals raised money for Scout troops in Langa to counter juvenile delinquency in the township, which they equated with the "skolly menace" of Coloured youth gangs. Yet Cape Town officials hindered their efforts on the grounds that the Coloured and African townships were temporary settlements that would eventually be razed when their inhabitants were relocated to "black areas." African and Coloured troops on the Cape Flats persevered throughout the 1950s but faced constant harassment from the security forces and members of their own communities who considered them government sympathizers.[1]

Ironically, we know more about the original Grace Dieu Pathfinder company in the 1920s than we do about the township troops. Few people remember these groups because the communities that supported them were reordered or destroyed during the South African government's removal campaigns. The South African Boy Scout Association (SABSA) was only dimly aware of the scope of township Scouting and preserved few records of the urban troops. As a result, the former Scouts themselves are often the only sources of information on township Scouting. Jonathan Ndima, a member of one of the Langa troops in the mid-1950s, recalled that it was difficult to wear a Scout uniform on the Cape Flats as life in its townships became more dangerous. He was taunted by his peers and questioned by white policemen, who did not believe that Africans could really be Scouts. The troop's African Scoutmaster had little affection for the government or the Scout authorities. Ndima eventually dropped out of school, but he enjoyed being a Scout and begged his parents to let him continue in the movement. "[Scouting] was fun. I learned to be a man and found many useful skills that helped me [in school] and life. As a Scout I learned how to stand up for myself and take care of things."[2]

It took real commitment for an African boy to remain a Scout during these troubled times. Many of the schools sponsoring township Scouting burned during antigovernment riots in 1960. Scout troops collapsed when the security forces cracked down on illegal urban migration by destroying "temporary" settlements in the townships. In the aftermath of the government's massacre of antiapartheid protestors at Sharpeville, membership in the movement dropped off precipitously. The annual report for the African Cape Western Scout Division sadly observed that the unrest lent credence to the anti-Scout faction in the townships, which considered the Scouts an arm of the apartheid regime. Nevertheless, John Thurman, the BSA's Gilwell Camp chief, observed that the Cape troops were some of the best in African Scouting. Although many parents withdrew their children from the movement during mounting tensions in the townships, the boys who remained in Scouting did so because it offered a limited escape from the grinding life in urban South Africa. Even though the police harassed Coloured and African Scouts, they were less inclined to beat or mistreat boys in uniform than they were urban youths who were not in the movement.[3]

The experiences of the Cape Flats Scouts demonstrate that South African Scouting was deeply caught up in the struggle over apartheid. The Nationalist Party's segregationist policies and the settler regimes' bitter defense of the color bar in Nyasaland and the Rhodesias were rearguard actions against African nationalism. Worried that international criticism of imperialism and the increasingly marginal value of African colonies in the 1950s would convince Britain to retreat from Africa, European communities asserted their independence by giving legal sanction to racial privilege. In South Africa the Nationalist Party tried to legitimize its segregationist policies by claiming to act as the trustee for "primitive" African societies. In reality, the Afrikaner nationalists and their industrialist allies used apartheid to produce cheap labor and divide the African majority along ethnic lines. British oversight prevented the Central African Federation (CAF), which comprised Nyasaland and the Rhodesias, from enacting similar explicitly racist legislation, but the Rhodesian settlers used the limited autonomy that came with federation to restrict African political participation and protect their economic interests.

The white minority regimes of southern Africa looked to the schools to teach acceptance of this new explicitly racial political and social order. The South African government used the perceived failings of liberal and mission education initiatives as an excuse to take over almost all private African schools in the Union. Territorial governments in the CAF also assumed a more direct role in African education in the postwar era. To some extent they were motivated by their "civilizing" mission, but colonial officials also sought to strengthen white minority rule in the federation by restructuring African education to produce economically useful and politically compliant graduates.

These political and educational changes had a direct impact on African Scouting in South Africa, and, by extension, the CAF and High Commission Territories. The trajectory of the postwar movement in the Union diverged markedly from the path followed by East African Scouting. Where the territorial Scout associations grew closer to the Kenyan, Ugandan, and Tanganyikan governments after war, the SABSA lost much of its claim to political legitimacy after the 1948 elections. The Nationalist Party's insistence on strict legal and social racial segregation under apartheid put South African Scouting in a vulnerable position. The Nationalists viewed Scouting as a fundamentally British institution and cut off most state support for the movement when they came to power. Nevertheless, they recognized that Scouting was a useful tool in disciplining African youth and allowed it to remain a fixture in state-run schools.

The SABSA agonized over its loss of official status. Yet it was still unwilling to fulfill its obligation to African boys by adhering to the spirit of the Fourth Scout Law. It vainly hoped to repair its relations with the government and draw Afrikaner youth into the movement. Although most Scout officials claimed to deplore the racialization of South African society, they shied away from challenging apartheid directly because they did not believe that Africans could interact with Europeans as political and social equals. The SABSA therefore continued to promote African Scouting within the confines of the strictly segregated "parallel" racial associations created by the 1936 Pathfinder compromise. The Scout associations in the CAF shared South African doubts about integration but were more receptive to African Scouting so long as their troops were segregated.

The Scout movement continued to draw large numbers of African boys throughout southern Africa in spite of the territorial associations' lukewarm support for non-European Scouting. In South Africa the Bantu Education Act disrupted African troops severely by closing or taking over the mission schools that had nurtured the movement. Yet enrollment levels recovered in the 1960s as government schools, churches, urban community centers, and large corporations sponsored Scouting to reduce social tensions under apartheid. African radicals and youth gang members had little use for Scouting, but many students, particularly those from (relatively) middle-class backgrounds, still embraced the movement as an extracurricular activity. Being a Scout was an enjoyable diversion and brought self-respect and small privileges that helped make apartheid more bearable. Scouting's international character also provided African and Coloured Scouts and Scoutmasters with sympathetic foreign allies in the international Scout movement.

Finally, and most important, the Fourth Scout Law was still a potent weapon in the struggle against colonialism and apartheid. To be sure, the South African Scout establishment's frayed relations with the government provided independent African churches with fewer incentives to follow the East African model by founding their own unauthorized troops to appropriate the movement's legitimacy and respectability. However, African Scouts, Scoutmasters, and community leaders still reinterpreted the Scout canon to challenge institutional racial discrimination. Their approach was far less radical or dangerous than the armed struggle favored by radical nationalist groups, but Scouting's egalitarianism remained a powerful challenge to the legitimacy of white minority rule. The Fourth Scout Law was a constant reminder to the English-speaking leadership of the SABSA that they had an obligation to work for the true brotherhood of all Scouts in South Africa.

SOUTH AFRICAN EDUCATION IN CRISIS

As in East Africa, explicitly adapted education was no longer viable by the close of the Second World War. Nevertheless, African students and their parents were entirely dissatisfied with the limitations of state-directed educational initiatives in postwar southern Africa. Both South African and British colonial education "reforms" envisioned a narrow education system where advanced schooling remained closed to all but a small handful of the most able students. In other words, schooling was still not a viable means of social mobility. Students and community leaders therefore challenged the right of South African and British colonial officials to control the schools. These conflicts often turned violent when the education establishment refused to listen to student grievances.

With state support at a minimum, the missions that bore the heaviest responsibility for African schooling in South Africa could not meet the growing demand for universal primary and advanced secondary education. By the 1940s African students finally lost patience with the unwillingness of liberal and mission educators to challenge the academic limits under the color bar. To make matters worse, wage cuts during the depression and inflation during the Second World War severely eroded the earning power of African teachers. Most African secondary school graduates seeking professional careers gravitated to teaching, and a small but vocal core of teachers were politicized by the vocational and educational failings of the mission schools.[4]

Many young educators in the Transvaal joined the ANC Youth League and actively recruited students into their movement. Radicalized students, teachers, and young professionals formed the League in 1944 to push the congress's older leadership to be more aggressive in attacking political and social discrimination. Led by Walter Sisulu, Peter Mda, and Nelson Mandela, the Youth Leaguers became a driving force in the ANC five years later and challenged the most oppressive apartheid laws through passive resistance.[5] From the Scout authorities' standpoint, joining the Youth League violated the Second Scout Law requiring Scouts to be "loyal" to the government. Nevertheless, the ANC Youth League drew some of its members from African secondary schools and thus became a key political competitor with the Boy Scout movement for the loyalties of African students.

In most cases, however, political tensions over education came to a head in student strikes. Between 1937 and 1946 there were forty-nine incidents of student unrest at twenty-eight of the Union's forty-six main mission schools.[6] The education authorities blamed the disturbances on petty student grievances over food and living conditions, but in reality they were popular expressions of frustration with the inequities of the African school system, and, by extension, segregated society on the whole. Even Lovedale—one of the premier secondary schools in South Africa and whose students arguably enjoyed some of the best employment prospects for Africans in the entire Union—was not immune to these tensions. On 7 August 1946, simmering anger over poor food and the authoritarian school administration erupted into a riot when over one hundred male students stoned the houses of the senior staff and set fire to school buildings.

In 1947 South African education authorities called a commission of enquiry to examine the causes of the widespread scholastic unrest. Under the chairmanship of D. M. Malcolm, chief inspector of native education in Natal and a founding member of the Pathfinder Council, the commissioners heard testimony from teachers, staff, "native education" inspectors, and chiefs. Their report blamed the strikes on the students' youthful frustrations and recommended introducing "sexual hygiene" instruction and expanding extracurricular "character-building" activities to keep them directed and occupied.[7] Although they did not specifically mention Scouting by name, it is clear that the commissioners believed that the movement was a partial solution to the strife in the schools.

In practice, the Scout movement lacked the scope and resources to solve the fundamental institutional failings of African schooling. Formal African and Coloured Scouting would have probably collapsed in the late 1940s had it not been for the intervention of the South African Scout authorities. In 1947 the European controlling body of the SABSA assumed direct clerical responsibility for the African, Coloured, and Indian Scout organizations as an "expression of good will." Kenneth Fleischer, the SABSA's onetime representative on the old Pathfinder Council, became the full-time general secretary of the SABSA to handle the correspondence, bookkeeping, and minutes of the subbranches of the movement. N. S. Mokgoko, a professional organizing commissioner paid by the Bantu Welfare Trust and the European Transvaal Divisional Scout Council, helped him maintain supervisory control over African troops in the Transvaal. The African Scout association, which was still run by white liberals and the old African Pathfinder leadership, did not have the resources to hire commissioners to cover the rest of the Union.[8] The SABSA did not prop up African Scouting out of a commitment to the Fourth Scout Law; rather they feared a return to politically embarrassing outbreaks of unauthorized scouting if the African association collapsed.

6.1. Blind Transvaal troop greets Lord Rowallan, Chief Scout of the Empire and Commonwealth (not pictured), ca. 1950. Reproduced with permission of the Trustees of the National Library of Scotland.

SCOUTING UNDER APARTHEID, 1948–60

Southern African Scouting became more precarious after the Second World War because changing political realities in the region complicated the Scouts' ability to link themselves to institutions of political authority and social legitimacy. The Nationalist Party's rise to power in South Africa made the movement's imperial ties a considerable liability. The increasingly totalitarian nature of European minority rule in the Union and the CAF made it more difficult for the Scout leadership to adhere to the Fourth Scout Law at a time when international criticism of imperialism made their tolerance of segregation harder to defend. When the metropolitan British government began to openly consider giving up its African colonies in the late 1950s, territorial Scout associations throughout southern Africa became caught up in the efforts of local European communities to preserve their privileges through institutionalized racial discrimination.

In South Africa the Nationalists exploited popular Afrikaner dissatisfaction with the United Party's wartime support of the British Empire and general white anxiety about rising African militancy to win the 1948 elections. Hendrik Verwoerd, minister of native affairs and a future prime minister, laid out the party's commitment to strict racial segregation. Asserting that integration led to crime, slums, "tribal clashes," and assaults on European women, Verwoerd argued that rigid separation of whites and blacks would protect the cultural integrity of both communities. The "native reserves" would become "homelands" for the various South African "tribes," thereby allowing each group to develop "in accordance with their own traditions." Invoking the language of the United Nations, Verwoerd depicted apartheid as the fulfillment of the government's obligation of "Christian trusteeship" toward backward peoples.[9] These views were clearly in conflict with Scouting's commitment to universalism and egalitarianism.

The Nationalists put their segregationist ideology into practice in the 1950s by transforming race into a legal category. The apartheid laws reserved specific jobs for whites, required all adult Africans to carry reference, or "pass," books, and criminalized interracial sexual relations. The geography of apartheid divided South Africa into white and black spheres and reserved the urban centers for Europeans. The Group Areas Act empowered the government to "relocate" Africans, Coloureds, and Asians living in white areas. In practice, this meant destroying the urban communities that supported township Scouting. Those Africans fortunate enough to secure permission to remain in urban areas had to move to planned townships on the fringes of major cities.[10]

Yet even Verwoerd had to accept that African labor was vital to the South African economy. Although he argued for cultural separation, a primary purpose of the Group Areas Act was to transform the African reserves, which constituted only 13 percent of the Union, into vast labor repositories. South African industry boomed during the Second World War and replaced mining and farming as the biggest contributor to the gross national product. This growth continued into the postwar era and created a powerful demand for cheap African labor.[11] The Nationalist Party had a tacit accord with the industrialists, who were predominately English speakers, whereby the mining and industrial interests supported racial segregation in return for government assistance in keeping labor costs low.

The apartheid regime accomplished this in part by using the Group Areas Act to perpetuate the fiction that every African was the citizen of a "tribal homeland." These Bantustans, as they were more commonly known, were essentially jury-rigged rural ghettos where overpopulation, severe erosion, and overgrazing made subsistence or commercial

CHAPTER 6

agriculture a virtual impossibility. Most Bantustan residents worked in South Africa's mines, farms, and expanding industrial sector as "temporary" labor migrants. The ten Bantustans also reduced the isolation and minority status of Europeans by dividing Africans into theoretically distinct "tribal" communities.

Verwoerd and the Nationalists considered education an important tool of apartheid. They sought to refocus African schooling to produce semiskilled laborers, teach "tribal" cultures in the Bantustans, and stifle political dissent. Recognizing that they could not deny non-Europeans at least some form of literary education, they sought to ensure that Africans learned to be docile but productive contributors to the South African economy. Afrikaner education officials understood that formal schooling had the potential to turn subversive if left in the wrong hands and declared a state monopoly on "native education" in an effort to reengineer African communities according to apartheid's blueprint.

Although right-wing Afrikaners had no sympathy for the social aspirations of educated Africans, the Nationalist Party recognized that the overtaxed school system was a potential source of political subversion. Moreover, they looked to education to divide and remake the Union's African population to fit their political and economic agendas. In 1949 the Nationalists appointed a commission chaired by Dr. W. W. M. Eiselen, a prominent Afrikaner expert on African education. Eiselen's formal task was to devise a plan for "the formation of the principles and aims of education for Natives as an independent race, in which . . . their inherent racial qualities [and] their distinctive characteristics and aptitude . . . are taken into account." As minister of native affairs, Verwoerd justified the racialization of education on the grounds that it was "unhealthy" to teach Africans "white collar ideals" when they would enter European society as manual laborers.[12]

Beginning in 1953 the South African government enacted most of the Eiselen Commission's recommendations into law as the Bantu Education Act. The act ended provincial supervision of non-European schooling and put African education under the jurisdiction of the Department of Native Affairs. Five years later, the government created a separate Department of Bantu Education (DBE) to strengthen state control over the African school system. In 1963 the Division of Education within the Department of Coloured Affairs took over all state-financed Coloured schools. Similarly, the Department of Indian Affairs assumed direct responsibility for the provincial Indian schools. The Bantu Education Act reorganized African schools along ethnic lines and introduced a mandatory curriculum stressing obedience, piety, and communal loyalty. It also mandated teaching in "tribal" languages for the first four years of school, with instruction at the upper-primary level split between English and Afrikaans. In practice, a shortage of Afrikaans-speaking teachers and textbooks meant that English remained the dominant language of advanced instruction until the government's ill-considered attempts to impose Afrikaans touched off the Soweto riots in 1976. Thus, English also remained the primary language of African Scouting.[13]

Under the new education regime it became illegal to operate a school without a permit. The missions initially had the choice of running their schools without government aid or turning them over to state-directed Bantu community organizations. The African teaching staff at these schools came under direct government supervision and could be dismissed easily for disciplinary or political reasons. Few missions had the economic resources to continue without state support, and the government simply refused to register many of the surviving schools that tried to remain autonomous. As a result, the number of mission schools in the Union dropped from roughly five thousand in the early 1950s to just seven hundred in 1959.[14]

Bantu education put South African Scouting in a tenuous position. Afrikaner ideologues were openly hostile to the movement, but the Nationalist education authorities recognized its value in disciplining African students. The Eiselen Commission recommended that the DBE offer moral and financial assistance to "youth organizations" and directed state school inspectors to encourage the schools to form strong links with these groups to encourage students to make proper use of their leisure time.[15] The commission's report did not mention Scouting or Guiding by name, but it clearly did not expect African schools to begin Voortrekker groups. The Fourth Scout Law was a problem, but government educationalists were willing to tolerate, and even promote, African Scouting for as long as the SABSA maintained four racially segregated associations.

Although the South African government devoted considerable resources to these new laws, Bantu education failed to bring social and political stability to the Union. The sugar coating of apartheid as paternalism was an obvious ruse because it consigned Africans, Coloureds, and Asians to permanent underclass status. Many educated Africans who had previously been willing to work with white liberals during the interwar period now turned to direct political action. Under the ANC's 1952 Defiance Campaign over eight thousand Africans, Coloureds, and Indians refused to carry passes and "trespassed" in white areas. The ensuing government crackdown sparked unrest in major cities throughout the Union and contributed to the problems experienced by the Langa troops. Three years later, this multiracial alliance drew up a manifesto, known as the Freedom Charter, calling for a nonracial democratic South Africa. The ideals of the Freedom Charter were entirely compatible with the Scout Law, but the government responded by prosecuting its drafters for treason.

Similarly, Bantu schooling did not resolve the crisis in African education and failed to address the growing juvenile delinquency problem. The collapse of agriculture in the reserves, coupled with rapid industrialization, produced an explosive growth in urban poverty after the Second World War. Although the apartheid regime tried to check urban migration through draconian pass laws, state security forces could not prevent large numbers of Africans from illegally moving to the cities to seek work. Lacking residency permits, they settled in slums, where homelessness and low pay led to crime and politicized labor unrest. Young people were at the heart of this urban crisis. By 1957 roughly half the Africans in South Africa's cities and towns were children. Most of the older boys had either never attended school or dropped out due to financial problems or a general frustration with Bantu education. The inability of older Africans to provide a sustainable future for these children intensified the generational crisis that had been building in most communities since the turn of the twentieth century. Bantu education might have defused these tensions by offering viable opportunities for accumulation and social mobility, but many young people dropped out of school upon realizing how little educational credentials mattered in the new South Africa.[16]

The brutality of apartheid drove many boys to delinquency. Young urban males who remained outside the Bantu schools gravitated to street gangs, whose members were known as tsotsis in the 1940s and 1950s. As with the youth gangs of Dar es Salaam, the tsotsis took their lead from American gangster and cowboy movies and glorified violence and the defiance of authority. The inability of the liberal voluntary social welfare agencies to cope with this problem forced the government to take a greater interest in youth matters. Rather than improving and expanding African schooling, the apartheid regime tried to round up the urban delinquents. In practice, mass detentions and the "repatriation" of juveniles to the countryside did little to solve the problem.[17]

These problems created an opportunity for the Scouts to rebuild their ties to the government by offering at least a partial solution to the youth problem. In practice, however, the Scout authorities were in no position

6.2. South African "inter-racial" Scout rally, ca. 1950. Reproduced with permission of the Trustees of the National Library of Scotland.

to seize this opportunity. Although the European branch of the SABSA was well organized and funded, the African, Coloured, and Indian parallel branches of the association were in disarray by the close of the Second World War and were entirely unprepared to deal with the Bantu Education Act.

To be sure, Scouting was still popular with African boys. In 1949 the Eiselen Commission counted 14,885 Scouts formally enrolled in the African Boy Scout Association, the new name for the Pathfinders. Most belonged to rural troops sponsored by mission schools or urban troops funded by liberal welfare agencies and corporate donors like the Anglo American Corporation and Colgate-Palmolive-Peel, Ltd. Although many of these boys were enthusiastic Scouts, when Lord Rowallan, Baden-Powell's successor, visited South Africa in 1950 he noted that African and Coloured Scouting lacked national leadership and depended entirely on Fleischer for its survival. He found no African King's Scouts in the entire Union and only a handful of First Class Scouts. A senior British Scout official blamed this lack of progress on poor training and groused that "when in doubt, sing" was the line of least resistance taken by the majority of African Scouters.[18]

The South African Scout leadership could offer little support because they were preoccupied with building ties to the new Nationalist regime. Where the SABSA had struggled to reconcile the Fourth Scout Law with the Union's racial sensibilities in the interwar era, the 1936 Pathfinder compromise that created the four parallel branches of the movement now made Scouting doubly suspicious in the eyes of right-wing Afrikaners. Not only were the Scouts an explicitly British imperial institution, their selective "multi-racial" reading of the Fourth Scout Law was now too liberal for the strict segregationism of apartheid. In 1950, Mokgoko, the only African organizing commissioner in the Union, had to sign an affidavit swearing that he had no communist loyalties, and he was followed by the police on his rural tours.[19] It is difficult to believe that the police truly suspected that African Scouters were communists. Rather, the Scout canon had the potential to become a subversive ideology under the new apartheid regime.

Union education authorities therefore tried to make the movement a formal extension of the Bantu school curriculum. The government takeover of the mission schools disrupted established troops and robbed Scouting of the services of the priests and mission teachers, who were often the most able and enthusiastic Scoutmasters in the Union. The Bantu school boards that assumed control of the schools imposed teachers with no Scout training on surviving troops and blocked the SABSA from instructing principals and teachers on the ideals of the movement. The DBE's de-emphasis of English made it harder for African boys to understand key Scouting texts, and the Scout authorities scrambled to translate the Scout canon into vernacular languages. Finally, the South African government cut off the small trickle of state aid that had flowed to the non-European Scout associations before 1948 and made future funding contingent upon the Scouts' willingness to embrace the government's apartheid policies.[20]

The Nationalist regime's takeover of African schools might well have spelled the death of African Scouting in South Africa. It survived in the Union because Scout officials convinced suspicious government authorities that the movement was still an effective method of disciplining young

Africans. Right-wing Afrikaners had little love for Baden-Powell's movement, but they were willing to tolerate it as part of the African school curriculum. Bantu school inspectors became more receptive to Scouting by the end of the 1950s and notified school officials that it was a "recognized extra-mural activity."[21]

By comparison, the Boy's Brigade was less willing to compromise with the apartheid regime. There were only segregated European and Coloured companies in South Africa in the mid-1950s, but brigade officials in the Union, mostly churchmen, took the Bantu Education Act as a challenge and tried to revive the brigade in the African community to put "backbone into Bantu youth."[22] Their defiance reflected the missions' anger over losing their schools and their overall hostility to the ideals of apartheid. However, it was also much easier for them to stand up to the government because they had no functioning African companies left in the Union that might suffer because of their defiance.

Most African and Coloured Scouts certainly expected the South African Scout leadership to uphold the letter of the Fourth Scout Law. The SABSA's accommodationist policies put African Scouters in a difficult position. Troops in the Cape Midlands Division lost members during the Defiance Campaign when their African Scoutmasters refused to openly embrace the ANC's political goals. The Cape Western Division, which included Cape Town, experienced a similar drop in membership during the mid-1950s. Cape Scout authorities blamed these problems on the "insidious activities" of African and Coloured political leaders who charged the movement with supporting the Bantu Education Act and preparing boys to become secret policemen and government spies. The Scouts' failure to take a stand against apartheid in the Cape also drove African Scoutmasters and officials to quit. Yet the movement revived by the end of the decade when many parents concluded that Scouting's role in preventing juvenile delinquency was more important than its lack of political backbone.[23]

The controversy over Scouting and apartheid was even sharper in the Transvaal. Led by Job Rabethe, founding secretary of the Bantu Men's Social Centre and an original member of the old Pathfinder Council, the African Southern Transvaal Division broke with the SABSA in the mid-1950s when disagreements over oversight, funding, and standards led to acrimony between African and European Scouters. The Union Scout authorities worried that there were too many unsupervised African troops in the division run by unwarranted scoutmasters with no knowledge of the movement. They complained that the African Divisional Council failed to pay its dues to the SABSA but still had £1,500 to send a delegation of five Scouts to the 1957 jamboree in Britain.[24]

In early 1956, J. D. Fraser, the SABSA's general secretary, accused Rathebe, Mokgoko, and other African council members of misappropriating Scout funds. Fraser portrayed Rathebe as a dictator and pushed for greater European supervision of the African division. This was the last straw for Rathebe. As deputy chairman of African Scouting in the Transvaal, he had worked with white liberals in the YMCA and the SAIRR for over thirty years, but he finally lost patience with the white Scout establishment. Openly attacking the hypocrisy of the 1936 Pathfinder compromise, he declared that African Scouters were capable of running their own affairs without European assistance. This was a battle that Rathebe could not win in apartheid-era South Africa. Fraser branded him a "menace to Scouting" and used the threat of prosecution for embezzlement to drive him from his post in 1959.[25]

This challenge from the old Pathfinder leadership played a role in inspiring South African Scout officials to reorganize the SABSA. Worried that they were losing control of African Scouting, the Scout leadership created the position of executive chief Scout to strengthen their authority over the three subassociations. This new chief Scout presented a more integrated and unified face of South African Scouting to the world and had the power to appoint the division commissioners and headquarters staff for the African, Coloured, and Indian Scout organizations. Each racial Scout association retained a separate chief Scout, but the African, Coloured, and Indian leaders were just figureheads; in reality, the new unitary organization was largely for stricter internal control and international consumption. It did little to change the segregated nature of South African Scouting.[26]

The South African Scout establishment had to balance the necessity of appeasing the government with international pressure from African and Asian national Scout associations to fulfill their obligations under the Fourth Scout Law. Apartheid's new racial order posed a serious challenge to organized Scouting. The Group Areas Act barred African Scouters from visiting the homes of their European colleagues. The SABSA's legal advisors concluded that interracial rallies, mixed training programs for Scoutmasters, and African Scout camps run by white Scouters were still legal if held in "non-white" public areas. The Union Scout leadership claimed to oppose the apartheid laws but justified their acceptance of them on the grounds that they had to observe "the letter of the Law."[27] Many white Scouters were most worried about African political unrest,

6.3. Integrated South African contingent to the World Scout Jamboree in Britain, 1957. Courtesy of the University of Cape Town Libraries, Special Collections. Reproduced with permission of the South African Scout Association.

and were not ready to use the movement to further racial integration at the personal level.

Although they claimed to make no distinction on the grounds of "race, colour or creed," and affirmed that "A Scout is a brother to every other Scout," Scout authorities maintained that strong "social borders" in the Union made four segregated associations a necessity. The SABSA tried to avoid international condemnation by projecting a more egalitarian image to the world. It sent an integrated delegation to the 1957 World Scout Jamboree in Britain and was relieved not to face "difficult questioning and criticism" of their racial policies from fellow Scouters. The image of racial harmony projected by the mixed delegation fooled no one in South Africa. Although the European leaders of the African association declared the jamboree a success, most of the white boys in the delegation resisted mixing with nonwhites and quit after returning to South Africa.[28]

Moreover, the integrated jamboree delegation was open fraud, and the SABSA had few allies in international Scouting. When Thurman visited the Union in 1960, the Scout authorities forced him to eat separately from the African Scouters he was training lest he be arrested for dining in mixed company. Thurman was not impressed and shared meals with his African students. Daniel Marivate, an African deputy camp chief, was deeply appreciative: "I have sat next to my Chief and eaten with him and my people will be happy to know that. I cannot go to Gilwell as our laws do not permit it, but you have brought Gilwell to me."[29] Clearly, the appeal and potency of the Fourth Scout Law under apartheid stemmed from more than just the right to camp with members of other races.

SCOUTING IN CENTRAL AFRICA

Apartheid put the neighboring British colonies and protectorates in a difficult position. Their strong links to South Africa meant that Afrikaner nationalists had the opportunity to dominate, and possibly absorb, the Rhodesias, Nyasaland, and the High Commission Territories. Colonial officials worried that apartheid might become an even greater international embarrassment by spreading to the British protectorates in the region. In 1953, Britain therefore linked Nyasaland and the Rhodesias in the Central African Federation to create a more viable economic and political unit to balance the Union's influence in southern Africa.[30] British officials kept Basutoland, Swaziland, and Bechuanaland out of the CAF, but the Nationalist Party's 1948 electoral victory ended the possibility that the High Commission Territories might eventually become part of the Union. British administrators had little choice but to set the protectorates on the path to self-government and independence as apartheid became more invasive in the 1960s.

In creating the CAF the British government paid little heed to the concerns of Africans in Northern Rhodesia and Nyasaland who did not want to be governed by the Southern Rhodesia settlers. African delegates boycotted the Lancaster House conferences that drafted the federal constitution, and many of the official celebrations scheduled by the Nyasaland and Northern Rhodesian authorities to mark the birth of the CAF in 1953 turned into riots. British officials promised that the federation's constitution would protect African rights and hoped to win African support by reducing racially discriminatory legislation and fostering the growth of a cooperative African middle class.[31] As in East Africa, their "multi-racialism" created opportunities for the Scouts to curry official support by teaching interracial cooperation and loyalty to the colonial regime. In practice, the Southern Rhodesian settlers blocked imperial efforts to promote social

Table 6.1. The Education Pyramid in the Central African Federation

	Total Students	Secondary School Students	Secondary School Graduates Passing the Cambridge Overseas School Certificate
Southern Rhodesia, 1949	223,918	344	37
Northern Rhodesia, 1951	161,061	248	12
Nyasaland, 1950	219,667	162	6

Source: Lord Arthur Hailey, An African Survey (London: Oxford University Press, 1957), p. 1165.

mobility for Westernized Africans. As a result, most people in Nyasaland and Northern Rhodesia remained passionately opposed to the Federation.

These political tensions had a direct impact on education policy in central Africa. Colonial officials and educators sought to use education to promote "multi-racialism" within the framework of the CAF by demonstrating that the empire could serve African interests. Moreover, economic necessity created a need for African teachers, artisans, veterinarians, and clerks to lower the costs of colonial rule. Yet African schooling remained largely unchanged in the 1950s. Primary and secondary African education in the CAF remained a territorial responsibility under the federal constitution. On the eve of federation, in the early 1950s, only several hundred students reached the secondary level in the Central African territories, with a just a fraction of these passing the Cambridge Overseas School Exam (table 6.1). This educational bottleneck exposed the hypocrisy of multiracialism. Africans would never achieve parity with the European community when the settlers could use African primitiveness as an excuse not to share political power.[32]

The failings of central African schooling stemmed primarily from the legacy of earlier misguided experiments in adapted and technical education that stunted literary secondary schooling. In Southern Rhodesia the missions still ran most rural African schools with state grants providing roughly 70 percent of their operating costs. In 1951 the government assumed direct responsibility for urban schools but left the education of children in the countryside to the overtaxed and underfunded missions. Roughly 65 percent of African children were in school by the mid-1950s, but they were overwhelmingly concentrated in the lower primary grades. In Northern Rhodesia, the Munali Training Centre in Lusaka was the only African institution in the territory offering a full secondary curriculum in the late 1940s, but it retained a focus on industrial schooling. Most children in the territory still attended rudimentary bush schools. It was only on the Copperbelt, where colonial officials worried about the danger of rootless and unsupervised African youth, that the government provided free and mandatory primary education for all African children.[33]

In Nyasaland government educators deemed a liberal arts education too expensive and irrelevant to the needs of most of the population and focused instead on developing African commercial agriculture. In 1951 the Nyasaland Education Department's primary school syllabus still devoted twice as much time to "rural science and handcrafts" as it did to spoken and written English. Nevertheless, the Nyasaland authorities drew up a postwar development program calling for universal primary and expanded secondary education by 1960. Yet, as in most British colonies, these ambitious plans faltered in the early 1950s due to budget problems and a shortage of qualified teachers.[34]

The failings of the Nyasaland school reforms were typical of the education problems that beset the Central African Federation. Although the CAF did not experience juvenile delinquency on the South African scale, by the late 1950s its schools had to cope with frustrated African students who opposed the federation's backward education policies. As in East and South Africa, these tensions created an opportunity for the Scouts to strengthen their ties to the government by promising to bring a measure of social and political stability to the restless younger African generation. Yet racial segregation also complicated Scouting in the CAF and the High Commission Territories. White Scout officials in the Rhodesias were no more willing than their South African counterparts to adhere to the spirit of the Fourth Scout Law. Their segregationist sentiments even carried into Nyasaland, where European Scouting was virtually nonexistent. Nevertheless, Britain's federation of the three territories made it harder for the Rhodesian settlers to defend rigid social segregation. The CAF's embrace of multiracialism put pressure on Scout authorities in the Rhodesias to combine the African and European branches of their movement into single territorial associations. Throughout the 1950s, European Scouters sought a balance between their commitment to social segregation and pressure from British authorities and international Scouting to follow the Fourth Scout Law more closely. Conversely, Scout leaders in the High Commission Territories were critical of segregated Scouting and distanced themselves from the better-funded and -organized South African and Rhodesian Scout associations.

Scouting in Southern Rhodesia virtually collapsed during the war due to financial and leadership problems. African Scouting, or Pathfinding as it was still known in the territory until 1948, continued on at mission schools without much oversight. As in Kenya, government and Scout officials worried about the potentially subversive activities of these largely independent "unwieldy [and] inefficient troops." Rhodesian Scout leaders revived the formal movement after the war but insisted on a segregated "African branch." The African and European organizations maintained separate organizing commissioners and training programs. White Scouters insisted that they could not adhere to the letter of the Fourth Scout Law because Africans would lower the overall standards of Scouting in the territory. A district Pathfindermaster at Que-Que typified this kind of thinking and made openly racist remarks about his African Scouts.[35]

These prejudices were harder to defend as Southern Rhodesia prepared to join the Central African Federation. European Scout leaders rewrote their constitution in 1950 to create a single Rhodesian Boy Scout Association. The CAF's multiracial legitimizing philosophy created an opportunity for the Scouts to build ties with the government by disciplining advanced students. In 1951 the RBSA asked for state funds to hire paid African organizing commissioners and to include Scouting in the formal school curriculum to provide "character training" for African students. Southern Rhodesian educators were far less enthusiastic about the pedagogical value of the movement and rejected the RBSA's proposal on the grounds that Scouting was a voluntary movement. Moreover, many white Scouters believed that it was premature to treat Africans as equals, and they did their best to keep the movement as segregated as possible. Certain that the Scouts should not get ahead of European public opinion, the chief commissioner of the African branch resigned his position in 1958 to protest the RBSA's qualified embrace of integration.[36]

European Scouters in Northern Rhodesia were equally unwilling to bring the Fourth Scout Law into conflict with the color bar. Although the Pathfinders won the right to call themselves Scouts in 1946, the territory had a separate Scout council and chief commissioner for each racial branch of the movement. The liaison committee that was supposed to coordinate policy between the two factions never met. F. J. H. Dahl found the African branch to be the stronger of the two and considered the Reverend David Maxwell Robertson's troop at the Chalimbana Jeanes School to be the best in the colony. European Scouters on the Copperbelt were the strongest opponents of integration, and Dahl considered that many of the white leaders of African troops in the mining compounds to be conceited and arrogant tyrants. Despite the African lead in Scouting, European officials justified segregation on the grounds that Africans could not grasp the meaning of the Scout Law and Promise. These sentiments complicated the plans for the CAF, and the Northern Rhodesian governor pushed the Scouts to create a single territorial association. In the 1950s the Scout leadership finally combined the two branches at the administrative level but kept individual troops strictly segregated. Nevertheless, Reverend Robertson became the chief commissioner for the new association.[37]

The Northern Rhodesian government was more supportive of African Scouting than was its southern counterpart. Colonial officials were particularly worried that unsupervised boys and teenagers on the Copperbelt might provoke more strikes and riots in the mining compounds. First, they tried experimental mandatory "community service camps" to give secondary school students "character training" through manual labor on public works projects. Although education officers made these camps relatively popular through recreation and a Scout-type program, they reached only schoolboys. Government officials hoped that Scouting would serve nonstudents on the Copperbelt. In 1950 they approached the Scouts with an offer of state funding to expand their African operations. In a reversal of the negotiations that played out in virtually every other British colony, Robertson was actually hesitant to accept the grant because he worried the salaries of European organizing commissioners would take money away from African troops. The director of African education convinced him to accept a greater official role for African Scouting on pedagogical grounds. Northern Rhodesian education experts believed that the movement would counter detribalization and made sure that every African teacher received some Scout training.[38]

Robertson was unique among European Scout leaders in anglophone Africa in that he held that the movement could and should act as an agent of social change. Arguing that "we must lead public opinion, not wait for it," he pushed for fully integrated Scout councils, training camps, and rallies. Although he stopped short of proposing interracial troops, he declared that "there is no room for any such thing as the 'colour bar' in Scouting. The last vestige of it must go as soon as possible if we are to make Scouting what it should be in this country." Robertson made little headway in winning over the Northern Rhodesian settlers, but his willingness to challenge social conventions in the territory illustrates that it was possible to embrace the Fourth Scout Law without jeopardizing the movement's relationship with the colonial state. In 1954 the government counted 4,598 African Scouts in the colony. The fact that Africans outnumbered Europeans in the movement by roughly seven to one certainly made it easier for Robertson to make his principled stand.[39]

African Scouting in postwar Nyasaland had fewer complications. Despite the extensive political influence of a small but vocal settler community, the protectorate was very much an "African country." European Scouting was limited, and the colonial government embraced the movement to discipline students and promote loyalty to the empire. In 1948, Nyasaland's chief secretary directed his provincial commissioners to support Scouting. The Nyasaland Boy Scout Association (NBSA) drew up a formal constitution that same year, and influential European planters endorsed the association's request for state funding for an organizing commissioner. The NBSA therefore enjoyed close ties with the territorial administration, and two years later, the protectorate allocated £1,500 to the Scouts and £200 to the Girl Guides. This official support helped African Scouting in Nyasaland expand nearly tenfold between 1948 and 1960. Ida Kiswigho Ndovie's informants, who joined the movement during this period, attributed this rapid growth to Scouting's role in the elite school curriculum and the appeal of marching and outdoor activities. Its ties to colonial institutions of authority conferred respect on uniformed Scouts and made it prestigious to be a member of the movement. Strong government support made Scouting a central extracurricular activity at the best secondary schools, and the Nyasaland battalions of the King's African Rifles ran troops in the barracks for soldiers' children.[40]

However, Scouting also faced a more significant challenge from the Boy's Brigade in Nyasaland that it did in the East African colonies. Dahl found the Scottish missions "very, very cool" to his movement because the Presbyterians were strong Brigade supporters. By the late 1950s there were over thirty companies at mission schools throughout the protectorate, plus an additional company at the Mkhoma teacher-training college. Nevertheless, the Boy's Brigade had limited appeal among the general populace because many parents suspected that its focus on drilling made it a military institution. Others asked if it was, in the words of a frustrated Brigade organizer, "a kind of dance or concert party." This may also indicate that people associated the Brigade with malipenga (trumpet), a local version of the Beni dance societies that satirized Scouting on the East African coast.[41]

British officials in Nyasaland favored Scouting over the Boy's Brigade as a tool of colonial administration and used the movement to co-opt

African political leaders. In 1948 the protectorate's Scout Council included an African member from each province in addition to representatives from the missions and colonial administration. Even J. F. Sangala, a key figure in the Nyasaland African Congress and a strong critic of the colonial regime, did not turn down a personal invitation from the governor to join the council. Yet there were distinct limits to Scouting's egalitarianism in Nyasaland. The NBSA's supposedly interracial training courses and camps maintained segregated bathing, dining, sleeping, and latrine accommodations for African, Indian, and European Scouters.[42] In other words, the small European population in the protectorate allowed Nyasaland Scouting to appear more egalitarian than it actually was, and the NBSA's segregated Woodbadge courses more accurately reflected the true racial sentiments of the Nyasaland Scout leadership.

The failure of official Scouting to abide fully by the Fourth Scout Law helps explain why African Scouts joined the widespread protests against the Central African Federation in 1953. Officially, each territorial association embraced the federation to maintain ties with political authority in the region. The Scouts created the position of chief Scout commissioner for the CAF and made the federal governor their ceremonial chief Scout. They also sponsored federal jamborees to bring together African Scouts from the three territories.[43] Many Africans therefore considered the Scouts active accomplices in the federation plans.

Urged on by their parents, large numbers of Scouts embarrassed their European Scoutmasters by boycotting the 1954 ceremonies in Nyasaland and Northern Rhodesia celebrating Queen Elizabeth's coronation one year earlier. School officials in Northern Rhodesia fired African teacher-Scoutmasters for their role in the protests at Broken Hill, and students at the Lubwa mission defaced coronation medals and uprooted the school's special coronation tree. The Nyasaland Boy Scout Association faced similar problems and disbanded several African troops that joined the boycott. Interestingly, the Nyasaland Boy's Brigade declined to take part in the coronation ceremonies to avoid becoming embroiled in the political controversy over the CAF, and brigade officials criticized the protectorate government for trying to use the queen to force the African population to accept federation. The Nyasaland Scout authorities blamed their problems on "impudence and unjust criticism" from African parents. Concluding that the trouble had passed by the end of 1954, they consoled themselves that the African Scouts who stayed in the movement were more reliable than the feckless boys who had quit for political reasons.[44]

With the exception of rare individuals like David Maxwell Robertson, most European Scouters took their lead from colonial officials. Anxious to preserve their links to the institutions of political authority and legitimacy, they shaped Scouting to suit the needs of the state. In the High Commission Territories, however, political trends in the 1950s favored African autonomy. As a result, European Scout leaders in Basutoland, Swaziland, and Bechuanaland adopted a stricter interpretation of the Fourth Scout Law. Bechuanaland Scouters, who had warily accepted the South African Pathfinder model in the interwar years, became harsh critics of segregated Scouting in the Union. Jack Leech, a government welfare officer and divisional Scout commissioner in Bechuanaland, declared, "If South African Scouts are not prepared to accept the principles and ideals of the Movement in them entirely [sic], there should be no Scouts in South Africa." Leech scorned the SABSA's attempts to reach an accommodation with the Afrikaner nationalists, and declared "condoning apartheid is obnoxious." The last straw broke for Leech in 1951 when European employees of the Public Works Department secured the South African association's help in starting a segregated Cub Scout pack for their sons in Bechuanaland's capital, Gaberones. Worried that Bechuana parents would see this as an attempt to export apartheid to the protectorate, Leech transformed Bechuanaland Scouting from a subordinate division of the SABSA into an autonomous organization. Although Scouting in the protectorate could not escape its affiliation with South Africa, Leech made it clear that the South Africans' failure to abide by the Scout canon was the sole reason for the de facto break.[45]

Scout authorities in Swaziland and Basutoland, who were also technically part of the SABSA, followed Leech's lead in severing working ties with South African Scouting. Swaziland, which had the only significant settler population of the three territories, merged its African and European branches in late 1951. Interestingly, the Scout leadership's principled stand in the High Commission Territories did not lead to a jump in African membership. In the 1950s, Swaziland had approximately two hundred fifty African Scouts, Basutoland one thousand, and Bechuanaland two thousand. Although African boys in the three territories were less likely to be suspicious of Scouting as a colonial institution, the movement still suffered from an adult leadership shortage and dependence on the schools for funding and institutional support. Ironically, Scouting was probably less appealing after the territories repudiated apartheid and laid the groundwork for independence. The Fourth Scout Law was far less significant and controversial once the threat of overt racial discrimination receded.[46]

African resistance to apartheid in South Africa had more dire consequences. Hardcore Afrikaner nationalists regarded even the mildest forms of nonviolent protest as a serious threat to white privilege and political authority. In March 1960 the security forces responded to the Pan-African Congress's anti–pass law campaign by massacring sixty-seven unarmed protestors in the Transvaal township of Sharpeville. In response, thousands of apartheid's opponents marched on the South African parliament in Cape Town. The government called out the army reserves to undertake mass arrests and outlawed the ANC and the more radical Pan-African Congress.[47] Sharpeville demonstrated the limits of passive resistance and convinced many in the ANC that apartheid could be defeated only by military means. Although the government arrested Nelson Mandela and much of the ANC's senior leadership, younger nationalists waged an intermittent guerrilla struggle against the apartheid regime for the next thirty years.

The Sharpeville murders marked the beginning of South Africa's status as a pariah state, which placed the liberal backers of African Scouting in a difficult position. By continuing to emphasize gradual social change through economic growth after Sharpeville, they lost most of their credibility with the ANC and like-minded African nationalists. Few in the liberal, largely English-speaking establishment were willing to challenge the economic bases of the apartheid state. Many South African liberals worried about mass African unrest and continued to believe that the long-term solution to the Union's racial tensions lay in Westernizing and modernizing "tribal" Africans.[48] Their gradualist program became increasingly irrelevant as the apartheid regime grew more brutal. Faced with harsh condemnation from India, Canada, and newly independent African states, the Afrikaner nationalists withdrew from the commonwealth to give themselves total autonomy in solving their "racial question." The South African government's declaration of a republic in 1961 deepened the liberals' isolation by severing ties with Britain, thereby making interracial compromise even more unlikely.

South Africa's political isolation had few immediate consequences as rising foreign investment from Europe and the United States sparked an economic boom in the 1960s. Low-cost, semiskilled African labor made mining and industry increasingly profitable. The South African government tried to tailor Bantu education to address these new political and economic realities, but the inherent structural failings of the apartheid regime's education policies made this impossible. There was little money for African education because the Bantu Education Act made African taxes the primary source of funding for African education and direct government grants to the schools remained frozen at 1950s levels. As a result, the Department of Bantu Education ran an annual deficit of R2 million by 1968. Yet Bantu education did substantially expand the scope of African education. Enrollment levels increased steadily throughout the 1950s and 1960s, thus demonstrating the importance of education to the apartheid regime. By the 1960s, South African industry needed black semiskilled machine operators with at least four years of primary education. Most of these students came from urban primary schools, which the DBE authorities grudgingly expanded to meet the republic's economic needs.[49]

In the short term the South African government won over some African parents by making schooling more accessible, particularly in urban areas, where families with residency rights looked on the schools as a refuge from urban violence and delinquency. Yet the DBE shortened the school day, increased the student-teacher ratio, and lowered academic standards across the board. In 1961 less than 3 percent of African teachers had a teaching degree or professional qualification and only 53 percent held even a lower-primary school certificate. By transferring the bulk of the costs of education from the state to parents, the new system kept the African schools chronically underfunded. As a result, urban juvenile delinquency remained a significant problem under the Republic. In 1955 only 10 percent of Africans under the age of eighteen were in school and, despite the success of the government in expanding the scope of African education, just 21 percent were enrolled in 1975. Disdaining their elders for failing to stand up to the racist state, many teenagers turned either to political activism or to juvenile delinquency.[50]

African Scouting therefore had to operate in an increasingly tense environment. The Afrikaner nationalists' decision to make South Africa into a republic complicated the Scouts' relationship with the state. Loyalty to the British Crown and the Union Jack were originally a central focus of the Scout Law and Promise in South Africa. These tenets of the Scout canon became political liabilities once the Nationalist Party broke with Britain. The SABSA was far more troubled by the political necessity of severing their ties with the Crown than it was by its pragmatic decision to water down the Fourth Scout Law to avoid coming into conflict with apartheid.

The Scout leadership became fully aware of the magnitude of their political problems in the late 1950s. The South African Scout Council tried to avoid provoking the government by dropping the Union Jack and "God Save the Queen" from its Tenderfoot tests. These overtly "imperial" requirements offended Afrikaner sensibilities and complicated the Scouts' relationship with the state education system. Moreover, the Scout Council's legal advisors warned that the use of the Union Jack violated the 1957 revisions of the Flag Act, which outlawed flying the British flag on government buildings. These modifications to the core of the Scout canon touched off a bitter internal debate within the SABSA between those who wanted to preserve the original versions of the Scout Law and Promise and those who argued for political pragmatism. The latter faction carried the day and in 1958 the SABSA dropped most of its references to the queen with the rationalization that accommodation between white English and Afrikaans speakers was for the ultimate good of European boys. Needless to say, the African branch of the movement bitterly opposed these changes, and most African troops changed their programs to de-emphasize the symbols of political authority in South Africa. They particularly wanted to avoid replacing "Nkosi Sikelel i Afrika" (God Bless Africa) with "Die Stem," the Afrikaners' new state anthem.[51]

The Scouts' concessions did not bring about a rapprochement between the SABSA and the South African government. Throughout the 1950s each of the Nationalist Party's prime ministers refused to become the ceremonial chief Scout of the Union. The Voortrekkers also declined the Scouts' invitation to cooperate on youth-related projects. Lt. Col. A. H. Johnstone, the SABSA's executive chief Scout, complained that the Afrikaner community treated the Scouts like a banned organization and unsuccessfully petitioned Prime Minister Verwoerd to meet with him personally so that he could explain that Scouting made Africans and Coloureds "better citizens . . . in a multi-racial society." Johnstone vainly hoped to persuade Verwoerd to make a public statement that the Scouts were not "un-national" and that white parents should let their sons join the movement.[52]

These snubs did not dissuade the SABSA from its determination to rebuild its ties to the South African state. In 1961 it further modified the Scout canon after South Africa became a republic. Brushing aside earlier concerns, the association dropped remaining references to the queen from the Scout Law and Promise. Coming on the heels of the Sharpeville massacre, these concessions cost the SABSA much of its African support. The British Scout Association assumed formal responsibility for Scouting in the High Commission Territories, and African troops in the Transvaal and Cape Province collapsed as parents withdrew their sons from what they now considered a "racialist" institution.[53]

Most of the remaining senior leadership of the old Pathfinder movement also broke with the South African Scout establishment during this period. In 1961 the South African government banned J. A. Calata, an Anglican bishop and the African commissioner of the Cape Midlands Scout Division, for showing public support for the now outlawed African National Congress. Although Calata was a former secretary general of the ANC who had been tried and acquitted for treason in the 1950s, he remained active in Scouting until this point. Lord Rowallan considered him one of the ablest Scouters in South Africa, but Calata also employed Scouting for political purposes by keeping in touch with key Cape Province African leaders through the divisional Scout organization. The SABSA refused to come to his rescue when he ran afoul of the security forces and was relieved that newspaper accounts of his banning did not link him with the movement.[54]

To be sure, some European Scouters genuinely disapproved of the compromises they had to make to operate under the apartheid regime. Colin Inglis, the chief Scout who would oversee the integration of the SABSA in the 1970s, maintained that although it was necessary for the movement not to get too far ahead of public opinion, most Scout leaders personally disliked the political status quo in the republic. The SABSA did its best to convey this distaste to its peers in the international Scout community. In presenting an award to Lord Rowallan in 1959, a Union Scout official declared, "He who confuses South African politics with South African Scouting could only do so from ignorance or malice." Yet some Scouters also clearly sympathized with the goals of apartheid, and the African association's leaders complained that European Scoutmasters often made loud derogatory comments about African Scouts.[55]

The SABSA never openly challenged the South African government's apartheid policies in the 1960s. In 1965, European Scout troops took part in a national jamboree honoring the creation of the republic. African troops were not invited and instead "expressed their love of their country" by collecting litter and building drinking fountains for birds. That same year, the Scout authorities refused to act on the SAIRR's plea to sue Cape Town's town clerk before the Supreme Court for his refusal to issue a permit for an interracial Scout gathering. The commissioner for the European Natal Scout Division considered that it would have been "fatal" to openly oppose the government, and he asserted that segregated Scout rallies did not conflict with the ideals of the movement.[56]

As in the interwar era, the South African Girl Guide Association was generally more willing to take a stand against racial segregation. Where the SABSA used the government's refusal to issue permits for interracial functions as an excuse to duck the Fourth Scout law, the Guides simply held their rallies without official permission. Much of their backbone came from Lady Baden-Powell, who served as chief Guide of the world until her death in 1977. She openly antagonized right-wing Afrikaner politicians in 1969 by insisting on inspecting a mixed gathering of African and European Guides. Unlike the Scouts, the Guide association refused to ask for state funding because had the funds been granted, the state would have required the group to follow the apartheid laws more closely. The Guides developed programs like the Guide Friendship Badge, which required a girl to meet a person from another racial group, learn common greetings and twenty-five other words in that community's language, and describe their customs and basic foods. The Guides were still neither brave nor farsighted enough to push for integrated companies, but their willingness to stand up to the apartheid regime undermined the Scouts' assertion that challenging official segregation would have been fatal.[57]

The SABSA retained the parallel-association model laid out in the Pathfinder compromise until the mid-1970s. The African, Coloured, and Indian Scout associations each had their own ceremonial chief Scout commissioners but remained firmly under the direction of the European association. Coloured Scouting was essentially divided between Cape Town and Johannesburg. Lord Rowallan admired the high standards of Cape Scouts in 1950, but eleven years later John Thurman criticized the low quality of Coloured Scouting in Johannesburg. These divisions stemmed from cultural tensions in the Coloured community and a general political disagreement over how to confront the apartheid state. Most of the Transvaal Coloured troops registered with the African association and rejected the SABSA's attempts to get them to accept official supervision and training. Coloured Scouts in the Cape, however, were generally more willing to cooperate with the government and accepted state funding from the commissioner for Coloured affairs. In 1971 three Coloured Cape Scouts won government money to attend the world jamboree in Japan by demonstrating their "loyalty and devotion to South Africa." In return, the Coloured chief Scout commissioner promised the commissioner for Coloured affairs that he could call on the Scouts to "assist in work connected with the cultural uplift of Coloureds."[58]

Indian Scouting was based almost entirely in Natal. There was no Indian chief Scout commissioner or national headquarters council for most of the apartheid years, and the provincial Natal Indian Scout Association essentially ran the movement under the republic. As in the interwar era, the Indian Scouts insisted on segregating themselves from Africans to claim greater social and political privileges as a "civilized" people. They refused to join the Pathfinders and were originally satisfied to become Scouts under the terms of the 1936 compromise. By the 1960s, however, Indian Scouts chafed under the direction of the European association. Some charged that Scouting had become a "platform to propagate Christianity" and were more open in using the movement to attack legal segregation. Nevertheless, the Indian association also accepted direct funding from the Indian Affairs Department.[59]

African Scouting, on the other hand, posed a much bigger problem for the SABSA. Granting Africans greater, if not equal, status within South African Scouting had broad political implications under apartheid because full Scout status implied full citizenship. The African association was therefore the only Scout organization that did not receive some state funding. Nevertheless, African Scouting quickly recovered from the political turmoil of the early 1960s. Not only did Scouting's egalitarian ideology stand as an obvious challenge to government-sponsored segregation, it still conferred a measure of sophistication and self-respect on its members. Ironically, rising African membership numbers posed a political problem for the South African Scout authorities. With South African Scouting on tenuous ground under the republic, Scout officials again worried about unsupervised and unofficial troops in the countryside. These troops had no ties to the SABSA and were unaffected by the backlash against official Scouting after Sharpeville. Some groups numbered over two hundred members but could not provide their boys with scout badges, much less uniforms. Many were little more than marching bands and lacked the resources, training, and inclination to follow a formal Scout curriculum. The Scout establishment worried that these unofficial scouts might embarrass the movement politically by getting caught up in the protests against apartheid or supporting the banned ANC.[60]

Technically the African association was responsible for supervising unstructured rural troops and ensuring that they did not tarnish the reputation of South African Scouting. However, most of the original African Pathfinder leadership had quit the movement by 1961, and in reality the African association was a handful of European administrators based at the national Headquarters Scout Council. The Group Areas Act made it difficult for them to oversee African troops, and they barely understood what was going on in the townships or the countryside. There were a few strong African divisional councils in the association but by the mid-1960s most African divisions had either collapsed or depended on European funding and leadership to remain active. Therefore the SABSA had little direct influence over African Scouting. The logical solution was to hire paid African organizing commissioners to supervise these troops and train their leaders in proper Scouting methods. But this was impossible once the South African government denied the movement funding. In 1964 the entire SABSA depended on private donations and interest on investments and was running in the red. Many African Scout divisions lacked the resources to run even the simplest programs.[61]

Despite these problems the SABSA raised enough money from private individuals, the Baden-Powell Memorial Fund, and business and mining interests to fund a new training program targeting the unofficial rural troops. The Scout leadership's primary goal was to shut down any unregistered group that failed to pay its dues or meet minimal Scout standards. They also hoped to co-opt the leaders of promising troops through Scoutmaster training courses. The SABSA drew up a shortened and simplified Scout curriculum for these troops that was based theoretically on the "African outlook and way of life." It hoped that the revised Scout tests would make Scouting a "practical possibility for the African boy, without lowering standards." In practice, most African Scouts viewed the training program as a reversion to the failed interwar policies of adaptation. They insisted on a full European Scout curriculum to demonstrate that they were entitled to equal status within the movement and, by extension, South African society on the whole.[62]

The primary burden of implementing the new training program fell on a small cadre of African field organizing commissioners. In 1961 the SABSA's development plan called for a national commissioner and one field commissioner each for the Natal, Southern Transvaal, and Orange Free State Scout divisions. It also left open the possibility of hiring commissioners for the Cape Border, Cape Midlands, and Transkei divisions. The commissioners' responsibilities included registering and monitoring rural Scout groups, meeting with key African Scout personalities, courting local political figures and Bantu education authorities, and recruiting new Scout leaders. In fulfilling these duties as national commissioner, Micksey N'thaba, who got his name from the American cowboy movie star Tom Mix, covered over three thousand miles a year by car, public transportation, and foot. John Thurman considered him the best African

Scouter in South Africa, but N'thaba's health suffered as he struggled to live up to the grueling expectations of his job. Only Mack Omega Shange, the commissioner for Natal and a strong advocate of African Scouting there, was up to N'thaba's standards. Most other African field commissioners were ineffectual, and the Scout authorities fired several over the course of the 1960s for lack of initiative and financial improprieties. The SABSA never raised enough money to fully fund their salaries, which averaged roughly half what an African teacher earned. The field commissioners received a minimal allowance for the long periods they spent away from home. They also faced continual harassment from the security forces. The police in the Transkei arrested N'thaba in 1964 on the suspicion that he was an "undesirable and political intimidator."[63]

From the standpoint of the SABSA, Shange and N'thaba presented the ideal face of African Scouting. They were personally and passionately committed to raising the standards of African troops and improving rural African society as a whole, and they had no patience for African Scoutmasters who did not take their jobs seriously. Both men were more than willing to shut down a poorly run troop. N'thaba expelled a Port Elizabeth Scoutmaster for "unscoutingly escapades," which may have referred to political or criminal activities, and for refusing to follow the "advice" of the national Scout headquarters. "I have since taken this drastic measure to bring him down on his knees only to make him realise his responsibility to the church authority and the Movement."[64] N'thaba's reference to church authority reflects that many of the most committed African Scouters were also devoutly religious.

These commissioners were powerful promoters of Scouting. After interrogating N'thaba for the Orange Free State police, an African security officer enraged his white colonel by asking permission to become a Scoutmaster. Yet neither N'thaba nor Shange were political radicals. Shange had close ties with Inkatha in the 1970s but remained relatively apolitical when he was in a Scout uniform. N'thaba was even more circumspect in telling the European press that while his primary goal was a "non-racial" South African Scout association, "I would not want to rush it, just to see it develop gradually."[65] This was exactly how the SABSA wanted the public and the international Scout authorities to interpret their attempts to keep the movement alive under apartheid.

Nevertheless, N'thaba, Shange, and their less able peers had considerable difficulty implementing the SABSA's approved version of African Scouting. DBE authorities presented a particular problem. In 1962 schools sponsored all but one of the registered troops in the Southern Transvaal

Division. School boards and principals considered Scouting part of the curriculum and vied with the SABSA for control of the movement. Teacher-Scoutmasters ran their troops as classes and refused to sacrifice their free time to Scouting. School authorities also seized funds raised by troops through the Bob-a-Job program. The SABSA instructed its field commissioners to deregister troops that became extensions of the school curriculum, but in practice there was little they could do to compel principals and teachers to follow the official guidelines of the movement. N'thaba and Shange also often had their work undone by the Group Areas Act. Some of their best troops disappeared when the security forces uprooted entire communities from "white areas" in the cities and the countryside.[66]

Shange had the greatest success among his own Zulu community. The original scarf clasp that marked the completion of the Woodbadge training course for Scoutmasters was made up of beads that Baden-Powell claimed to have taken from a twelve-foot-long necklace belonging to King Dinizulu. Official Scout lore held that the Zulu royal family demanded the necklace's return until they learned that the Scouts used the beads as symbols of loyalty and bravery. Scout authorities in Natal played up this ethnic connection during the interwar era, and John Thurman remarked that Dinizulu's Woodbadge beads were a "passport to anything one wants from the Zulus." By the 1960s many Natal troops included Zulu dancing and "war cries" in their programs. The Scouts' embrace of "Zulu tradition" played into the hands of Zulu intellectuals and nationalists, who sought to use Zulu ethnic symbols to acquire political and social authority under apartheid. Beginning in the 1930s, they tried to convince the South African government to recognize Dinizulu's son Solomon as the Zulu paramount chief. Scouting's celebration and valorization of all things Zulu served these goals nicely. In 1966, Shange invested Cyrian Bhekuzulu Nyangayizwe, Dinizulu's grandson, as a Scout in a public ceremony at the Zulu royal kraal before an audience of fifteen hundred Zulu Scouts and five thousand members of the local community. Shange had the full backing of the Department of Bantu Affairs, and after Chief Nyangayizwe died, the Zulu Scout commissioner convinced Prince Goodwill Zewlithini to replace him as the official patron of African Scouting in Natal. These official ties made Shange's job much easier, and by 1974 the 13,343 officially enrolled Zulu Scouts accounted for 45 percent of the entire African membership of the SABSA.[67]

By comparison, urban African Scouting waxed and waned during the 1960s and early 1970s. The SABSA won support and funding for African

6.4. Mack Omega Shange (left) invests King Cyrian Bhekuzulu Nyangayizwe as a Scout, 1965. Courtesy of the University of Cape Town Libraries, Special Collections. Reproduced with permission of the South African Scout Association.

troops in the cities and mining compounds by portraying the movement as a tool for promoting labor stabilization, strengthening student discipline, and combating juvenile delinquency. In the early 1960s several corporations in Johannesburg and Durban sponsored Scout troops and Rover crews to provide structured leisure activities for their African workers. Similarly, municipal governments, social welfare experts, and urban principals looked to Scouting as a partial solution to youth unrest. N'thaba promised the African community of Port Elizabeth: "If parents and teachers keep the movement alive, many boys will be saved. More will attend church services and school. There will be less lawlessness in the townships and better hope for a responsible community." Supervision of urban troops was less of a problem, but N'thaba was overpromising. Scouting was popular in urban schools but could not compete with the tsotsis on the streets. Urban gangs still vied with the Scouts for members and also taught physical toughness and self-respect. The tsotsis, however, rejected the authority of their elders and celebrated alcohol, drugs, violence, and an aggressive conceptualization of masculinity. They harassed uniformed Scouts, stole their Bob-a-Job money and, in many cases, monopolized the available young women. Urban students valued Scouting for its respectability and sophistication, but most township boys could not afford to belong to a troop and saw little reason to submit to the movement's conformist code of discipline.[68]

But the European community also had a juvenile delinquency problem in the 1960s. Social and cultural dislocation stemming from South Africa's rapid postwar industrialization and urbanization also led rootless young white men to form violent gangs and flout the symbols of social conformity. Neither European Scouting nor the Voortrekkers made headway in drawing these white "ducktails" (a name based on their favorite hairstyle) back into the realm of respectability. The Voortrekkers in particular faced a significant membership decline in the 1960s. The European Scouts and Guides outnumbered the coed Afrikaner movement fifty thousand to thirty thousand. Pieter le Rux recalls that his Afrikaner peers were more interested in listening to popular music from Mozambique than joining a uniformed youth group. High school students who stayed in the movement faced the mocking chant: "Voortrekkers, Voortrekkers, Draadtrekkers." The latter term was a play on the Afrikaans phrase om draad te trek, meaning "to masturbate." Clearly, the SABSA had lost its only serious competitor and could no longer reasonably claim that it had to discriminate against Africans to recruit Afrikaner youth.[69]

The final end of the Scouts' embarrassing courtship of the Voortrekkers created more opportunities for Africans and Coloureds in the movement. By the early 1970s, a younger generation of European Scouters began to push tentatively at the racial boundaries of South African Scouting. Recognizing that the Guides had demonstrated that the government would not bother them if they did not publicize their activities, they began slowly by holding low-key mixed camping trips and jamborees. Most of the push for change in the SABSA came from Scout officials in the Cape Province. As commissioner of the European Cape Western Division, Colin Inglis held a "multi-racial Jambo Join-in Canoes Hike" for European, African, and Coloured Scouts who traveled together in mixed patrols. Inglis was a successful executive with Shell Oil and typified a push by South African business leaders to dismantle the most obnoxious social elements of apartheid. They were not yet ready, however, to share political and economic power.[70]

On the surface, it appeared that the SABSA was taking the first steps toward the creation of an integrated national Scout organization. In 1973 Carveth Geech made what sounded like a revolutionary declaration in a speech to the Scout association marking the end of his tenure as European chief Scout:

> Ladies and gentlemen, we live in a land where the searing symbols of insecurity abound. We have become anaesthetized to things which say "right of admission reserved, *Blankes alleen*." It can't go on ladies and gentlemen, it can't. . . . We Scouts must recognize that there are twenty million South Africans, and we must recognize, and insist, by our actions, and operating within the laws of our land, that greater recognition must be given to those of our brother Scouts, who have striven, and in terms of the preamble of our constitution, deserve equal admiration for that which they have achieved.[71]

However, Geech's open criticism of apartheid did not mean he was calling for an end to the parallel association model created by the 1936 Pathfinder compromise. He was careful to conclude with the qualification that Scouts might have, "for the foreseeable future, to live as separate races, each pursuing his own race purity and pride." Charles Martin, Geech's successor, was even more cautious. Although he professed to personally dislike apartheid, Martin maintained that the Scouts had to respect the law. This was the SABSA's primary defense against domestic and international critics who charged South African Scouting with being soft on apartheid. Scout officials claimed that the Second Scout Law ("A Scout is loyal"), which they interpreted as national loyalty, was more important than the Fourth. In other words, the Scouts were still unwilling to sacrifice their links to political authority in service of the more dangerous idealistic pursuit of universal brotherhood. The SABSA's public relations officer advised the South African delegation to the 1975 World Scout Jamboree in Norway to answer their critics with the common prayer asking for God's help "to change the things I can; to accept the things I cannot change; and the wisdom to know the difference."[72]

International revulsion over apartheid eventually had political and economic repercussions in South Africa. In 1973 the United Nations General Assembly labeled apartheid a "crime against humanity," which generated support for an economic boycott of the republic. Sanctions did not shut down foreign investment in South Africa, which totaled $26.3 billion in 1978, but they limited markets for South African exports.[73] The resulting overproduction drove South Africa's economy into decline. Moreover, the collapse of Portugal's African empire in the mid-1970s brought the armed African resistance struggle to the republic's borders.

The South African government tried to weather these storms through military action and economic retrenchment. To improve the productivity of South African industry, it sought to create a better-trained African labor force by improving urban schooling. To placate hardcore Afrikaner nationalists, who objected to increased African education spending, the government ordered African schools to shift much of their instruction to Afrikaans. Laws requiring African schools to teach in Afrikaans had been on the books since the early 1950s, but the government's decision to enforce them came at a particularly bad time. African students' long-standing grievances against Bantu education turned violent as the end of the economic boom of the 1960s made decent jobs scarce. Their resistance to instruction in Afrikaans touched off widespread rioting in mid-1976. Young people often turned to open political defiance as education became an increasingly dead end, and a slogan chalked on a wall in Soweto read: "enter to learn, leave to serve." Security forces killed 176 protestors in Soweto when approximately twenty thousand children took to the streets to demand a return to instruction in English and the opportunities it provided. The violence spread to 160 urban communities throughout the republic by the end of the year.[74]

The state's murder of unarmed children in Soweto provoked an international backlash that strengthened the call for sanctions and deepened the isolation of the apartheid regime. Moderate Afrikaners and English-speaking whites concluded that South Africa needed to remake apartheid to make it more economically efficient and internationally acceptable. Multinational corporations like Polaroid, Reckitt and Coleman, and Anglo American provided much of the inspiration and financing for these "reform" efforts. Reviving the interwar liberal agenda of defusing unrest through social welfare, they sought to answer their international critics by improving African living and working conditions. Although right-wingers in the Nationalist Party opposed any retreat from strict racial segregation, the South African government was willing to modify the most extreme apartheid laws to preserve white minority rule. It tried to divide the African opposition by seeking common ground with conservative African leaders in the Bantustans and relaxing restrictions on employment, labor activism, and urban settlement. These "reforms" did not appease the African National Congress or its international allies. By the early 1980s the hard-line opponents of apartheid would settle for nothing less than universal democracy and the complete destruction of the racist South African state.[75]

The regime's relaxed stance on segregation allowed the SABSA to play a more active role in promoting African social welfare without jeopardizing its relations with the government. It took three quarters of a century, but by the late 1970s South African Scouting could finally begin to bridge the racial boundaries that had made a mockery of the Scout Law. The Scout authorities recognized the opportunities presented by the changing political landscape. Charles Martin raised the possibility of ending the racial compartmentalization of the SABSA even as he reminded his senior Scout colleagues of the need to respect the laws of the land. There were also more pragmatic reasons for the Scouts to reconsider their racial policies. Both African and European membership levels were falling by the mid-1970s and plunged after the 1976 Soweto riots. The SABSA also faced a steep budget deficit of R6,000. The Scout leadership's hesitance in openly challenging the apartheid laws cost them popular African support and even eroded their strong position in the Zulu community. In 1975, Mangosuthu Buthelezi, the leader of the Inkatha Freedom Party, proposed to create a new youth movement in the KwaZulu Bantustan. F. W. Drysdale, organizing commissioner for the Natal Scout division, blamed Oscar Emanualson, the DBE inspector who still ran the African Scout division in the province. He complained that Emanualson still called Africans "natives," and thus typified "a patronising arrogance of the worst kind." Most troubling of all, Shange and Otty Nxumalo, the chief Scout of the African association, were deeply involved in the new movement but refused to discuss their role with Scout officials. Finally, the SABSA faced mounting criticism from the international Scout community. Scout authorities worried that they might be caught in the international sanctions against South Africa and ostracized within the movement if they did not create a unified national Scout organization by the next World Scout Conference, in 1977.[76]

Recognizing the necessity of reform, the Scout leadership created a special committee to study the future of the movement in South Africa. Known as the Quo Vadis committee, from the Latin meaning "whither are you going?" the working group consisted of the SABSA's headquarters staff, the chief Scouts of the four racial associations, and the African field commissioners. They first met in March 1975 and recommended that the SABSA shift from a federal structure to a single association open to all boys. Quo Vadis led to a new Scout constitution in 1977 that made no reference to race or color. South African Scouting became integrated at the national and divisional level, but individual Scout groups and troops had the option of remaining segregated. The Scout leadership emphasized that the reforms would conserve manpower and produce economies of scale by eliminating duplication of services in the four parallel associations. Hoping not to provoke the South African government, they appealed to the liberal press not to devote too much attention to the changes. Although he had a more radical agenda, Colin Inglis, who became chief Scout in 1977, portrayed Quo Vadis in public as a movement to promote good interracial manners.[77]

Nevertheless, many European Scouters objected strenuously to the Quo Vadis reforms. Some questioned whether Africans could be trusted with large sums of money, while others wondered whether South African Scouting was ready to have African commissioners oversee white Scouts. The Northern Transvaal European division led the opposition. Its training team refused to run courses for African Scoutmasters on the grounds that interracial gatherings were still illegal. More than half of the team had civil service jobs, which they claimed would be jeopardized if they trained Africans. The Northern Transvaalers tried to ignore Quo Vadis by hiding behind the government's refusal to issue permits for integrated events. In Natal the secretary of the Durban Scout association resigned to protest the "immorality" of multiracialism, and in South-West Africa a district Scout commissioner refused to train Owambo Scouts because "everything that I teach them now, they are going to use against me later on." Even the leadership of the Coloured Scout association in Cape Town opposed Quo Vadis, on the grounds that the lines of authority at the local level were unclear. In fact, they were unwilling to surrender the authority and status that came with having their own separate association. Inglis dealt with these problems quietly. He eased reactionary Scouters into retirement and used his considerable charm and tact to reassure the doubters that the reforms would strengthen South African Scouting.[78]

For the most part, Quo Vadis did bring about substantial changes to the movement. Although Inglis maintained full control over the SABSA as chief Scout, Sam Motsuenyane, a successful African businessman, became its president. In 1979, Micksey N'thaba told the Orange Free State divisional Scout council that there would be no racial distinctions in choosing candidates for senior Scout posts. He explained that districts would be made up of African and European groups and that individual European troops had the option of "inviting" African or Coloured boys to join. In a few cases, Quo Vadis actually produced integrated Scout troops of a sort. In Kokstad, a small town near the Transkei border, a European Scoutmaster went against the wishes of his school sponsors by integrating his troop. He did, however, maintain three separate white, African, and Coloured patrols.[79]

In reality the geography of apartheid kept South African Scouting largely segregated after Quo Vadis. The Group Areas Act ensured that few Africans and Europeans lived close enough to attend the same schools, much less join the same Scout troops. Scouting almost disappeared from African townships following the Soweto riots, and most rural troops still had to fend for themselves. Moreover, European Scouters retained most senior posts by virtue of their greater experience, despite N'thaba's guarantee that the Scout leadership would be integrated. Many Africans therefore remained suspicious of the Scouts' commitment to real integration. J. Motsimato, an African area secretary, refused an order from the SABSA to resign on the grounds of "inefficiency." Maintaining that his replacement would be just a "window dress of multi-racialism," he defiantly declared: "I think all the Big Heads shout about [regulations] and they don't understand it that [they] made one of our Black Brothers who was one of [our] best leaders left [sic] Scouting."[80]

Yet despite this simmering resentment African Scouting began to recover from the Soweto riots by the early 1980s. As a result, the SABSA found that its greatest problem was more economic than political. Under the unified Scout association the European Scout leadership now bore direct financial responsibility for African Scouting. Few African Scouts could afford their annual dues, and Inglis worried that that the SABSA would become insolvent if more affluent white boys did not join the movement. In Natal there were fifteen thousand officially registered African Scouts and just two thousand Europeans.[81] Scouting faced the same problems confronting the rest of South African society in the 1980s. As with many South African social institutions, the SABSA struggled to undo the legacy of apartheid by including large numbers of lower-class and less educated African and Coloured boys in the movements as full partners.

Most of our information on African Scouting under apartheid comes from official sources. Although tens of thousands of African boys passed through the Scout ranks in the decades after the Second World War, the government's takeover of the mission education system, destruction of urban African communities, and rigid pass laws meant that African Scout troops were largely ephemeral institutions. Ex-Scouts who belonged to relatively short-lived urban troops or unofficial groups in the countryside are difficult to locate, but there is a trove of rich personal information for the researcher who has the time and resources to track them down. For the purposes of this broader study, however, it is still possible to uncover a basic picture of what it meant to be an African Scout during the apartheid era by using select oral histories and archival sources. On the surface, it would seem questionable that so many young Africans would join a movement that put its good relations with the hostile racist regime ahead of its duty to promote egalitarianism under its own Fourth Scout Law. Many African boys rejected Scouting for just these reasons. Students at Marian Hill College in the Transkei grilled N'thaba on how Scouting could claim to be apolitical if it maintained four segregated associations. Others considered the movement a government-sponsored system of political indoctrination, and Shange also had to deny accusations that he was a military trainer for the government.[82]

Moreover, African Scouting usually suffered significant defections when the SABSA demonstrated its unwillingness to openly confront apartheid. Political upheavals, school strikes, and forced removals during the apartheid era can be roughly tracked in rising and falling African membership levels (see fig. 6.5). Yet new generations of Africans invariably returned to both official and unofficial scouting after these upheavals. They may have been frustrated by the SABSA's unwillingness to challenge the political status quo, but they reaped real personal benefits from being a Scout. Wearing a Scout uniform brought them a measure of respect from South Africans of all walks of life. Scouting's seemingly esoteric curriculum of first aid, knots, camping, and folklore taught self-respect and self-confidence at a time when widespread racial discrimination and

Figure 6.5. Registered African Scouts by Year

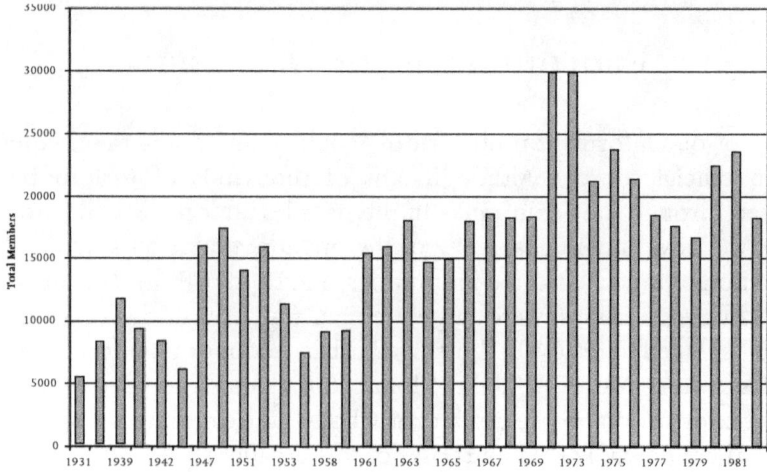

Figure 6.5. Registered African Scouts by Year

Source: SASA, BC 956/F/Census Returns.

government oppression made life barely tolerable. With the majority of troops based at schools, African Scouts used the movement to demonstrate their sophistication and respectability. They generally glossed over the SABSA's official imperial and patriotic rhetoric and interpreted the Second Scout Law to mean loyalty to an egalitarian and nonracial vision of South Africa.[83] It is most likely that Africans in unauthorized or unsupervised troops (who are not accounted for in the official census figures shown in fig. 6.5) shared most of these views and had even greater freedom to put them into practice.

Nevertheless, the realities of life under apartheid made it difficult for African boys to demonstrate their ability and sophistication through Scouting. Only the most affluent Scouts could pay their dues or purchase a uniform. In the 1960s African subscription fees were only ten to thirty cents per year, but many Scoutmasters still had to pay their entire troop's dues out of their own pockets. Some troops had only a few Scout badges, which their members shared by taking turns attaching them to their everyday clothes with safety pins. The SABSA subsidized badges to the point where they sold for just one cent, but many Scouts still could not afford them. In the early 1960s the Scout establishment tried to make the African Scout uniform more affordable by making it simpler, but many Scouts objected on the grounds that the new styles were too different from the European uniform. Scoutmasters in KwaZulu complained that the lack of pockets and belt loops in the new Scout shorts made them too tight fitting and thus too much like the clothing worn by the tsotsis.[84]

Scout standards also suffered when DBE authorities took over most of the African troops in the 1950s. Few of the teachers dragooned into becoming Scoutmasters had Scout training. As a result, Africans had a great deal of difficulty earning badges and advancing to senior Scout ranks. The Scout authorities caught some boys forging badge certificates to overcome this problem. Yet African Scouts objected to the SABSA's attempt to draft an easier "Native" Scout curriculum because they wanted to use the movement to demonstrate that they were as able and resourceful as European boys. The Scout authorities tried to solve this problem in the 1970s by creating a two-tiered curriculum offering alternate, less rigorous tests that had no defined requirements. In theory, any Scout, regardless of race, could choose either option, but in practice European boys had to take the harder tests and most African and Coloured Scouts took the easier ones.[85]

As in East Africa, the African troops also experienced significant problems with the Bob-a-Job fundraising program. They did not win the right to raise money by doing simple tasks until 1952 because their European counterparts argued that Africans could not be trusted with money. The African association convinced the SABSA to let them take part in the program by arguing that it would teach African boys the value of labor. In practice, it was asking a great deal of poor boys to work for no pay. In some cases parents took their sons' Bob-a-Job money to cover basic living expenses. To make matters worse, boys and young men in Scout uniforms, who were probably both official Scouts and impostors, used the program to solicit money from affluent Europeans. By 1954 the Scout authorities received complaints of poorly dressed Scouts "begging" in the streets of Johannesburg. In some cases, the security forces arrested legitimate Scouts while they were working in white neighborhoods.[86]

Rathebe's Transvaal African Scout division argued that the Bob-a-Job problems were overblown and blamed the call to ban Africans from taking part in voluntary fundraising activities on "indigenous prejudice on the part of the [Transvaal] European Section." The African Scouters could not, however, prevent the SABSA limiting fundraising activities by Scouts to their own racial groups. The Scout authorities also reserved the name Bob-a-Job for the exclusive use of the European association. Nevertheless, the African association continued to sponsor similar fundraising activities until the SABSA outlawed the practice altogether in 1966. African Scouts had to compete with unemployed adults for simple jobs and were often exploited by European employers who assigned them unreasonable tasks for minimal pay. Finally, the growing unrest in the townships made it unsafe for uniformed Scouts to engage in public fundraising.[87]

Yet there were still enough perquisites attached to Scouting to inspire impostors to pose as Scouts by wearing the uniform. African teachers often falsely claimed to be Scouts to get jobs. As in East Africa, many African boys also considered Scouting to be a form of employment. An East London student published his own scout paper in which he claimed that the benefits for Scouts included free rail travel, vocational training, and exemption from the pass laws. In other cases, scout imposters appear to have been motivated by simple greed. Throughout the 1960s and 1970s the South African press carried warnings about conmen posing as Scoutmasters collecting money, hawking trinkets, or selling raffle tickets to fund their troops. Although the Afrikaner regime denied the Scouts official status during the apartheid years, the movement still had enough prestige and public respect to make it a suitable vehicle for these kinds of scams.[88]

Sometimes the bogus African scoutmasters were genuinely interested in starting their own troops. When the SABSA pushed to improve the standards of African Scouting in the early 1960s, its field commissioners discovered a host of unauthorized and unregistered scout groups in the countryside. Some troops numbered as many as seven hundred boys at a time when the Scout authorities considered the ideal African troop size to be thirty Scouts. The independent African churches that sponsored most of the unofficial troops during the interwar years appear to have given up their interest in scouting in the apartheid era. By the 1960s independent scouting was primarily in the hands of well-meaning amateurs and former African Scoutmasters who left formal Scouting for disciplinary or political reasons. In some cases they simply took their troops out of the movement to avoid paying dues to the SABSA.[89]

Freed from the oversight of official Scouting, these independent troop leaders had near total autonomy in reinterpreting the movement to suit their personal and political agendas. In some cases they changed the Scout Law and Promise to reflect their religious beliefs. In others they broke with the SABSA because they would no longer tolerate oversight by white Scouters. Interestingly, some of these independent troops also flouted official Scouting's gender doctrines. As in East Africa, African parents and scoutmasters occasionally took it upon themselves to add "girl Scouts" to their troops to conserve financial and leadership resources. Professing not to see the necessity of gender segregation, they argued that coed Scouting was cheaper and more useful in addressing the needs of the entire community. Although the SABSA shut down as many of these mixed troops as it could find, it was hard to exclude girls from the movement because many African school troops had female teachers as Scoutmasters. The Scout authorities consoled themselves that this was a necessary evil on the grounds that African men were unwilling to become Scoutmasters because "African tradition" did not include them in bringing up children.[90]

Thus, as in East Africa, the southern African Scout associations focused on strengthening their ties to political authority after the Second World War. The Central African Federation provided an ideal opportunity for official Scouting in Nyasaland and the Rhodesias to achieve this goal. South African Scouting, on the other hand, lost most of its semiofficial status after the Nationalist Party came to power in 1948. Right-wing Afrikaners viewed the movement as an instrument of British imperialism but were willing to let the Scouts discipline African students. The SABSA was so committed to rebuilding its relations with the state that it did little to contest apartheid's rigid segregation even though segregation violated its Fourth Scout Law. In the postwar era European Scouters were more concerned with political and economic stability than with political justice.

The survival of the color bar in the CAF and brutal racial segregation under apartheid undermined the liberal interpretation of Scouting. The Afrikaner regime's violent reaction to African dissent made the Scouts' gradualism appear irrelevant and craven, and Africans quit the movement in large numbers when the SABSA failed to speak out against the worst abuses of the state. Nevertheless, the movement remained popular in most African communities. Wearing a Scout uniform in South Africa conferred status and respectability and brought some relief from the pass laws and from harassment by the security forces. Scholastic Scouting provided an opportunity for African students to prove their worth in comparison with European boys.

As in East Africa, official Scouting's prevarication on the Fourth Scout Law did not entirely undermine its prestige and status in African communities. The movement therefore remained a tempting target for African independency. African Scouts in Nyasaland and the Rhodesias reinterpreted the Second Scout Law to transfer their loyalties to anticolonial nationalist movements and openly challenged the legitimacy of the CAF. The South African police state made it impossible for Scouts to engage in overt political activity, and African Scouting had difficulty competing with the political radicalism of the ANC and the charismatic nihilism of the tsotsis. Yet it still offered a strong measure of legitimacy and self-respect to boys who sought a middle ground by making a respectable life for themselves within the narrow confines of apartheid society.

7

Independence and After

THE PROSPECT OF INDEPENDENCE, popularly known in Swahili as uhuru, and African majority rule put official Kenyan Scouting in a difficult position that typified the problems faced by territorial Scout associations throughout anglophone Africa. The Kenya Boy Scout Association (KBSA) had allied itself with the colonial regime against African nationalism and had specifically demonized Jomo Kenyatta as the sinister force behind the Mau Mau Emergency. In the late 1950s the European Scouters who made up the Kenyan Scout establishment were largely unaware of, or chose to ignore, the increasingly obvious indications that Britain intended to withdraw from Africa. They were slow to promote Africans to senior leadership positions and to adopt an interpretation of the Fourth Scout Law that would integrate the movement at the local level. In 1962, with Kenyan independence just two years away, the KBSA was still telling African boys that the colony's segregated school system prevented them from joining European troops.[1]

Many young Africans found Scouting less appealing as its imperial and settler connections became more obvious. The KBSA's African membership plunged as uhuru grew closer. Scouting's close ties to the colonial regime now became a liability. Instead of deferring to uniformed Scouts, many Africans, emboldened by the prospect of independence, now scorned them as government lackeys. In the Kikuyu districts, members of the Kenya African National Union's youth wing threw stones at Scouts who wore their uniforms in public. Even more problematic from the standpoint of the Scout establishment, African Scoutmasters and Scouts attended anti-government rallies as partisans of the new political parties. The Girl Guides were also troubled a growing lack of deference from their African Guiders. Kikuyu Guides in Kiambu refused to drill or get out of bed on time on camping expeditions, and their African leaders were openly hostile to the European Guide establishment. Nyeri Guide authorities complained that Kikuyu girls had become "flippant, giggly, inclined to be cheeky." Clearly the appeal of the uniformed colonial youth movements wore thin during the waning days of British rule in Africa.[2]

The Scout authorities in Africa tried to defend their monopoly on legitimacy, limit the scope of independency, and codify their reading of the Scout canon by forming close ties with the colonial regime. Most European Scouters were administrators, missionaries, teachers, businessmen, and settlers. Few doubted the morality or utility of the British imperial enterprise. Decolonization and independence reconfigured the lines of political authority in Africa and shifted the ground under the feet of the territorial Scout associations. The Scout leadership had to scramble to court the new African political leaders, come to terms with African nationalism, and abandon their toleration of racial segregation. In only a few years the KBSA went from condemning Kenyatta as the sinister force behind Mau Mau to pleading with him to become their ceremonial chief Scout once he became prime minister, and later president, of Kenya. South African Scouting, which did not have to deal with an African head of state until 1994, struggled to forge a working relationship with the new national African Scout associations, most of whom were harshly critical of the SABSA's interpretation of the Scout canon. Independent African scouting lost much of its appeal once Africans took control of the Scout establishment after the transfer of power. Yet the Scout canon still remained open to interpretation in the postcolonial era. Informal and unauthorized scouting survived throughout the continent because the failure of the postcolonial states to bring about widespread prosperity created an incentive for individuals to trade on the respectability of the movement to either eke out a living or, in the case of the more audacious imposters, enrich themselves.

The most serious challenge to official Scouting came from the youth wings of ruling parties and government-sponsored youth groups, which competed with the Scouts for legitimacy, resources, and members. The new states often concluded that uniformed youth movements had too much potential power and influence to be left in private voluntary hands. Many preferred the Israeli model of a paramilitary youth organization that

combined military training for national defense with agricultural training for economic development.[3] Worried that the failing and overtaxed
school system they had inherited from the colonial regime could not accommodate the growing numbers of children who sought a formal education, African rulers hoped to channel primary school dropouts and
unemployed youths into regimented youth organizations.

Kwame Nkrumah's Ghana took the lead in creating the National Workers' Brigade to reduce unemployment, mobilize labor for rural development, and provide "patriotic" training for the nation's youth. The capacity
of these movements to strengthen the ruling party's hold on power in
addition to disciplining the increasingly restless younger generation was
no small bonus.[4] Nkrumah used some ex-Scout organizing commissioners to train his brigade leaders, but, for the most part, the new political
youth wings and pioneer movements directly threatened Scouting. As
the first generation of postcolonial African rulers grew more authoritarian they became more inclined to keep the politically volatile field of
youth work under strict government control.

SCOUTING AND THE TRANSFER OF POWER IN AFRICA

Few of the territorial Scout associations in anglophone Africa were prepared for the political and social realities that came with Britain's retreat
from the continent. As close allies of colonial authority they were too
caught up in the struggle to suppress African nationalism to realize that
the metropolitan British government had developed serious doubts
about the value of its African empire. The United Nations' insistence on
self-determination for subject peoples, coupled with Britain's participation in the failed Suez invasion in 1956, made imperialism a diplomatic
embarrassment. The recovery of the British pound from its postwar value
crisis and the growing dollar deficits run by many territorial governments also made the African colonies less important to the British economy.[5] Furthermore, violent resistance to British rule in the 1948 Gold
Coast riots and the Mau Mau Emergency threatened to make the cost of
colonial administration unacceptably expensive. Once a significant number of Africans withdrew their tacit consent from the colonial enterprise,
Britain could not afford the economic, diplomatic, and military costs of
retaining its African empire by force.

Although the imperially minded Conservative Party returned to power
in the early 1950s, many of its younger leaders had no great attachment to

the African colonies and had little sympathy for their entrenched settler communities. Led by Prime Minister Harold Macmillan, the Conservatives calculated Britain could best maintain influence in postcolonial Africa by withdrawing before the nationalist movements turned violent. Macmillan was acutely aware that the French and Belgians were preparing their territories for independence and worried that Britain might become the last colonial power in Africa.[6] Metropolitan officials accepted the inevitability of African independence by the late 1950s and sought to ensure that the new governments would remain pro-British when they were courted by the Americans and their Eastern Bloc rivals.

It was relatively easy for the British to give up their West African territories because they had no permanent European residents. The colonies in eastern and southern Africa were a much thornier problem. Appalled at the thought of living under African majority rule, the settlers used all the political capital at their disposal to block the transfer of power. Many were even opposed to granting Africans limited communal political rights under multiracialism. Yet the African colonies' falling stock meant that the settlers were fighting a losing battle. Macmillan and his Conservative successors were not willing to sacrifice Britain's long-term national interests to preserve the privileges of a group of white colonialists whose passionate defense of the color bar had become a political embarrassment. The West African territories were well on the way to independence by the late 1950s, and in February 1960 Macmillan served formal notice of Britain's intention to surrender its remaining African colonies in an address to the South African parliament. Warning that there was no political or military solution to African nationalism, he declared, "The wind of change is blowing through this continent, and, whether we like it or not, this growth of national consciousness is a political fact."[7]

These shifting political realities put international Scout authorities in an awkward position. For the previous four decades, Britain's national Scout association had directed African Scouting through its Imperial Headquarters (IHQ). Acknowledging the hostility to imperial institutions in Africa and Asia, British Scout officials created a new Commonwealth Department to replace the old IHQ. Although British Scout officials accepted the realities of the transfer of power, they were intensely uneasy about the prospect of turning the movement over to Africans. John Thurman, the Gilwell Camp chief, worried that most Africans just "played the game of Scouting" to please Europeans and warned that more had to be done to prepare the African associations for independence. Echoing

Macmillan, Thurman warned, "The 'Wind of Change' is reaching gale force in Africa as a whole and somehow we must make sure that Scouting is not blown off the continent."[8] In 1962, British Scout authorities created the Committee on Africa to examine Scouting in anglophone Africa and suggest ways to give the postcolonial governments a stronger understanding of the ideals and practices of the movement. The committee recommended "Africanizing" the senior ranks of the national associations and sought to reassure African politicians that Scouting was not an imperial institution by stressing that it "does not produce imitation Europeans but good Africans."[9] Scout leaders hoped this initiative would rebuild their alliance with political authority in postcolonial Africa.

The British Scout Association tried to make this possible by drawing up a simple set of guidelines for the Scout "transfer of power." To be recognized as a national Scout association an organization had to show a commitment to "basic Scouting principles" as outlined in the Scout canon. Its sponsors and leadership had to have good reputations and provide the Commonwealth Department with copies of its constitution and official charter. The international Scout authorities were willing to accept a federation of associations on the South African model. Their only explicit requirement for recognition was that the Scout constitutions had to disavow explicitly all military connections. The new national Scout associations had an entirely free hand in modifying Scout badges, uniforms, tests, and curricula to reflect the new political order. Thus, the rank of Queen's Scout became the Springbok in South Africa, the Simba (lion) in Kenya, and the Crested Crane in Uganda. The Scout Law and Promise remained largely unchanged, with "my country" replacing references to the queen in most territories. In short, Scouting was flexible enough in mirroring established social and political values to serve both the colonial and the post-colonial African state.[10]

CONSEQUENCES OF INDEPENDENCE FOR EAST AFRICAN SCOUTING

The transition to African majority rule was relatively straightforward in Tanganyika and Uganda because the territories lacked significant settler communities. In 1958, Julius Nyerere, an ex-Scout and the leader of the Tanganyika African National Union (TANU), forced the pace of independence through a national strike and boycott of elections under the failed multiracial constitutional model. Recognizing the inevitability of African rule, the British government called new elections for an African majority government as a transitional step to independence. On 9 December 1961, Tanganyika became an independent member of the commonwealth with Nyerere as its prime minister. Two years later he became president of the Tanganyikan Republic, and in 1964 he joined the nation with Zanzibar to form Tanzania.[11]

Although Nyerere had been an enthusiastic Scout, his transformation of Tanzania into a single-party state with an official youth organization threatened the autonomy of the movement. Nyerere envisioned that the TANU Youth League (TYL) would serve several functions. As with the Ghanaian National Worker's Brigade, it would instruct young people in the ideals of African socialism, supply labor for development projects, provide a useful occupation for the tens of thousands of students who failed to win a place in secondary school, and prepare recruits for military service. Nyerere had approached the Scouts to train youth wing leaders in the late 1950s, but when he formed the National Youth Council to coordinate the nation's youth groups, Tanganyikan Scout officials worried that their movement might be absorbed into the TYL. They went to great lengths to reassure the African public that Scouting was no more English than the postal system and asserted that the movement was entirely compatible with Nyerere's doctrines of self-reliance and socialism. L. D. Stirling, a Scout leader of long standing, claimed that Tanganyikan Scouting had helped pave the way for independence by adopting the song "Mungu ibarika Africa" (God Bless Africa) in place of "God Save the King" fourteen years before uhuru.[12]

Although the Tanganyika Boy Scout Association had the fewest official ties of the East African Scout associations, Stirling was stretching the truth when he depicted it as an anticolonial institution. Few Tanganyikans were willing to believe that Scouting was an instrument of African nationalism. Nyerere was personally sympathetic to the ideals of the movement, but his government offered Scouting little official support. Cut off from official funding, the TBSA relied on Williamson Diamonds Ltd. to pay the salary of Tanganyika's only field commissioner in 1963. Scout officials unrealistically hoped to raise enough money from private sources to hire two more by the end of the decade. Instead, Tanzanian Scouting remained a school-based organization and floundered because the government required headmasters to run TYL chapters in every school. Some education officers even banned the movement altogether in their districts. Scouting suffered from the loss of its official status, and boys who wanted to be Scouts had to find the money for both a TYL and a Scout uniform. The TBSA recovered somewhat in the 1970s when Nyerere relaxed TANU's grip on Tanzanian society. Recalling his own roots as a Scout, the president appealed to local TANU leaders to support Scouting on the grounds it was actually an African movement that Baden-Powell had adapted to British circumstances. This argument echoed James W. C. Dougall's rationalization for creating an adapted Scout movement at the Kenyan Jeanes School in the 1920s.[13]

In Uganda the most serious problem complicating the transfer of power was the status of the Kingdom of Buganda in the postcolonial Ugandan state. The kabaka's allies boycotted the constitutional deliberations and the 1961 independence elections because Britain refused to guarantee Buganda's autonomy. The kabaka's retreat from the political arena opened the way for Benedicto Kiwanuka, a Gandan commoner, to become prime minister. Kiwanuka was unseated a year later by Milton Obote's Uganda People's Congress, which had formed a pragmatic alliance with the disgruntled Gandan elites. Obote repaid the Gandans for their help with a constitutional amendment granting federal status to Buganda and Uganda's other historical kingdoms. The kabaka also became the largely ceremonial president.[14] Obote lacked Nyerere's popular mandate and tried to solidify his hold on power by developing his own populist version of African socialism.

Ugandan Scouting was not drawn directly into the political controversy over the Kingdom of Buganda. Nevertheless, although the Uganda Boy Scout Association made substantial progress in "Africanizing" its senior leadership, the movement's position was less than secure on the eve of Ugandan independence in 1961. Having previously collected two-thirds of the colonial government's spending on youth welfare, the Scouts faced competition from the Boy's Brigade, the YMCA, and even the charity Save the Children. A professional white brigade organizer had been working in Uganda since 1955, and the Anglican Church hoped to expand the movement after the protectorate became independent. Brigade officials joined the other competing organizations in questioning whether Uganda's youth problems could be addressed through an elite school-based movement like Scouting. In 1964 the Ugandan Labour Department warned that there was work for neither unskilled primary school leavers nor for three-quarters of the sixteen thousand students who graduated from secondary school each year.[15]

The Ugandan government proposed to address this problem by bringing all the nation's youth organizations under state control. Following Nyerere's lead in Tanganyika, Obote packed the National Union of Youth Organisations (NUYO) with members of the Uganda People's Congress youth wing.

Although the NUYO threatened to swallow the Scouts, it gave them some room to maneuver by defining a youth as anyone less than thirty years of age. Uganda Scout officials tried to retain their autonomy and state funding by embracing Obote's socialist goals and asking the government to assign them primary responsibility for working with eight- to sixteen-year-old boys. The NUYO's ambitious development plans came to nothing, as Obote made military expansion rather than social welfare his greatest priority. The UBSA's state funding dried up, and the political turmoil surrounding Obote's declaration of a single-party state made private fundraising difficult. The Ugandan Scout authorities therefore had no choice but to discharge their paid commissioners. The resulting leadership vacuum led to a decline in standards and membership levels over the course of the 1960s. The collapse of Ugandan Scouting was due primarily to the increasing authoritarianism of the Obote regime and demonstrates that it is almost impossible for Scouting to survive when the state monopolizes youth work.[16]

Uhuru was even more problematic for the Kenya Boy Scout Association. While it was relatively easy for Britain to withdraw from Tanganyika and Uganda, the Kenyan settlers bitterly fought the transfer of power. Yet Mau Mau had cost the metropolitan government roughly twenty million pounds.[17] Britain did not have the military manpower or financial resources to maintain a permanent garrison in the colony, and the Colonial Office served notice on the territorial government that it would have to come to terms with African nationalism. Lacking the means to retain their privileges by force, the settlers grudgingly shared power with the African majority under a multiracial format. The 1958 Lennox-Boyd Constitution preserved their political dominance by assigning seats in the legislative council on a disproportionate communal basis whereby Europeans retained a parliamentary majority despite their minority status. African politicians understandably rejected the constitution as a thinly veiled ploy to protect white privilege.

The failure of multiracialism set Kenya on the path to independence. The metropolitan government tried to guarantee the settlers a measure of security by leaving in place a new federal constitution that guaranteed minority rights by dividing the nation into seven autonomous regions. The leaders of Kenya's smaller ethnic groups, who comprised the Kenya African Democratic Union (KADU), supported the plan because they worried the more populous Kikuyu and Luo communities would monopolize the spoils of independence. Acting in the name of Jomo Kenyatta, who remained in detention for alleged Mau Mau crimes, Kikuyu and Luo leaders formed the Kenya African National Union (KANU) to contest the 1961 elections for a transitional African led government. KANU won in a landslide but boycotted the new government until the British freed Kenyatta. Kenyatta then shared power with KADU under British supervision until KANU won a crushing victory in the May 1963 elections, which paved the way for independence. Taking his electoral success as a mandate to dismantle the federal constitution, Kenyatta transformed Kenya into a de facto single-party state after taking power in December 1963.[18] Although Kenya remained in the commonwealth, he followed Nyerere's lead in remaking Kenya as a republic with himself as president.

As in Tanganyika and Uganda, the new nation inherited a narrow and inadequate school system. British efforts to build support for multiracialism in the 1950s by improving African educational standards collapsed for lack of funds and trained African teachers. Kenyan Scouting remained segregated during the transition to independence because the colonial authorities used the necessity of preserving educational standards as an excuse not to integrate the schools. It took a threat by KANU to nationalize the school system to convince European educators and parents to abandon their commitment to segregation. With independence fast approaching, departing colonial administrators embraced mixed schooling as a means of instilling British values in future generations of African leaders. The Kenyan government opened the settler secondary schools to Africans in late 1960 to prepare non-Europeans to "take part in the educational and political life of the country." They did not lower tuition rates, which ensured that only the most elite African families could take advantage of the new educational opportunities.[19]

The gradual desegregation of the upper levels of Kenyan education offered no relief to the growing youth problem that awaited Kenyatta's new government. In 1962, 60 percent of the Kenyan population, which numbered between seven and eight million, was under the age of twenty-one. The population was growing 2.5 percent per year, and approximately 1.2 million children were not in school. These poorly educated boys and girls faced a grim labor market. The 1960 Dalgleish Report found that between 120,000 and 150,000 adult men were unemployed and warned that there was no work for the approximately one hundred thousand children who either dropped out of or graduated from school each year. To further complicate matters, the vast majority of Africans expected independence to bring improved schooling and well-paying jobs. Colonial officials and their KANU successors worried that their inflated, and sadly unrealistic, expectations might destabilize the new Kenyan nation.[20]

These youth problems created an opportunity for the KBSA to rebuild its alliance with political authority in the postcolonial era, but the Scout authorities were too closely tied to the settlers to accept the new political realities in Kenya. Geoffrey Rhodes, the Kenyan chief Scout commissioner, criticized the Ugandan association's plans to drop references to the queen from the Scout Law and openly opposed granting Africans the right to vote. It is therefore not surprising that senior European Scouters resisted pressure from the international Scout authorities to Africanize the upper ranks of the KBSA. George Witchell, one of the British Scout Association's overseas commissioners, frankly told the Kenyan leadership: "If after 50 years of Scouting in Kenya we still haven't produced people of the right calibre, there is something wrong somewhere." Rhodes claimed that Africanization was unnecessary because Kenyan Scouting was color-blind.[21] By comparison, the Guide authorities were theoretically more receptive to Africanizing their senior leadership but claimed that there were no qualified candidates because educated African women lacked a tradition of voluntary service.[22]

Kenyan Scout officials also resisted desegregating the KBSA's leadership because they worried that African Scouters might draw the movement into politics. Thurman noted that some African Scouters used their prestige as Scoutmasters to run for political office, and both the Scouts and Guides were embarrassed when their members attended political rallies while in uniform. Scout officials published an article in *Batian*, the KBSA's official magazine, reminding Scouts that the movement was officially nonpartisan: "Remember that the Scout Movement as such is completely outside politics. No Scout or Scouter is allowed to wear a Scout uniform at any political meetings or activities. The Scout Promise of Loyalty means that a Scout gives his whole-hearted support to the lawful Government of the time."[23] As a close ally of the colonial regime, Scouting was hardly apolitical, but the Scout authorities worried that the movement might lose its official status if it became linked with a particular party. Loyalty for the KBSA meant allegiance to the dominant political order, not a specific political faction.

The Scouts found it difficult to stand above the political fray as the lines of political authority in Kenyan blurred in the turbulent years leading up to independence. The transitional government preferred to spend its social welfare money on schools and hospitals, and it cut the KBSA's yearly subsidy from nine to four thousand pounds in 1962. Rhodes's outraged protest that the cuts spelled disaster for the movement fell on unsympathetic ears. Scout officials appealed to Jeremiah

Nyagah and Musa Amalemba, government ministers with close Scouting ties, to restore their funding, but it took an anonymous donation of £7,000 from a "Kenya resident" to cover the salaries of the KBSA's organizing commissioners for 1963.[24] Realizing that they now had to justify their existence to the African public, the Scout authorities began a belated publicity campaign outlining the movement's contributions to the new nation.

Yet it was not easy for the KBSA to find its way through the political thickets of late colonial Kenya. The Scout leadership eventually hired some African training and organizing commissioners, and a handful of nonscholastic "open" European troops in Nairobi admitted African and Indian Scouts. The KBSA also enlisted Musa Amalemba, an ex-Scout and the new African housing minister, to serve as deputy chief Scout commissioner. In seeking to protect the Scouts from the KADU and KANU youth wings, Amalemba told the press: "I should like to think that the Boy Scouts represented the real 'youth wing' of this country instead of one which brings intimidation, death and fear." But Scouting inevitably became ensnared in the political tensions of the day. When the Kenyan National Union of Teachers went on strike to demand better pay in 1962, teacher-Scoutmasters tried to stop their troops from meeting on the grounds that Scouting was a school activity. The SABSA also had to move Godwin Gathu, one of the new African organizing commissioners, out the Rift Valley Province because he faced harassment in some Kalenjin communities. Gathu was a Kikuyu and thus linked with KANU, while most Kalenjin were strong KADU supporters. Moreover, Kenyan Scouting had trouble letting go of its segregated past. A settler faction threatened to create a rival all-white Scout organization, and the supposedly open Nairobi Scout troops attracted few non-European members.[25]

Eventually, however, Kenyan Scouting had to make its peace with African majority rule. Beginning in 1961 it established a Forward Planning Committee composed of European Scouters and African political leaders, many of whom were former Scouts, to chart the path to independence. The committee removed imperial references from the Kenyan Scout constitution and curriculum over Rhodes's increasingly faint objections. The Kenyan Scout leadership set 12 December 1963, Independence Day, as the point when the KBSA would cease to be an overseas branch of the BSA and become simply the Kenya Scout Association (KSA). On that date, the Scouts and Guides participated in a special youth rally at Nairobi's Uhuru Stadium marking the end of British rule. Before an audience that included Jomo Kenyatta and the Duke of Edinburgh they put on displays demonstrating the Scout Law. An honor guard of African Scouts, escorted by Asian and European Scouts, then received a new Scout flag that symbolized the independent status of Kenyan Scouting.[26]

Nevertheless, the Scouts' intimate relationship with Kenyan political authority was over. Kenyatta declined their invitation to become the ceremonial chief Scout. Rhodes filled the position temporarily before Kenyatta appointed his vice-president, Daniel arap Moi, to the post. Jeremiah Nyagah, a cabinet minister who held several portfolios in Kenyatta's government, eventually replaced Rhodes as chief Scout commissioner. The Scout authorities hoped that these appointments would ensure them a measure of official status in postcolonial Kenya. In asking for a limited renewal of state aid they appealed to the minister for labor and social service to make a public declaration that Scouting was a national institution, not one associated with the empire.[27]

The new Kenyan government, however, did not believe that the Scouts could deal with the nation's youth problems. Scouting remained a school-based movement and had little success in reaching boys outside the education system. Moreover, Kenyatta needed a way to reign in the KANU youth wing, whose members grew increasingly defiant of governmental and generational authority. Many were out of work and some declared they would replace the police in the Rift Valley after independence. Scouting had little hope of disciplining the youth wingers, many of whom were in their twenties. Kenyatta therefore created the National Youth Service (NYS) to bring unemployed young men and women under the direct government authority. As in Tanzania, the NYS provided labor for development projects and served as a military recruiting pool. The Scouts were not entirely shut out of the new youth program. They helped train NYS leaders, and Kenyatta chose Geoffrey Griffin, the Wamumu Scoutmaster, to run the service.[28]

The Kenyan government eventually recognized that Scouting had its uses. Education and social welfare officials gave the movement a limited role in extracurricular school life, assisting in rural development, and alleviating urban poverty. Kenyatta restored some of the Scouts' legitimacy by drawing public attention to the similarities between the Scout Promise and his ideology of harambee (self-help). In 1971 he declared: "I am satisfied that the Scout Movement in Kenya is our own. It is loyal to the Government and, whatever the movement sets out to achieve, has the backing of my Government."[29] In the late 1960s the KSA counted 13,365 registered Scouts and Cubs and received 70 percent of its funding from public sources and donations. Only a small percentage of this money came from government grants, but the association managed to retain three salaried field commissioners at a time when the Ugandan and Tanzanian associations dismissed most of their paid staff because they were near bankruptcy. Ultimately, however, the Kenyan Scouts found it extremely difficult to operate without substantial state funding. By 1966, 90 percent of all Scouts belonged to school-sponsored troops, which often collapsed when the Education Department transferred their teacher-Scoutmasters. The KSA eventually fell victim to the financial problems that plagued its Ugandan and Tanzanian counterparts. In the 1970s many of the European donors who had anonymously supported Scouting after independence had either died, moved away, or found other uses for their money. Overseas funding dried up as well, and the KSA discharged its traveling commissioners and rented out its headquarters at Baden-Powell House to private organizations. As in Tanzania and Uganda, Scouting survived in Kenya but in a much smaller and less influential role than under British rule.[30]

Interestingly, the end of the colonial era did not end unauthorized scouting in East Africa. Although independency no longer had overtly political implications, harsh postcolonial economic conditions provided sufficient incentives for individuals to trade on the respectability and legitimacy of the movement. All three national associations tried to continue Bob-a-Job fundraising to compensate for the reduction in government aid. In some cases poor Scouts kept the money for their families, and in others imposters used illegally acquired uniforms to solicit funds from the unsuspecting public. In 1963 gangs of boys in Nairobi posing as Scouts collected money to attend the world jamboree in Greece, which suggests they had some knowledge of the movement. The Tanzanian government also arrested and imprisoned several con-men who made a good living by pretending to be Scouts, one of whom claimed to be a nephew of President Banda of Malawi. The Scout authorities tried to crack down on illegal fundraising by maintaining stricter controls over the Scout uniform and issuing identity cards to their members. In 1971, the Kenya Scout Association released an official warning that boys who did not followed set Bob-a-Job guidelines were most likely impostors. However, self-interested Scouts and outright charlatans got around these membership controls by forging badge tests and Scout membership certificates. It is unlikely that these larcenous activities were as lucrative as they had been under British rule. Nevertheless, the national Scout associations' partial success in reestablishing their links to postcolonial political legitimacy and authority continued to make unauthorized scouting an economically rewarding endeavor in East Africa.[31]

THE CONSEQUENCES OF INDEPENDENCE FOR SOUTHERN AFRICAN SCOUTING

Official Scouting's close ties with the Central African Federation were also a liability during the transfer of power. Popular opposition to the CAF in Northern Rhodesia and Nyasaland became a rallying point for African nationalists. They organized tax resistance, boycotts, and strikes to press for universal suffrage leading to African majority rule. In 1957 riots broke out in Nyasaland and Northern Rhodesia when the federal assembly announced revisions in the constitution that would dilute direct African representation. At the same time, African miners on the Northern Rhodesian Copperbelt struck over pay and working conditions. The unrest grew so violent by 1959 that Federation Prime Minister Roy Welensky deployed the mostly European federal army to restore order. Federation forces killed fifty-one civilians in Nyasaland and wounded seventy-nine more. "Counterinsurgency" operations in Northern Rhodesia provoked widespread accusations of murder, rape, and beatings by the police and army. African Scouts were invariably drawn into the antifederation struggle, and the Nyasaland Boy Scout Association was particularly embarrassed when the security forces arrested some of its most accomplished Scoutmasters.[32]

The international attention generated by the 1959 riots, coupled with growing doubts about the value of African colonies, led the British government to rethink its commitment to the Central African Federation. In 1960 the Monckton Commission tried to salvage the federation through constitutional reform, but the vast majority of Africans would settle for nothing less than the dissolution of the CAF and universal suffrage leading to majority rule. In assessing the potential for violent unrest in central Africa, a confidential War Office minute concluded that the federal army would not be able to restore order if Nyasaland and Northern Rhodesia "went bad." Colonial officials in Nyasaland refused to sanction the further use of force against the nationalists and opened negotiations with Kamuzu Hastings Banda and his Malawi Congress Party (formerly the Nyasaland African Congress).[33] They had detained Banda during the riots but released him to take part in the transfer of power. After holding several ministerial portfolios in the transitional government he became prime minister in 1963 and led the protectorate to independence as the new nation of Malawi.

Banda proved far more hostile to Scouting than were his East African counterparts. Although the NBSA dutifully hired African organizing commissioners and appointed Africans to leadership positions at the district level, Banda still considered it a colonial institution. He refused to become the national chief Scout and cut off state funding to the movement. It took a grant from the Beit Trust to keep official Scouting running in the 1960s. The Boy's Brigade did not fare much better during this period. Although brigade officials counted twenty-seven hundred registered African members in 1960, the movement's links with the CAF also cost it popular and political support. The Boy's Brigade had wisely stayed out of the federation celebrations in 1953 and 1954, but by the close of the decade several of its senior European leaders were members of the federal parliament. The Nyasaland brigade organizer had close links with the Southern Rhodesian brigade, and many Africans suspected he was a federal agent. Thus, the brigade was in no position to take advantage of the Scouts' problems.[34]

As in East Africa, Malawian Scouting faced a serious challenge from the youth wing of the ruling party. Founded in 1958, the Malawi Congress Party's Youth League played an active role in the 1959 riots that helped bring about independence. Banda recognized the political value of a disciplined youth movement and sent representatives to Ghana to study Nkrumah's National Workers' Brigade. After deciding that the Ghanaians lacked sufficient discipline, he turned to Israel for assistance in developing a paramilitary youth organization modeled on Gadna, the Israeli youth corps. Banda won funding for the plan from the World Bank and other international donors by depicting it as a development project. In reality, Banda's Young Pioneers were a paramilitary political organization that helped him transform Malawi into a single-party state. Recruits studied Kamuzism, the "teaching, philosophy and life of Ngwazi Dr. Kamuzu Banda, Father and Founder of the Nation of Malawi." By the late 1960s, there were approximately three thousand Young Pioneers, five hundred of whom received full military training. They served as Banda's personal bodyguard and had total immunity from arrest by the civil police. By the 1970s the Young Pioneers were better trained and equipped than the regular Malawian army and provided the coercive underpinning of Banda's authoritarian regime.[35]

The Scouts tried to show Banda that they were not in competition with the Pioneers. Having given up hope of convincing to him to renew their official status, the Scout authorities now sought simply to dissuade him from shutting them down. In hindsight, it is clear that Banda wanted a government monopoly on youth work for political reasons, but at the time he dismissed Scouting and Guiding on the grounds that they did not teach "young men and women the essence of manual and physical labour, as well as the old African customs." Promising that the Young Pioneers would cleanse Malawian youth of "colonial attitudes," he severed Scouting's remaining official ties with the government. The end finally came in the early 1970s when the government ordered the Malawi Scout Association to disband entirely. In an interesting reversal of the South African attempts to export their Pathfinder model during the interwar years Banda approached the African leaders of the Bantustans with an offer to help them create their own pioneer organizations. The South African Boy Scout Association headed off the threat by pointing out that membership in Scouting would bring the Bantustans greater international recognition. Moreover, Scouting never really disappeared from Malawi. When Banda finally lost power in 1994 many former Scouts revealed they had kept the movement alive in secret and have subsequently revived the national Scout association.[36]

Scouting fared slightly better in Northern Rhodesia, which its prime minister (later president) Kenneth Kaunda renamed Zambia. Unlike Banda, Kaunda was both a former Scout and an accomplished Scoutmaster at the Lubwa mission. When Scout troops faced intimidation from the youth wing of the ruling United National Independence Party, Kaunda issued a statement endorsing Scouting. He was one of the few first generation African leaders to accept the invitation to become chief Scout, and he praised the movement as the best tool for teaching discipline and helping boys to become men. Kaunda also allowed Jack Leech, the ex-Bechuanaland Scouter who stood up to the SABSA over apartheid, to continue serving as an organizing commissioner while on leave from the Zambian welfare department. Nevertheless, the Zambian Scout Association still faced most of the same institutional problems of the other postcolonial African Scout organizations. There was no money to pay professional Scouters after Leech left, and Zambian Scouting became an extension of the school curriculum.[37]

Not surprisingly, Southern Rhodesian Scouting took its lead from South Africa once Britain withdrew from Africa. After the dissolution of the CAF in 1964, the Rhodesian settlers tried to convince the British government to hand over power to them rather than the African majority. When this gambit failed, Ian Smith, leader of the right-wing Rhodesian Front Party, declared Rhodesia unilaterally independent in 1965. Four years later he broke with Britain entirely by following the South African example in transforming Rhodesia into a republic.[38] Smith's intransigence touched off a brutal guerilla war where African nationalists led by Robert Mugabe tried to win independence by force of arms.

As in South Africa, the Rhodesian Boy Scout Association interpreted the Second Scout Law as a mandate, and an excuse, to remain loyal to Smith's regime. As a result, Rhodesian Scouting had to fend for itself when sanctions made Rhodesia an international pariah. Having finally done away with its separate African section in 1970, the RBSA's approximately six thousand members in 1976 demonstrated that African Scouting remained viable during the independence struggle. Yet the association remained segregated at the local level, and many Africans viewed it with suspicion because they confused Scouting with the Selous Scouts, a particularly brutal arm of the Rhodesian army. The European Scout leadership tried to distance the movement from the security forces, but the chief Scout commissioner still told Scouters to offer their services to the civil defense authorities as part of their "duty to country" under the Second Scout Law. When the expense of the war, coupled with intense international pressure, forced Smith to negotiate with Mugabe in 1978, the Scouts scrambled to adapt to the new political order by offering their services in helping the country recover from war. The RBSA had kept just enough distance from Smith's regime to avoid antagonizing the African nationalists. It therefore managed to elicit a declaration from the new government endorsing its value in building the Zimbabwean nation.[39]

Decolonization in southern Africa, coupled with international disdain for apartheid, left the South African Boy Scout Association increasingly isolated in the international Scout community. In the late 1950s, before the scope of the transfer of power was fully apparent, South African Scout officials pushed for the creation of a separate "African Region" within world Scouting that would link the Scout associations in the High Commission Territories, the Central African Federation, Portuguese Africa, the Belgian Congo, and the British East African colonies. By building bridges to the rest of the continent South African Scout officials sought to export their pragmatic interpretation of the Scout canon and ensure that African Scouters did not shun the SABSA as a result of apartheid. Needless to say, none of the former colonial Scout associations in the rest of Africa wished to jeopardize their relations with the postindependence nationalist governments by linking themselves with South Africa. John Thurman warned it would be "political suicide" to accept South African help, which led South Africa's international Scout commissioner to complain that British Scouting was trying to isolate the SABSA. Thurman was of course correct, and most of the new national associations were openly contemptuous of the South African model of segregated Scouting.[40] As a result, the SABSA had few open friends in postcolonial African Scouting.

The primary focus of the South African Scout authorities in the 1960s and 1970s was to avoid being included in the international sanctions against the apartheid regime. In 1967 the SABSA proposed to create a southern zone within the African Scout Region to strengthen its ties to the remaining settler regimes in Southern Rhodesia and Portuguese Africa. It also drew in the former High Commission Territories, whose economies remained entirely subordinate to South Africa despite their political independence. The offer to assist with training, equipment, and grants to visit South Africa enticed the Scout associations in Rhodesia, South-West Africa, Swaziland, Lesotho, Botswana, Angola, and Mozambique to join South Africa in the Southern Zone in 1973. Yet the SABSA's success was short-lived. Portuguese decolonization and boycotts over the Soweto riots effectively reduced the Southern Zone to just Lesotho, Rhodesia, and South Africa by 1977.[41]

The South African Scout leadership's search for regional allies did little to blunt international criticism of their failure to confront apartheid aggressively. The Scandinavian Scout associations led the campaign to expel the SABSA from the International Scout Federation. South African Scouting blunted some of this criticism in the early 1970s by sending multiracial delegations to international Scout events. The SABSA issued careful instructions advising Scouters that they could voice a hope that apartheid would come to an end and that conditions in South Africa were changing for the better. It warned them to beware of making more explicit statements that might end up in the South African press and suggested pointing out that there were similar ethnic tensions between the French and English in Canada, the Flemish and Walloons in Belgium, and the English and Irish in Belfast. South African Scout representatives were less convincing in claiming that the movement's apolitical character prevented them from challenging segregation because most of the world recognized that even tacit accommodation of apartheid was an inherently political act. The SABSA escaped censure and sanctions because Scouting remained a largely conservative institution worldwide. The World Scout Bureau resisted political pressure from the more activist national associations because it believed Scouting remained a force for good in South Africa. Foreign Scouters were impressed by African and Coloured South African Scouts and took the integrated overseas delegations as evidence of the SABSA's attempts to push racial boundaries in the republic.[42]

Yet this cautious vote of support was not enough to protect South African Scouting from its international critics. After overseeing the creation of a unified Scout association, Colin Inglis played down the SABSA's previous efforts to win state support and emphasized that his association had undertaken the Quo Vadis reforms entirely without government approval (see chapter 6). He stressed that the SABSA was more independent of government supervision than most African Scout associations.

Yet Scouting was not as divorced from South African political authority as Inglis suggested. The SABSA supported government efforts to secure international recognition for the Bantustans by lobbying the World Scout Bureau to treat the Transkei Scout organization, which was entirely run by South African Scouting, as a national association. When the international Scout authorities refused the petition the South Africans made Transkei a Scout "area" within the SABSA. Nevertheless, they worked hard to maintain the fiction that the Bantustans had their own national Scout movements. President Kaiser Matanzima remained the patron of Transkei Scouting, and African Scouts formed honor guards for political dignitaries in Bophuthatswana. The Quo Vadis reforms also complemented the South African government's efforts to undercut international sanctions and counter African radicalism by fostering the development of a cooperative black middle class. It was relatively easy for the SABSA to abandon the segregated parallel association model of the 1936 Pathfinder compromise once the government began to dismantle the most restrictive social regulations that were known as petty apartheid. The Scouts assisted these efforts, albeit indirectly, by working to reestablish Scouting in the townships. As the SABSA's 1977 Community Development Report put it: "The youth in the urban townships are both our future employees and customers. These people will form the rising Black middle class, but at the present there is little evidence that these people share the Western standards and ideals normally associated with a middle class structure." Inglis used his business connections to secure grants from major South African corporations to pay for professional Scoutmasters and equipment for urban African troops. In addition to teaching the formal Scout canon these troops also served corporate interests by offering rudimentary vocational training.[43]

By 1979 the SABSA had raised one hundred thousand rand for Scout training centers in Soweto and Cape Town's Guguletu Township. The Scout authorities hoped to eventually put similar centers staffed by African training teams in every major urban center in South Africa. They also used their increased resources to hire African field commissioners for Soweto and Cape Town, plus a pair of Coloured commissioners for the Cape Province. These commissioners did a good job recruiting new Scouts, but the SABSA's ambitious urban development plans soon ran into trouble. The townships remained transitory and precarious places where Africans, Coloureds, and Indians were still subject to arbitrary "removal" by the security forces. Between 1960 and 1983 the government forced over 3.5 million people to move to the Bantustans. African Scout troops had trouble finding safe places to meet, and Scout officials admitted that the boys had to choose between Scouting and the increasingly militant opposition youth organizations. Moreover, there were still few parents who could afford to buy their sons uniforms or even pay their dues. The end result was that only the most committed boys stayed in Scouting, and the SABSA's ambitious expansion plans generally lost steam by the mid-1980s.[44]

Nevertheless, the Scout establishment's renewed focus on urban development and welfare left the movement relatively well prepared for the end of apartheid. Inglis felt sufficiently confident to publicize the Quo Vadis reforms by the early 1980s, and the SABSA became much more open about promoting itself as a fully integrated organization with strong international ties. The Scout authorities were thus able to convince Nelson Mandela to become their patron when he became president of South Africa in 1994. Nkwenkwe Nkomo, an ex-Scout who spent six years imprisoned on Robben Island for his role as a national organizer for the Black People's Convention, became the new chief Scout. Moving away from the South African Scout Association's segregated history, Nkomo declared: "Scouting is a premium youth movement, there to enable us, especially now, to move towards healing this country, to train leaders and empower people." This statement also laid out the philosophy of the Phakamani Project, taken from the Nguni word for "rise," which seeks to burnish South African Scouting's nationalist credentials by promoting community-based Scouting as a tool for economic and social development.[45]

Scouting began in Africa as an extension of colonial authority. Administrators, educators, missionaries, and social welfare experts hoped the movement would reinforce the colonial social order by giving young African males a tacit stake in the British Empire. They also expected Scouting would buttress indirect rule and smooth over intergenerational tensions by reducing social friction stemming from Western education, wage labor, and urbanization. Yet the movement's emphasis on egalitarianism made it a tempting target for independent schools and churches, which developed unauthorized versions of Scouting to claim its legitimacy and respectability. Baden-Powell built official support for his movement around the world by making its core values adaptable enough to suit the needs of diverse political and social orders. The references to honor, loyalty, duty, obedience, and brotherhood in the Scout Law and Promise were sufficiently vague to allow boys from widely different backgrounds to become Scouts. Although the British Scout Association and its subordinate colonial branches made loyalty to the Crown a central focus of the Second Scout Law, it was not difficult for the African independents to propose alternative outlets for the loyalty and duty of their unofficial troops. The Boy Scout movement thus became a site of intense contestation as Africans reinterpreted the Scout canon to challenge the political and social legitimacy of the colonial regime.

Ironically, Scouting's openness and vulnerability to adaptation was the key factor that allowed the movement to survive the transfer of power. Although the Scout authorities had been archenemies of the African nationalist movements, they successfully transformed what had been an instrument of colonial authority into a national institution. Yet independence marked the demise of the authoritarian and bureaucratic model of colonial Scouting. Under British rule, the Scout leadership was made up almost entirely of European missionaries, settlers, and administrators. Many of these men remained in Africa after the end of empire, but they lacked the official support and financial resources to keep the old colonial Scout associations intact.

The movement survives in Africa to this day because of the grassroots efforts of teachers, parents, and boys who continue to see value in Scouting. Modern African troops still teach the values of integrity, sophistication, and self-respect that made the movement so popular in colonial times, but Scouting is obviously no longer a means of contesting colonial and political authority. The first generation of African Scout leaders lacked the will and resources to exert much influence over Scouting at the local level, but they reestablished their ties to political authority in most nations by reinventing the movement as a tool of (national and) economic development. Although contemporary African Scout associations now emphasize loyalty to the postcolonial state, they are generally far less political than their colonial predecessors. Yet the survival of Scouting in Malawi after it was banned by the Banda regime demonstrates that it retains the capacity to be reinterpreted as an expression of political and social opposition. Moreover, Scouting's semiofficial status continues to provide a powerful temptation for informal scouts and impostors to make money by trading on the respectability and legitimacy of the movement.

Appendix

1. A Scout's honour is to be trusted.
2. A Scout is loyal to the King, his country, his Scouters, his parents, his employers, and to those under him.
3. A Scout's duty is to be useful and helpful to others.
4. A Scout is a friend to all, and a brother to every other Scout, no matter to what country, class or creed, the other may belong.
5. A Scout is courteous.
6. A Scout is a friend to animals.
7. A Scout obeys orders of his parents, Patrol Leader or Scoutmaster, without question.
8. A Scout smiles and whistles under all difficulties.
9. A Scout is thrifty.
10. A Scout is clean in thought, word and deed.

THE SCOUT PROMISE

On my honour I promise that I will do my best
To do my duty to God, and the King,
To help other people at all times,
To obey the Scout Law.

Source: Lord Robert Baden-Powell, *Scouting for Boys*, 30th edition (London: C. Arthur Pearson, 1957).

Notes

All interviews were conducted by the author.

MNA	Malawi National Archives
MUR	Muranga (Fort Hall) District [Kenya]
NBI	Nairobi
NNZA	North Nyanza District [Kenya]
NP	Northern Province [Kenya]
NR	Northern Rhodesia
OFS	Orange Free State
PC	Provincial Commissioner
PCEA	St. Andrews Presbyterian Church of East Africa Archives
PEO	Principle Education Officer
PRO	British Public Records Office
RVP	Rift Valley Province [Kenya]
SA(A)BSA	South African (African) Boy Scout Association
SABSA	South African Boy Scout Association
SAGGA	South African Girl Guide Association
SAIRR	South African Institute of Race Relations
SASA	South African Scout Association
SASC	South African Scout Council
SNA	Swaziland National Archives
TBSA	Tanganyika Boy Scout Association
TNA	Tanzania National Archives, Dar es Salaam
UBSA	Uganda Boy Scouts Association
UW	University of Witwatersrand
WO	War Office

PREFACE

1. The U.S. Postal Service no longer includes uniforms on the list of restricted items.

2. Frank Crego, "Local Boy Scout Council Aims to Try to Alter Anti-Gay Policy," *Rochester Democrat and Chronicle*, 13 March 2001.

CHAPTER 1

1. *Daily Nation*, 26 February 2001; 21 February 2003.

2. Jeremiah Nyagah, interview, June 1998; J. G. Kiano, July 1998; Kiraithe Nyaga, July 1998.

3. Evelyn Baring, Speech to KBSA AGM, 20 May 1955, MNA 17/BSA/8/13.

4. Matthew Kipoin, interview, June 1998.

5. Kiraithe Nyaga, interview, July 1998.

6. Guha, "Dominance without Hegemony and Its Historiography," 212–13.

7. Berman and Lonsdale, *Unhappy Valley*, 79–81; Mamdani, *Citizen and Subject*, 18.

8. Kirk-Greene, "The District Officer as the Man in the Middle in West Africa"; **countryside:** Chanock, "Paradigms, Policies and Property," 62–64.

9. **Africans as primitive:** Mangan, "Imperialism, History and Education," 10; Lugard, *The Dual Mandate in British Tropical Africa.*

10. The phrase is from Kennedy, *Islands of White.*

11. Tanganyika Education Conference, *Conference between Government and Missions,* 76.

12. Quoted in Rawson, ed., *Education for a Changing Commonwealth,* 80.

13. **Communal rights:** Comaroff and Comaroff, *The Dialectics of Modernity on a South African Frontier,* 61; Huxley, *Africa View,* 359; **civil society:** Mamdani, *Citizen,* 19.

14. Cooper, "Conflict and Connection," 1517; Martin, *Leisure and Society in Colonial Brazzaville,* 3.

15. **Local circumstances:** Newman, "Archbishop Daniel William Alexander and the African Orthodox Church," 628; Peterson, *Creative Writing,* 147–55.

16. Comaroff and Comaroff, *Dialectics,* 35.

17. Baden-Powell, *Scouting for Boys,* 21.

18. Mugomba and Nyaggah, introduction to *Independence without Freedom,* 1; S. Ball, "Imperialism, Social Control and the Colonial Curriculum in Africa," 260.

19. **Superior culture:** Bogonko, "Education as a Tool of Colonialism in Kenya," 1; Okoth, "The Creation of a Dependent Culture," 135; **colonial schools:** Kallaway, "An Introduction to the Study of Education for Blacks in South Africa," 9; Molteno, "The Historical Foundations of the Schooling of Black South Africans," 59.

20. **Technical elites:** Whitehead, "British Colonial Educational Policy," 222; **social mobility:** Carnoy, *Education as Cultural Imperialism,* 13, 16; Apple, *Ideology and Curriculum,* 6; Nasson, "Perspectives on Education in South Africa," 95.

21. Inter-Territorial Jeanes Conference, *Findings,* 7.

22. Parpart, "Sexuality and Power on the Zambian Copperbelt," 119; White, "Separating the Men from the Boys," 4; Stoler, "Empire," 374; the term *gender chaos* was coined by Jean Allman and Victoria Tashjian in *"I Will Not Eat Stone,"* xxxvi.

23. **Alternate masculinities:** Hansen, *African Encounters with Domesticity,* 6; Morrell, "Of Boys and Men," 606–8; "The Times of Change," 7; **manliness:** Mangan and Walvin, introduction to *Manliness and Morality,* 1; Kimmel, "Rethinking 'Masculinity,'" 13; MacDonald, *Sons of the Empire,* 17.

24. **Abnormal state:** Sinha, "Gender and Imperialism," 228; Jeal, *The Boy-Man,* 92–95, 101, 509–10.

25. **Western "perversion":** Epprecht, "The 'Unsaying' of Indigenous Homosexualities in Zimbabwe," 646; Moodie, "Migrancy and Male Sexuality on the South African Gold Mines," 254; Shire, "Men Don't Go to the Moon," 155.

26. **Official quotes:** in Great Britain, Board of Education, *Special Reports on Educational Subjects,* 13:133, 166; **colonial regime:** Epprecht, "'Good God Almighty, What's This!'" 641; **urban women:** White, *The Comforts of Home,* 11, 39.

27. Huxley, *Africa,* 402; Obermyer, "Do Native Customs Prepare for Pathfinding?" 20.

28. Epprecht, "'Good God!,'" 211; Morrell, "Boys," 627; Glaser, *Bo-Tsotsi,* 4; Burton, "Urchins, Loafers and the Cult of the Cowboy," 206.

29. School Supervisor's Annual Report, 1953, KNA, AB 15/56/9a.

30. **Autonomy of adulthood:** Gillis, Youth in History, 2, 138, 172; Kahane, The Origins of Postmodern Youth, 12; **political activism:** Stachura, The German Youth Movement, 2; Kahane, Origins, 2, 43–44.

31. Kahane, Origins, 56; Springhall, "The Boy Scouts, Class, and Militarism in Relation to British Youth Movements," 158.

32. Carton, "Impotent African Patriarchs, Unruly African Sons," 33; Mager, "Youth Organisations and the Construction of Masculine Identities in the Ciskei and Transkei," 657.

33. **Smallest units:** Burman, introduction to Growing Up in a Divided Society, 8; **structuring leisure:** Martin, Leisure, 71.

34. Fussell, Uniforms, 164.

35. Comaroff, "The Empire's Old Clothes," 402; Martin, Leisure, 154; Comaroff and Comaroff, Dialectics, 251.

36. Bonami, Frisa, and Tonchi, Uniform, 14.

37. **Historians:** Springhall, "Boy Scouts," 125–58; Rosenthal, The Character Factory; Warren, "Sir Robert Baden-Powell, the Scout Movement and Citizen Training in Great Britain"; Springhall, "Baden-Powell and the Scout Movement before 1920," 934–42; **pedagogical applications:** British Boy Scouts, Scouting and Education; Wyland, Scouting in the Schools; Nicholson, Education and the Boy Scout Movement in America; MacLeod, Building Character in the American Boy; **B-P:** Jeal, Boy-Man; Baden-Powell, Scoutmastership; Scouting and Youth Movements; Scouting for Boys.

38. **India:** Watt, "The Promise of 'Character' and the Spectre of Sedition," 37–62; Brownfoot, "Sisters under the Skin"; **Guiding:** Gaitskell, "Upward All and Play the Game"; Proctor, "'A Separate Path,'" 605–31; **extracurricular activity:** Horrell, Bantu Education to 1968; Anderson, The Struggle for the School; Furley, A History of Education in East Africa; Kallaway, ed., Apartheid and Education; Küster, African Education in Colonial Zimbabwe, Zambia and Malawi; **social historians:** J. Lewis, Empire State-Building; Martin, Leisure.

39. Warren, "Citizens of the Empire," 236.

CHAPTER 2

1. This account is drawn primarily from Jeal, Boy-Man, 383–86.

2. Iliffe, A Modern History of Tanganyika, 32–34.

3. This was the case in Kenya, where colonial administrators hoped that cross-tribal adoptions would relieve population pressure in the overcrowded Kikuyu "native reserves." In the late 1940s the policy became known as interpenetration.

4. Iliffe, Tanganyika, 318; **mouthpieces:** Huxley, Africa, 112; **leadership roles:** Leroy Vail, introduction to The Creation of Tribalism in Southern Africa, 12.

5. Tanganyika Education Conference, Conference between Government and Missions, 77.

6. Great Britain, Board of Education, Special Reports, 164–65.

7. Great Britain, Education in the United Kingdom Dependencies, 1–3.

8. **Proselytizing skills:** S. Ball, "Imperialism," 238; **LMS:** Goodall, *A History of the London Missionary Society*, 458.

9. **Social revolution:** Hetherington, *British Paternalism and Africa*, 111; **education committee:** S. Ball, "Imperialism," 243; King, *Pan-Africanism and Education*, 45.

10. **Lovedale:** Rich, "The Appeals of Tuskegee," 274; **mission schools:** Molteno, "Schooling," 57.

11. Great Britain, Board of Education, *Special Reports*, 185.

12. Quoted in Ghosh, "'English in Taste, in Opinions, in Words and Intellect,'" 185.

13. Tanganyika, *Conference*, 79.

14. **Industrial schooling:** Spring, *Deculturalization and the Struggle for Equality*, 63–64; King, "Africa and the Southern States of the USA," 661–63; Orr quoted in Sifuna, *Short Essays on Education in Kenya*, 14.

15. Anderson, *Struggle*, 39; Küster, *Education*, 104.

16. **1925 plan:** Advisory Committee on Native Education, *Education Policy in British Tropical Africa*; Hailey, *African Survey*, 1166; **1935 report:** Great Britain, Colonial Office, *Memorandum on the Education of African Communities*.

17. Advisory Committee, *Policy*, 4; Proceedings of Conference of East African Directors of Education, June 1933, KNA, ED 1/1494/113; Advisory Committee, *Policy*, 4; Mumford, "Native Schools in Central Africa," 238.

18. Sivonen, *White-Collar or Hoe Handle?* 145; GB Colonial Office, *Memorandum*, 7.

19. Inter-Territorial Jeanes Conference, *Findings*, 9; Phillips, *The Bantu in the City*, 146.

20. Ranger, "Missionary Adaptation of African Religious Institutions."

21. **Individualism and materialism:** GB Colonial Office, *Memorandum*, 9; Dougall, *Christianity and the Sex-Education of the African*, 12; **"Tribal restraint":** Steytler, *Educational Adaptations with Reference to African Village Schools*, x.

22. Remarks by R. H. W. Wisdom, School Inspector, 19 July 1928, KNA, AV 7/7/6.

23. Heyman, "The Initial Years of the Jeanes School in Kenya," 109; Benson, "The Jeanes School and the Education of the East Africa Native," 421.

24. Conference of East African Directors of Education, June 1933, KNA, ED 1/1494/113; Southern Rhodesia, Department of Native Development, *Junior School Syllabus*; Bechuanaland Protectorate, *Annual Report on Education, 1935*.

25. S. Ball, "Imperialism," 253; R. F. Gaunt, "The Place of the Vernacular in Native Education," by Nyasaland Director of Education, 25 February 1927, KNA, AV 2/69/117; Furley, *Education*, 197–99; Bude, "The Adaptation Concept in British Colonial Education," 344.

26. **Schools:** Bogonko, "Education," 8–10; **use of skills:** Mason, *Education of Rural Communities*, 2; Union of South Africa, *Report of the Commission on Native Education*, 43.

27. Hargreaves, *Decolonization in Africa*, 105.

28. Nuffield Foundation and the Colonial Office, *African Education*, 4; Hailey, *An African Survey*, rev. ed., 1167.

29. **Staffing:** Southern Rhodesia, Education Commission, *Report of the Commission Appointed to Enquire into the Matter of Native Education*, 120; Furley, *Education*, 190; **"The aim":** Uganda Protectorate, *Annual Report of the Education Department 1932*, 6; **a thousand years:** Mumford and Parker, "Education in British African Dependencies," 22.

30. Steytler, *Adaptations*, 14.

31. Tanganyika Territory, *Syllabus of Instruction for African Schools*, 3, 24–27.

32. Kershaw, *Mau Mau from Below*, 169; Thompson, *South Africa*, 172.

33. David Njoroge, interview, June 2000; Kershaw, *Mau Mau*, 170.

34. Kiambu PCEA Supervisory Team Circular, 22 July 1952, KNA, MK 1/4/46; Callander, *Handbook for Teachers*, 50; M. K. Nzioli, interview, November 1993.

35. The average age of children entering school in Bechuanaland was 10.5 years in 1936, and South African Form V students (the last year of school) averaged 19.3 years in the 1970s. Bechuanaland, *Annual Report*, 1936, 16; Kane-Berman, *Soweto*, 8.

36. Bogonko, "African Political Associations and the Quest for Secular Education in Kenya," 10; J. G. Kiano, interview, July 1998.

37. Rosenthal, *Character Factory*, 231–32; Springhall and Fraser, *Sure and Stedfast*, 20; Birch, *The Story of the Boy's Brigade*, 101–3.

38. **Militarism:** Springhall and Fraser, *Sure*, 25; Springhall, "Boy Scouts," 129; **"The Object":** McVicker, "The Boys' Brigade," 87; **non-Presbyterian:** Springhall and Fraser, 69–71; Kadish, *"A Good Jew and A Good Englishman,"* xvi, 23, 39.

39. Rosenthal, *Character*, 3–4; MacDonald, *Sons*, 3–4, 19.

40. Baden-Powell, *The Matabele Campaign*, 63–64.

41. Lord Rosmead, Governor Cape Colony, to Chamberlain, Colonial Secretary, 22 December 1896, PRO, WO 32/5626.

42. Jeal, *Boy-Man*, 338–40.

43. Rosenthal, "Knights and Retainers"; Springhall, "Boy Scouts," 131.

44. Springhall and Fraser, *Sure*, 101–2; Rosenthal, *Character*, 52; Baden-Powell, *Scouting and Youth*, 26; Jeal, *Boy-Man*, 400; Warren, "Baden-Powell," 388.

45. Jeal, *Boy-Man*, 408; Springhall, "Boy Scouts," 137; Baden-Powell, *Scouting and Youth*, 49; Baden-Powell, *Scoutmastership*, 33.

46. South Africa (African) Boy Scout Association, "What Are These Boy Scouts?" ca. 1969, SASA, BC 956/A/CSIC, 1969.

47. MacDonald, *Sons*, 11, 153–56.

48. **Religious brigades:** Wilkinson, "English Youth Movements," 3; **Haldane:** Springhall and Fraser, *Sure*, 99; Springhall, "Boy Scouts," 145; **not militaristic:** Chief Scoutmaster P. F. F. White, "Aims, Objects and Methods of the Baden-Powell Boy Scout Association," Pretoria Division, 27 May 1912, SASA, BC 956/G/Speeches; Warren, "Baden-Powell," 386–87, 391; **critics:** Springhall, "Baden-Powell," 935; Springhall, "Boy Scouts," 151; Rosenthal, *Character*, 191.

49. **Pacifism:** Baden-Powell, *Scoutmastership*, 48; Warren, "Citizens," 241; Warren, "'Mothers for the Empire'?" 106; **universal movement:** Baden-Powell, *Scouting and Youth*, 95; *Scouting for Boys*, 25.

50. Warren, "Baden-Powell," 390–91; Springhall, "Boy Scouts" 140; Proctor, "(Uni)Forming Youth," 104.

51. Jeal, *Boy-Man*, 503.

52. Smith, *Aids to Scoutmasters in East A`frica*, 7–13; White, "Aims," SASA, BC 956/G/Speeches.

53. MacDonald, *Sons*, 5, 132; Baden-Powell, *Scoutmastership*, 82.

54. **Martial tribe:** Hamilton, *Terrific Majesty*, 112; **cultural institutions:** Uganda Boy Scout Association, *Quarterly Newsletter*, no. 5 (April 1948), KSA, KBSA/C/54/34; Baden-Powell, *Scouting for Boys*, 51; *Scouting and Youth*, 27; **necklace:** Organizing Commissioner, Nyasaland Boy Scout Association to Private Secretary of the Governor, 16 November 1951, MNA, 17/BSA/1/210; Jeal, *Boy-Man*, 134; **lore:** South African Boy Scout Association, "Dinizulu's Necklace," SASA, BC 956/H/1967 Jamboree.

55. Baden-Powell, *Scouting for Boys*, 269; *Scouting and Youth*, 49; **figurative equals:** Rosenthal, *Character*, 117; Baden-Powell, *Scoutmastership*, 144.

56. Baden-Powell, *Scouting and Youth*, 77; **"desirable":** Religious Advisory Panel, 15 January 1947, MNA 17/BSA/1/209; **flexibility:** Baden-Powell, *Scoutmastership*, 120; British Boy Scouts Association, *A Challenge to Scouting*, 5; Draft Revisions of South African Boy Scout Association, POR, ca. 1976, SASA, BC 956/F/Quo Vadis.

57. **Moral education:** Baden-Powell, *Aims, Methods and Needs; Scouting for Boys*, 288; West, "The Educational Philosophy of Baden-Powell," 60; **Montessori:** Baden-Powell, *Scouting and Youth*, 15; *Scouting for Boys*, 21; British Boy Scouts, *Education*, 14; **pride:** Baden-Powell, *B.-P.'s Outlook*, January 1912 entry, 27.

58. Jeal, *Boy-Man*, 75–83; Baden-Powell, *Scoutmastership*, 89, 90–91.

59. Voeltz, "Adam's Rib," 93; Baden-Powell, *Scouting and Youth*, 21.

60. Baden-Powell, *Scouting for Boys*, 273; "White Men in Black Skins," 7.

61. John Thurman, Commissioners Training Course, British Boy Scouts Association, November 1948, SASA, BC 956/H/Jubilee Souvenirs; SABSA, "Boy Scouts?" SASA, BC 956/A/CSIC, 1969.

62. Quoted in Jeal, *Boy-Man*, 162; MacLeod, *Building Character*, 212.

63. Baden-Powell, *Scouting and Youth*, 101; "White Men," 6.

64. Baden-Powell, "Aims, Methods and Needs," no page.

65. West, "Scouting as an Educational Asset," 1016.

66. **Segregation:** "The Extension of the Privileges of Boy Scouts to the Negro Boys," ca. September 1919, Memorandum, papers of NAACP, pt. 2: Special Projects 1912–39, ser. A, reel 23; MacLeod, *Character*, 213–14; **1919:** notes on Mary White Ovington's Meeting with James West, 12 August 1919; James West to Mary White Ovington, 20 August 1919, NAACP papers, reel 23.

67. Roy Wilkins, Assistant Secretary, NAACP, to James West, 4 June 1937, NAACP papers, reel 23.

68. SASA, BC 956/G/Habonim 1930s–40s.

69. **Official resistance:** Watt, "Promise," 43–44; Warren, "Citizens," 248–49; **unauthorized troops:** Watt, "Promise," 48–50; Jeal, *Boy-Man*, 496.

70. Montagu, *An Indian Diary*, 95–97.

71. Watt, "Promise," 52–54; Jeal, *Boy-Man*, 542; Rosenthal, *Character*, 266.

72. **Leisure time:** Opper, "Education in the Copperbelt of Northern Rhodesia," 337; **cleanliness:** Nigerian Chief Scout Commissioner, "Scouting in Nigeria," 286; HQ Council of African BSA, Cub Test Amendments, 1960, UW, Calata Papers, A1729/B6.1; **expert:** Dougall, *Christianity*, 15; **song:** "I want to be a Pathfinder," by a "Natal Boy," *The Pathfinder* 2 (April 1935).

73. **"Duty to God":** Smith, *Aids,* 7; Rhodesia Boy Scouts Association, *Good Scouting,* 19; **non-Christians:** Inter-Territorial Jeanes Conference, *Findings,* 245; Minutes of Conference of Sponsoring Authorities, 2 November 1960, KNA, DC KMG 1 / 1 / 100 / 23; "Bid to Stop Scout Show," *Leader,* 8 March 1979.

74. E. Ball, "The Pathfinder Movement," 1 November 1931, 225; T. Lewis, "The Problem of the Semi-Educated African," 268, 273.

75. "General Comments on East African Scouting," by Lord Rowallan, 22 December 1950, BSA, TC/ 315 Visit of Lord Rowallan to EA 1950; **political role:** in comparison, the leaders of the Boys' Brigade shared the Scouts' faith in Britain's colonizing mission but were unwilling to adapt African traditions to their programs on the grounds they were anti-Christian. W. H. McVicker, BB Overseas Secretary, to Rheinallt Jones, 24 May 1935, UW, SAIRR, RJ Papers, AD 843/B 25. 1 (1).

76. **Colonial school system:** B. K. ole Kantai, interview, July 1998; **jamborees:** Uganda, *Annual Report,* 1947, 42; Stirling, *History of Scouting in Tanzania,* 11.

77. **Prestige:** Kiraithe Nyaga, July 1998, and J. G. Kiano, interviews, July 1998; **uniform:** Notes of Chief Scout's Tour of Rhodesia, Nyasaland, and South Africa by Traveling Commissioner IHQ, 1950, BSA, TC Zimbabwe; Matthew Kipoin, interview, June 1998.

78. **Imposters:** "Starting and Running a Scout Group in the African Boy Scouts Association," draft by SAHQ, ca. 1964, SASA, BC 956/C/File 91; **Uganda:** Uganda Boy Scouts Association Ordinance, 1922, BSA, TC Uganda; **badges:** Samuel Kazungu s/o Shadrack to KBSA, 1958, KSA, A/MSA/75; Micksey N'thaba, Natal Report, 11 November 1962, SASA, BC 956/D/D52.

79. Report by District Pathfinder Master, St. Augustine's Mission Penhaouja, 1940, BSA, TC Zimbabwe.

80. Smith, *Aids,* 22; L. S. Colchester, Kenya Scout Council Secretary to A. Yussuf, AC Kitui, 26 October 1962, KSA, A/KTI/ 133.

CHAPTER 3

1. Mokwele, "The Pedagogy of Pathfinding and the Boy Scout Movement in South Africa," 74; "How Did the Pathfinder Movement Start," by S. P. Woodfield, Divisional Pathfinder, Transvaal, 8 April 1934, UW, SAIRR, AD 1715/19.

2. Grace Dieu Training College Pathfinder Minutes, 17 February, 24 March, 7, 14 April, 19 May, 28 August, 10 November 1923, UW, Grace Dieu, AB 750/B3.

3. In South Africa, "Coloured" refers to a community of mixed European, African, and Malayan descent.

4. **Afrikaner majority:** Thompson, *South Africa,* 145–47; **Afrikaners vs. English speakers:** Dubow, "Afrikaner Nationalism, Apartheid and the Conceptualization of 'Race,'" 210.

5. Freund, *The Making of Contemporary Africa,* 176; Thompson, *South Africa,* 163.

6. **Social place:** Union of South Africa, *Native Education,* 40; **Tuskegee:** Loram, "The Phelps-Stokes Education Commission in South Africa," 505.

7. Rev. G. P. Geldenhuys, "Opinions Concerning Boys' Brigade Work in the Coloured

Churches of Cape Province," Union Congregational Church, Port Elizabeth, 27 March 1935, UW, SAIRR, RJ Papers, AD 843/B 25. 1(1); Springhall and Fraser, *Sure*, 90.

8. Jeal, *Boy-Man*, 364; Mokwele, "Pedagogy," 65.

9. Baker, "Discipline of Boys Today Is Not What It Used to Be," 85.

10. White, "Aims," SASA, BC 956/G/Speeches; **Natal:** Secretary, Natal BSA to J. Thorpe Legg, Transvaal BSA, 10 March 1921, SASA Minute Book, 1921; **provincial bodies:** SA(A)BSA, "Boy Scouts," SASA, BC 956/A/CSIC, 1969.

11. **Lovedale:** "The Pathfinder Movement," *South African Outlook*, 1 December 1931, 222; Proctor, "'Path,'" 613; **Cape Colony:** Baden-Powell to Colonel H. S. Brownrigg IHQ, 2 December 1916, BSA, TC/51 BP's Visits to Kenya, 1934–37; "Pathfinder Movement," by Woodfield, UW, SAIRR, AD 1715/19; Mokwele, "Pedagogy," 68.

12. **Transvaal:** Minutes of Conference of Pathfinder Representatives, 27 August 1924, UW, SAIRR, AD 1715/19; "Pathfinder Movement," by Woodfield, UW, SAIRR, AD 1715/19; Draft History of South African Scouting, 1980, SASA, BC 956/D/General Correspondence 1980; **innovations:** G. W. Dickson to Rheinallt Jones, 25 May 1935, UW, SAIRR, AB 843/B 25 (2).

13. **Platform:** Thompson, *South Africa*, 158; **color bar:** Dubow, "Nationalism," 224.

14. Freund, *Making*, 186.

15. **SAIRR:** Brookes, *Rheinallt Jones*, 6–7; **Joint Council movement:** Rich, *White Power and Liberal Conscience*, 17; Elphick, "Mission Christianity and Interwar Liberalism," 76.

16. **Population:** Marks, "Southern Africa," 552–53; **views on race:** Parpart, *Labor and Capital on the African Copperbelt*, 26.

17. **1940:** Marks, "Southern Africa," 553; **territories:** Pachai, *Malawi*, 100; Adult Male Population and Labor Statistics, Nyasaland Protectorate, October 1937, MNA, S1/96/37.

18. Grieveson, "Educational Needs of Urbanised Natives in South Africa," 234; Bonner, "Family, Crime and Political Consciousness on the East Rand," 394.

19. **State vs. church:** Couzens, "'Moralizing Leisure Time,'" 314; Elphick, "Christianity," 66; Cross, *Imagery of Identity in South African Education*, 170; **Loram:** Hunt Davis, "Charles T. Loram and the American Model for African Education in South Africa," 113, 121; Cross, *Imagery*, 179.

20. Southern Rhodesia, Education Commission, *Report of the Native Education Inquiry Commission*, 86.

21. C. Summers, *From Civilization to Segregation*, 133.

22. **Technical courses:** Küster, *Education*, 95, 113; C. Summers, *Civilization*, 174; **kraal schools:** Grimston, "Survey of Native Educational Development in Southern Rhodesia," chapter 7, 2; Southern Rhodesia, Education Commission, *Native Education*, 1951, 4; **Northern Rhodesia:** Küster, *Education*, 232; Ipenburg, "All Goodmen," 96.

23. Nyasaland Protectorate, Department of Education, *Annual Report*, 1954, 1; Steytler, *Adaptations*, 12.

24. Bechuanaland, *Education*, 1936, 19; Swaziland, Department of Education, *Annual Report of the Director of Education*, 6; Booth, *Historical Dictionary of Swaziland*, 293.

25. **Natal support:** Horrell, *Bantu Education*, 1, 39; Hunt Davis, "The Administration and Financing of African Education in South Africa," 130; **African graduates:** Horrell, *Bantu Education*, 1, 51.

26. **Political aims:** Kros, "They Wanted Dancing and Not Merely the Lambeth Walk," 8; Union of South Africa, *Native Education*, 61; **church schools:** Edgar, "African Educational Protest in South Africa," 144.

27. Percy Mokwele, the primary authority on African Scouting in the Union, believes that Baden-Powell probably instructed the Transvaal authorities to give way on the issue. Mokwele, "Pedagogy," 66, 74.

28. Woodfield, "Pathfinder Movement," UW, SAIRR, AD 1715/19.

29. Minutes of Conference of Pathfinder Representatives, 27 August 1924, UW, SAIRR, AD 1715/19.

30. **African Guides:** Gaitskell, "Upward," 229; **Wayfarers:** "Wayfarers in the Cape Province," *South African Outlook*, 62 (1932): 112; "Résumé of Guide Wayfarer Situation," by Lady Baden-Powell, 20 January 1936, BSA, TC South Africa.

31. Minutes of Meeting at Transvaal Scout Association HQ, 25 August 1923, UW, SAIRR, AD 1715/19; Palmer to IHQ, 5 May 1923, UW, SAIRR, AD 1715/19.

32. Secretary IHQ to Palmer, 12 June 1923, UW, SAIRR, AD 1715/19; Minutes of Transvaal Scout Assn., 25 August 1923, UW, SAIRR, AD 1715/19; E. Ball, "Movement," 1 November 1931, 224.

33. **Constitution:** Pathfinder Council, *Constitution and Regulations of the Pathfinder Movement*; **trinity:** Transvaal Scout Council, "Transvaal Pathfinders," August 1923, UW, SAIRR, AD 1715/19; S. P. Woodfield to Byrnes, Transvaal Scout Association, ca. December 1923, UW, SAIRR, AD 1715/19; *Pathfinder* 2 (September 1935).

34. **Divisions:** SASA Minute Book, 1921; **council:** Woodfield, "Pathfinder Movement," 8 April 1934, UW, SAIRR, AD 1715/19; **veto:** Pathfinder Council, *Constitution*.

35. **Twenties:** South Africa Girl Guide Association, AR 1975, SASA, BC 956/G/Girl Guides, 1970s; "Work amongst the Youth of Africa of All Races Work," by Rheinallt Jones, UW, SAIRR, AB 843/B 25 (2); **1930s:** *Pathfinder* 1 (June 1933); McVicker, "Brigade," 88; Bechuanaland, *Annual Report*, 1 January 1937 to 31 March 1938, 7, 23.

36. Lamba, "Moulding the Ideal Colonial Subject," 64–65; "Work," by Rheinallt Jones, UW, SAIRR, AB 843/B 25 (2).

37. **Southern Rhodesia:** Landau, "A Brief History of the Boy Scout Association of Rhodesia and Zimbabwe"; "Summary of Proceedings of Conference on Youth Movements in Africa," by T. G. Benson, June 1935, KSA, loose files; **Stanley:** "Commissioner for Northern Rhodesia," by H. C. Parkin, Boy Scout Association Northern Rhodesia, February 1928, BSA, TC Zambia; Ranger, "Making Northern Rhodesia Imperial," 351, 367.

38. **Pathfinder council:** D. M. Robertson, *History of Scouting amongst African Boys of Northern Rhodesia*, ca. 1947, BSA, TC Zambia; Greig, *Education in Northern Rhodesia and Nyasaland*, 41 7; Jones, "Work," UW, SAIRR, AB 843/B 25 (2); Robertson to S. Knutzen, Northern Rhodesian Scout Council, 18 March 1930, BSA, TC Zambia; Legat to Knutzen, NRBSA Commissioner, 20 June 1930, BSA, TC Zambia.

39. S. P. Woodfield to Byrnes, Transvaal Scout Association, ca. December 1923, UW, SAIRR, AD 1715/19; **tests:** Pathfinder Council, "Constitution and Regulations of the Pathfinder Movement," *Pathfinder* 1 (June 1933); **Pathfinder meetings:** Pathfinder HQ Council Minutes, 16 December 194, SASA, BC 956/A/SASC, 1940.

40. Williams, *From the South African Past*, 240; Thompson, *South Africa*, 171.

41. Freund, *Making*, 184; Thompson, *South Africa*, 162.

42. "Findings of the Bantu Juvenile Delinquency Conference," *South African Outlook* 68 (1938): 268; Grieveson, "Needs," 333, 325.

43. "Bantu Delinquency Conference," 266.

44. **Urban unrest:** Great Britain, Commission on Disturbances in the Copperbelt, *Report of the Commission Appointed to Enquire into the Disturbances in the Copperbelt*, 60; Henderson, "Early African Leadership," 87, 90; Greig, *Education*, 20; **Copperbelt schools:** C. J. Opper, "Education," 334–36; Chizinga, *The Politics of Education on the Zambian Copperbelt since the 1930s*, 18.

45. Quoted in Phillips, *Bantu*, 102.

46. Glaser, *Bo-Tsotsi*, 6, 31.

47. **Indian troop:** Minutes of Conference of Pathfinder Representatives, 27 August 1924, UW, SAIRR AD 1715/19; SA Branch BSA Council Minutes, 20 July 1928; **SABSA:** SA Branch BSA Council Minutes, 25 November 1929, SASA Minute Book, 1921; Mokwele, "Pedagogy," 86.

48. **Acrimony:** Baden-Powell to Lord Passfield, 9 January 1931, BSA, TC/51 BP's Visits to Kenya, 1934–37; **a general:** Malherbe, *Education in South Africa*, 2:400; Cross, *Imagery*, 36.

49. **Allegiance:** Meeting SASC on Making Scouting More Acceptable to Afrikaans-Speaking Boys, 12 June 1930, SASA Minute Book, 1921; "Voortrekkers and Scouts," *Die Burger*, 29 November 1930, SASA, BC 956/C/SA Scout History; **editorial:** "Our Own Organization for Our Youths," *Die Volksblad*, 26 November 1930, SASA, BC 956/C/SA Scout History; **Voortrekkers:** Making Scouting More Acceptable; SASC Minutes, 4 July 1930, SASA Minute Book, 1921.

50. Kadish, "*Good Jew*," 18, 119–21; Habonim Council, "The Aims of the Movement," February 1936, SASA, BC 956/G/Habonim 1930s–40s; SASC Minutes, 26 November 1937, SASA, BC 956/G/Habonim 1930s–40s.

51. Sir William Campbell, SASC Minutes, 16–17 May 1935, SASA Minute Book, 1921; **incomplete knowledge:** SASC Minutes, 26 November 1937, SASA, BC 956/G/Habonim 1930s–40s; A. Israel, Pretoria Scoutmaster, to K. Fleischer, 10 February 1938, SASA, BC 956/G/Habonim 1930s.

52. **Resolution:** Rheinallt Jones to Baden-Powell, 16 September 1931, BSA, TC South Africa; "The Pathfinder Movement: A State of Affairs Which Should Not Continue," *Ikwezile Afrika*, 5 September 1931, BSA, TC South Africa; **branch:** Phillips, *The Bantu Are Coming*, 102; SASC Minutes, 16 February 1931, SASA Minute Book, 1921.

53. *Scouter*, August 1931, UW, SAIRR, AD 1715/19; Baden-Powell to Rheinallt Jones, 16 October 1931, BSA, TC South Africa; **"buck up":** Pilson, "Pathfinders in the Cape Border Division," 230.

54. "Kaffir" is a derogatory term for Africans in South Africa. **1933:** Proctor, "'Path,'" 621; Mokwele, "Pedagogy," 105, 111; **meeting:** Rheinallt Jones to Sir Herbert Stanley, 1 April 1935, UW, SAIRR, AB 843/B 25 (2).

55. Memorandum by Clemmens on Non-Europeans, 29 July 1935, BSA TC South Africa; Memorandum by Assistant Division Commissioner Natal, 6 August 1935, BSA TC South Africa.

56. Rey, *Monarch of All I Survey*, 196; Points Raised by Rheinallt Jones with F. Raleigh and P. Whitely (SASC), 10 September 1935, BSA, TC South Africa; Alan Hattersley to E. H. Clemmens, Divisional Commissioner Natal, 21 August 1935, BSA, TC South Africa; Proctor, "'Path,'" 620.

57. SASC Minutes, 27 November 1936, SASA Minute Book, 1921; Pathfinder HQ Council Minutes, 16 December 1940, SASA, BC 956/A/SASC, 1940.

58. **Legal ownership:** SASC Minutes, 25–27 February 1936, SASA Minute Book, 1921; SA(P)BSA HQ Council Minutes, 14 December 1936, SASA, BC 956/A/Africa Scouts, 1936–60; Grant, "Scouts and Pathfinders," 85; The Pathfinder Movement, 1936 Fund Raising Appeal, UW, SAIRR, AD 1715/19; **funding:** Constitution of SABSA, section 3(p), 18 January 1937, SASA, BC 956/B/Original Constitution; Pathfinder HQ Council Minutes, 16 December 1940, ASA, BC 956/A/SASC, 1940.

59. **"True conception":** SA(A)BSA, "What Are These Boy Scouts?" ca. 1969, BC 956/A/CSIC, 1969; Lugard, *Dual Mandate,* 86; **declaration:** *Natal Mercury,* 2 March 1936; **"comrades":** Baden-Powell, "A Federation of Scouts: Race Problems in Africa," *Times,* 3 June 1936.

60. SA(P)BSA Executive Committee Minutes, 14 July 1938, SASA, BC 956/A/Africa Scouts, 1936–60; Arthur Amor, Ex-Principal St. Augustine School, to Rheinallt Jones, 30 May 1940, BSA, TC South Africa; Pathfinder HQ Council Minutes, 16 December 1940, SASA, BC 956/A/SASC, 1940; Union of South Africa, *Report of the Commission on Native Education,* 1949–1951, 94.

61. Gaitskell, "Upward," 245.

62. **1936:** "Résumé," by Lady Baden-Powell, BSA, TC South Africa; Memorandum by SAGGA, 1936, BSA, TC South Africa; **appeal:** F. Raleigh to Baden-Powell, 13 February 1936, BSA, TC South Africa; **"no question":** *South African Outlook,* March 1936, 51; **controversy:** Lady B-P, "Résumé"; Mrs. MacNeillie to Lady Read, 26 February 1936, BSA, TC South Africa; **Transvaal:** Gaitskell, "Upward," 250; *Grace Dieu Bulletin,* June 1937, UW, Grace Dieu, AB 750.

63. **Enrollment:** "South African Pathfinder Council," *South African Outlook,* 1 December 1931, 229; SA(P)BSA HQ Council Minutes, 14 December 1939, SASA, BC 956/A/Africa Scouts, 1936–60; **Chief Pathfinder:** Grant, "Scouts," 85; SA(P)BSA Executive Committee Minutes, 14 July 1938, SASA, BC 956/A/Africa Scouts, 1936–60.

64. **Federated Scouting:** Bechuanaland, *Annual Report,* 1937–38, 26; Rey, Resident Commissioner Bechuanaland, to Col. G. Walton, IHQ, 14 February 1936, BSA, TC South Africa; **Bangwato and Batwana:** John Shaw, Bechuana Protectorate Pathfinder Association, to Rheinallt Jones, 29 May 1940, BSA, TC South Africa; "Memorandum on Youth Movements in Bechuanaland," by J. Leech, 18 March 1950, SASA, 956/H/International Commissioner.

65. Grimston, "Survey," chapter 4, 275; Stanley to Baden-Powell, 3 August 1937, BSA, TC South Africa; Mokwele, "Pedagogy," 79.

66. CO Minute by J. A. Calder, 25 September 1935, PRO, CO 849/5/2; Secretary NRBSA to CSNR, 19 October 1935, BSA, TC Zambia; Robertson, *History of Scouting,* BSA, TC Zambia; W. F. Cartmel-Robinson, NR Commissioner, to IHQ, 13 June 1941, BSA, TC Zambia.

67. Rheinallt Jones to Ugandan Director of Education, 14 November 1934, UW, SAIRR, AB 843/B 25; Conference on Youth Movements, Draft Agenda, Salisbury, 7–8 June 1935, UW, SAIRR, RJ Papers, AD 843/B 25. 1 (1).

68. W. H. McVicker, BB Overseas Secretary, to Rheinallt Jones, 24 May 1935, UW, SAIRR, RJ Papers, AD 843/B 25. 1 (1).

69. Findings of Conference on Youth Movements in Africa, 7–8 June 1935, UW, SAIRR, RJ Papers, AD 843/B 25. 1 (1); Use of Indigenous Arts and Crafts and Traditional, Proposed Memorandum for African Youth Conference, Salisbury 1935, UW, SAIRR, AB 843/B 25 (2).

70. I am particularly grateful to Alan Booth for providing me with his notes and personal insights on Swazi history in general and the emabutfo controversy in particular. Booth, Dictionary, 8–10, 93; Lowe, "Swaziland's Colonial Politics," 29.

71. **Emabutfo:** Lowe, "Swaziland," 25; Swazi National School Committee Minutes, 24 November 1932, SNA, RCS 328/33; **Sobhuza's goals:** Paramount Chief of Swaziland, Memorandum upon Native Education, 10 March 1933, SNA, RCS 328/33; Lowe, "Swaziland," 439.

72. Notes of a Meeting at Mbabane, 3 May 1933, SNA, RCS 328/33; Hoernle and Schapera, "Joint Report on the Advisability and Possibility of Introducing the Ibuto System of the Swazi People into the Educational System," August 1934, SNA, RCS 328/33; Marwick, The Swazi, 87. For a discussion of similar practices in Xhosa and Zulu society, see Mager, "Youth," 660; T. Dunbar Moodie, "Migrancy," 231.

73. **Debate:** Marwick to Schapera, 28 February 1934, SNA, RCS 328/33; W. W. M. Eiselen to H. J. E. Dumbrell, 17 March 1934, SNA, RCS 328/33; **safeguard:** Committee of Advice on Native Education Minutes, 3 October 1934, SNA, RCS 328/33; **dismissal:** Malinowski, "Report on the Age Grade System of the Swazi People," 13 August 1934, SNA, RCS 328/33.

74. Rheinallt Jones, Chief Pathfinder, to Swaziland Resident Commissioner, 13 November 1934, SNA, RCS 328/33.

75. **Traditional authorities:** "Notes upon the Chief Pathfinder's Memorandum upon the Pathfinder Movement and Swazi Youth," by A. G. Marwick, Acting Resident Commissioner, 24 January 1935, SNA, RCS 328/33; **funding:** "The Use of Indigenous Age-Grade Organisations: The Swazi Ibutho," by Rheinallt Jones, ca. 1935, UW, SAIRR, RJ Papers, AD 843/B 25. 1 (1); W. Byrant Mumford, Comments on the Possible Introduction of the Amabuto System in the Swazi National School, 14 August 1934, SNA, RCS 328/33.

76. Principal G. E. P. Broderick, Report on the Experimental Ibuto System at Swazi National School, 8 October 1935, SNA, RCS 328/33.

77. Meeting between Resident Commissioner Marwick and Paramount Chief, 4 May 1933, SNA, RCS 328/33; Pathfinder HQ Council Minutes, 14 December 1939, SASA, BC 956/A/SASC, 1940; Mokwele, "Pedagogy," 80. Although the Emabutfo-Pathfinder hybrid faded from popular memory, many of its former members went on to have distinguished political careers. These included Prince Makhosini Dlamini, Swaziland's first prime minister; Mfundza Sukati (the school induna who supposedly drank too much), the first deputy prime minister; and J. S. M. Matsebula, secretary to King Sobhuza and a leading Swazi historian. H. Macmillan, "Swaziland," 652.

78. Grimston, "Survey," chapter 4, 81; Pathfinder 2 (April 1935), UW, SAIRR, RJ Papers, AD 843/B 25. 1 (1).

79. **Beating/punishment:** P. C. Sykes, "Lubwa TTC," UW, Sykes AB 2589f; **Christianity:** Ipenburg, "All Goodmen," 123; **Lubwa Scouts:** *African Scout* (Northern Rhodesian Branch of BSA) 5 (October–December 1949), BSA, TC Zambia; Kaunda, *Zambia Shall Be Free*, 12–13.

80. **Retribalization:** Obermyer, "Customs," 20; **"never forget":** D. McMalcolm, Chief Inspector of Native Education in Natal, to Baden-Powell, 8 June 1940, BSA, TC South Africa; **royal family:** Harries, "Imagery Symbolism and Tradition in a South African Bantustan," 111–12.

81. **Liberals:** Ball, "Movement," 1 November 1931, 225; *The Pathfinder* 1 (June 1933), UW, Calata Papers A1729/B6.1; **urban Pathfinding:** Pathfinder HQ Council Minutes, 14 December 1939, SASA, BC 956/A/SASC, 1940; Grieveson, "Needs," 334; Phillips, *Bantu in City*, 301; Glaser, "The Mark of Zorro," 50.

82. James Arthur Calata, SASA, Biographies; Tetelman, "We Can," 61–63, 179, 556–58.

83. Pathfinder HQ Council Minutes, 14 December 1939, SASA, BC 956/A/SASC, 1940; SA(P)BSA HQ Council Minutes, 6 January 1942, 25 June 1948, SASA, BC 956/A/Africa Scouts, 1936–60.

84. *Pathfinder*, 2 April 1935, 1–3.

85. Pathfinder Council, *Constitution; Pathfinder* 1 (August 1931).

CHAPTER 4

1. AHS, AR 1932, Church Missionary Society Archives (CMS), G3 A5/01933/98.

2. Inspection Report AHS, March 1933, KNA, ED 1/1023/147; AHS, AR, 1934, PCEA, I/12/EE2/27; AHS Principal's Report, 1941, KNA, ED 1/1020/295.

3. **Future leaders:** *Alliance High School Old Boys Magazine* 1 (June 1937), PCEA, I/12/EEI-V; "How Scouting Came to Africans in Kenya," *Batian*, no. 18 (September 1954); **Kiano:** J. G. Kiano, interview, July 1998.

4. Quoted in Hailey, *Survey* (1938), 135.

5. Kenya, Land Commission, *Evidence*. The actual percentage of usable land in African hands depends on the definition of what was arable. The Kenyan Agriculture Department did not count the Laikipia Plateau and the lowest portions of the Rift Valley as fully arable. By its reckoning, Africans held 80 percent of the colony's productive land.

6. East Africa Protectorate, *Evidence of the Education Commission*, 185.

7. *Kikuyu News* 18 (April 1910).

8. **1st Kikuyu:** *Kikuyu News* 13 (August 1909), 17 (March 1910); **Kareri:** Charles Muhoro Kareri, *The Life of Charles Muhoro Kareri*, 23.

9. "Boy's Brigade Report, 1931," by Rev. A. Christie Johnson, *Kikuyu News* 116 (June 1931); Circular by H. M. Lamont, 24 April 1942, CSM ACC 7548-B275.

10. "A Short History of Scouting in Kenya," *Batian* 3 (1957); Kenya Scout Association, "Short History of Scouting in Kenya," in Souvenir Programme, Kenya Scouts Camporee at Princess Park Mombasa, 11–18 August 1961.

11. **Zanzibar:** Stirling, *Scouting*, 1–4; "Report on Zanzibar Scouting," by Charles Simp-

son, ca. 1921, BSA, TC Tanzania; **1930s:** Informal East African Scout Commissioners Meeting, 14 January 1935, UW, SAIRR, AB 843/B 25 (2).

12. **Uganda:** UBSA Quarterly Newsletter, no. 5 (April 1948), Nairobi (KSA), KBSA/C/54/34; McGregor *King's College Budo*, 55; **Lukiko:** Commissioner E. L. Scott, UBSA, to Overseas Commissioner, 11 May 1922, BSA, TC Uganda; **"true" aims:** Special Meeting at Kazi Camp, 11 June 1952, KSA, KBSA/C/54.

13. **Bukoba District:** Stirling, *Scouting*, 1–2; Jones, *Education in East Africa*, 184; **officials:** Acting TG Gov to Colonial Secretary, 30 March 1923, TNA, AB 898/5; Tanganyika Secretariat Minute to CST, 8 March 1922, TNA, AB 898/3; *Tanganyika, Conference*, 88.

14. **Uganda:** Jenkins, "Girl Guide Activities in Uganda," 14–17; **other countries:** *Tanganyika, Conference*, 90; KGGA AR, 1962–63, KNA, OPE 2/65/2; *East Africa Standard*, 22 February 1963.

15. Parsons, "African Participation in the British Empire."

16. **"Sacred trust":** Hailey, *Survey* (1938), 435–37; **indirect rule:** Iliffe, *Tanganyika*, 322, 336.

17. **Assemblies/councils:** Berman, *Control and Crisis in Colonial Kenya*, 310; **Kenyan groups:** for example, the East Africa Association became the Kikuyu Central Association in 1925 to concentrate on more specifically on Kikuyu land claims. The Kavirondo Taxpayers Association became similarly more focused on Luo concerns. See Lonsdale, "Political Associations in Western Kenya"; Furedi, "The African Crowd in Nairobi," 279; Strayer, *Making of Mission Communities in East Africa*, 128; Clough, *Fighting Two Sides*, 48. **Uganda:** Pirouet, *Historical Dictionary of Uganda*, 74; **Tanganyika:** Westcott, "An East African Radical," 87.

18. **Western curriculum:** Jones, *Education*; **efficiency:** Furley, *Education*, 160; Hewitt, *The Problems of Success*, 246.

19. Kay, "African Roles, Responses, and Initiatives in Colonial Education," 279–80.

20. **Religious character:** J. W. Arthur to Dougall, 24 June 1940, CSM, ACC 7548-B274; **basic pedagogy:** Heyman, "Jeanes School," 111–15; Sivonen, *White-Collar*, 40; **Jeanes teachers:** "Jeanes School AR 1928," by James W. C. Dougall, CMS G3/X/A5/12; Dougall, *The Village Teacher's Guide*, 113–14; Report by T. G. Benson, Inter-territorial Jeanes Conference, *Findings*, 62.

21. "Notes on African Scouting," by Jeremiah Segero, Jeanes Teacher, ca. 1935, UW, SAIRR, RJ Papers, AD 843/B 25. 1 (1). Having proved his reliability to the colonial authorities, Segero went on to have a distinguished career as a judge. He eventually became senior chief of Isukha Location, near Kakamega in western Kenya.

22. "Jeanes School," by Dougall, CMS G3/X/A5/12.

23. **"Leader":** Segero, "Notes on African Scouting," UW SAIRR, RJ Papers, AD 843/B 25. 1 (1); **Atsinwa:** "Notes on Native Scouting in Kavirondo,' by Stefano Atsinwa, Jeanes Teacher, ca. 1935, UW, SAIRR, RJ Papers, AD 843/B 25. 1 (1); **mission help:** Raphoto, "The Jeanes School in Kenya," 127–28; Kay, "The Southern Abaluyia, the Friends Africa Mission, and the Development of Education in Western Kenya," 233.

24. **Scout law:** "Notes on Native Scouting in Kikuyu," by Justin Itotia, Jeanes Teacher, ca. 1935, UW, SAIRR, RJ Papers, AD 843/B 25. 1 (1); **individual interests:** Jeanes School Circular, no. 2/34, 24 June 1934, KNA, PC NZA 3/6/124/30.

25. Cameron, *My Tanganyika Service*, 127; Furley, *Education*, 140; Iliffe, *Tanganyika*, 338–40.

26. **Tribal houses:** Tanganyika Education, *Conference*, 80–81; Mumford, "Schools," 240–41; **warrior tradition:** Tanganyika Education, *Conference*, 88–90; Mumford, Education Department Bukoba, to Secretary BBSA, 8 July 1924, BSA, TC Tanzania; **Mashujaa:** Tanganyika Education, *Conference*, 81.

27. **Literary curriculum:** Furley, *Education*, 110; **Huxley:** Huxley, *Africa*, 298.

28. **Ugandan troops:** Huxley, *Africa*, 298; E. L. Scott, Commissioner UBSA, to Overseas Commissioner IHQ, 11 October 1921, BSA, TC Uganda; H. Wood, "The Boy Scout Movement as part of the Educational System," 66; **countryside:** "Notes on the Scout Movement in Uganda," by Uganda Scout Commissioner, ca. 1935, UW, SAIRR, RJ Papers, AD 843/B 25. 1 (1); Uganda, *Annual Report*, 1944, 31.

29. The name Alliance referred to the close cooperation of the Protestant missions in theological and educational matters. Sifuna, *Essays*, 50–54, 66–67.

30. **Alliance:** "How Scouting Came to Africans in Kenya," *Batian* 18 (September 1954); AHS AR 1932, CMS G3 A5/01933/98; **1930s:** John Arthur CSM to W.W. McLachlan, General Secretary Foreign Mission Committee, 23 July 1931, PCEA, I/12/EE7/91; AHS AR, 193, PCEA, I/12/EE5/15.

31. **European movement:** Stephen Smith, *The History of Alliance High School*, 39; Kenya Scout Association, Assistant Commissioner's AR 1934, by T. G. Benson, UW, SAIRR, AB 843/B 25 (2); "Short History of Scouting," *Batian* 3 (1957); **administrator:** Senior Commissioner Central Province to CSK, 12 March 1924, KNA, DC MKS 10B/16/1.

32. **Percentages:** Mumford and Parker, "Education," 22; Grimston, "Survey," chapter 2, 30; **1924:** Jones, *Education*, 118; Kenya Colony, *Education Department Annual Report*, 1935, 16. European schooling in Kenya was also subpar in the interwar era. Julian Huxley criticized the European Nairobi schools for low standards and noted that students at the local Indian schools took more rigorous exams. Huxley, *Africa*, 160; Cameron, *Service*, 128; Anderson, *Struggle*, 138.

33. **Vernaculars:** Sheffield, *Education in Kenya*, 21; Sivonen, *White-Collar*, 188; **English:** Hewitt, *Problems*, 248; KMC Standing Education Committee Report 1942, CMS AF35/49 G3 A5/2–4.

34. "Kenya Missionary Council Statement on Educational Policy," by L. B. Greaves, 29 December 1939, CMS, AF35/49 G3 A5/2/A5/4.

35. Quoted in Bogonko, "African Political Associations," 12.

36. Barrett et al., *Kenya Churches Handbook*, 111.

37. "African Separatist Churches in Kenya," by Rev. L. J. Beecher, December 1952, CSM ACC 7548-B277; Iliffe, *Tanganyika*, 363; Furley, *Education*, 106; Welbourn, *East African Rebels*, 79–81, 98.

38. Kovar, "Kikuyu," 115, 155; Clough, *Fighting*, 148; Anderson, *Struggle*, 116.

39. Peterson, *Creative Writing*, 144.

40. Peterson, "Writing in Revolution," 77–79.

41. **Ordaining:** Superintendent CID Uganda to Superintendent CID Kenya, 14 September 1932, KNA, SEC 1/7/9/18a; Newman, "Archbishop Daniel William Alexander and the African Orthodox Church," 616; **raising money:** Confidential Letter, no author,

n.d., KNA, SEC 1/7/9/7a; Assistant Inspector i/c Thika Unit to Kenya Superintendent of CID, 17 December 1935, KNA, SEC 1/7/9/13c; **Kikuyu culture:** Ndungu, "Gituamba and Kikuyu Independency in Church and School," 140, 145; Anderson, *Struggle*, 118; **Pentecostal Church:** Kovar, "Kikuyu," 178; Natsoulas, "The Kenyan Government and the Kikuyu Independent Schools," 298.

42. Kenya, *Education Annual Report*, 1935, 15–16.

43. Johana Kunyiha to Kenya Governor, 13 June 1936, KNA, Sec 1/7/9/26.

44. Jeanes School Meeting on Independent Schools, 11 August 1936, KNA, SEC 1/7/9/39a.

45. Inspection Report, Rironi Karinga School, 6 November 1937, KNA, MK 2/5/8; Notes of Meeting at CNC's office, 6 February 1939, KNA, ED 1/3284/9; Natsoulas, "Schools," 292

46. CNC Minute, 2 February 1939, KNA, ED 1/3284/7; Meeting at CNC, 6 February 1939, KNA, ED 1/3284/9; Anderson, *Struggle*, 123.

47. Kershaw, *Mau Mau*, 194; Anderson, *Struggle*, 125; Kovar, "Kikuyu," 250, 256.

48. **Segero:** Lonsdale, "State and Peasantry in Colonial Africa," 114; **Jeanes graduates:** Raphoto, "Jeanes School," 42; King, *Pan-Africanism*, 161; Heyman, "Jeanes School," 114.

49. **Alliance requirements:** AHS Circular, Admission, 5 December 1931, PCEA, I/12/EE7/75; Clayton and Savage, *Government and Labour in Kenya*, 244; **"training place":** Colin Maher, Memorandum on Agricultural Education at AHS, 21 October 1940, KNA, ED 1/1020/233.

50. **Success:** Tanganyika, *Conference*, 80–81; **reality:** Mumford, "Schools," 243; Ranger, "African Attempts to Control Education in East and Central Africa," 69.

51. Mumford, "Schools," 243–44; "Tentative Suggestions and Comments on Amabuto System in the Swazi National School," by W. Byrant Mumford, 14 August 1934, SNA, RCS 328/33.

52. **Independent troops:** B. A. Astley, Education Department, to Chief Commissioner G. Rhodes, 2 May 195, KNA, AB 13/2/157; **Mohindra:** Secretary Mombasa Scout Association to Secretary KBSA, 11 February 1934, KNA, AG/3/1/16; **1934:** KSC Minutes, 26 March 1934, KSA, Minute Book, 1934–1939; Commissioner of Police to AGK, 26 June 1934, KNA, AG 3/1/2.

53. **Beni dance:** Ranger, *Dance and Society in Eastern Africa*, 5; Freund, *Making*, 152; **legislation:** Boy Scouts Ordinance 1935, KNA, AG 3/1/20a.

54. **Last resort:** H. Legat, HQ Commissioner Overseas Scouts, to Benson, Acting CC, 26 February 1934, KSA, Correspondence with Imperial HQ; "Proceedings," by Benson, June 1935, KSA, loose; **Scoutmasters:** KSC Minutes, 26 March 1934, KSA, Minute Book, 1934–1939; "For Information of the Committee of the Council," by Baden-Powell, 19 November 1935, Rhodes House Library, Oxford, Afr. S. 1120/III/8/12; Baden-Powell to Kenya governor Joseph Byrne, 3 December 1935, BSA TC/51 B.P.'s Visits to Kenya, 1934–37.

55. Informal East African Scout Commissioners Meeting, 14 January 1935, UW, SAIRR, AB 843/B 25 (2).

56. Nigerian Chief Scout Commissioner, "Scouting in Nigeria," *Nigeria* 16 (1938): 284; Slater, "The Guides and Brownies of the Gold Coast," 161; Cardinall, *The Gold Coast*, 200.

57. **UBSA:** "The Importance and Extent of Work amongst the Youth of Africa of All Races," by Rheinallt Jones, ca. 1935, UW, SAIRR, AB 843/B 25 (2); **Tanganyika:** TBSA to H. Legat, Overseas Commissioner IHQ, 6 June 1940, BSA, TC Tanzania; **Nyerere:** Stirling, *Scouting*, 5.

58. **African representative:** ExCom Report, 1939–40, KSA Library; Chief Native Commissioner Hosking to PCs, 18 December 1939, KNA, AB 14/15/3; **finances:** G. R. B. Brown, DC FH, to ACC, 2 April 1938, KNA, DC, MUR 3/4/13/7; KBSA ExCom Report, 1939–40, KSA Library; Chair KGGA and CC KBSA to Trustee King George Memorial Fund, 6 June 1941, KGGA Minute Book, 1939–43.

59. **Brigade exclusion:** J. A. Arthur to A. Kydd, Foreign Mission Committee CSM, 18 June 1936, SA I/B/10; CMS Executive Council Minutes, n.s., no. 29, 8–10 March 1938, CMS AF35/49 G3 A5/4: CMS ExCO Minutes, 1935–45, vol. 1; CMS Coast Missionary Committee Minutes, 24–25 August 1938, CMS AF35–49, G3 A5/3; **Kenyan Guides:** *Kikuyu News*, no. 134 (March 1938).

60. **1930s expansion:** KSC Minutes, 20 January 1936 and 9 January 1939, KSA, Minute Book, 1934–1939; "A Short History of Scouting," *Batian* 10 (1957); Machakos AR, 1938, KNA, DC MKS 1/1/27; **circular:** PC, CP Circular, 1 July 1937, KNA, DC MUR 3/4/13/1; **6th Nairobi influence:** *Alliance High School Old Boys Magazine* 1 (June 1937), PCEA, I/12/EEI-V; *Batian*, October 1953.

61. **Money for uniforms:** Jeanes School, AR 1936, KNA, PC NZA 3/6/124/46; Jeanes School AR 1938, CMS AF35–49, G3 A5/03; **collapse of troops:** Jeanes School, AR 1936; Inspection Report, Kima Central School, by T. G. Benson, 19 September 1940, KNA, AV 1/18/298.

62. CMS Buxton School Inspection Report, 5 November 1935, KNA, CA 3/15; CMS Maseno Inspection Report, 30 November 194, KNA, DC KSM 1/10/39; Underwood to Benson, KBSA, 26 October 1938, KSA, Scouts General, TSB.

63. Mason, *Education*, 3; Memorandum to Kenya Scout Council by DC of Scouts NZA, September 1938, KSA, Scouts General, TSB.

64. KBSA ExCom Report, 1939–40, KSA Library Nairobi LA Circular, January 1944, KNA, MAA 2/5/91; Nyanza Education Annual Report, 1945, KNA, EAYMF 134/80/147; CC, UBSA, AR 1945, KSA, KBSA/C/54/19.

65. **1940s:** KGGA ExCom Minutes, 2 December 1941, KGGA Minute Book, 1939–43; Dougall to R. G. M. Calderwood, Secretary CSM Council, 4 January 1944, CSM, ACC 7548-B275; Dougall to J. W. Muggoch, 10 January 1944, CSM, ACC 7548-B275; **war activities:** Uganda Protectorate, *Annual Report of the Education Department* 1940 (Entebbe: Government Printer, 1941), 2; Saunders, *Left Handshake*, 195; KBSA ExCom Report, 1939–40, KSA Library; Nairobi LA Circular, January 1944, KNA, MAA 2/5/91.

66. Matthew Kipoin, interview, June 1998.

67. Interviews, Matthew Kipoin, June 1998, J. G. Kiano, July 1998, and B. K. ole Kantai, July 1998; **heckling:** (Kenyan) *Scouting News*, January 1947.

68. Uganda, *Annual Report*, 1932, 15; Jenkins, "Activities," 15.

69. "Notes on the Scout Movement in Uganda," by Uganda Scout Commissioner, ca. 1935, UW, SAIRR, RJ Papers, AD 843/B 25 1 (1).

70. DC of Scouts NZA to T. G. Benson, 2 November 1938, KSA, Scouts General, TSB; KSA, "Short History of Scouting in Kenya"; Wood, "Boy Scout Movement," 67.

71. Director of Education to Inspector of Schools KBU, 15 June 1938, KNA, MK 2/5/20; "Report on Rironi Scout Troop," by Kiambu School Inspector, 1 July 1938, KNA, MK 2/5/21.

72. KGGA ExCom Minutes, 9 May 1944, KGGA Minute Book, 1943–47.

73. P. K. Allen AIP Machakos to Commissioner of Police, 17 September 1938, KNA, SEC 1/1/6/18.

74. KSC Minutes, 20 January 1936, KSA, Minute Book, 1934–1939; NZA LA Minutes, 13 March 1939, KNA, AK 1/32.76.

CHAPTER 5

1. Hewitt, *Problems*, 136; CNC Minute, 2 February 1939, KNA, ED 1/3284/7; Kahuhia Normal School, AR 1939, KNA, ED 1/2097/48.

2. **Staff:** Kahuhia Normal School AR 1940, CSM, ACC 7548-B274; **1944:** 2d Fort Hall Troop, Report 1944, KNA, DC MUR 3/4/13; **1948:** Kahuhia Normal School, Principal's Report 1948, KNA, DC MUR 3/4/21; **best organized:** Lord Rowallan, Commonwealth Chief Scout, Report on Visit to Kenya, 31 January 1951, BSA, TC/315 visit of Lord Rowallan to EA 1950; **Mbugua:** Francis Kamau Mbugua, interview, July 1998.

3. **Rebellion:** PEO Nairobi to Director of Education, 27 February 1953, KNA, AB 13/2/137; Hooper to M. A. C. Warren, 2 November 1952, CMS, AF59 G3 A5/6/1/1952–53; Circular Letter by Pearl Read, Kahuhia Mission, 18 June 1953, CMS, AF59 G3 A5/6/1/1953; **Minae:** Diary of C. T. F. Bewes, 18 January 195, CMS, AF59 G3 A5/6/2/Diary of C. T. F. Bewes.

4. **"Schemes":** Quoted in Seeley, "Social Welfare in a Kenyan Town," 545; **arguments:** J. Lewis, *Empire*, 98; Iliffe, *Tanganyika*, 437; Cain and Hopkins, *British Imperialism*, 231–33.

5. Freund, *Making*, 195.

6. **Territorial level:** Great Britain, Colonial Office, *Education for Citizenship in Africa*, 5; J. Lewis, *Empire*, 126; Iliffe, *Tanganyika*, 482; **Labourite experts:** J. Lewis, *Empire*, 78, 313; Seeley, "Welfare," 541.

7. **Education pyramid:** Kenya Colony, *Report of the Development Committee*, 1:11; Nuffield Foundation, *African Education*, 72.

8. **English:** Uganda, *Annual Report*, 1952, 17; NBI Region PEO Circular, Teaching of English in Primary Schools, 24 July 1953, KNA, MK 3/9/111.

9. **1948 report:** GB, CO, *Citizenship*, 10–18, 29; **1949 report:** Kenya Colony and Protectorate, *African Education in Kenya* (Nairobi: Government Printer, 1949), 34.

10. **Education:** J. Lewis, *Empire*, 317; Nuffield Foundation, *Education*, 69; **Scouts and Guides:** Great Britain, Colonial Office, *Summer Conference on African Administration*, 140.

11. Furley, *Education*, 225–27; Kenya, *African Education*, 10–11; R. A. Lake, "A Kenya Government African School in 1948," 1004; Iliffe, *Tanganyika*, 444.

12. African Education in Kenya, December 1950, KNA, AV 1/43/15/1; Kenya, *African Education*, vii–viii, 54.

13. **Protest:** Draft Despatch to Colonial Secretary, 13 February 1951, KNA, AV 1/43/19; Brief for Minister of State on Parliamentary Debate on Beecher Report, 13 December 1950, PRO, CO 533/565/4/38; **practical constraints:** R. F. Dain, CCK Education Secretary, to C. T. F. Bewes, 14 October 1955, CMS, AF59 G3 A5/2/5/4; Speech by Norman Larby, Education Director, to CCK Education Committee, 27 February 1956, CMS, AF59 G3 A5/2/5/4.

14. Kenya, *Legislative Council Debates*, vol. 55, 2d sess., question no. 80 by M. G. Kanyo, 6 May 1953; Sheffield, *Education*, 32; Kershaw, *Mau Mau*, 170; Furley, *Education*, 230.

15. Iliffe, *Tanganyika*, 356; PCEA Kiambu Supervisory Team AR 1954, by F. Welch, KNA, MK 3/7; "CCK Report on Kabere Village Embu," by G. Sluiter, May 1956, CMS AF59 G3 A5/4/502.

16. **Kenyatta:** B. E. Kipkorir, "Mau Mau and Western Education," University Nairobi Department of History, Staff Seminar Paper no. 7, 16 November 1977, 8; **Beecher Report:** "Kikuyu Independence Schools: Extract from 1953 Report from Kenyan Education Department," *Oversea Education* 27 (1953): 61; Kovar, "Kikuyu," 272–74.

17. Uganda, *Annual Report*, 1947, 17, 21, 35; *Annual Report*, 1950, 18; Furley, *Education*, 285.

18. Iliffe, *Tanganyika*, 38–39; Burton, "Urchins," 201.

19. **Training schools:** "Proposal for Rural Schools in Central Province," by M. G. Capon and N. Langford-Smith, 8 November 1948, CMS, AF59 G3 A5/e15/1; Diary of C. T. F. Bewes, 26 January 1953, CMS, AF59 G3 A5/6/2/Diary of C. T. F. Bewes; **Williams:** "Youth Camps: A Proposal," by P. E. Williams, Director of Training, 1945, KNA, DC, KSM 1/10/74/1; Williams to Dickson, 21 February 1945, KNA, DEF/10/64/14; **plan dismissed:** Governor Richards to G. F. Sayers, 1 August 1945, MNA, S41/1/5/3/7; Memorandum on Social Welfare, PC's Meeting, January 1946, KNA, CA 3/93/43.

20. **Kenya:** Secretary TBSA to Secretary KSC, 28 November 1946, KSA, KBSA/C/47; **Tanganyika:** TBSA HQ Committee Minutes, 31 March 1948, BSA, TC Tanzania; **"headless":** "Tour of Tanganyika," by Dahl, 1948, BSA, TC/264 Tours.

21. **Inspiration:** Lord Rowallan to Kenya Governor Sir Philip Mitchell, 2 June 1945, KNA, AB 14/15/23; **Rowallan:** Lord Rowallan to Chief Scouts, Overseas Branches, 21 September 1945, BSA, TC/274 Overseas Organizing Commissioners.

22. **Uganda:** Committee of TSC Minutes, 9 May 1947: No Funds for Commissioner, KSA, KBSA/C/47/3; CC UBSA, AR 1945, KSA, KBSA/C/54/19; Uganda, *Annual Report*, 1944, 31; **Kenya:** Governor Mitchell to Chief Commissioner A. J. Kingsley-Heath, 29 July 1945, KNA, AB 14/15/20; Mitchell to Rowallan, 19 September 1945, KNA, AB 14/15/36; KSC ExCom Minutes, 24 October 1945, KNA, DC, MUR 3/4/13.

23. **KBSA:** *Kenya Scouting News*, December 1945, KNA, DC MUR 3/4/13; CSK to Social Welfare Advisor, 17 June 1946, KNA, AB 14/15/78; **Smith:** *East Africa Standard*, 3 May 1946; **Vincent:** "Tour of Kenya," by Dahl, 1948, BSA, TC/264 Tours.

24. **1947:** Uganda, *Annual Report*, 1947, 43; CSK to KSC, 3 April 1947, KNA, AB 14/15/105; H. H. Wood CC KBSA to Mrs. P. Maslin, KGGA Colony Treasurer, 15 July 1947, KGGA, Correspondence with Scouts; **"integrate":** Rhodes to CSK, 2 March 1949, KNA, AB 14/15/167; **Tanganyika:** TBSA, HQ Committee Minutes, 3 September 1948, KSA,

KBSA/C/47/40; TSBA Extraordinary Meeting Minutes, 19 October 1950, KSA, KBSA/C/47; TBSA, ExCom Minutes, 27 November 1951, KSA, KBSA/C/47.

25. **Allocation:** Organizing Commissioner's Report on Nyanza, April 1948, KSA, KBSA/C/39; **media:** *Batian* 17 (July 1954); **Nyanza DC:** DC CNZA to CNC, 16 August 1948, KNA, MAA 2/5/91/74.

26. **1948:** CO, Social Welfare in the Colonies, January 1948, KNA, CA 3/93/166a; **Uganda:** acting CC UBSA, AR 1946, KSA, KBSA/C/54/4; Conference of Uganda Social Welfare Staff, 5 December 1947, KNA, AB 17/80/20; **Jeanes:** Social Welfare Course, Ex-Servicemen's Training Centre C, Jeanes School, June 1947, KNA, CA 3/93/105; **officers:** Organizing Commissioner's Tour of Coast Province, 30 June 1948, KSA, KBSA/C/39; FH LA 1948 AR, by C. Hooper, AC, KNA, DC, MUR 3/4/13/21.

27. **School discipline:** Uganda, *Annual Report*, 1947, 24; **constructive outlet:** "General Comments on East African Scouting," by Lord Rowallan, 22 December 1950, BSA, TC/315 Visit of Lord Rowallan to EA 1950; **Kenya:** W. J. D. Wadley, Education Director, to CNC, 9 December 1948, KNA, MAA 2/5/91/96; I. C. Freeman, Education Department Mombasa to Local Principals, 16 December 1948, KNA, CC 7/12/12; SEO Coast to DC Kwale, 11 January 1949, KNA, CC 7/12/13; Lake, "African School," 1006; **Tanganyika:** BSA ExCom Minutes, 3 April 1952, KSA, KBSA/C/47; G. K. Reakes-Williams, Area Commissioner, to Brother Scouts and Scouters, 1 May 1956, TNA, ACC 71.

28. **Limited resources:** KSC to CSK, 20 July 1948, KNA, AB 14/15/82; **Kenya:** Circular to Standing Finance Committee, 29 March 1949, KNA, AB 14/15/173; Acting KCC to J. G. Throughton, Member for Finance, 4 January 1949, KNA, AB 14/15/150; **warning:** Betty Brooke-Anderson, KCC, to Director of Education, 25 June 1949, KNA AB 14/18/16/1.

29. **Boy's Brigade threat:** W. H. McVicker, BB Overseas Secretary, to R. G. M. Calderwood, Secretary CSM Council, 17 June 1946, CSM, ACC 7548-B275; "Tour of Kenya," by Dahl, 1948, BSA, TC/264 Tours; **KBSA victory:** CCK Occasional Bulletin, September-October 1948, CMS, AF35/49 G3 A5/4: KMC 1946–49, vol. 2; KBSA Statement of Expenditure, January–June 1952, KSA, Finances, loose file; KBSA Circular to LA's, 25 March 1952, KSA, Finances, loose file: ExCom Minutes, 30 July 1952, KNA, DC, KMG 1/1/82/30; Kenya Colony, *Annual Report of the Department of Community Development and Rehabilitation*, 1957, 3.

30. **1949:** Uganda Protectorate, *Report of the Commission of Inquiry into the Disturbances in Uganda during April 1949*, 44, 71–74; **Tanganyika:** Iliffe, *Tanganyika*, 481.

31. **Mau Mau:** Rosberg and Nottingham, *Myth of "Mau Mau*," 223; **Kariuki:** Obadiah Kariuki to C. T. F. Bewes, 26 June 1953, CMS AF59 G3 AF/6/1/1953; **proxies:** Throup, *Economic and Social Origins of Mau Mau*, 11; **Mau Mau constituents:** Lonsdale, "Mau Maus of the Mind," 418.

32. **1952:** Clayton, *Counterinsurgency in Kenya*; **hymn:** Waciuma, *Daughter of Mumbi*, 114.

33. **Near collapse:** The Ugandan independent churches and schools also established a number of troops in the southern provinces, but these enjoyed relatively cordial relations with the Ugandan Boy Scout Association and did not become embroiled in the most controversial political issues that roiled the protectorate in the late 1940s and 1950s. UBSA Meeting Minutes, 26 July 1955, MNA/17/BSA/8/17; UBSA, AR 1955, MNA/17/BSA/13/8; **local association:** KSC ExCom Minutes, 25 January 1953, KNA, DC,

KMG 1/1/82/56; **observers impressed:** Organizing Commissioner's Report on Kiambu LA, 26 May 1948, KSA, KBSA/C/39; "Tour of Kenya," by Dahl, 1948, BSA, TC/264 Tours; **Smith:** Kiambu LA Minutes, 31 March 1952, KNA, AB 15/56/3.

34. **"Heterogenous collection":** extract from school supervisor's report, 1953, KNA, A315/56/9a; **"Scouts":** James William Wambugu, interview, July 1998.

35. **Unauthorized Guides:** KGGA ExCom Minutes, 14 March 1950, KGGA Minute Book, 1947–50; **1951:** KGGA Minutes, 9 May 1950, KGGA Minute Book, 1947–50; KGGA Commissioners' Conference Minutes, 19 May 1950, 27 July 1951, KGGA, Commissioners Conference Minute Book, 1937–60; **new postings:** Smith to F. L. Megson, AC Nairobi, 23 February 1954, KNA, AB 15/56/14.

36. Letter to the author from David Hemphill, 27 July 1996.

37. **Kenyan report:** Historical Survey of Origins and Growth of Mau Mau, chapter 5, app. J, Commissioner of Police to Member for Law and Order, 14 July 1952, KNA, GO 3/2/72; **Scouts' loyalties:** KSC ExCom Minutes, 25 January 1953, KNA, DC, KMG 1/1/82/56; "Kikuyu Boy Scouts Renew Pledges," *East Africa Standard*, 20 March 1953; PEO Nairobi to EO Kiambu, 30 January 1954, KNA, MK 2/1/1; director of education, W. J. S. Wadley, to PEO NBI, 28 January 1954, KNA, MK 2/1/1a.

38. Kiambu AR 1952, KNA, DC KBU 1/43; Kiambu DEB Minutes, 12 December 1952, KNA, MK 3/9/77; Kipkorir, "Mau Mau," 10.

39. Kiraithe Nyaga, interview, July 1998.

40. Organizing Commissioner's Report, October 1952, KSA, KBSA/C/39; "East Africa Tour," by Dahl, 1955, BSA, TC/11 Tours; Report on Guiding in RVP, February 1956, KGGA, RVP File, 1953–58.

41. **Schools:** Neville Langford-Smith to W. H. Carey, 16 February 1954, CMS AF59 G3 A5/6/1/1952–53; Report on Church in Embu District, March 1954, CMS, AF59 G3 A5/6/1/1952–53; **Alliance:** Extract from CMS AC Meeting, 10 October 1952, CMS AF59 G3 A5/6/1/1952–53; Hooper to M. A. C. Warren, 2 November 1952, CMS AF59 G3 A5/6/1/1952–53; E. Cary Francis AHS to Warren, 3 November 1952, CMS AF59 G3 A5/6/1/1952–53; Diary of C. T. F. Bewes, 10 January 1953, CMS AF59 G3 A5/6/2/Diary of C. T. F. Bewes.

42. **Oath taker:** "Report of ACC Churches & Schools of Embu Deanery," by Keith Cole, 31 August 1953, CMS, AF59 G3 A5/6/1/1953; **naming names:** PC CP to Minister for Education, Labour and Lands, 26 July 1954, KNA, OPE 1/690/9; KBU DEB Circular, Teacher's Confessions—Gitundu Division, 9 February 1955, KNA, MK 3/7/51.

43. Fort Hall District Training Report, 15–20 September 1952; ExCom Minutes, 26 November 1952, KNA, AB 14/17/57; Embu LA AR, 1953, KNA, AB 15/56/16/1; KBSA ExCom Minutes, 12 January 1955, KNA, OPE 1/5/81; "Monthly Report, Central Province, July 1955," by R. C. Tyers, MNA/17/BSA/13/9.

44. **KBSA:** W. J. D. Wadley to Rhodes, 15 March 1954, KNA, OPE 1/5/40/1; **blame:** Governor Sir Evelyn Baring, Speech to KBSA AGM, 20 May 1955, MNA/17/BSA/8/13; "East Africa Tour," by Dahl, 1955, BSA, TC/11 Tours; **leaders' loyalty:** "Central Province Monthly Report," by R. C. Tyers, May–June 1956, MNA/17/BSA/13/9; Application for Warrant for Edward Ayub, 24 September 1958, KSA, A/RV/108; Application for Warrant for Elijah Mukayagi Ominde, 24 September 1958, KSA, A/RV/105.

45. **1953 oath:** "Kikuyu Boy Scouts Renew Pledges," *East Africa Standard* (20 March 1953); **Malaya:** Rhodes to G. Smyth-Osbourne, ACNC, 19 November 1953, KNA, OPE 1/5/27; Rhodes to Baring, 19 November 1953, KNA, AB 15/4/53/1; **Baring receptive:** Extraordinary Meeting of KBSA, 16 November 1953, KNA, DC MUR 3/4/13/82; Baring's Address to KBSA AGM, 27 May 1954, MNA/17/BSA/1/209; Baring's Address to KBSA AGM, 20 May 1955, MNA/17/BSA/8/13.

46. D. J. Wilson-Haffeden, BB Secretary, to Leonard Beecher, 24 February 1955, CMS AF59 AFG 06; C. T. F. Bewes to D. J. Wilson-Haffeden, BB Secretary, 28 February 1955, CMS AF59 AFG 06; Max Warren to Bewes, 29 March 1956, CMS AF59 AFG 06.

47. **KBSA success:** Rhodes to Baring, 2 February 1953, KNA, AB 15/4/1; "African Recreation and Welfare in Town and Country," by R. G. Turnbull, Member for Education, 12 May 1953, KNA, AB 15/4/38/1; **KBSA funding:** "Note on Boy Scouts and Girl Guides," by Assistant Secretary, Education, Labour and Lands, 1 September 1954, KNA, OPE 1/5/64/1; Kenya Secretariat Minute, 4 September 1954, KNA, OPE 1/5/65; KGGA Colony Commissioner's AR, 1956, KGGA, National Council Meetings, 1952–63; Kenya Colony, *Annual Report of the Department of Community Development and Rehabilitation*, 1955, 1; **windfall:** L. S. Colchester, HQ Commissioner and Secretary, KSC, to AC Mombasa, P. E. Sandall, 13 August 1958, KSA, A/MSA/72; Extraordinary General Meeting of Scout Council of Kenya, 27 January 1960, KNA, DC KMG 1/1/100/15; Minute by Principal Finance Officer, Ministry of Social Services, 5 July 1962, KNA, XH 3/11/13; **at-risk troops:** Rhodes to E. H. Windley, CNC, 4 April 1954, KNA, OPE 1/5/43; Education Officer Minute, 23 April 1954, KNA, OPE 1/5/48.

48. Rhodes to Minister for Community Development, 14 October 1955, KNA, OPE 1/5/91/1; KBSA ExCom Minutes, 24 November 1954, KNA, OPE 1/5/80.

49. "Nairobi Extra-Provincial District HoR," by A. C. Small, KNA, OPE 1/408/1/1; "Judgment Must Begin," Interim Report on the African Anglican Church in the Northern Highlands, 10 January 1953, CMS, AF59 G3 A5/6/1/1952–53; Kershaw, *Mau Mau*, 325–26, 336.

50. Kenya, *Rehabilitation*, 1955, 1; Carothers, *The Psychology of Mau Mau*, 12–15; **"demonic upsurge":** "Mau Mau Movement in Kenya," by R. G. M. Calderwood, 21 December 1952, CSM, ACC 7548–B271.

51. **"Christian values":** CCK ExCo Minutes, 25 February 1954, CMS, AF59 G3 A5/4/599; Church, State, and Rehabilitation, September 1954, CMS AF59 G3 A5/6/3; Kenya Survey and CCK, September 1954, CMS AF59 G3 A5/6/5; Kabiro, *The Man in the Middle*, 74; Kenya, *Rehabilitation*, 1955, 25, 33; White, "Separating," 19.

52. **Numbers:** Commissioner of Prisons to Secretary for Community Development, 17 May 1956, KNA, AB 2/45/13; **redeemable:** CCK ExCom Minutes, 24 February 1955, CMS AF59 G3 A5/4/522; **"repentance":** Rhodes to G. W. Griffin, 23 September 1955, KNA, AB 1/116/28; Rhodes to C. M. Johnston, 11 October 1955, KNA, OPE 1/5/90/1; "The Rehabilitation of Youth," by G. Gardner, ca. 1957, KNA, VQ 21/3/54.

53. Kenya, *Rehabilitation*, 1954, 30–31; *Rehabilitation*, 1955, 3; Record of Meeting between CCK Representatives and Kenya Governor, 8 October 1955, CMS, AF59 G3 A5/6/1/1954–57; Policy for Wamumu Approved School, February 1957, KNA, AB 1/118/57.

54. Kabiro, *Man in the Middle*, 70; Geoffrey Griffin, interview, July 2000.

55. **First-rate institution:** Empire Day Parade, Wamumu Approved School, 1956, KNA, AB 1/116/151; Wamumu Approved School and Youth Camp, AR 1956, KNA, AB 1/118/88; Policy for Wamumu Approved School, February 1957, KNA, AB 1/118/57; Geoffrey Griffin, interview, July 2000; **graduates:** Special Assistant to Special Commissioner Central Province, December 1956, KNA, VQ 21/3/26; Kenya, *Rehabilitation*, 1957, 12.

56. "East Africa Tour," by Dahl, 1955, BSA, TC/11 Tours; "Scouting at Wamumu Approved School," by G. W. Griffin, *Batian* 3, no. 7 (August 1956); Wamumu Approved School and Youth Camp, AR 1956, KNA, AB 1/118/88; "Rehabilitation," by Gardner, ca. 1957, KNA, VQ 21/3/54.

57. **Standards:** Wamumu Approved School and Youth Camp, AR 1956, KNA, AB 1/118/88; "Rehabilitation," by Gardner, KNA, VQ 21/3/54; **Gikubu:** Joseph Kamira Gikubu, interview, July 2002.

58. "Report on Inter-Racial Boy Scout & Boy's Camp, Thiba River, Mwea Embu, 26 March–3 April 1958," by G. W. Griffin, 5 April 1958, KSA, A/EMB/13; Geoffrey Griffin, interview, July 2000.

59. **"Some boys":** "Vocational Training Project," by Chalres Tett, March 1957, CMS AF59 G3 A5/e11/589; **parents' strategy:** PS Community Development to PC Central Province, 9 April 1958, KNA, VQ 21/3/91; Minute by PS Community Development, 23 April 1958, KNA, VQ 21/3/93a; J. C. Nottingham, DO N. Tetu, to Commissioner for CD, 26 February 1959, KNA, DC EMB 2/1/1/16/1; **embarrassment:** Community Development Circular, Admission to Wamumu, 21 May 1958, KNA, VQ 21/3/109; Kenya, *Rehabilitation*, 1958, 11; **Griffin's career:** "Geoffrey Griffin: A Brilliant Career in Education," *Standard Now Magazine*, 12 July 1998.

60. **Uganda:** Pirouet, *Dictionary*, 130–32; Hargreaves, *Decolonization*, 144–45; **Tanganyika:** Hargreaves, *Decolonization*, 143–44.

61. **Census:** This was in comparison to the Uganda Boy Scout Association's 1953 census, which recorded 5,019 Scouts (almost all of them African) in 213 groups. Report of CC Kenya, 20 May 1955, KNA, OPE 1/5/86/1; UBSA, AR, 1953, KSA, UBSA/II; **viable institution:** "East Africa Tour," by Dahl, 1955, BSA, TC/11 Tours; "Monthly Report for Central Province," by R. C. Tyers, June 1955, KNA, DC KMG 1/1/85/17; Education Department Meeting on Loyalty to the Crown, 29 February 1956, KNA, CS 8/9/17/25/1; **army support:** KBSA, AR, 26 April 1950, KNA, JZ 6/21; Army Welfare in East Africa Command, 10 May 1951; *Batian* 3, no. 1 (July 1955); EALF Standing Orders, I/XIII, Welfare, 1957, KNA, DEF/13/470.

62. **Immorality:** KBU Intermediate School Principals Meeting Minutes, 20 February 1955, KNA, MK 4/6/116a; Director of Education to AC Nairobi, 13 April 1955, KNA, AB 15/4/18; KBSA ExCom Minutes, 31 July 1957, KNA, GH 7/8/40; PEOs Meeting Minutes, 7–9 May 1958, KNA, AV 2/38/3; "Machakos District Annual Report, 1958," by T. A. Watts, KNA, DC/MKS/1/1/34; **partial success:** Kiambu LA Minutes, 6 June 1957, KNA, MK 2/1/127; General Meeting NNZA LA Minutes, 8 March 1958, KNA, DC KMG 1/1/85/73; "Report on Central Province, 1954–59," by R. C. Tyers, KSA, A/NER.

63. Diary of John Thurman, Gilwell Camp Chief, SA Tour, 1960, BSA, TC/265 Tours;

Minutes of Extraordinary General Meeting of Scout Council of Kenya, 27 January 1960, KNA, DC KMG 1/1/100/15; Minute by Principal Finance Officer, Ministry of Social Services, 5 July 1962, KNA, XH 3/11/13.

64. **Delinquents:** Youth Program in Nyeri District, July 1957, KNA, VT 1/1/3; East African Director of Education conference Minutes, 3–4 October 1957, KNA, AV 2/39/2; "Interim Report to the Council of the Kenya Association of Youth Clubs," by G. W. Griffin, 8 June 1958, KNA, PC NZA 4/5/12/46; **Nairobi:** Kenya Survey and CCK, September 1954, CMS, AF59 G3 A5/6/5; Report of CC Kenya, 20 May 1955, KNA, OPE 1/5/86/1; Notes on Community Centres in Nairobi, March 1957, CMS AF59 G3 A5/e11/589; Nairobi City Council Department of Social Services and Housing, AR 1958, KGGA Archives.

65. Report on Tour of Central Province on Development of Youth Clubs, July 12–23, 1957, KNA, VT 1/1/21.

66. Kenya, *Rehabilitation*, 1957, 10; *Rehabilitation*, 1958, 9; Youth Program in Nyeri District, July 1957, KNA, VT 1/1/19; "Youth Organization Progress Report," by Chief ExO, Kenya Association of Youth Clubs, January 1960, KNA, VT 1/1.

67. **Scouting vs. clubs:** O/C Community Development Nyeri to DC NYI, 25 July 1957, KNA, VT 1/1/10; CDO NYI to PS CD, 1 August 1957, KNA, VT 1/1/13; T. Askwith, PS Community Development, to Minister for Community Development, 31 August 1957, KNA, AB 16/11/16; "Interim Report to the Council of Kenya Association of Youth Clubs," by G. W. Griffin, 8 June 1958, KNA, PC NZA 4/5/12/46; **Rhodes:** PS for Community Development to Minister for Community Development, 16 April 1958, KNA, OPE 1/5/120; G. A. Farell, Community Development Officer Machakos, to Rhodes, 24 December 1960, KSA, A/MKS/124; KBSA Commissioners Conference Minutes, 2–3 September 1960, KNA, GH 7/9/89.

68. Report on Central Province, 1954–9, by R. C. Tyers, KSA, A/NER.

69. **Problems in Uganda and Tanganyika:** Bukoba LA Minutes, 23 June 1951, TNA, ACC 71; TBSA Treasurer's Report, 31 December 1957, KSA, K/T/I/19; TGGA Conference, 20 May 1958, KGGA, Correspondence with TGGA; **nationalist criticism:** Uganda, *Annual Report*, 1950, 57; AGM, Tanganyika Annual Report, 1955, MNA/17/BSA/13/7; **better equipped:** Uganda, *Annual Report*, 1947, 79; "East Africa Tour," by Dahl, 1955, BSA, TC/11 Tours; UBSA AR, 1959, KSA, K/U/103.

70. Organising Commissioner's Report, Tanganyika AR, 1956, MNA/17/BSA/13/7; TBSA AR, 29 June 1960, MNA/17/BSA/13/7.

71. B. K. ole Kantai, interview, July 1998.

72. *Batian* 18 (September 1954); I. R. Gillespie to PEO NBI, 31 March 1955, KNA, MK 2/1/23; Treasurer KBU LA to CC KBSA, 3 May 1955, KNA, MK 2/1/32; Service of Queen's Scout Candidates, 1960–61, KSA, 136/Queens Scouts/II.

73. Minutes of Conference of Sponsoring Authorities, 2 November 1960, KNA, DC KMG 1/1/100/23; Francis Kamau Mbugua, interview, July 1998.

74. AHS, AR 1946, CSM, ACC 7548-B287; AHS Principal's Report, 6 December 1947, CSM ACC 7548-B287; "Tour of Kenya," by Dahl, 1948, BSA, TC/264 Tours; *Batian* 19 (December 1954); AHS Principal's Report, 1 October 1955, CMS AF59 G3 A5/e6/1; *Batian*,

February 1956; **first aid:** interviews, J. G. Kiano, July 1998, and B. K. ole Kantai, July 1998.

75. Machakos District AR, 1949, KNA, DC/MKS/1/1/30; Scout Advisory Council for Nairobi, Minutes, 29 December 1955, KNA, JW 4/2; Scout Shop Price List, 1955, KNA, JW 4/2; Kiraithe Nyaga, interview, July 1998.

76. **English:** TBSA ExCom Minutes, 7 March 1949, KSA, KBSA/C/47/47; "Report on Scouting in Dar-Es-Salaam," by F. D. Henry, November 1949, KSA, KBSA/C/47/55; UBSA AR, 1953, KSA, UBSA/II; USC Sub-Committee on Publicity, 1956, KSA, UBSA/II; **Sixth Law:** KBSA Commissioners Conference Minutes, 2–3 September 1961, KNA, GH 7/9/89; *Batian* 8 (January 1965); **Kikuyu versions:** KBSA ExCom Minutes, 29 April 1953, KNA, DC KMG 1/1/82/69; **magaidi:** Phyllis Moffett, Territory Commissioner, TGGA, to EA Literature Bureau, 8 June 1953, KGGA, Correspondence with TGGA.

77. **Integration efforts:** FH LA AR 1949, KNA, DC MUR 3/4/13/31; *Batian* 18 (September 1954), 19 (December 1954); R. Brian Carter, Rover Crew Leader, to P. E. Walters, DC Thika, 4 February 1956, KNA, AMC 8/8/35; ExCom Minutes, 26 September 1956, KNA, DC KMG 1/1/85/45; **limited contact:** Kiraithe Nyaga and Jeremiah Nyagah, interviews, July 1998.

78. **Unwilling:** USC Minutes, 7 November 1955, KSA, UBSA/II; **Tanganyika:** "Scouting in Dar-Es-Salaam," by Henry, KSA, KBSA/C/47/55; TBSA ExCom Minutes, 27 November 1951, KSA, KBSA/C/47.

79. Nairobi LA Minutes, 13 August 1957, KSA, Nairobi LA Minute Book; Colchester to R. H. Cauldwell, Organizing Commissioner TBSA, 15 March 1960, KSA, K/T/I/67.

80. Uganda, *Annual Report*, 1951, 68; CNC's Meeting with F. M. J. Dahl, 19 July 1948, KNA, AB 17/46/12; Colony Secretary to Guide DC Embu, 23 January 1953, KGGA, Embu File, 1955–61; Education Supervisor, Friends Elgon Schools, to CC, 13 June 1957, KSA, Jamboree Sub-Committee/89.

81. **Testimonial:** KBSA ExCom Minutes, 24 November 1948, KNA, JZ 6/21; Colchester to P. R. Scott, CSS Shimo-la-Tewa, 22 December 1958, KSA, A/MSA/97; HQ Secretary UBSA to Colchester, 18 March 1966, KSA, K/U/III/3/63; **Alliance High School:** Evans to R. Ngala, Kaloleni School, 23 October 1948, KSA, A/Mombasa/5; KBSA ExCom Minutes, 24 November 1954, KNA, OPE 1/5/80; J. G. Kiano and Jeremiah Nyagah, interviews, July 1998.

82. **"Good fraction":** "Future of Scouting in Mumias Division," by Peter Leo Omurunga, 58 Troop Kakamega, ca. 1963, KSA, A/KAK/II/33; **job seekers:** Masudi Nassaro to Secretary KBSA, 1958, KSA, A/MSA/66; Eliphaz Mputhia Manene to Traveling Commissioner, 8 October 1959, KSA, A/MER; John Wakhunga to KBSA, 15 October 1959, KSA, A/KTL; **continue education:** Gbuyu s/o Josephy Gede to KBSA, 11 April 1950, KSA, KBSA/C/95; Geoffrey Kariuki s/o Njuguma to KBSA, 21 July 1950, KSA, KBSA/C/44; Executive Commissioner ISB to Secretary KBSA, 2 May 1960, KSA, A/KTL/21; Stephan Tomasi Muliro to Editor *Batian*, 22 December 1961, KSA, A/NN/170.

83. *Kenya Scouting News*, December 1945, KNA, DC MUR 3/4/13; UBSA Quarterly Newsletter, no. 5 (April 1948), KSA, KBSA/C/54/34; "Tour of Tanganyika," by Dahl,

1948, BSA, TC/264 Tours; Report by George Witchell, Traveling Commissioner, 11 September 1961, KNA, GH 7/9/87; Colchester to AC NNZA, 20 July 1965, KSA, A/KAK/II/81.

84. "KBSA, Woodbadge Course, Rowallan Camp, August 1952," by ACC F. J. Bedford, KNA, DC KMG 1/1/82/45; KBU PCEA Supervisory Team Circular, 27 July 1955, KNA, MK 1/4/137; "Nairobi (Rural) Area Report," by Stephen Smith, 1957–58, KSA, Nairobi LA Minute Book; L. S. Colchester to Mrs. Purdy, Honorary Secretary, Embu LA, 24 July 1958, KSA, A/EMB/59; Colchester to C. Ramsey, Secretary CNZA LA, 15 November 1958, KSA, A/CN/66; David Hemphill, interview, July 1996.

85. Rift Valley Guide DC to Colony Commissioner, 31 May 1956, KGGA, RVP File, 1953–58; M. Nganga, 27th Rift Valley (1st Kinangop Troop), to Colony Secretary KGGA, 24 January 1958, KGGA, RVP File, 1953–58.

86. Nairobi and District LA, Summary of Reports, 5 April 1949, KNA, DC KMG 2/1/122b; AHS Principal's Report, 12 October 1957, CMS AF59 G3 A5/e6/1; Colchester to Sandall, 21 November 1957, KSA, A/MSA/203; Colchester to Andrew Musumba, AC Elgon Nyanza, 21 November 1959, KSA, A/EN/82.

87. **Bob-a-Job:** *East Africa Standard*, 28 April 1955; **imposters:** KBSA ExCom Minutes, 30 August 1950, KNA, JZ 6/21; KBSA ExCom Minutes, 25 March 1959, KNA, DC KMG 1/1/100/2; Colchester to Noyes, 22 May 1961, KSA, K/U/130; Buers to Colchester, 20 June 1961, KSA, A/CN/II/6.

88. Assistant Commissioner V. Alawi to Secretary KBSA, 29 March 1950, KSA, Zanzibar, no. 58; Colchester to Executive Commissioner Kiambu, September 1958, KSA, A/KBU.

89. Colchester to Area Commissioner Rift Valley, June 1958, KSA, A/RV/45); Colchester to A. L. Shaunak, Lake Victoria Primary, 14 May 1959, KSA, A/CN; C. Ramsay, Secretary CNZA LA, to Colchester, 23 July 1959, KSA, A/CN; Colchester to Wilson, 13 July 1963, KSA, K/T/III/46.

90. Ex Com Minutes TBSA, 18 May 1956, KSA, TBSA 1953/47; "Report on Central Province," by Tyers, September/October 1956, KNA, DC KMG 1/1/85/47; Nairobi LA Minutes, 8 January 1957, KSA, Nairobi LA Minute Book; ExCom Minutes, 27 February 1957, KNA, DC KMG 1/1/85/55; KBSA ExCom Minutes, 31 July 1957, KNA, DC KMG 1/1/85/62; Secretary KBSA to Tyers, 14 July 1958, KSA, A/NER/38.

CHAPTER 6

1. Minute February 1953, SASA, BC 956/D/Cape Town Minute Book.

2. **Township troops:** Wilson and Mafeje, *Langa*, 7–8; Western, *Outcaste Cape Town*, 122–23; **Ndima:** Jonathan Ndima, interview, August 1998.

3. **Membership:** Minute, February 1953, SASA, BC 956/D/Cape Town Minute Book; Cape Western Division (A), AR 1960, SASA, BC 956/A/AS24; **report:** Cape Western Division (A), AR 1961, SASA, BC 956/A/AS24/1962; **Thurman:** Diary of John Thurman, 1960, BSA, TC/265 Tours.

4. Hyslop, "'A Destruction Coming In,'" 394, 399.

5. Glaser, "Students, Tsotsis and the Congress Youth League," 1.

6. Bolnick, *Double-Cross*, 2.

7. Kros, "Dancing," 5, 24.

8. SA(P)BSA HQ Council Minutes, 4 January 1947, SASA, BC 956/A/Africa Scouts, 1936–60; SAHQ Circular, Reorganization, 10 June 1947, SASA, BC 956/F/Census, 1930s–40s; SA(P)BSA HQ Council Minutes, 25 June 1948, SASA, BC 956/A/Africa Scouts, 1936–60.

9. Williams, *Past*, 253–55.

10. Thompson, *South Africa*, 194–95; Freund, *Making*, 265.

11. Hargreaves, *Decolonization*, 56; Bonner, "Family," 393.

12. **Eiselen quote:** South Africa, *Native Education*, 7; **Verwoerd:** Horrell, *Bantu Education*, 5; Verwoerd, *Bantu Education*, 7.

13. **Act, departments:** Horrell, *Bantu Education*, 10–13; *The Education of the Coloured Community in South Africa*, 95; **curriculum:** Molteno, "Schooling," 89; **riots:** Kane-Berman, *Soweto*, 11.

14. Hyslop, "State Education Policy and the Social Reproduction of the Urban African Working Class," 451.

15. South Africa, *Native Education*, 156.

16. **Slums:** Hyslop, "Policy," 448; **1957:** Bonner, "Family," 394.

17. **Tsotsis:** Glaser, *Bo-Tsotsi*, 47; **government response:** Glaser, "'When Are They Going to Fight?'" 309.

18. **Enrolled Scouts:** Union of South Africa, *Native Education*, 94; **corporate donors:** SA(A)BSA HQ Council Minutes, 12 July 1950, SASA, BC 956/A/Africa Scouts, 1936–60; Transvaal Division (A), AR 1952, SASA, BC 956/D/AS3; **Rowallan's visit:** Notes of Chief Scout's Tour by Traveling Commissioner IHQ, 1950, BSA, TC Zimbabwe; **official quote:** Mokwele, "Pedagogy," 287.

19. SA(A)BSA HQ Council Minutes, 12 July 1950, SASA, BC 956/A/Africa Scouts, 1936–60.

20. **Disruption:** SA(A)BSA HQ Council Minutes, 5 January 1957, SASA, BC 956/A/Africa Scouts, 1936–60; Transvaal Division (A) AR 1956, SASA, BC 956/A/Africa Scouts, 1936–60; Griqualand West Division, AR 1959, SASA, BC 956/A/AS24; **translation:** General Secretary SABSA to CSSA, 30 March 1953, SASA, BC 956/D/CS17; Transkei Division, AR 1965, ASA, BC 956/A/AS24/1966.

21. SA(A)BSA HQ Minutes, 5 January 1957, SASA, BC 956/A/Africa Scouts, 1936–60; Letter of Authority, 23 November 1962, SASA, BC 956/D/African Field Commissioner.

22. Rev. J. A. Anderson to J. M. Hamilton, FML, 17 June 1955, CSM ACC 7548-406B.

23. **Midlands:** SA(A)BSA HQ Council Minutes, 7 January 1953, SASA, BC 956/A/Africa Scouts, 1936–60; **membership drop:** Cape Western Division (A) AR 1957, SASA, BC 956/A/Africa Scouts, 1936–60; Cape Western Division (A) AR 1958, SASA, BC 956/A/Africa Scouts, 1936–60.

24. J. D. Fraser to CSC (A), 2 February 1956, SASA, BC 956/D/AS3; Fraser to CSSA, 3 February 1956, SASA, BC 956/D/AS3.

25. **Accusation:** Fraser to CSC (A), 8 February 1956, SASA, BC 956/D/AS3; Fraser to

CSSA, 15 February 1956, SASA, BC 956/D/AS3; Fraser to CSC (A), 20 April 1959, SASA, BC 956/D/AS3; Fraser to CSC (A), 24 April 1959, SASA, BC 956/D/AS3.

26. **Chief Scout:** CSSA to Executive Committee SABSA, 18 August 1958, SASA, BC 956/B/SA Constitution, 1960s–70s; "Draft Memo to Executive Council SABSA," by Johnstone, ca. 1958, SASA, BC 956/B/SA Constitution; SAHQ Council Circular, 19th World Conference Delegate Briefing, February 1963, SASA, BC 956/H/International Conference Misc.; **figureheads:** Confidential Memorandum to SABSA, 5 June 1960, SASA, BC 956/A/Admin and Training; SA(A)BSA, What Are These Boy Scouts? ca. 1969, SASA, BC 956/A/CSIC, 1969.

27. Executive Committee SABSA Memo by E. P. Fowle, CSSA, 25 April 1957, SASA, BC 956/A/African HQ Council 1957.

28. **1957 delegation:** Report from SA Delegates on 16th International Scout Conference, August 1957, SASA, BC 956/H/International Conference Misc; CSC (A) Circular, 28 November 1958, SASA, BC 956/A/AS24; **resistance:** Diary of John Thurman, 1960, BSA, TC/265 Tours.

29. Diary of John Thurman, 1960, BSA, TC/265 Tours.

30. Gifford, "Misconceived Dominion," 393–95.

31. Hargreaves, *Decolonization*, 146–49; Marks, "Southern Africa," 570.

32. Southern Rhodesia, Education, *Inquiry Commission*, 10.

33. **Mid-1950s:** Hailey, *Survey*, rev., 1164–65; **Northern Rhodesia:** "African Education in Northern Rhodesia," *Colonial Review* 5 (1947): 52.

34. Nyasaland Protectorate, Department of Education, *Primary School Syllabus*, 8; *Annual Report*, 2; Küster, *Education*, 226–27, 297.

35. **"Unwieldy":** "Report to Rhodesia Pathfinder Council," by H. H. Morely-Wright, Colony Commissioner, 9 July 1948, BSA, TC Zimbabwe; **Dahl:** "Tour of Southern Rhodesia," by Dahl, 1948, BSA, TC/264 Tours.

36. **Constitution:** Landau, "History"; **educators:** Southern Rhodesia, Education Commission, *Inquiry Commission*, 59; **resignation:** P. J. Kenworth, CC RBSA, to P. Cooke, Overseas Secretary IHQ, 29 June 1958, BSA, TC Zimbabwe.

37. **Separate council:** *The African Scout, Northern Rhodesian Branch of BSA* 5 (October–December 1949); **Dahl:** Dahl to Walton, 14 April 1948, BSA, TC/264 Tours; "Tour of Northern Rhodesia," by Dahl, 1948, BSA, TC/264 Tours; **justification:** Notes of Chief Scout's Tour by Traveling Commissioner IHQ, 1950, BSA, TC Zimbabwe; **push:** Notes of Chief Scout's Tour by Traveling Commissioner IHQ, 1950, BSA, TC Zimbabwe; "Central Africa Tour," by Dahl, 1954, BSA, TC/11 Tours.

38. **Public works:** H. Holmes, "Urban Schoolboys Go to the Country," 32; Milne, "Community Service Camps in Rhodesia," 22; Greig, *Education*, 42; **state funding:** Notes on Conversation with NR Scout Officials, 11 September 1950, BSA, TC Zimbabwe; Notes of Chief Scout's Tour by Traveling Commissioner IHQ, 1950, BSA, TC Zimbabwe; "Central Africa Tour," by Dahl, 1954, BSA, TC/11 Tours.

39. **"No room":** "NRBSA Chief Scout Commissioner Report, 1956–57," by D. M. Robertson, BSA, TC Zimbabwe; **1954:** Northern Rhodesia Social Welfare Report, 1954, BSA, TC/11 Tours.

40. **Chief secretary:** Lamba, "Moulding," 70; **constitution:** "Tour of Nyasaland," by

Dahl, 1948, BSA, TC/264 Tours; **allocations:** Colonial Office Report on Nyasaland, 1950, MNA, 17/BSA/1/210; **expansion:** *Round the Troops* 7 (11 December 1948); NBSA AGM Minutes, 11 June 1954, KSA, KBSA, C/67; Great Britain, Colonial Office, Nyasaland, 110; **appeal:** Ndovie, *The Origins, Growth and Decline of the Boy Scout Association of Nyasaland*, 17; Nyasaland, *Annual Report*, 14; **battalions:** Troop 45, KAR Troop Zomba, MNA, 17/BSA/1/42.

41. "Central Africa Tour," by Dahl, 1954, BSA, TC/11 Tours; Organizing Commissioner to PC NP, 23 August 1954, MNA, 17/BSA/1/210; **"party":** "BB Nyasaland Report #1, 30 September 1958," by Stewart McCollough, CSM 7548-406B; **malipenga:** Njoloma, "The King's African Rifles and Colonial Development in Nyasaland (Malawi)," 182.

42. **1948:** Scouting Nyasaland, Position, April 1948, MNA 17/BSA/6/1; **Sangala:** Lamba, "Moulding," 68; **limits:** Scouters Training Camp, Jeanes School, Preliminary Scout Course, 5–13 June 1948, MNA, 17/BSA/5/6; "Tour of Nyasaland," by Dahl, 1948, BSA, TC/264 Tours.

43. "African Tour," by P. B. Nevill, 1957–58, BSA, TC/265 Tours; Lamba, "Moulding," 74.

44. **Boycott:** Ndovie, *Origins*, 15; Ipenburg, "All Good Men," 212; "Central Africa Tour," by Dahl, 1954, BSA, TC/11 Tour; **Boy's Brigade:** Andrew Berg, BB Nyasaland, to W. H. McVicker, BB Overseas Secretary, 13 June 1953, CSM, ACC 7548–406B; **"impudence":** Richard Belcher to Camp Chief Boy Scouts Association London, 4 February 1954, MNA/17BSA/5/2; **consolation:** NBSA AGM Minutes, 11 June 1954, KSA, KBSA/C/67.

45. **"Not prepared":** "Youth Movements in Bechuanaland," by Leech, 18 March 1950, SASA 956/H/International Commissioner; **"obnoxious":** Leech to Fleischer, 27 November 1951; **last straw:** Leech to Fleischer, 9 November 1951; Rheinallt-Jones to Fleischer, 7 December 1951; Leech to Kenneth Fleischer, 10 December 1951, SASA, 956/H/International Commissioner.

46. **Numbers:** "Youth Movements in Bechuanaland," by Leech, 18 March 1950, SASA, 956/H/International Commissioner; Basutoland BSA, AR 1957, SASA, BC 956/A/Africa Scouts, 1936–60; Swaziland, *Annual Report*, 30; **leadership shortage:** Basutoland Branch, Territorial Report 1961, SASA, BC 956/A/AS24/1962.

47. Thompson, *South Africa*, 210.

48. Cross, *Imagery*, 195; Hyslop, "Policy," 463.

49. Hyslop, "Policy," 452, 459; Glaser, *Bo-Tsotsi*, 99–100; Hyslop, "Schools, Unemployment and Youth," 64.

50. **Urban areas:** Hyslop, "Destruction," 395, 405; **underfunding:** Tom Lodge, "The Parents' School Boycott," 268–69; Horrell, *Bantu Education*, 88; Hyslop, "Destruction," 401; **1955:** Glaser, *Bo-Tsotsi*, 98; Hyslop, "Schools," 65.

51. **Accommodation:** SASC Minutes, 16–17 May 1958, SASA, BC 956/A/SASC, 1940–58; Fraser to DCSSA, 13 June 1958, SASA, BC 956/H/IC35; CSSA Monthly Letter, 23 November 1958, SASA, BC 956/D/CS Monthly Letters; **African branch:** SA(A)BSA HQ Council Minutes, 4 January 1958, SASA, BC 956/A/Africa Scouts, 1936–60.

52. Draft, Johnstone to Prime Minister of South Africa, 18 November 1960, SASA BC 956/N/Miscellaneous.

53. **Scout canon:** SABSA Circular, 1 March 1961, SASA, BC 956/A/SASC, 1961; **loss of**

support: Cape Western Division (A), AR 1961, SASA, BC 956/A/AS24/1962; SA(A)BSA HQ Council Minutes, 10 January 1962, SASA, BC 956/A/AS24.

54. **Treason:** Notes of Chief Scout's Tour by Traveling Commissioner IHQ, 1950, BSA, TC Zimbabwe; Tetelman, "We Can," 111; **accounts:** "Anglican Canon Found Guilty," *Rand Daily Mail* (21 June 1961).

55. **Inglis:** Colin Inglis, interview, July 1995; **"malice":** Commonwealth Report by Geoffrey Hussey, 8 December 1959, SASA, BC 956/D/Commonwealth CS, 1950s–60s; **sympathizers:** Report by Dr. A. H. Tonkin, CSC (A), 25 January 1962, SASA, BC 956/D/General Correspondence 1960s.

56. **1965:** "National Jamboree in S. Africa in 1965," *Christian Record*, 27 August 1965; **African troops:** "Race Ruling: Scouts May Go To Court," *Sunday Tribune*, 28 November 1965; Divisional Commissioner Natal to Divisional Commissioner Cape Western, 15 December 196, SASA, BC 956/D/Cape Western.

57. **Guides:** "Girl Guides Will Beat Apartheid," *Star*, 9 September 1965; "Government's Scout Ban Is 'Ridiculous,'" *Sunday Tribune*, 8 February 1970; Medea Hussey, CC SAGGA, to J.C. Meinert, 6 June 1979, SASA, BC 956/G/Girl Guides, 1979–80; **refused funding:** Eleanor Murray, CCGGA, to HQ Council SABSA, July 1967, SASA, BC 956/A/CSIC, 1967–68; **Friendship Badge:** Miss Marjorie Grant, International Commissioner SAGGA, to Charles Martin, CSSA, 27 January 1975, SASA, BC 956/D/General Correspondence 1970s.

58. **Rowallan:** Notes of Chief Scout's Tour by Traveling Commissioner IHQ, 1950, BSA, TC Zimbabwe; **Thurman:** Excerpts of Report by John Thurman, 15 February 1961, SASA, BC 956/F/D1; **Coloured community:** Fraser to CSC (S), 2 October 1963, SASA, 956/D/D61; A. Domingo, CSC (C), to Commissioner for Coloured Affairs, 21 October 1969, SASA, BC 956/D/CS17; **"assist":** Commissioner for Coloured Affairs to A. Domingo, CSC (C), 5 October 1970, SASA, BC 956/A/CSIC, 1969–73.

59. Fleischer to Governor-General South Africa, 25 September 1947, SASA, BC 956/B/SA Constitution II; **chafed:** Fraser to D. G. Shepstone, 15 August 1960, SASA, BC 956/B/SA Constitution II; **"platform":** National Treasurer SABSA to Secretary for Bantu Education, 9 July 1975, SASA, BC 956/D/African BSA; "Bid to Stop Scout Show," *Leader*, 8 March 1979.

60. **State funding:** Geech, CSSA, to Rev. C. L. Gittens, 23 October 1971, SASA, BC 956/D/General Correspondence 1968–73; National Treasurer SABSA to Secretary for Bantu Education, 9 July 1975, SASA, BC 956/D/African BSA; **unofficial Scouts:** Cape Midlands Division (A), AR 1961, SASA, BC 956/A/AS24/1962; Fraser to CSC (A), ca. 1962, SASA, BC 956/D/D51; "Natal Report," by N'thaba, 11 November 1962, SASA, BC 956/D/D52.

61. **African divisions:** Fraser to Lt. Col. R. Gold, International Commissioner BSIB, 19 September 1962, SASA, BC 956/C/File 91; Bezencon to Mrs. M. Wettergreen, 13 May 1976, SASA, BC 956/D/D58; **1964:** Diary of John Thurman, 1960, BSA, TC/265 Tours; Divisional Commissioner Natal (A) to SAHQ Development Commissioner, 2 July 1962, SASA, BC 956/D/African Field Commissioner; "What SAHQ Does," by CSSA, ca. 1964, SASA, BC 956/B/National Organization.

62. **Funders:** Fraser to General Spry, WSB, 5 December 1961, SASA, BC 956/F/D1; Fraser to CSC (A), 18 September 1962, SASA, BC 956/D/D53; **Scoutmaster courses:** "Starting and Running a Scout Group," draft by SAHQ, ca. 1964, SASA, BC 956/C/File 91; **curriculum:** Report by John Thurman, 15 February 1961, SASA, BC 956/F/D1; Fraser to Lt. Col. R. Gold, International Commissioner BSIB, 19 September 1962, SASA, BC 956/C/File 91.

63. **1961 plan:** SAHQ Council Circular, SAHQ Field Commissioners, 21 December 1961, SASA, BC 956/D/General Correspondence 1960s; **responsibilities:** SAHQ Circular, Duties of SAHQ Field Commissioners, 24 March 1970, SASA, BC 956/B/African Field Commissioners; Traveling Report by N'thaba, 16 November 1970, SASA, BC 956/D/D58; **N'thaba:** Diary of John Thurman, 1960, BSA, TC/265 Tours; Fraser to N'thaba, 3 February 1967, SASA, BC 956/D/African Field Commissioner; SABSA ExCom Minutes, 7 January 1962, SASA, BC 956/A/Executive, 1960–62; N'thaba to SA(A)BSA HQ Council, 5 December 1964, SASA, BC 956/A/AS24/1965; Transkei Division Circular, 27 November 1968, SASA, BC 956/A/African, 1968–70s; Otty Nxumalo, CSC (A), to CSSA, 23 January 1974, SASA, BC 956/B/African Field Commissioners.

64. "Report on Port Elizabeth District," by N'thaba, 23 June 1965, SASA, BC 956/D/African Field Commissioner.

65. **Security officer:** Inglis, interview, July 1998; **N'thaba:** "'It Is Wonderful,' Says N'thaba As He Goggles at Life in America," *Star*, 27 April 1961.

66. **Bob-a-Job:** SA(A)BSA HQ Council Minutes, 10 January 1959, SASA, BC 956/A/Africa Scouts, 1936–60; Report by Dr. A. H. Tonkin, CSC (A), 25 January 1962, SASA, BC 956/D/General Correspondence 1960s; Memo to CSC (A), 1962, SASA, BC 956/D/D51; **official guidelines:** SAHQ Circular, Duties of SAHQ Field Commissioners, 24 March 1970, SASA, BC 956/B/African Field Commissioners; **Group Areas Act:** Shange to Fraser, 5 December 1969, SASA, BC 956/F/Census 1969.

67. "Dinizulu's Necklace," by South African Boy Scout Association, SASA, BC 956/H/1967 Jamboree; **ethnic connection:** Inter-Territorial Jeanes Conference, *Findings*, 341; **Thurman:** Diary of John Thurman, 1960, BSA, TC/265 Tours; **1960s:** Programme for Annual Rally Natal Division (A), 25 August 1962, SASA, BC 956/D/D56; **Zulu nationalists:** Harries, "Symbolism," 112; Hamilton, *Majesty*, 170; **1966:** Report by SAHQ Commissioner for Development, 17 January 1966, SASA, BC 956/A/Council Circulars, 1964–65; Natal Division (A), AR 1968, SASA, BC 956/A/African, 1968–70s; "Prince Heads Scouts," *Natal Mercury*, 7 August 1972; **1974:** "Zulus Flock to Join Scouts," *Natal Witness*, 24 May 1974.

68. **Structured leisure:** SA(A)BSA HQ Council Minutes, 10 January 1962, SASA, BC 956/A/AS24; "A Boost for African Scouts," *Natal Mercury*, 14 May 1962; **N'thaba promise:** "P.E. African Boyscouts: Plan to Revive Movement," *Port Elizabeth Post*, 14 June 1965; **tsotsis:** Glaser, "Zorro," 50, 55; **stole:** Bob-a-Job Instructions, Natal Division (A), September 1962, SASA, BC 956/D/D56.

69. **White gangs:** Mooney, "'Ducktails, Flick Knives and Pugnacity,'" 754–55; **membership decline:** "Apathy Hits Afrikaner Groups," *Cape Times*, 15 April 1962; le Roux, "Growing Up an Afrikaner," 189–91.

70. **Tentative push:** "An Adaptable Phenomenon: Scouting's Prospects in a Permissive Age," *Star*, 21 February 1970; Group Information Officers Working Kit, "How We Should Deal with the Press," ca. 1973, SASA BC 956/J/Scout Digest; **Cape:** C. J. Inglis, Division Commissioner Western Cape, to CSSA, 22 May 1974, SASA, BC 956/D/General Correspondence, 1973–74; Cape Western Division (E) to CSSA, May 1974, SASA, BC 956/D/General Correspondence, 1973–74.

71. Valediction Speech by C. H. Geech, CSSA, 3 February 1973, SASA, BC 956/G/Speeches.

72. **Respect:** Martin, CSSA, to Carveth Geech, 8 February 1974, SASA, BC 956/D/General Correspondence, 1973–4; **public relations:** "Pointers on Coping with Political Questions While Overseas," by D. Drysdale, 1975, SASA, BC 956/G/Politcal Questions.

73. Thompson, *South Africa*, 217.

74. **1976 riots:** Kane-Berman, *Soweto*, 24; **dead end:** Hyslop, "Schools," 62; **protestors:** Hyslop, "Policy," 469, 473; Kane-Berman, *Soweto*, 1–3.

75. **Liberal agenda:** Hyslop, "Policy," 466; **minority rule:** Thompson, *South Africa*, 223–26.

76. Martin, CSSA, to Geech, 8 February 1974, SASA, BC 956/D/General Correspondence, 1973–74; **deficit:** Quo Vadis Conference Notes, Lexton Maritzburg, 15–16 March 1975, SASA, BC 956/F/Quo Vadis; **Shange and Nxumalo:** Martin, CSSA, to P. Knightly, ca. October 1975, SASA, BC 956/F/Quo Vadis; **international criticism:** HQ Council SA(E)BSA, 6 March 1976, SASA, BC 956/A/CSIC, 1970s.

77. **1975:** Quo Vadis Conference Notes, Lexton Maritzburg, 15–16 March 1975, SASA, BC 956/F/Quo Vadis; **1977:** Minutes of Natal Division (E) Scout Council, 3 March 1977; SABSA Newsletter, 2 July 1977, SASA, BC 956/B/SA Constitution II; **leadership:** Synopsis of "Quo Vadis" Report on Integration of Scout Movement in South Africa, n.d., SASA, BC 956/A/CSIC Reports, 1970s.

78. **Objections:** Unsigned Memorandum, "Closer Cooperation or Integration," ca. 1976, SASA, BC 956/F/Quo Vadis; Minutes of Natal Division (E) Scout Council, 3 March 1977; **Cape Town:** Cape Western Division (C) to CSC (C), 29 March 1976, SASA, BC 956/F/Quo Vadis; "'Mixing Is Devil's Work,' Says Ex-Scout Official," *Sunday Tribune*, 16 September 1979; Brother Egidius, GM 3d Windhoek, to Inglis, September 1980, SASA, BC 956/D/SWA; CSSA to VP BSA, 6 March 1980, SASA, BC 956/D/VPs; **Inglis:** Inglis to CC SAGGA, 2 February 1980, SASA, BC 956/G/Girl Guides, 1979–80; Inglis, interview, July 1998.

79. **N'thaba:** Extraordinary Meeting, OFS Divisional Council, 26 May 1979, SASA, BC 956/D/Central Area; **Kokstad:** Alan Ritchie to Inglis, 26 September 1978, SASA, 956/D/D61.

80. **Reality:** Legal Opinion by L. R. Dison, Consultant's Counsel, 18 October 1978, SASA, BC 956/D/Community Development, 1980s; Extraordinary Meeting, OFS Divisional Council, 26 May 1979, SASA, BC 956/D/Central Area; Planning and Development of Gilweto Training Centre, Mofolo Park, Soweto, 1982, SASA, BC 956/D/Transvaal Area Correspondence; **"window dress":** J. Motsimato, Central Area Secretary, 21 December 1981, SASA, BC 956/D/Central Area.

81. Transvaal Area AGM Minutes, 14 March 1981, SASA, BC 956/D/T7; Inglis, interview, July 1998.

82. Report on Natal Division (A) by N'thaba, 5 March 1961, SASA, BC 956/D/D56; Transkei Division, AR 1961, SASA, BC 956/A/AS24; Natal African Field Commissioner to SAHQ Development Commissioner, 21 April 1964, SASA, BC 956/D/African Field Commissioner.

83. SA(A)BSA HQ Council Minutes, 4 January 1958, SASA, BC 956/A/Africa Scouts, 1936–60; Report by South African Development Commissioner, 25 April 1961, SASA, BC 956/F/D1; Jonathan Ndima, interview, August 1998.

84. **Dues:** Shange to Fraser, 5 December 1969, SASA, BC 956/F/Census 1969; Natal and Zululand African Boy Scout Development Fund, ca. 1975, SASA, BC 956/D/African Scouts, 1975–76; **badges:** Jack Pettersen, AS Natal and KwaZulu, to Director of Administration, 15 June 1961, SASA, BC 956/D/General Correspondence 1980–81; "Confidential Report on Natal Tour," by J. D. Fraser, 5 June 1962, SASA, BC 956/F/D1; Fraser to Lt. Col. R. Gold, International Commissioner BSIB, 19 September 1962, SASA, BC 956/C/File 91.

85. **Curriculum:** J. A. Joel to North Transvaal Division Commissioner (A), 19 March 1968, SASA, BC 956/D/African Scouts, 1960s–70s; Memorandum by Division Commissioner Transkei, Murray McGregor, March 1968, SASA, BC 956/D/African Scouts, 1960s–70s; **tests:** Inglis, interview, July 1998.

86. SA(A)BSA HQ Council Minutes, 5 January 1952, SASA, BC 956/A/Africa Scouts, 1936–60; Transvaal Division (A), AR 1952, SASA, BC 956/D/AS3; Fraser to C. N. Wallace, April 1954, SASA, BC 956/D/AS3; SA(A)BSA HQ Council Minutes, 7 January 1956, SASA, BC 956/A/Africa Scouts, 1936–60; Cape Western Division (A) AR 1957, SASA, BC 956/A/Africa Scouts, 1936–60; Transvaal Division (A) AR 1958, SASA, BC 956/A/Africa Scouts, 1936–60.

87. **Reserved name:** C. N. Wallace, Chair Transvaal Division (A), to CSC (A), 14 February 1956, SASA, BC 956/D/AS3; **African association:** SAHQ Circular, Bob-a-Job, 11 July 1956, SASA BC 956/N/Miscellaneous; SAHQ Administration Commissioner to Division Cape Midlands, 20 August 1968, SASA, BC 956/D/Cape Midlands; Secretary OFS LA to SAHQ Administration Commissioners, 12 December 1970, SASA, BC 956/D/OFS Division; Inglis, interview, July 1998.

88. **Benefits:** *Ikhwezi Boy Scouts Morning Star, Scouts Paper Monthly* 4 (November 1949), SASA, 956/H/International Commissioner; SAHQ Circular, Extra-Mural Activities—School Teacher Scouters, 20 December 1963, SASA, BC 956/A/AS24/1964; **conmen:** "Appeals for Scout Funds," *Rand Daily Mail*, 26 June 1962; "Bogus Scout Collector Has 'Blankets Tale,'" *Cape Times*, July 1962; S. R. Ngosheng, DC Polieteurus, to Mrs. Hunt, 14 December 1976, SASA, BC 956/B/Reports.

89. **Unregistered groups:** Fraser to CSC (A), 2 February 1956, SASA, BC 956/D/AS3; Fraser to Lt. Col. R. Gold, International Commissioner BSIB, 19 September 1962, SASA, BC 956/C/File 91; **amateurs:** Transkei Division, AR 1961, SASA, BC 956/A/AS24; Fraser to Dr. A.H. Tonkin, CSC (A), 29 March 1962, SASA, BC 956/F/D12; Fraser to CSC (A), 18 September 1962, SASA, BC 956/D/D53.

90. **Autonomy:** J. V. Hanratty, Division Commissioner Natal, to Bezencon, 3 December 1976, SASA, BC 956/D/General Correspondence, 1976–79; African Association, ca. 1976, SASA, BC 956/B/People and Personalities; **girl scouts:** Cape Midlands Division (A), AR 1960, SASA, BC 956/A/AS24; Southern Transvaal Division (A), AR 1960, SASA, BC 956/A/AS24; N'thaba to H. W. A. Young, Divisional Commissioner (A) Midlands, 13 July 1966, SASA, BC 956/H/Africa Southern Zone, 1979.

CHAPTER 7

1. Linzee Colchester, HQ Commissioner, to Indiozi, 24 February 1962, KSA, A/NN/181.

2. **Scorn:** Area Secretary Rift Valley LA to Linzee Colchester, HQ Commissioner, 28 September 1960, KSA, A/RV/105; **Kikuyu:** Nairobi LA Minutes, 12 September 1961, KSA, Nairobi LA; CP Report, June 1962, by Ron Tyers, KSA, A/CR/42; Geoffrey Rhodes, Kenyan Chief Scout Commissioner, to Jeremiah Nyagah, 16 October 1962, KSA, A/CR/49; **Girl Guides:** Guide DC Kabete, Report on Limuru Camp, January 1959, KGGA, Kiambu File, 1952–62; Guide DC Kiambu to Colony Secretary, 28 January 1960, KGGA, Kiambu File, 1952–62; Colony Commissioner to Guide DC Nyeri, 23 January 1960, KGGA, Nyeri File, 1956–63.

3. Graaff, *Youth Movements in Developing Countries,* 11; Sachar, *A History of Israel,* 363.

4. Hodge, "The Ghana Workers Brigade," 113–15; Mangoche, "The Role of Youth Movements and Voluntary Organisations in Education in Rural Countries," 81.

5. Hargreaves, *Decolonization,* 171.

6. Douglas-Home, *Evelyn Baring,* 285.

7. Macmillan, *Pointing the Way,* 475.

8. Diary of John Thurman, 1960, BSA, TC/265 Tours.

9. Committee on Africa, 1st Meeting, 26 July 1962, BSA, TC/194 Report of Sub-Committee on Africa; Committee on Africa, 4th Meeting, 25 October 1962, BSA, TC/194 Report of Sub-Committee on Africa.

10. **Military connections:** Summary Procedure as to Recognition and Registration of National Scout Organizations, 1962, KSA, FP/74; **modifications:** Siebold to Colchester, 21 August 1961, KSA, K/BSWB/21.

11. Iliffe, *Tanganyika,* 564; Area Handbook Series, *Tanzania: A Country Study* (Washington DC: American University, 1978), 62–64.

12. **TYL functions:** Iliffe, *Tanganyika,* 532; Bienan, *Tanzania,* 375; **TYL:** TBSA Training Report, 1959, MNA/17/BSA/13/7; "East Africa Tour," by G. F. Witchell, Traveling Commissioner IHQ, 1961, BSA, TC/11 Tours; Stirling, *Scouting,* 23–25.

13. **Private sources:** CSIC Minutes TBSA, 11 February 1963, KSA, K/T/III/26; TBSA Five Year Plan, 12 October 1964, KSA, K/T/III/151; **school-based:** "Tour of Africa," by G. F. Witchell, Traveling Commissioner CWHQ, 1968, BSA, TC/265 Tours of Traveling Commissioner; Stirling, *Scouting,* 24; **appeal:** "Africans Started Scouting and Europeans Developed It," *Zambian Daily Mail,* 7 October 1975.

14. Leys, *Politicians and Policies*, 6.

15. **Competition:** Diary of John Thurman, 1960, BSA, TC/265 Tours; P. A. Wilson to W. H. McVicker, BB Overseas Secretary, 6 September 1955, CMS AF59 AFG 06; **organizer:** Uganda BB QR December 1959, by Geoffrey Hewitson, CMS AF59 AFG 06; **Labour Department:** *Uganda Argus*, 10 January 1964.

16. **State control:** Colchester to Siebold, 30 April 1964, KSA, K/BSWB/204; Peter Marsh, British Council Representative Uganda, to R. A. Frost, British Council Representative to Kenya, 2 May 1964, KSA, K/U/II/85; Draft Constitution of National Union of Youth Organisations, 8 May 1964, KSA, K/U/II/84; **funding:** W. Lloyd Jenkins, HQ Commissioner for Training UBSA, to Colchester, 31 July 1964, KSA, K/U/II/106; **discharge:** Brief Review of Ugandan Scouting, 1964, MNA/17/BSA/13/8; UBSA ExCom Minutes, 11 September 1965, KSA, K/U/III/3/40; UBSA ExCom Minutes, 15 November 1966, KSA, K/U/III/3/102.

17. Oliver and Atmore, *Africa since 1800*, 227.

18. "What a KANU Government Offers You," 18 April 1963; Gertzel, *The Politics of Independent Kenya*, 12–13.

19. **African standards:** Sheffield, *Education*, 64; **segregation:** Christian Churches Educational Association Meeting on Non-Racial Secondary School, 6 December 1960, CMS AF59 G3 A5/e10; **"take part":** "Confidential British Council of Churches Memorandum, Proposed Non-Racial Secondary Schools for Boys in Kenya," by Janet Lacey, 22 June 1960, CMS AF59 G3 A5/e10; Furley, *Education*, 261.

20. **Population:** Griffin, "The Development of Youth Centres in Kenya," 52–53; **unemployment:** Note for Colonial Secretary, Unemployment in Kenya, October 1960, PRO, CO 822/2851.

21. Rhodes to Uganda CC, 5 October 1959, KSA, K/U; Comments on G. F. Witchell's Report, by Rhodes, 5 October 1961, KNA, GH 7/9/93/2; **"50 years":** KBSA Commissioners Conference Minutes, 2–3 September 1961, KNA, GH 7/9/89.

22. KGGA Commissioners Conference Minutes, 12 November 1960, KGGA, Commissioners Conference Minute Book, 1937–60.

23. **Politics:** Nairobi LA Minutes, 12 September 1961, KSA, Nairobi LA; Bridget Culley CC KGGA to Ministry of Education, 2 October 1961, KNA, MK 2/1/166; Camp Chief's Report (Thurman) on Kenyan Training Team Course, January 1962, BSA, TC/265 Tours; **nonpartisan:** *Batian* 6, no. 10 (November 1961).

24. **Cut:** Minutes by PS Department of Social Services, 23 May 1962, KNA, XH 3/11/7; Rhodes, CC, to PS Minister of State, 2 May 1962, KNA, GH 7/9/140; **appeal:** Minute by PS Social Services, 13 July 1962, KNA, XH 3/11/18; **donation:** ExCom Minutes, 24 September 1962, KNA, DC TTA 3/3/29/20.

25. **Amalembe quote:** *Daily Nation*, 10 April 1963; **Gathu:** CC KBSA to Chair, Kenya National Union of Teachers, 3 October 1962, KGGA, Correspondence with Scouts; Colchester to T. A. David, Rift Valley LA, 8 November 1963, KSA, A/RV/III/59; **trouble letting go:** Report of Rev. A. St. J. Lemon, AC Nairobi City, 10 April 1962, KSA, Nairobi LA; Colchester to Schweingruber, 20 November 1961, KSA, K/BSWB/25; Nairobi LA Minutes, 10 July 1962, KSA, Nairobi LA.

26. **Rally:** *Batian* 8 (January 1964).

27. **Nyagah:** Extraordinary Meeting of KSC, 25 November 1963, KNA, DC TTA 3/3/29/60; **declaration:** CC KSA to Minister for Labour and Social Services, 26 March 1964, KGGA, Correspondence with Scouts.

28. Coe, *The Kenya National Youth Service*, 5–7; *Tanganyika Standard*, 1 February 1964; Colchester to J. S. Ameete, Organizing Commissioner UBSA, 22 November 1964, KSA, K/U/II/132.

29. Presidential Address to KSA, 1966, KSA AR, 1966; *Daily Nation*, 27 July 1971.

30. **Late 1960s:** Response to Questionnaire on World Scouting Conducted by Lazlo Nagy, August 1966, KSA, Boy Scouts World Bureau, 1966–68; Annual Report 1966, KSA, Annual Report 1966; G. K. Gathu, Acting HQ Commissioner, to Executive Commissioner, WSB, 28 February 1967, KSA, K/BSWB; **1966:** Colchester to M. B. Nunn, AC CNZA, January 1965, KSA, A/CN/II/208; Response to Nagy Questionnaire; KBU BS and GG Circular, 24 April 1974, KNA, MK 2/1/87; **1970s:** KBSA AGM, 7 August 1970, KNA, XH 3/11/149.

31. **Imposters:** *East Africa Standard*, 7 June 1963; Colchester to Wilson, 13 July 1963, KSA, K/T/III/46; TBSA Minutes of 1st Field Commissioners Conference, November 1964, BSA, TC Tanzania; KBSA Circular, Bob-a-Job Week, 1964, KNA, CB 4/33/12; KBSA AGM, 5 April 1966, KNA, XH 3/11/132; **crackdown:** J. S. Ameete, Organizing Commissioner UBSA, to Colchester, 12 January 1965, KSA, K/U/III/3/50); UBSA ExCom Minutes, 23 April 1968, KSA, K/U/III/3/119; *Daily Nation*, 4 June 1971.

32. **1957:** Gifford, "Dominion," 403–4; Great Britain, Colonial Office, *Report of the Nyasaland Commission of Inquiry*, 14–15; **miners:** Commission of Inquiry, 3–4; Casualties 1959 Operations, MNA, F/248/2072/CAC/155/3f/G (Ops); **"counterinsurgency":** Director FISB to GOC CAC, 18 February 1959, MNA, F/248/2072/CAC/155/3c/G (Ops); **arrest:** PC NP to R. C. Belcher, Organizing Commissioner, 27 May 1959, MNA/17/BSA/1/210.

33. Gifford, "Dominion," 409; WO Minute to CIGS, 25 February 1960, PRO, WO 216/923; Meeting at Nyasaland Government House, 14 July 1960, MNA, F/248/2072/CAC/155/3/G (Ops).

34. **Banda:** Central African Tour of CSCW, 1962, BSA, TC/265 Tours; "Nyasaland Threat to Boy Scouts," *Star*, 20 August 1963; Belcher to Lewis, 3 January 1964, MNA/71/BSA/1/1; A. Dow, Chief Scout Commissioner, to Governor Sir Glyn Jones, 10 January 1964, MNA/17/BSA/1/220; Colonial Office, *Nyasaland*, 110; Lamba, "Moulding," 73; **Boy's Brigade:** BB Nyasaland Report no. 6, 31 December 1959, by Stewart McCollough, CSM ACC 7548–406.

35. **Plan:** League of Malawi Youth, Malawi Young Pioneers Youth Leadership Course: Education, Malawi, March 1966, 66–68; Graaff, *Youth Movements*, 20; **paramilitary:** Nelson et al., *Area Handbook for Malawi*, 310; William, *Malawi*, 227; Graaff, *Youth Movements*, 19.

36. **"Essence":** "Nyasaland Threat"; **Bantustans:** "Tour of Africa," by Witchell, BSA, TC/265 Tours of Traveling Commissioner; **secret:** Kiraithe Nyaga and Colin Inglis, interviews, July 1998.

37. Kaunda, *Zambia Shall Be Free*, 21; Leech, Organizing Commissioner ZMBSA, to IHQ, 12 November 1963, BSA, TC Zimbabwe; Kaunda, Prime Minister of Zambia, to Scout Commissioners Conference, 24 September 1964, BSA, TC Zimbabwe; "Kaunda Is Chief

Scout," *Daily Mail*, 22 September 1965; **institutional problems:** Notes on Scouting in Zambia, 23 December 1968, BSA, TC Zambia.

38. Hargreaves, *Decolonization*, 216, 237; Marks, "Southern Africa," 571.

39. **RBSA:** Landau, "History"; "Scouts, Guides for CD Duties?" *Sunday News Bulawayo*, 4 July 1976; "There Are Scouts and Scouts . . ." *Rhodesia Herald*, 5 October 1977; **negotiation:** "Scouts and Guides Will Be Helped," *Rhodesia Herald*, 12 June 1978; **offer:** "Boy Scout Association," by Charles Martin, International Commissioner ZWBSA, July 1979, SASA, BC 956/H/Zimbabwe; **declaration:** Address by G. M. Magaramombe, Joint Minister of Manpower and Social Affairs, to ZWBSA, ca. 1981, SASA, BC 956/H/Zimbabwe.

40. **"African Region":** G. M. Hussey, International Commissioner SA Association, 8 July 1958, KSA, K/SA/4; **export:** CC UBSA to Hussey, 5 November 1958, KSA, K/SA/7; SASA International Commissioners Report, May 1959–February 1960, KSA, K/SA; CSSA to Commonwealth Commissioner, 29 January 1960, SASA, BC 956/D/Commonwealth CS; **"suicide":** Diary of John Thurman, 1960, BSA, TC/265 Tours.

41. **Offer:** CSIC Minutes, 24 October 1970, SASA, BC 956/A/CSIC, 1969–73; **1973:** Report to CSIC on 2nd Africa Regional Conference, by C. A. Martin, 4 October 1973, SASA, BC 956/A/CSIC Reports, 1970s; **1977:** Martin, CSSA, to Lazlo Nagy and Percy Siebold, BSWB, 5 April 1977, SASA, BC 956/B/SA Constitution II.

42. **Scandinavian Scouts:** SABSA International Department Report, ca. 1970, SASA, BC 956/A/HQ Council, 1970–71; "Scouting Boycott for South Africa?" *Star*, 26 November 1970; Inglis, interview, July 1998; **delegations:** SA(A) BSA, Division Commissioners Meeting, 27 September 1975, SASA, BC 956/A/African, 1968–70s; **instructions:** "Pointers," by Drysdale, 1975, SASA, BC 956/G/Political Questions.

43. **Bantustans:** SA(A)BSA HQ Council Minutes, 15 January 1977, SASA, BC 956/A/African, 1968–70s; Inglis to Rev. Albert Sliep, 15 May 1978, SASA, BC 956/D/General Correspondence, 1977–78; P. Mokgobo, Bophuthatswana Minister for Education, to Secretary for Education, 17 December 1979, SASA, BC 956/C/File 91; AC Transkei to Group Scouters, 13 August 1980, SASA, BC 956/D/D55; **1977 report:** Community Development Report, by CSSA, 29 March 1977, SASA, BC 956/D/Urban Development; **urban troops:** Guidelines for Development of Soweto, Transvaal Area, March 1979, SASA, BC 956/D/Urban Development.

44. **1979:** Conference on Black Urban Scouting Development, ca. 1979, SASA, BC 956/D/Urban Development; SABSA Press Release, April 1980, SASA, BC 956/D/General Correspondence 1980; **Cape commissioners:** Report on Development in Cape Western Area, 31 August 1980, SASA, BC 956/D/General Correspondence 1980; Thompson, *South Africa*, 194–95; Report on Urban Black Scouting Project for Period Ending 31 March 1980, SASA, BC 956/D/Urban Development; Report on Development in Cape Western Area, 31 August 1980, SASA, BC 956/D/General Correspondence 1980; Field Commissioners Report, Cape Western Area, 2 December 1980, SASA, BC 956/D/General Correspondence 1977–79; Cape Western Field Commissioner's Report, June 1982, SASA, BC 956/D/Urban Development.

45. **Well prepared:** Transvaal Area AGM, 14 March 1980, SASA, BC 956/D/General Correspondence 1980–81; **publicize:** Inglis to Mobil Oil Manager Community Affairs, 26 September 1980, SASA, BC 956/D/Urban Development; South African Scout Association website: www.scouting.org.za.

Selected Bibliography

ARCHIVAL SOURCES

BSA British Scout Association, London, England
CMS Church Missionary Society, Birmingham, England
CSM Church of Scotland Mission, Edinburgh, Scotland
KNA Kenya National Archives, Nairobi, Kenya
MNA Malawi National Archives, Zomba, Malawi
PCEA Presbyterian Church of East Africa, Nairobi, Kenya
PRO Public Records Office, Kew, England
SASA South African Scout Association, Cape Town, South Africa
SNA Swaziland National Archives, Mbabane, Swaziland
TNA Tanzania National Archives, Dar es Salaam, Tanzania

OFFICIAL AND SEMIOFFICIAL SOURCES

Advisory Committee on Native Education in the British Tropical African Dependencies. *Education Policy in British Tropical Africa.* Command paper 2374. London: HM Stationery Office, 1925.

Bechuanaland Protectorate. *Annual Report on Education, 1 January 1937 to 31 March 1938.* N.p.

———. *Annual Report on Education, 1 January 1938 to 31 March 1939.* Krugersdorp: West Rand Publications, n.d.

———. *Annual Report on Education, 1935, 1936.* Mafeking, n.d.

Callander, J. F. *A Handbook for Teachers.* Nairobi: East African Literature Bureau, 1961.

Cameron, Donald. *My Tanganyika Service.* London: Allen and Unwin, 1939.

Colony and Protectorate of Kenya. *Education Department Annual Report, 1935.* Nairobi: Government Printer, 1936.

Colony and Protectorate of Kenya. Legislative Council Debates, volume 55, Second Session, 5 May–15 May 1953.

East Africa Protectorate. *Evidence of the Education Commission of the East Africa Protectorate, 1919.* Nairobi: Education Commission, 1919.

Frisby, A. W. *African Education Development Plans, 1945–55.* Lusaka: Government Printer, 1945.

Goodall, Norman. *A History of the London Missionary Society, 1895–1945.* London: Oxford University Press, 1954.

Grant, E. W. "Scouts and Pathfinders." *South African Outlook,* 1 April 1936.

Great Britain. Board of Education. *Special Reports on Educational Subjects.* Vol. 13, *Educational Systems of the Chief Crown Colonies and Possessions of the British Empire, Including Reports on the*

Training of Native Races. Part 2, *West Africa, Basutoland, Southern Rhodesia, East Africa Protectorate, Uganda, Mauritius, Seychelles*. London: HM Stationery Office, 1905.

Great Britain. Colonial Office. *Education for Citizenship in Africa*. London: HM Stationery Office, 1948.

————. *Memorandum on the Education of African Communities*. London: HM Stationery Office, 1935.

————. *Nyasaland: Report for the Year 1960*. London: HM Stationery Office, 1961.

————. *Report of the Nyasaland Commission of Inquiry*. London: HM Stationery Office, 1959.

————. *Summer Conference on African Administration: African Local Government, First Session*. London: HM Stationery Office, 1947.

Great Britain. Commission on Disturbances in the Copperbelt. *Report of the Commission Appointed to Enquire into the Disturbances in the Copperbelt, Northern Rhodesia*. London: HM Stationery Office, 1935.

Inter-Territorial Jeanes Conference. *Findings of the Inter-Territorial "Jeanes" Conference, held in Salisbury, Southern Rhodesia, 27th May to 6th June, 1935*. Lovedale, South Africa: Lovedale Press, 1935.

Jones, Thomas Jesse (African Education Commission). *Education in East Africa* (Phelps-Stokes Report). London: Edinburgh House, Press, 1924.

————. *A Ten-Year Plan for the Development of African Education*. Nairobi: Government Printer, 1948.

Kenya. African Affairs Department. *Annual Report, 1949, 1950, 1957*. Nairobi: Government Printer, 1951–58.

Kenya. Department of Community Development and Rehabilitation. *Annual Report of the Department of Community Development and Rehabilitation, 1954, 1955, 1957, 1958*. Nairobi: Government Printers, 1955–59.

————. *Community Development Organization Annual Report, 1953*. Nairobi: Government Printers, 1954.

Kenya. Education Department. *Annual Report, 1946*. Nairobi: Government Printer, 1947.

————. *Report of the Development Committee*, 2 vols. Nairobi: Government Printer, 1946.

Kenya. Land Commission, *Evidence*. Vol. 2. Nairobi: Government Printer, 1933.

Nuffield Foundation and Colonial Office. *African Education: A Study of Educational Policy and Practice in British Tropical Areas*. Oxford: Oxford University Press, 1953.

Nyasaland Protectorate. Department of Education. *Primary School Syllabus*. Zomba: Government Printer, 1951.

————. *Annual Report, 1954*. Zomba: Government Printer, 1955.

Provincial Administration of the Cape of Good Hope. *Report of the Coloured Education Commission, 1953–1956*. Cape Town: Premier Printing, 1956.

Southern Rhodesia. Department of Native Development. *Junior School Syllabus*. Salisbury: Rhodesian Printing Company, 1932.

Southern Rhodesia. Education Commission. *Report of the Commission Appointed to Enquire into the Matter of Native Education in All Its Bearing in the Colony of Southern Rhodesia*. Salisbury: Government Printer, 1925.

————. *Report of the Native Education Inquiry Commission, 1951*. Bulawayo: Rhodesian Printing and Publishing Company, 1952.

Swaziland Education Department. *Annual Report of the Director of Education*. Mbabane: Education Department, 1956.

Tanganyika Education Conference. *Conference between Government and Missions: Report of Proceedings, 5–12 October 1925*. Dar es Salaam: Government Printer, 1925.

Tanganyika Territory. *Syllabus of Instruction for African Schools: Primary*. Dar es Salaam: Government Printer, ca. 1934.

Uganda Protectorate. *Annual Report of the Education Department*. Entebbe: Government Printer, 1933–60.

———. *Report of the Commission of Inquiry into the Disturbances in Uganda During April, 1949*. Entebbe: Government Printer, 1950

Union of South Africa. *Report of the Commission on Native Education, 1949–1951*. Pretoria, Government Printer, 1951.

Verwoerd, H. F. *Bantu Education: Policy for the Immediate Future*. Pretoria: Department of Native Affairs, 1954.

OFFICIAL AND SEMIOFFICIAL SCOUT SOURCES

Baden-Powell, Lord Robert. *Aims, Methods and Needs*. London: Boy Scouts Association, n.d.

———. *B.-P.'s Outlook: Selections from the Founder's Contributions to The Scouter from 1909–1941*. Ottawa: Boy Scouts of Canada, 1979.

———. *The Matabele Campaign, 1896*. Westport: Negro Universities Press, 1970.

———. "A New Development in the Scout Movement in South Africa." *Journal of the Royal African Society* 36 (1936): 368–71.

———. *Scouting and Youth Movements*. New York: Jonathan Cape and Harrison Smith, 1931.

———. *Scouting for Boys*. 30th ed. London: C. Arthur Pearson, 1957.

———. *Scoutmastership: A Handbook for Scoutmasters on the Theory of Scout Training*. London: G. P. Putnam's Sons, 1920.

———. "White Men in Black Skins." *Elders Review of West African Affairs* 8, no. 30 (July 1929): 6–7.

Ball, E. A. "The Pathfinder Movement." *South African Outlook*, 1 September, 1 November, 1931.

Boy Scouts of America. *Handbook for Scoutmasters: A Manual of Leadership*. New York: National Council of Boy Scouts of America, 1923.

———. *Scouting for Negro Boys in Methodist Churches*. New York: N.p., 1949.

British Boy Scouts Association. *A Challenge to Scouting: The Menace of Communism*. London: Staple Printers, 1951.

———. *Scouting and Education*. London: Bradley and Son, n.d.

Kenya Scout Association. "Short History of Scouting in Kenya." In souvenir program, Kenya Scouts Camporee at Princess Park Mombasa, 11–18 August 1961.

———. Souvenir program, Chief Scout's Rally, Rowallan Camp, 1963.

Pathfinder Council. *Constitution and Regulations of the Pathfinder Movement*. N.p., [ca. 1932].

Rhodesia Boy Scouts Association. *Good Scouting*. Salisbury: Mambo Press, 1963.

Smith, J. Stephen. *Aids to Scoutmasters in East Africa*. Nairobi: Eagle Press, 1951.

Tanganyika Scout Association. *Constitution of the Tanganyika Boy Scout Association*. Ndanda Mission Press, 1963.

SECONDARY SOURCES

Allman, Jean, and Victoria Tashjian. *"I Will Not Eat Stone": A Women's History of Colonial Asante*. Portsmouth: Heinemann, 2000.

Anderson, John. *The Struggle for the School: The Interaction of Missionary, Colonial Government, and Nationalist Enterprise in the Development of Formal Education in Kenya.* London: Longman, 1970.

Apple, Michael. "Reproduction and Contradiction in Education: An Introduction." In *Cultural and Economic Reproduction in Education: Essays on Class, Ideology, and the State,* ed. Michael Apple. London: Routledge and Kegan Paul, 1982.

———. *Ideology and Curriculum.* London: Routledge and Kegan Paul, 1979.

Baker, W. "Discipline of Boys Today Is Not What It Used to Be." *Outspan* 42, no. 1101 (2 April 1948).

Ball, Stephen. "Imperialism, Social Control, and the Colonial Curriculum in Africa." *Journal of Curriculum Studies* 15, no. 3 (1983): 237–63.

Barrett, David, George Mambo, Janet McLaughlin, and Malcolm McVeigh, eds. *Kenya Churches Handbook: The Development of Kenyan Christianity, 1498–1973.* Kisumu: Evangel Publishing House, 1973.

Beinart, William. "The Origins of the Indlavini Male Associations and Migrant Labour in the Transkei. In *Tradition and Transition in Southern Africa,* ed. Andrew Spiegel and Patrick McAllister. New Brunswick, NJ: Transaction Publishers, 1991.

Benson, T. G. "Some Problems of Education To-Day." *Oversea Education* 7, no. 1 (1935): 10–15.

———. "The Jeanes School and the Education of the East Africa Native." *Journal of the Royal African Society* 36 (1936): 418–31.

Berger, Elena. *Labour, Race, and Colonial Rule: The Copperbelt from 1924 to Independence.* Oxford: Clarendon Press, 1974.

Berman, Bruce. *Control and Crisis in Colonial Kenya: The Dialectic of Domination.* Nairobi: East African Publishers, 1990.

Berman, Bruce, and John Lonsdale. *Unhappy Valley: Conflict in Kenya and Africa.* London: James Currey, 1992.

Berman, Edward. "Africans and Their Schools." *History of Education Quarterly,* Summer 1977, 209–19.

Bienan, Henry. *Tanzania: Party Transformation and Economic Development.* Princeton: Princeton University Press, 1970.

Birch, Austin. *The Story of the Boys' Brigade.* London: F. Muller, 1965. Birmingham, Jack. "Perspectives on Colonial Education in Botswana." In *Independence without Freedom: The Political Economy of Colonial Education in Southern Africa,* ed. A. Mugomba and M. Nyaggah. Santa Barbara: ABC-Clio, 1980.

Blood, A. G. *The History of the Universities' Mission to Central Africa.* Vol. 2, 1907–1932. London: UMCA, 1957.

Bogonko, S. N. *African Political Associations and the Quest for Secular Education in Kenya, 1920–1934.* Kenyatta University College Department of History Staff Seminar Paper no. 8, February 1984.

———. "Education as a Tool of Colonialism in Kenya: The Case of the First Government African Schools." *Transafrican Journal of History* 12 (1983): 1–32.

Bolnick, Joel. *Double-Cross: Potlako Leballo and the 1946 Riots at Lovedale Missionary Institution.* African Studies Seminar Paper no. 265, University of Witwatersrand, February 1990.

Bonami, Francesco, Louisa Maria Frisa, and Stefano Tonchi, eds. *Uniform: Order and Disorder.* Milan: Edizioni Charta, 2000.

Bonner, Philip. "Family, Crime, and Political Consciousness on the East Rand, 1939–1955." *Journal of Southern African Studies* 14, no. 3 (1988): 393–420.

Bonner, Philip, Peter Delius, and Deborah Posel, eds. *Apartheid's Genesis, 1935–1962.* Johannesburg: Ravan Press, 1993.

Booth, Alan. *Historical Dictionary of Swaziland.* 2d ed. Lanham: Scarecrow Press, 2000.

Breckenridge, Keith. "The Allure of Violence: Men, Race, and Masculinity on the South African Goldmines, 1900–1950." *Journal of Southern African Studies* 24 (1998): 669–92.

Brookes, Edgar. R. J.: *In Appreciation of the Life of John David Rheinallt Jones and His Work for the Betterment of Race Relations in Southern Africa.* Johannesburg: South African Institute of Race Relations, 1953.

Brown, Arthur. "The Development of the Scout Movement in Nigeria." *African Affairs* 46 (1947): 38–42.

Brownfoot, Janice. "Sisters under the Skin: Imperialism and the Emancipation of Women in Malaya, c. 1891–1941." In *Making Imperial Mentalities: Socialisation and British Imperialism,* ed. J. A. Mangan. Manchester: Manchester University Press, 1990.

Bryan, H. S. *The Troublesome Boy.* London: C. Arthur Pearson, 1936.

Bude, Udo. "The Adaptation Concept in British Colonial Education." *Comparative Education* 19, no. 3 (1983): 341–55.

Burke, Timothy. *Lifebuoy Men, Lux Women: Commodification, Consumption, and Cleanliness in Modern Zimbabwe.* Durham: Duke University Press, 1996.

Burman, Sandra. Introduction to *Growing Up in a Divided Society: The Contexts of Childhood in South Africa,* ed. Burman and Pamela Reynolds. Evanston: Northwestern University Press, 1986.

Burton, Andrew. "Urchins, Loafers, and the Cult of the Cowboy: Urbanization and Delinquency in Dar es Salaam, 1919–61." *Journal of African History* 42 (2001): 199–216.

Cain, P. J., and A. G. Hopkins. *British Imperialism: Crisis and Deconstruction, 1914–1990.* London: Longman, 1993.

Capon, M. G. *Towards Unity in Kenya.* Nairobi: Christian Council of Kenya, 1962.

Cardinall, A. W. *The Gold Coast, 1931.* Accra: Government Printer, [ca. 1931].

Carnoy, Martin. *Education as Cultural Imperialism.* New York: David McKay, 1974.

Carothers, J. C. *The Psychology of Mau Mau.* Nairobi: Government Printer, 1955.

Carpenter, David Bailey. "The Boy Scouts of America: A Social Evaluation of the Organization in Terms of Its Measurable Influence on Its Past and Present Membership." MA thesis, Washington University, 1938.

Carton, Benedict. "Impotent African Patriarchs, Unruly African Sons in Colonial South Africa. In *The Politics of Age and Gerontocracy in Africa,* ed. Mario Aguilar. Trenton: Africa World Press, 1998.

Chanock, Martin. "Paradigms, Policies and Property: A Review of the Customary Law of Land Tenure." In *Law in Colonial Africa,* ed. Kristin Mann and Richard Roberts. Portsmouth, NH: Heinemann, 1991.

Chizinga, L. M. *The Politics of Education on the Zambian Copperbelt since the 1930s.* Oslo: U-Landsseminaret, 1984.

Clayton, Anthony. *Counterinsurgency in Kenya: A Study of Military Operations against the Mau Mau, 1952–1960.* New York: Sunflower University Press, 1984.

Clayton, Anthony, and Donald Savage. *Government and Labour in Kenya, 1895–1963.* London: Frank Cass, 1974.

Clough, Marshall. *Fighting Two Sides: Kenyan Chiefs and Politicians, 1918–1940.* Niwot: University of Press of Colorado, 1990.

Coe, R. L. *The Kenya National Youth Service: A Governmental Response to Young Political Activists*. Ohio University: Center for International Studies, 1973.

Cole, Keith. *The Cross over Mount Kenya: A Short History of the Anglican Church in the Diocese of Mount Kenya, 1900–1970*. Nairobi, 1970.

Comaroff, Jean. "The Empire's Old Clothes: Fashioning the Colonial Subject." In *Situated Lives: Gender and Culture in Everyday Life*, ed. Louise Lamphere, Helena Ragone, and Patricia Zavella. New York: Routledge, 1997.

Comaroff, John, and Jean Comaroff. *The Dialectics of Modernity on a South African Frontier*. Vol. 2 of *Of Revelation and Revolution*. Chicago: University of Chicago Press, 1997.

Coombs, R. H. "Non-Formal Education: Myths, Realities, and Opportunities." *Comparative Education Review* 20, no. 3 (1976): 287–93.

Cooper, Frederick. "Conflict and Connection: Rethinking Colonial African History." *American Historical Review* 99, no. 5 (1994): 1516–45.

———. *Decolonization and African Society: The Labor Question in French and British Africa*. Cambridge: Cambridge University Press, 1996.

Cornwall, Andrea, and Nancy Lindisfarne. Introduction to *Dislocating Masculinity: Comparative Ethnographies*, ed. Andrea Cornwall and Nancy Lindisfarne. New York: Routledge, 1994.

Couzens, Tim. "'Moralizing Leisure Time': The Transatlantic Connection and Black Johannesburg, 1918–1936." In *Industrialisation and Social Change in South Africa: African Class Formation, Culture, and Consciousness, 1870–1930*, ed. Shula Marks and Richard Rathbone. New York: Longman, 1982.

Cross, Michael. *Imagery of Identity in South African Education, 1880–1990*. Durham: Carolina Academic Press, 1999.

Deane, Dee Shirley. *South Africans: A Who's Who*. Cape Town: Oxford University Press, 1978.

Dougall, J. W. C. *Missionary Education in Kenya and Uganda*. London, 1936.

———, ed. *Christianity and the Sex-Education of the African*. London: Society for Promoting Christian Knowledge, 1937.

———, ed. *The Village Teacher's Guide: A Book of Guidance for African Teachers*. London: Sheldon Press, 1931.

Douglas-Home, Charles. *Evelyn Baring: The Last Proconsul*. London: Collins, 1978.

Dubow, Saul. "Afrikaner Nationalism, Apartheid and the Conceptualization of 'Race.'" *Journal of African History* 33 (1992).

Edgar, Robert. "African Educational Protest in South Africa: The American School Movement in the Transkei in the 1920s." In *Apartheid and Education: The Education of Black South Africans*, ed. Peter Kallaway. Johannesburg: Ravan Press, 1984.

Elphick, Richard. "Mission Christianity and Interwar Liberalism." In *Democratic Liberalism in South Africa: Its History and Prospect*, ed. Jeffrey Butler, Richard Elphick, and David Welsh. Middletown, CT: Wesleyan University Press, 1987.

Epprecht, Marc. "'Good God Almighty, What's This!': Homosexual 'Crime' in Early Colonial Zimbabwe. In *Boy-Wives and Female Husbands: Studies of African Homosexualities*, ed. Stephen Murray and Will Roscoe. New York: St. Martin's Press, 1998.

———. "The 'Unsaying' of Indigenous Homosexualities in Zimbabwe: Mapping a Blindspot in an African Masculinity." *Journal of Southern African Studies* 24, no. 4 (1998): 631–51.

Fleischer, Kenneth. "Training Youth to Become Good Citizens." *Outspan*, no. 1051 (25 April 1947): 57, 77.

Freund, Bill. *The Making of Contemporary Africa:The Development of African Society since 1800.*
    Bloomington: Indiana University Press, 1984.
Furedi, Frank. "The African Crowd in Nairobi: Popular Movements and Elite Politics."
    Journal of African History 14 (1973).
Furley, O. W. *A History of Education in East Africa.* New York: NOK Publications, 1978.
Fussell, Paul. *Uniforms:Why We AreWhatWeWear.* Boston: Houghton Mifflin Company,
    2002.
Gaitskell, Deborah. "Race, Gender, and Imperialism: A Century of Black Girls' Education
    in South Africa." In *"Benefits Bestowed"? Education and British Imperialism,* ed. J. A. Man-
    gan. Manchester: Manchester University Press, 1988.
———. "Upward All and Play the Game:The Girl Wayfarers' Association in the Trans-
    vaal, 1925–1975." In *Apartheid and Education:The Education of Black South Africans,* ed. Peter
    Kallaway. Johannesburg: Ravan Press, 1984.
Gertzel, Cherry. *The Politics of Independent Kenya, 1963–68.* Evanston: Northwestern University
    Press, 1970.
Ghosh, Suresh Chandra. "'English in Taste, in Opinions, in Words and Intellect': Indoc-
    trinating the Indian through Textbook, Curriculum and Education." In *The Imperial
    Curriculum,* ed. J. A. Mangan. New York: Routledge, 1993.
Gifford, Prosser. "Misconceived Dominion:The Creation and Disintegration of Federa-
    tion in British Central Africa." In *The Transfer of Power in Africa,* ed. Prosser Gifford and
    Wm. Roger Louis. New Haven:Yale University Press, 1982.
Gillis, John. *Youth in History:Tradition and Change in European Age Relations, 1770–Present.* New York:
    Academic Press, 1974.
Glaser, Clive. *Bo-Tsotsi:TheYouth Gangs of Soweto, 1935–1976.* Portsmouth, NH: Heinemann,
    2000.
———. "The Mark of Zorro: Sexuality and Gender Relations in theTsotsi Subculture
    on the Witwatersrand." *African Studies* 51, no. 1 (1992): 47–67.
———. "Students,Tsotsis, and the CongressYouth League:Youth Organisation on the
    Rand in the 1940s and 1950s." *Perspectives in Education* 10, no. 2 (1988–89): 1–15.
———. "'When Are They Going to Fight?':Tsotsis,Youth Politics, and the PAC." In
    Apartheid's Genesis, 1935–1962, ed. Philip Bonner, Peter Delius, and Deborah Posel. Jo-
    hannesburg: Ravan Press, 1993.
Graaff, J. F. de V. *Youth Movements in Developing Countries.* Bournemouth: Manchester Mono-
    graphs, 1982.
Greig, Jack C. E. *Education in Northern Rhodesia and Nyasaland: Pre-Independence Period.* Oxford: Ox-
    ford Colonial Records Project, 1985.
Grieveson, E. T. "Educational Needs of Urbanised Natives in South Africa." *Journal of the
    African Society* 36 (1937): 321–36.
Griffin, G. W. "The Development ofYouth Centres in Kenya." *International Labour Review* 88,
    no. 1 (1963): 52–65.
Grimston, Brian. "Survey of Native Educational Development in Southern Rhodesia,
    1939." N.p., [ca. 1939].
Guha, Ranajit. "Dominance without Hegemony and Its Historiography." In *Subaltern Stud-
    iesVI:Writings on South Asian History and Society,* ed. Ranajit Guha. Delhi: Oxford Uni-
    versity Press, 1989.
Hailey, William Malcom, Baron. *An African Survey: A Study of Problems Arising in Africa South of the
    Sahara.* London: Oxford University Press, 1938.

———. *An African Survey: A Study of Problems Arising in Africa South of the Sahara.* Rev. 1956. London: Oxford University Press, 1957.

———. *Native Administration and Political Development.* London: HM Stationary Office, 1944.

Hamilton, Carolyn. *Terrific Majesty: The Powers of Shaka Zulu and the Limits of Historical Invention.* Cambridge, MA: Harvard University Press, 1998.

Hansen, Karen Tranberg. *African Encounters with Domesticity.* New Brunswick, NJ: Rutgers University Press, 1992.

Hantover, Jeffrey P. "The Boys Scouts and the Validation of Masculinity." *Journal of Social Issues* 34, no. 1 (1978): 184–95.

Hargreaves, John. *Decolonization in Africa.* 2d ed. London: Longman, 1996.

Harries, Patrick. "Imagery Symbolism and Tradition in a South African Bantustan: Mangosuthu Buthelezi, Inkatha, and Zulu History." *History and Theory* 32, no. 4 (1993): 105–25.

Hattersley, Alan F. *The Boy Scout and the Future of Education.* Pietermaritzburg: Times Printing, 1918.

Hellman, E. *Problems of Bantu Urban Youth.* Johannesburg: South African Institute of Race Relations, 1940.

Henderson, Ian. "Early African Leadership: The Copperbelt Disturbances of 1935 and 1940." *Journal of Southern African Studies* 2, no. 1 (1975): 83–97.

Hewitt, Gordon. *The Problems of Success: A History of the Church Missionary Society, 1910–1942.* Vol. 1. London: SCM Press, 1971.

Heyman, Richard. "The Initial Years of the Jeanes School in Kenya, 1924–1931." In *Essays in the History of African Education,* ed. Vincent Battle and Charles Lyons. New York: Teachers College Press, 1970.

Hodge, Peter. "The Ghana Workers Brigade." *British Journal of Sociology* 15, no. 2 (1964): 113–29.

Holmes, Brian. "British Imperial Policy and the Mission Schools." In *Educational Policy Mission Schools: Case-Studies from the British Empire,* ed. Brian Holmes. London: Routledge and Kegan Paul, 1968.

Holmes, H. "Urban Schoolboys Go to the Country." *Rhodes-Livingstone Journal* 9 (1950): 31–36.

Hooper, C. J. D. "Teacher Training and the Community." *Oversea Education* 24, no. 3 (October 1952): 22–25.

Horrell, Muriel. *Bantu Education to 1968.* Johannesburg: South African Institute of Race Relations, 1968.

———. *The Education of the Coloured Community in South Africa 1652 to 1970.* Johannesburg: South African Institute of Race Relations, 1970.

Hunt Davis, R. "The Administration and Financing of African Education in South Africa, 1910–1953." In *Apartheid and Education: The Education of Black South Africans,* ed. Peter Kallaway. Johannesburg: Ravan Press, 1984.

———. "Charles T. Loram and the American Model for African Education in South Africa." In *Apartheid and Education: The Education of Black South Africans,* ed. Peter Kallaway. Johannesburg: Ravan Press, 1984.

———. "Producing the 'Good African': South Carolina's Penn School as a Guide for African Education in South Africa." In *Independence Without Freedom: The Political Economy of Colonial Education in Southern Africa,* ed. A. Mugomba and M. Nyaggah. Santa Barbara: ABC-Clio, 1980.

Huxley, Julian. *Africa View*. New York: Harper Brothers, 1931.

Hyslop, Jonathan. "'A Destruction Coming In': Bantu Education as Response to Social Crisis." In *Apartheid's Genesis, 1935–1962*, ed. Philip Bonner, Peter Delius, and Deborah Posel. Johannesburg: Ravan Press, 1993.

————. "Schools, Unemployment and Youth: Origins and Significance of Student and Youth Movements, 1976–1987." *Perspectives in Education* 10, no. 2 (1988–89): 61–69.

————. "State Education Policy and the Social Reproduction of the Urban African Working Class: The Case of the Southern Transvaal 1955–1976." *Journal of Southern African Studies* 14, no. 3 (1988): 446–76.

Iliffe, John. *A Modern History of Tanganyika*. New York: Cambridge University Press, 1979.

Ipenburg, At. *"All Good Men": The Development of Lubwa Mission, Chinsali, Zambia, 1905–1967*. Frankfurt: Peter Lang, 1992.

Jeal, Tim. *The Boy-Man: The Life of Lord Baden-Powell*. New York: Morrow, 1990.

Jenkins, A. O. "Girl Guide Activities in Uganda." *Uganda Teachers Journal* 2 (1940): 14–18.

Joseph, Nathan. *Uniforms and Nonuniforms: Communication through Clothing*. Westport, CT: Greenwood Press, 1986.

Kabiro, Ngugi. *The Man in the Middle: The Story of Ngugi Kabiro*. Ed. Don Barnett. Richmond, BC: Liberation Support Movement, 1973.

Kadish, Sharman. *"A Good Jew and A Good Englishman": The Jewish Lads' and Girls' Brigade, 1895–1995*. London: Vallentine Mitchell, 1995.

Kahane, Reuven. *The Origins of Postmodern Youth: Informal Youth Movements in a Comparative Perspective*. Berlin: Walter de Gruyter, 1997.

Kallaway, Peter, ed. *Apartheid and Education: The Education of Black South Africans*. Johannesburg: Ravan Press, 1984.

Kane-Berman, John. *Soweto: Black Revolt, White Reaction*. Johannesburg: Raven Press, 1978.

Kareri, Charles Muhoro. *The Life of Charles Muhoro Kareri*. Trans. Kariuki Muriithi, ed. Derek Peterson. Madison: African Studies Program, 2003.

Kaunda, Kenneth. *Zambia Shall Be Free*. New York: Frederick Praeger, 1962.

Kay, Stafford. "African Roles, Responses, and Initiatives in Colonial Education: The Case of Western Kenya." *Paedagogica Historica* 16 (1976): 272–93.

————. "The Southern Abaluyia, the Friends Africa Mission, and the Development of Education in Western Kenya, 1902–1965." PhD diss., University of Wisconsin, 1973.

Kennedy, Dane. *Islands of White: Settler Society and Culture in Kenya and Southern Rhodesia, 1890–1939*. Durham: Duke University Press, 1987.

Kershaw, Greet. *Mau Mau from Below*. Oxford: James Currey, 1997.

Kimmel, Michael. "Rethinking 'Masculinity': New Directions in Research. In *Changing Men: New Directions in Research on Men and Masculinity*, ed. Michael Kimmel. Beverly Hills: Sage Publications, 1987.

King, Kenneth James. "Africa and the Southern States of the USA: Notes on J. H. Oldham and American Negro Education for Africans," *Journal of African History* 10 (1969): 659–77.

————. *Pan-Africanism and Education: A Study of Race, Philanthropy, and Education in the Southern United States and East Africa*. Oxford: Clarendon Press, 1971.

Kirk-Greene, A. H. M. "The District Officer as the Man in the Middle in West Africa." In *The Transfer of Power in Africa*, ed. A. H. M. Kirk-Greene. Oxford: Oxford University Press, 1979.

Kovar, Michael H. "The Kikuyu Independent School Movement: Interaction of Politics and Education in Kenya, 1923–1953." PhD diss., University of California, Los Angeles, 1970.

Kros, C. J. *They Wanted Dancing and Not Merely the Lambeth Walk: A Reassessment of the 1940s School Disturbances with Particular Reference to Lovedale*. African Studies Seminar Paper no. 318, University of Witwatersrand, 27 July 1992.

Küster, Sybille. *African Education in Colonial Zimbabwe, Zambia and Malawi: Government Control, Settler Antagonism and African Agency, 1890–1964*. Hamburg: Lit Verlag, 1999.

Lake, R. A. "A Kenya Government African School in 1948." *Oversea Education* 21 (1950): 1004–8.

———. "The Outward Bound Mountain School of East Africa." *Oversea Education* 32 (1960): 54–60.

Lamba, Isaac. "Moulding the Ideal Colonial Subject: The Scouting Movement in Colonial Malawi up to 1961." *Transafrican Journal of History* 14 (1985): 63–77.

Landau, John. "A Brief History of the Boy Scout Association of Rhodesia and Zimbabwe, 1909–1996." Unpublished manuscript, ca. 1996.

le Roux, Pieter. "Growing Up an Afrikaner." In *Growing Up in a Divided Society: The Contexts of Childhood in South Africa*, ed. Sandra Burman and Pamela Reynolds. Evanston: Northwestern University Press, 1986.

League of Malawi Youth. *Malawi Young Pioneers Youth Leadership Course: Education*. Malawi, March 1966.

Leonard, Rev. M. P. G. *Scouts' Own*. Plymouth: Mayflower Press, 1933.

Leslie, W. Bruce. "Creating a Socialist Scout Movement: The Woodcraft Folk, 1924–42." *History of Education* 13, no. 4 (1984): 299–311.

Lewis, Joanna. *Empire State-Building: War and Welfare in Kenya, 1925–52*. Oxford: James Currey, 2000.

Lewis, Thomas H. "The Problem of the Semi-Educated African." *Oversea Education* 13, no. 2 (1942): 265–73.

Lewsen, Phyllis. "Liberals in Politics and Administration, 1936–1948." In *Democratic Liberalism in South Africa: Its History and Prospect*, ed. Jeffrey Butler, Richard Elphick, and David Welsh. Middletown, CT: Wesleyan University Press, 1987.

Leys, Colin. *Politicians and Policies: An Essay on Politics in Acholi, Uganda, 1962–1965*. Nairobi: East African Publishing House, 1967.

Listowel, Judith. *The Making of Tanganyika*. London: Chatto and Windus, 1965.

Lodge, Tom. "The Parents' School Boycott: Eastern Cape and East Rand Townships, 1955." In *Apartheid and Education: The Education of Black South Africans*, ed. Peter Kallaway. Johannesburg: Ravan Press, 1984.

Lonsdale, John. "Mau Maus of the Mind: Making Mau Mau and Remaking Kenya." *Journal of African History* 31 (1990): 393–421.

———. "Political Associations in Western Kenya." In *Protest and Power in Black Africa*, ed. R. I. Rotberg and Ali Mazrui. New York: Oxford University Press.

———. "State and Peasantry in Colonial Africa." In *People's History and Theory*, ed. Raphael Samuel. London: Routledge and Kegan Paul, 1981.

Loram, C. T. "The Phelps-Stokes Education Commission in South Africa." *International Review of Missions* 10 (1921): 496–508.

Lowe, Christopher. "Swaziland's Colonial Politics: The Decline of Progressivist South African Nationalism and the Emergence of Swazi Political Traditionalism, 1910–1939." PhD diss., Yale University, 1998.

Lugard, F. D. *The Dual Mandate in British Tropical Africa.* London: Frank Cass, 1965.

MacDonald, Robert H. *Sons of the Empire: The Frontier Movement and the Boy Scout Movement,* 1890–1918. Toronto: University of Toronto Press, 1993.

MacLeod, David I. "Act Your Age: Boyhood, Adolescence, and the Rise of the Boy Scouts of America." *Journal of Social History* 16, no. 2 (Winter 1982): 3–20.

————. *Building Character in the American Boy: The Boy Scouts, YMCA, and Their Forerunners,* 1870–1920. Madison: University of Wisconsin Press, 1983.

Macmillan, Hugh. "Swaziland: Decolonisation and the Triumph of 'Tradition.'" *Journal of Modern African Studies* 23 (1985).

MacMillan, W. M. "The Importance of the Educated African." *Journal of the African Society* 33 (1934): 137–42.

Mager, Anne. "Youth Organisations and the Construction of Masculine Identities in the Ciskei and Transkei, 1945–1960." *Journal of Southern African Studies* 24, no. 4 (1998): 653–67.

Mager, Anne, and Gary Minkley. "Reaping the Whirlwind: The East London Riots of 1952." In *Apartheid's Genesis, 1935–1962,* ed. Philip Bonner, Peter Delius, and Deborah Posel. Johannesburg: Ravan Press, 1993.

Maina wa Kinyati. *Thunder from the Mountains: Mau Mau Patriotic Songs.* Trenton: Africa World Press, 1990.

Malherbe, Ernst G. *Education in South Africa.* Vol. 2, 1923–75. Cape Town: Juta, 1977.

Mamdani, Mahmood. *Citizen and Subject: Contemporary Africa and the Legacy of Late Colonialism.* Princeton: Princeton University Press, 1996.

Mangan, J. A. "Images for Confident Control: Stereotypes in Imperial Discourse." In *The Imperial Curriculum,* ed. J. A. Mangan. New York: Routledge, 1993.

————. "Imperialism, History and Education." In *"Benefits Bestowed"? Education and British Imperialism,* ed. J. A. Mangan. Manchester: Manchester University Press, 1988.

————, ed. *Making Imperial Mentalities: Socialisation and British Imperialism.* Manchester: Manchester University Press, 1990.

Mangan, J. A., and James Walvin. Introduction to *Manliness and Morality: Middle-Class Masculinity in Britain and America, 1800–1940,* ed. Mangan and Walvin. New York: St. Martin's, 1987.

Mangoche, M. V. B. "The Role of Youth Movements and Voluntary Organisations in Education in Rural Countries." In *Educational Development in Predominately Rural Countries,* ed. J. D. Turner and A. P. Hunter. Mojira, Lesotho: Mojira Printing Works, 1968.

Marks, Shula. "Southern Africa." In *The Oxford History of the British Empire,* vol. 4, *The Twentieth Century,* ed. Judith Brown and Wm. Roger Louis. Oxford: Oxford University Press, 1999.

Martin, Phyllis. *Leisure and Society in Colonial Brazzaville.* Cambridge: Cambridge University Press, 1995.

Marwick, B. A. *The Swazi: An Ethnographic Account of the Natives of the Swaziland Protectorate.* London: Frank Cass, 1966.

Mason, R. J. *Education of Rural Communities: Suggestions for the Training of Teachers.* Dar es Salaam: Government Printer, 1938.

Mathu, Mohamed. *The Urban Guerilla: The Story of Mohamed Mathu.* Ed. Don Barnett. Richmond, BC: Liberation Support Movement, 1974.

McFarlan, Donald. *First for Boys: The Story of the Boys' Brigade, 1883–1983.* Glasgow: Collins, 1982.

McGregor, G. P. *King's College, Budo: The First Sixty Years.* London: Oxford University Press, 1967.

McVicker, W. H. "The Boys' Brigade." *South African Outlook,* 1 April 1936.

Milne, F. Douglas. "Community Service Camps in Rhodesia." *Oversea Education* 30, no. 1 (1958): 19–22.

Mokwele, Alfred Percy Phuti. "The Pedagogy of Pathfinding and the Boy Scout Movement in South Africa, 1911–1977." PhD diss., University of the North, 1992.

Molteno, Frank. "The Historical Foundations of the Schooling of Black South Africans." In *Apartheid and Education: The Education of Black South Africans,* ed. Peter Kallaway. Johannesburg: Ravan Press, 1984.

Montagu, Edwin. *An Indian Diary.* London: William Heinemann, 1930.

Moodie, T. Dunbar. "Migrancy and Male Sexuality on the South African Gold Mines." *Journal of Southern African Studies* 14, no. 2 (1988): 228–56.

———. *The Rise of Afrikanerdom: Power, Apartheid, and the Afrikaner Civil Religion.* Berkeley: University of California Press, 1975.

Mooney, Katie. "'Ducktails, Flick-Knives and Pugnacity': Subcultural and Hegemonic Masculinities in South Africa, 1948–1960." *Journal of Southern African Studies* 24, no. 4 (1998): 753–74.

Morrell, Robert. "Of Boys and Men: Masculinity and Gender in Southern African Studies." *Journal of Southern African Studies* 24, no. 4 (1998): 605–30.

———. "The Times of Change: Men and Masculinity in South Africa." In *Changing Men in Southern Africa,* ed. Robert Morrell. New York: Zed Books, 2001.

Motani, Nizar. "Makerere College, 1922–1940: A Study in Colonial Rule and Educational Retardation." *African Affairs* 78, no. 312 (1979): 357–69.

Mugomba, Agrippah, and Mougo Nyaggah. Introduction to *Independence without Freedom: The Political Economy of Colonial Education in Southern Africa,* ed. A. Mugomba and M. Nyaggah. Santa Barbara: ABC-Clio, 1980.

Muhoro Kareri, Charles. *The Life of Charles Muhoro Kareri.* Ed. Derek Peterson. Madison: University of Wisconsin African Studies Program, 2002.

Mumford, W. B. "Native Schools in Central Africa." *Journal of the African Society* 26, no. 103 (1927): 237–44.

Mumford, W. B., and B. N. Parker. "Education in British African Dependencies: A Review of the 1935 Annual Reports on Native Education in Nyasaland, N. Rhodesia, Tanganyika, Uganda, Gold Coast, Nigeria and Sierra Leone." *Journal of the Royal African Society* 36 (1936): 17–32.

Murray, Stephan, and Will Roscoe. "All Very Confusing." In *Boy-Wives and Female Husbands: Studies of African Homosexualities,* ed. Stephen Murray and Will Roscoe. New York: St. Martin's Press, 1998.

Nasson, Bill. "Perspectives on Education in South Africa." In *Growing Up in a Divided Society: The Contexts of Childhood in South Africa,* ed. Sandra Burman and Pamela Reynolds. Evanston: Northwestern University Press, 1986.

Natsoulas, Anthula, and Theodore Natsoulas. "Racism, the School and African Education in Colonial Kenya." In *The Imperial Curriculum,* ed. J. A. Mangan. New York: Routledge, 1993.

Natsoulas, Theodore. "The Kenyan Government and the Kikuyu Independent Schools: From Attempted Control to Suppression, 1929–1952." *Historian* 60, no. 2 (1998): 289–305.

Ndovie, Ida Kiswigho. *The Origins, Growth and Decline of the Boy Scout Association of Nyasaland.* University of Malawi Challenge College History Department Seminar Paper no. 15, May 1981.

Ndungu, J. B. "Gituamba and Kikuyu Independency in Church and School." In *Ngano: Studies in Traditional and Modern East African History.*, ed. B. G. McIntosh. Nairobi, 1969.

Nelson, Harold, et. al. *Area Handbook for Malawi.* Washington, DC: Government Printing Office, 1975.

Newman, Richard. "Archbishop Daniel William Alexander and the African Orthodox Church." *International Journal of African Historical Studies* 16, no. 4 (1983): 615–30.

Nicholson, Edwin. *Education and the Boy Scout Movement in America.* New York: Bureau of Publications, Columbia Teachers College, 1941.

Nigerian Chief Scout Commissioner. "Scouting in Nigeria." *Nigeria*, no. 16 (1938): 283–87.

Njoloma, James C. "The King's African Rifles and Colonial Development in Nyasaland (Malawi), 1890–1914." MA thesis, Chancellor College, University of Malawi, 1988.

Nwauwa, Apollos O. "University Education for Africans, 1900–1935: An 'Anathema' to British Colonial Administrative Policy." *Asian and African Studies* 27 (1993): 263–92.

Obermyer, Father Francis. "Do Native Customs Prepare for Pathfinding?" *South African Outlook,* 2 January 1935.

Okoth, P. G. "The Creation of a Dependent Culture: The Imperial School Curriculum in Uganda." In *The Imperial Curriculum,* ed. J. A. Mangan. New York: Routledge, 1993.

Oliver, Roland. *The Missionary Factor in East Africa.* London: Longmans, 1965.

Oliver, Roland, and Anthony Atmore. *Africa since 1800.* 4th ed. Cambridge: Cambridge University Press, 1994.

Opper, C. J. "Education in the Copperbelt of Northern Rhodesia." *Oversea Education* 3, no. 3 (1942): 334–39.

Pachai, Bridglal. "A History of Colonial Education for Africans in Malawi. In *Independence without Freedom: The Political Economy of Colonial Education in Southern Africa,* ed. A. Mugomba and M. Nyaggah. Santa Barbara: ABC-Clio, 1980.

———. *Malawi: History of the Nation.* London: Longman, 1973.

Parpart, Jane. *Labor and Capital on the African Copperbelt.* Philadelphia: Temple University Press, 1983.

———. "Sexuality and Power on the Zambian Copperbelt, 1926–1964." In *Patriarchy and Class,* ed. S. B. Stichter and J. L. Parpart. Boulder: Westview Press, 1988.

———. *Working Class Wives and Collective Labor Action on the Northern Rhodesian Copperbelt,* 1926–1964. Boston University African Studies Center, Working Paper no. 98, 1985.

Parsons, Timothy. "African Participation in the British Empire." In *Black Experience and the Empire,* ed. Philip D. Morgan and Sean Hawkins. Oxford: Oxford University Press, 2004.

Peterson, Derek. *Creative Writing: Translation, Bookkeeping, and the Work of Imagination in Colonial Kenya.* Portsmouth, NH: Heinemann, 2004.

———. "Writing in Revolution: Independent Schooling and Mau Mau in Nyeri." *Mau Mau and Nationhood: Arms, Authority and Nation,* ed. E. S. Otieno Odhiambo and John Lonsdale. Oxford: James Currey, 2003.

Phillips, Ray. *The Bantu Are Coming: Phases of South Africa's Race Problem.* Stellenbosch: Students' Christian Association of South Africa, 1931.

————. *The Bantu in the City: A Study of Cultural Adjustment on the Witwatersrand*. Lovedale: Lovedale Press, 1938.

Pilson, C. A. "Pathfinders in the Cape Border Division." *South African Outlook*, 1 December 1931, 230–31.

Pirouet, M. Louise. *Historical Dictionary of Uganda*. Metuchen, NJ: Scarecrow Press, 1995.

Proctor, Tammy. "'A Separate Path': Scouting and Guiding in Interwar South Africa." *Comparative Studies in Society and History* 42, no. 3 (July 2000): 605–31.

————. "(Uni)Forming Youth: Girl Guides and Boy Scouts in Britain, 1908–1939." *History Workshop Journal* 45 (1998): 103–34.

Ranger, T. O. "African Attempts to Control Education in East and Central Africa, 1900–1939." *Past and Present* 32 (1965): 57–85.

————. *Dance and Society in Eastern Africa, 1890–1970: The Beni Ngoma*. Berkeley: University of California Press, 1975.

————. "Making Northern Rhodesia Imperial: Variations on a Royal Theme, 1924–1938." *African Affairs* 79, no. 316 (1980): 349–73.

————. "Missionary Adaptation of African Religious Institutions: The Masasi Case." In *The Historical Study of African Religion*, ed. T. O. Ranger and I. N. Kimambo. Berkeley: University of California Press, 1972.

Raphoto, Thabo David. "The Jeanes School in Kenya, 1924–1964: A Social Experiment to Train Teachers for Rural Education and Community Development." PhD diss., Syracuse University, 1984.

Rawson, Wyatt, ed. *Education for a Changing Commonwealth: Report of a British Commonwealth Education Conference, July 1931*. London: New Education Fellowship, 1931.

Rey, Charles. *Monarch of All I Survey: Bechuanaland Diaries, 1929–37*. Ed. Neil Parsons and Michael Crowder. London: James Currey, 1988.

Rich, Paul. "The Appeals of Tuskegee: James Henderson, Lovedale, and the Fortunes of South African Liberalism, 1906–1930." *International Journal of African Historical Studies* 20, no. 2 (1987): 271–92.

————. *White Power and Liberal Conscience, Racial Segregation and South African Liberalism, 1921–1960*. Manchester: Manchester University Press, 1984.

Rosberg, Carl G., and John Nottingham. *The Myth of 'Mau Mau': Nationalism and Colonialism in Kenya*. Nairobi: TransAfrica Press, 1985.

Rosenthal, Michael. *The Character Factory: Baden-Powell's Boy Scouts and the Imperatives of Empire*. New York: Pantheon Books, 1984.

————. "Knights and Retainers: The Earliest Version of Baden-Powell's Boy Scout Scheme." *Journal of Contemporary History* 15 (1980): 603–17.

Sachar, Howard. *A History of Israel: From the Rise of Zionism to Our Time*. New York: Knopf, 1988.

Sayers, Gerald F., ed. *The Handbook of Tanganyika*. London: Macmillan, 1930.

Seeley, Janet. "Social Welfare in a Kenyan Town: Policy and Practice, 1902–1985." *African Affairs* 86 (1987): 541–66.

Sheffield, James R. *Education in Kenya: An Historical Study*. New York: Teachers College Press, 1973.

Shire, Chenjerai. "Men Don't Go to the Moon: Language, Space and Masculinities in Zimbabwe." In *Dislocating Masculinity: Comparative Ethnographies*, ed. Andrea Cornwall and Nancy Lindisfarne. New York: Routledge, 1994.

Sifuna, D. N. *Short Essays on Education in Kenya*. Nairobi: Kenya Literature Bureau, 1980.

Sinha, Mrinalini. "Gender and Imperialism: Colonial Policy and the Ideology of Moral

Imperialism in Late Nineteenth-Century Bengal." In *Changing Men: New Directions in Research on Men and Masculinity*, ed. Michael Kimmel. Beverly Hills: Sage Publications, 1987.

Sivonen, Seppo. *White-Collar or Hoe Handle? African Education under British Colonial Policy, 1920–1945*. Helsinki: Suomen Historiallinen Seura, 1995.

Slater, Lady. "The Guides and Brownies of the Gold Coast." *Elders Review of West African Affairs* 9, no. 36 (September 1930): 161–62.

Smith, Melvin. "Some Problems, Methods and Results in Scout Interracial and Intercultural Scouting." MA thesis, Highlands University, 1951.

Smith, Stephen. *The History of Alliance High School*. Nairobi: Heinemann, 1963.

South African Institute of Race Relations. *Record of Proceedings of a National Conference to Study the Report of the Native Education Commission*. Johannesburg: A. M. and I. Abrahams, 1952.

Spring, Joel. *Deculturalization and the Struggle for Equality*. 2d ed. New York: McGraw-Hill, 1997.

Springhall, John O. "The Boy Scouts, Class and Militarism in Relation to British Youth Movements, 1908–1930." *International Review of Social History* 16 (1971): 125–58.

———. "Baden-Powell and the Scout Movement before 1920: Citizen Training or Soldiers of the Future?" *English Historical Review* 102 (1987): 934–42.

———. *Youth, Empire and Society: British Youth Movements*. London: Croom Helm, 1977.

Springhall, John O., and Brian Fraser. *Sure and Stedfast: A History of the Boys' Brigade*. London: Collins, 1983.

Stachura, Peter. *The German Youth Movement, 1900–1945*. New York: St. Martin's Press, 1981.

Steytler, J. G. *Educational Adaptations with Reference to African Village Schools: With Special Reference to Central Nyasaland*. London: Sheldon Press, 1939.

Stirling, Leander Dominic. *History of Scouting in Tanzania, 1917–1992*. N.p., n.d. [ca. 1990].

Stoler, Ann. "Making Empire Respectable: The Politics of Race and Sexual Morality in Twentieth-Century Colonial Cultures." In *Situated Lives: Gender and Culture in Everyday Life*, ed. Louise Lamphere, Helena Ragone, and Patricia Zavella. New York: Routledge, 1997.

Strayer, Robert. *Making of Mission Communities in East Africa*. London: Heinemann, 1978.

Summers, Anne. "Scouts, Guides and VADs: A Note in Reply to Allen Warren." *English Historical Review* 102 (1987): 943–47.

Summers, Carol. *From Civilization to Segregation: Social Ideals and Social Control in Southern Rhodesia, 1890–1934*. Athens: Ohio University Press, 1994.

T. A. "Pathfinders Past and Present." *South African Outlook*, 1 December 1931, 231–33.

Taylor, John. *Processes of Growth in an African Church*. London: SCM Press, 1958.

Tetelman, Michael. "Generational Control, Political Protest, and Everyday Violence in Cradock, South Africa, 1984–85." In *The Politics of Age and Gerontocracy in Africa*, ed. Mario Aguilar. Trenton: Africa World Press, 1998.

———. "We Can: Black Politics in Cradock, South Africa, 1948–1985." PhD diss., Northwestern University, 1997.

Thompson, Leonard. *A History of South Africa*. 2d ed. New Haven: Yale University Press, 1985.

Throup, David W. *Economic and Social Origins of Mau Mau*. Nairobi: Heinemann Kenya, 1988.

Voeltz, Richard. "Adam's Rib: The Girl Guides and an Imperial Race." *San Jose Studies* 14, no. 1 (1988): 91–99.

Waciuma, Charity. *Daughter of Mumbi*. Nairobi: East African Publishing House, 1969.

Wamweya, Joram. *Forest Fighter*. Nairobi: East Africa Publishing House, 1971.

Warren, Allen. "Citizens of the Empire: Baden-Powell, Scouts and Guides, and an Imperial Ideal." In *Imperialism and Popular Culture*, ed. John MacKenzie. Manchester: Manchester University Press, 1986.

———. "'Mothers for the Empire'? The Girl Guides Association in Britain, 1909–1939." In *Making Imperial Mentalities: Socialisation and British Imperialism*, ed. J. A. Mangan. Manchester: Manchester University Press, 1990.

———. "Popular Manliness: Baden-Powell, Scouting, and the Development of Manly Character." In *Manliness and Morality: Middle-Class Masculinity in Britain and America, 1800–1940*, ed. J. A. Mangan and James Walvin. New York: St. Martin's Press, 1987.

———. "Sir Robert Baden-Powell, the Scout Movement and Citizen Training in Great Britain, 1900–1920." *English Historical Review* 101 (1986): 376–98.

Watt, Carey. "The Promise of 'Character' and the Spectre of Sedition: The Boy Scout Movement and Colonial Consternation in India, 1908–1921." *South Asia* 22, no. 2 (1999): 37–62.

Welbourn, F. B. *East African Rebels: A Study of Some Independent Churches*. London: SCM Press, 1961.

West, James. "Scouting as an Educational Asset." *Journal of the National Education Association of the United States* (1916): 1012–19.

West, Robert. "The Educational Philosophy of Baden-Powell." PhD diss., University of South Africa, 1987.

Westcott, N. J. "An East African Radical: The Life of Erica Fiah." *Journal of African History* 22 (1981).

Western, John. *Outcaste Cape Town*. Berkeley: University of California Press, 1996.

White, Luise. "Cars Out of Place: Vampires, Technology, and Labor in East and Central Africa." In *Tensions of Empire: Colonial Cultures in a Bourgeois World*. Berkeley: UCLA Press, 1997.

———. *The Comforts of Home: Prostitution in Colonial Nairobi*. Chicago: University of Chicago Press, 1990.

———. "Separating the Men from the Boys: Constructions of Gender, Sexuality, and Terrorism in Central Kenya, 1939–1959." *International Journal of African Historical Studies* 23 (1990): 1–25.

Whitehead, Clive. "The Advisory Committee on Education in the [British] Colonies, 1924–1961." *Paedagogica Historica* 27 (1991): 385–421.

———. "British Colonial Educational Policy: A Synonym for Cultural Imperialism?" In *"Benefits Bestowed"? Education and British Imperialism*, ed. J. A. Mangan. Manchester: Manchester University Press, 1988.

Wilkinson, Paul. "English Youth Movements, 1908–30." *Journal of Contemporary History* 4, no. 2 (1969): 3–23.

William, T. David. *Malawi: The Politics of Despair*. Ithaca: Cornell University Press, 1978.

Williams, John, ed. *From the South African Past: Narratives, Documents, and Debates*. Boston: Houghton Mifflin, 1997.

Wilson, E. G., ed. *Who's Who in East Africa*. Nairobi: Marco Publishers, 1966.

Wilson, Monica, and Archie Mafeje. *Langa: A Study of Social Groups in an African Township*. Cape Town: Oxford University Press, 1963.

Wood, A. W. "Training Malawi's Youth: The Work of the Malawi Young Pioneers." Community Development Journal 5, no. 3 (1970): 130–38.

Wood, H. H. "The Boy Scout Movement as Part of the Educational System." Uganda Teachers Journal 1 (1939): 65–68.

Wright, Harold Arthur. "A Comparative Study of Twenty-Five Negro Scouts and Twenty-Five Negro Non-Scouts of Pittsburg, Kansas." MA thesis, Kansas State Teachers College, 1940.

Wyland, Ray. Scouting in the Schools: A Study of the Relationships between the Schools and the Boy Scouts of America. New York: Bureau of Publications, Columbia Teachers College, 1934.

Index